ONE TO ONE

ONE TO ONE

Resources for Conference-Centered Writing
Third Edition

CHARLES W. DAWE

Orange Coast College

EDWARD A. DORNAN

Orange Coast College

Scott, Foresman and Company
Glenview, Illinois   Boston   London

Library of Congress Cataloging-in-Publication Data

Dawe, Charles W.
  One to one.

  Includes index.
  1. English language—Rhetoric. 2. Tutors and
tutoring. I. Dornan, Edward A. II. Title.
PE1408.D248 1987   808'.042   86-27572

ISBN 0-673-39205-8
ISBN 0-673-49120-X (Instructor's Edition)

678910-RRC-959493929190

Credits

To Kwang Ja Dawe
To Patti, Hugh, and Aaron Dornan

PREFACE TO
THE THIRD EDITION

As in the first and second editions, the changes in the third edition of *One to One* reflect the suggestions of teachers and students who have used the book over the past several years. Our meetings with teachers at workshops, conventions, and informal get-togethers have reaffirmed our belief that the personal interaction between student and teacher that one-to-one instruction promotes is an effective and rewarding way to teach composition.

In each edition of the text we tried to make the explanations, sample papers, and writing task directions thorough enough and clear enough to allow the teacher to devote class time (always precious) to the instruction of individual writers rather than to the explanation of assignments. In the third edition we continue to refine that aspect of the text and also to add fresh student and professional examples throughout Part One, Getting Started, and Part Two, Writing Tasks. We also revised Part Three, Daily Writing, to make this section even more independent of teacher direction. And, finally, we refined Part Four, Index for Writers, and added a full usage glossary.

Beyond such refinements, we also revised the text by integrating current research in the composing process and in audience analysis in such key chapters as "Listing and Writing for a Reader," "The Composing Process," and "Deductive Essay." Furthermore, to stress the composing process, we expanded the deductive essay chapter to include a second student essay and a professional essay, both with commentary in the margin that traces each writer's strategy.

In order to involve students more deeply in the writing process, we made one other significant change in this edition. Wherever possible, we have had student writers speak about their writing themselves — both in introductory comments and in comments in the margins alongside their works. We hope the addition of these additional voices in *One to One* deepens the lessons that student writers will draw from the examples.

ACKNOWLEDGMENTS

We wish to express our gratitude to the late Roger Garrison for helping us adapt the conference method of composition instruction to our classrooms and for encouraging us throughout the writing of this text. We'd also like to thank Charles Christensen, Elizabeth Philipps, Joan Feinberg, and Elizabeth Schaaf for their trust, patience, and guidance during the composition of the first edition and express our appreciation to Richard Andrews, Clackamas Community College; Peter Brunette, George Mason University; Judi Burken, Kellogg Community College; Judith R. Hert, San Bernardino Valley College; Robert G. Lesman, Northern Virginia Community College, Annandale Campus; and Harvey S. Wiener, LaGuardia Community College, for reviewing the manuscript in its early stages.

We owe a special debt to Richard Beal of Boston University whose cogent comments and suggestions helped us establish the final form of the manuscript.

We received indispensable assistance from our colleagues at Orange Coast College, especially those who listened to our ideas and shared with us their one-to-one teaching experiences over five years of lunches and coffee breaks: John Coates, Margaret Callanan, Robert Dees, Michael Finnegan, Judith Jernigan, Patricia Kubis, Richard Linder, Margaret Langhans, and Thomas O'Keeffe.

Finally, any acknowledgment would be incomplete that fails to thank those teachers who attended seminars, conferences, and workshops and shared with us their responses to our materials. The list is too long to include here, but certain names come immediately to mind: Patricia Barney, Citrus College; Edith Conn, Ventura College; Don Heidt, College of the Canyons; Sevia Kaye, Nassau Community College; Jan Lawson, College of the Desert; Nancy Roediger, Tarrant County Junior College; James Roman, Delaware County Community College; Ellery Sedgwick, Longwood College; Michael Seeley, Ventura College; Jo An

Simmons, Los Angeles City College; Gayle Smith, Pennsylvania State University; Norman Williamson, Mendocino College.

For the second edition of this text it has been our good fortune to receive suggestions from many students and instructors throughout the country. We would particularly like to thank Joyce Kinkead and Bill Smith of Utah State University, Margot Soven at La Salle College, and Jim Strickland at Trocaire College who met with us at 4 Cs in Detroit; Pauline Havens of California State University at Long Beach; Marian Gremmels of Wartburg College; and Charles Warnick of Orange Coast College.

We owe a special thanks to four diligent and perceptive reviewers: Robert J. Albrecht, SUNY, Alfred; Robert Bullock, Northeastern University; Betty Hughes, Beaufort County Community College; and Jane C. Hunt, College of DuPage.

For the third edition of *One to One* we wish to thank Lynda Adamson, Prince George's Community College; Edgar C. Alward, Westfield State College; Thomas K. Birmingham, Citrus Community College; Peter Brunette, George Mason University; Jefferson Carter, Pima Community College; James Coleman, Mohegan Community College; B. J. Craig, Del Mar College; Diana Y. Dreyer, Slippery Rock University; Elizabeth Hoffman, California State University — Long Beach; Linda T. Humphrey, Citrus Community College; Albert J. Husar, Mt. San Antonio College; Marsha Jeffer, Cypress College; Jim Jones, Citrus Community College; Jo Ann B. Little, Pima Community College; Robert Longoni, Pima Community College; Nancy A. Lusignan, Salem State College; Sam Lusk, Grayson County College; Phyllis Mael, Pasadena City College; Joyce Magnotto, Prince George's Community College; John Markley, San Diego City College; Shirley Morahan, Northeast Missouri State University; Jeanne O'Reilly, Mt. San Antonio College; Leonard Pellettiri, Grossmont College; Charles R. Plunkett, Cañada College; Ann D. Sova, Broome Community College; Robert K. Terrill, Mt. San Antonio College; Madelyn Troxclair, Bellevue Community College; and Clemewell Young, Manchester Community College for their sensitive reviews of the text.

As always we wish to express our deepest appreciation to our editors at Little, Brown and Company: Carolyn Potts and Virginia Shine.

TO THE STUDENT

Two activities are important to learn to write well. First is to write, and to write a lot. Second is to get sound advice about your writing from someone who knows how to write. The class you're in will bring these two activities together.

Your teacher has probably selected *One to One* in order to support conference-centered instruction. Although *conference-centered instruction* might sound a little fancy, the concept behind the phrase is quite simple. It involves nothing more than you and your teacher sitting side-by-side and talking about each paper you write. The conference will last from three to fifteen minutes, depending on the length of the assignment. But no matter how long the conference lasts, the major activities will be the same — the teacher will read your work, listen to your comments, and offer advice and directions to help you develop your writing strengths and weaknesses. Simple enough, but to make it work takes some effort. We want to give you a few suggestions that will make that effort easier.

First, we suggest you become an active participant in the conference. Don't just put yourself in the teacher's hands and wait for your fate. Instead, identify and talk about the problems you faced in the assignment. Ask specific questions about solving the problems. Take some brief notes that capture your teacher's responses and recheck them when the conference ends.

We also suggest you try to see your instructor as a writing coach rather than as a judge. Just as a coach wants an athlete to win in competition, your teacher wants you to succeed at writing. If you don't agree with a particular comment about your work, say so and present your view as clearly as you can without arguing or being defensive. Then let your teacher explain the reasons behind the comment. This way the two of you will be building a working relationship that fosters success.

Third, make an effort to treat your papers as works in progress. If you follow the advice of many successful writers who claim that to learn to write well, the beginning writer must learn to rewrite, then you'll have no difficulty improving your writing. But if you come to a conference convinced that you've attained perfection in your writing, you'll have some trouble because a conference will often end with an assignment that requires you either to revise or rewrite a paper. Our best advice is to relax and keep in mind that the purpose of the conference is not just to get your work accepted but to improve your skills. View each assignment as a stage in the process of mastering different kinds of writing. Sometimes that mastery comes faster by rewriting a flawed paper rather than by starting a new one.

Finally, you can help make your conferences work by carefully studying the material your instructor assigns. Read the explanations, analyze the illustrations, review the marginal notes — do all this before you start to write. If you work in this way, you'll save valuable conference time by keeping the focus on your writing and not on explanations of the assignments you didn't read thoroughly.

A quick glance at the book will show you it's divided into four main parts and that the first three are subdivided into several sections, each identified by number or week. (The fourth part is arranged alphabetically.) Since the book teaches writing by getting you to write, each sub-section ends with an assignment called a "Writing Task" that's designed to help you learn the information presented in the section. In Part One, Getting Started, you'll learn to write for a reader, how to work through a four-step composing process, and how to combine the particulars of an experience with your reactions to it. In Part Two, Writing Tasks, you'll learn different ways to develop paragraphs and several ways to develop essays. In Part Three, Daily Writing, you'll go through nine weeks of writing practice that will help you overcome the fears you might have when facing a blank page. By working through daily writing tasks you'll also generate subjects and material for the more formal assignments in the course. In Part Four, Index for Writers, you'll find help with common problems beginning writers face: how to get sentences to flow together; where to put commas, semicolons, and apostrophes; when to use quotation marks, and so on.

In closing we'd like to offer one last thought. Soon after completing Part One, Getting Started, you may discover that you are doing writing tasks that are different from the ones your neighbor is doing. Don't be concerned about that. In one-to-one instruction individual students work on what they need at the moment. Our advice is to take advantage of the flexibility in one-to-one instruction and use this text to help you find your own path to the common goal — good writing.

CONTENTS

2

PART THREE

DAILY WRITING   231

PART FOUR

INDEX FOR WRITERS 287

PART ONE

GETTING STARTED

    This part will introduce you — in three chapters, with Writing Tasks included in each — to the process of putting your thoughts on paper. You will base the writing you do in this section on your own observation and experience, not on your ability to collect material from other writers' thoughts. In other words, you will not be researching but will be collecting, recording, and organizing your personal experiences.

    Besides the primary question that plagues most beginning writers — "What should I write about?" — there is a second question usually linked to it — "How should I get started?" A third question, probably as fundamental as the other two, seldom gets consciously asked yet is important for the success of any written communication: "For whom am I writing?"

    As for the first question, for every Writing Task you do in this part of the book we will guide you to something to write about. So for now that problem is solved. Our main goals in this section are to give you a simple way to start writing and to make you aware of your reader.

1 LISTING AND WRITING FOR A READER

Getting started on a written project may be the most critical point in the entire enterprise. Perhaps the difficulty has something to do with facing a blank page and knowing that page, and most likely many other blank pages, will have to be filled with words. Moreover, the words must be nudged into sentences. The sentences must link logically together and be fitted into paragraphs. The paragraphs must be assembled into a coherent essay, report, or letter. Besides all the nudging, fitting, and assembling, you must put in the squiggles called punctuation. And then there is spelling — the mind shudders. The part of the brain that sends energy to the arm freezes. Writer's elbow sets in. It's too painful to shape the words with a pen. You're blocked.

There is a way to overcome the block. Instead of worrying about all the meticulous arranging you have to do to finish a piece of writing, concentrate on randomly collecting the raw material that will make up the content. One way to do the collecting is to draw up a list.

Listing

Everyone is familiar with grocery lists. Consumer advocates often advise shoppers to make grocery lists before shopping. With a list in hand, the expedition won't turn into a spending spree. Well, the advice is equally valid for a writer.

3

A list works as an ordering device through which you can quickly gather the material you want to communicate to a reader. By writing a list you can rapidly capture fleeting details. A list can also fire your imagination and guide your direction. No doubt you can see how a piece of writing could easily form around a list of joyful or frightening experiences or around a list of dreams, fears, or memories. Now let's see how a list works.

Imagine a homemaker who is planning an Italian supper. After surveying the cupboard, she realizes she needs a few items to complete the menu and sees she's also short of juice and coffee. She quickly makes a simple list to remind herself to get what she needs.

juice
tomatoes
coffee
bread
onions

Five simple items. About a ten-minute trip with the list in hand to keep her on target. Of course, the plan may change — she may rearrange the list as she goes. For instance, she would probably pick up the tomatoes and onions at the same time because they would be in the produce section, then go to the nearby frozen-food compartment before stopping for coffee located somewhere near the center of the market, and end up at the bread rack near the checkout counter. The simple list makes her shopping a breeze.

Now imagine that our homemaker is going to use this simple list to write a note to someone else who plans to stop at the grocery store for her. She must now communicate with an audience — a reader. Somehow, to make the communication clear, the writer must anticipate the reader's mind.

Audience

The reader you address will influence choices you make about content and vocabulary when writing. If you were separately to tell a police officer, a parent, and a friend about the events at a party, you would select different details to emphasize for each person and different words to describe what you experienced. In speech you make this adaptation instantly and naturally, but when writing you must actively adjust your thinking to make the adaptation. It is essential, therefore, that before you move too far into planning a piece of writing, you should identify who the reader will be and anticipate what he or she needs to know to understand what you are trying to communicate.

To illustrate the dangers in failing to identify the reader, consider our homemaker's grocery list again:

juice
tomatoes
coffee
bread
onions

Could she give this to her teenage son and expect him to gather what she wants?

If she were naive enough to do so, her teenage son might return with freshly squeezed guava juice when she wanted frozen orange juice. He might buy two green tomatoes when she wanted four ripe ones; instant coffee when she wanted regular grind; wheat bread when she wanted French; white onions when she had purple in mind. The confusion could deepen. Her teenager might even go to the wrong market — you know, the exclusive one where the goods cost a nickel or dime more.

For our homemaker to avoid the confusion, she would have to add specific detail to the list, anticipating her teenager's way of thinking, thus making her own written thought as clear as necessary in order to get what she wanted. The finished list might look something like this:

> I need some items from the market for tonight's dinner and tomorrow's breakfast. Please get them at Safeway.
> 1. four ripe tomatoes
> 2. two purple onions
> 3. a six-ounce can of frozen orange juice
> 4. regular grind coffee — whatever brand is on sale
> 5. French bread — the long kind, not the presliced

You can see how composing even a simple grocery list for a particular reader puts demands on the writer. The homemaker needs to include specifics, such as *four ripe* tomatoes, *two purple* onions, a *six-ounce can* of *orange* juice, and so on. Otherwise her teenager will interpret the note according to the characteristics of his own mind.

If the homemaker were writing for someone else, she might need to include more information. If she were writing the note for out-of-town guests or a grandparent or a child, what information would she have to give? Let's see.

Jean Bennett, a composition student, actually began with this simple grocery list as a basis for a note she invented for both her teenage and her ten-year-old sons. Since the note for her teenager did not give enough information for her ten-year-old to follow, Jean developed more specific information while keeping in mind what she knew about her ten-year-old's way of thinking. Fleshed out with more detail, the list then served as a rough guide for Jean's final note.

1. four ripe tomatoes — deep red, not orange; squeeze them for softness
2. two large purple onions, at least as big as a baseball
3. a small can of orange juice, the kind you've helped me make for breakfast
4. a small can of coffee with "regular grind" written at the top — buy the one that costs the least
5. French bread, the kind your brother says looks like a spyglass

For her ten-year-old, Jean has made the list even more specific than she did for her teenager. Aside from the details, she has made some comparisons: "at least as big as a baseball" and "looks like a spyglass." She also recalls previous experience: "the kind you've helped me make for breakfast." She even gives a brief lesson on how to select a ripe tomato. All this information is necessary because she knows it will help her ten-year-old understand her meaning. There will be less confusion in the communication.

With the list before her, Jean can begin to write the note. But while writing, she must envision her ten-year-old following the directions and anticipate his responses. For instance, her teenager would have no trouble with money transactions; her ten-year-old might. More than likely, her teenager would easily find his way around the market; her ten-year-old probably would not think in the neat categories in which most market managers arrange their merchandise. And, finally, it is doubtful that her teenager would get sidetracked on the way home; her ten-year-old might stop to play. So you see, even after developing a detailed list, the writer, when arranging the contents in a final draft, must continue to anticipate the reader's mind. In fact, the writer will often pause to assume the role of reader and reread what he or she has written to see if it is clearly expressed.

What follows is Jean Bennett's note to her ten-year-old son, based on the list developed above. Read it and see how she used the list for content and how, as she wrote the note, she added information as she thought of it so that the message would be clear to the child. Also notice how she arranged the information step by step to avoid confusing the communication.

Take this ten-dollar bill and hurry to Safeway to buy some groceries for dinner.

First, go to the vegetable and fruit section on the far side of the market and get four ripe tomatoes. The tomatoes should be deep red — not orange. Be sure to test them with a slight squeeze for softness. Don't buy mushy ones and don't buy hard ones — find some in between hard and mushy. Near the tomatoes, you'll see the onions. I need two purple ones about the size of your baseball or bigger.

Next, while you are on that side of the market, go to the frozen-food section for a small can of orange juice. A small can is the size you've helped me make for breakfast some mornings.

After getting the orange juice, go to the toy section — you should have no trouble finding it — and right behind it you'll find the coffee. I need one small can, the pound size, that says "regular grind" near the top. Check the prices and take the one that costs the least.

And finally, from the rack near the checkout counter, pick up a loaf of French bread, the kind your brother says looks like a spyglass.

After you've done all that, you may buy a treat. Not candy or ice cream, but some dried fruit or nuts.

When you've finished paying for the groceries and your treat, put the change in your pocket and rush home without stopping at the hobby shop to look at models or at the park to toss the football or at Jack's to watch *M*A*S*H* reruns.

"Now scoot!" Jean might have put at the close, sending her ten-year-old off in a swirl of uncombed hair and baggy clothes. Let's briefly review the process Jean followed to develop her note. After drawing up the details, she anticipates her child's mind right down to the distractions he might be drawn to on the way home. She even anticipated how much he would like a treat after facing all the temptations supermarket managers scatter along the aisles to ensnare children, and she guided him to a more healthful choice.

Of course, writing from a list and anticipating your reader will not solve all your writing frustrations, but they do give you a way to start working. Perhaps now facing a blank page seems a little easier.

WRITING TASK

Write a note in no more than 250 words. First, decide on a subject. Second, draw up a "grocery list" that captures the content of your note. Third, decide who the reader will be. Finally, write the note, using the list as a rough plan while anticipating how much the reader needs to know to understand what you wish to communicate.

Although you are free to select your own subject, you might want to direct a reader to a favorite spot of yours, such as a special hideaway,

restaurant, bookshop, or record store. Or perhaps you will send someone on a shopping errand to a nearby shopping center. You might offer
a set of guidelines for surviving a stressful situation, such as a trip to
the dentist, doctor, chiropractor, or traffic court. You might tell a
reader how to survive a fraternity party, rock concert, or a dull college
course. You might write a note that explains why you did or did not do
something, such as why you missed an appointment, abandoned a
project, or caught a cold.

Once you've selected a subject and developed a list that will make
up the content of the note, identify a reader who represents a challenge: a younger brother or sister, a parent or grandparent, an out-of-
town friend. Don't select a close friend with whom you talk daily —
that's too easy. While you write the note, try to create a personal tone,
the tone you would use if you were talking to the person.

Remember:

1. Build your note from a list.
2. Identify a reader and anticipate how much information he or she
   needs to understand what you are saying.
3. When writing and rereading, imagine the reader trying to follow
   your words.
4. Arrange your note in a step-by-step fashion.

2 THE COMPOSING PROCESS

This section is the beginning of four related assignments. We've assembled them to introduce you to a method of working we hope you'll use whenever you tackle a writing task. These assignments have been built around the idea that writing is a process best done in drafts. Paragraphs, essays, reports, or entire books do not hatch fully formed from the writer's imagination. Instead, works such as these are usually nudged and teased into life, sometimes unfolding in elaborate ways. After all — and you might be either disappointed or reassured by this knowledge — there is no secret formula for creating a successful piece of writing. All writers must develop their own processes to build their individual works. In fact, one of the secrets of becoming a good writer is to discover your own personal method of nudging and teasing experience and ideas into words.

In this series of tasks, you will first record the details of a brief experience — this will be called the prewriting phase. Second, we'll ask you to write a rough draft by arranging the details of the prewritten material in an orderly form. Once the rough draft is done, you will edit and revise it by tinkering with the arrangement of words, phrases, and sentences so that the entire piece reads smoothly. After editing and revising, the next step in the method will be to integrate the changes by writing a final draft, thus polishing the whole piece.

When you have completed this series of tasks you will have used one observed experience to work through the four main steps of the writing process:

Phase 1: prewriting
Phase 2: rough draft
Phase 3: editing and revising
Phase 4: final draft

Prewriting

If you consider the entire composing process, you'll see that it involves two different kinds of thought: (1) creative thought, which grows from a writer's intuition and allows the mind to connect ideas, events, and images, and (2) critical thought, which grows from the intellect and allows the mind to organize words into verbal structures, such as sentences, paragraphs, and essays. Creative thought is less self-conscious than critical thought, yet both are important. Prewriting stresses the creative process while restraining the more self-conscious critical process.

When prewriting, you are actually inventing the raw material you'll be working with at other writing stages. You need not be concerned with the nitty-gritty of writing — grammar, syntax, punctuation, and spelling — but you should be concerned with generating an abundance of raw material with which to work in future drafts. Therefore, while you are involved in prewriting activities, open yourself to the creative experience without making critical judgments. The reshaping and organizing — that is, the judging — will come later.

Begin with a List

The method of prewriting we present in this section is an extension of the list described in Chapter 1. (See listing, pp. 3–4) Although prewriting works for all kinds of written projects, for learning purposes you'll begin by working with a brief description that captures an experience you set out to record. After we've examined an illustration of prewriting, we'll ask you to stroll around your neighborhood, across campus, through a park, or wherever you wish to go in order to find something to describe.

Once you find something to describe, like a reporter using a notepad and pencil to capture colorful background for an article, you'll record the details of whatever it is that has caught your interest. These details will come to you through your senses — through sight, sound, smell, touch, and taste. The senses are involved to some degree in almost every type of writing. They are particularly important in descriptive writing.

SIGHT

The trees sway in the wind . . . Their dark silhouettes look like ink blots against the sky . . . Lightning streaks the night.

SOUND

Thunder rumbles over the plains . . . Rain beats a steady rhythm on the iron gas drum . . . The kettle whistles in the kitchen.

SMELL

The spicy aroma of curry . . . The air fresh and clean from the rain . . . The dog's wet fur smells wooly.

TOUCH

The water-smooth stones slip under my feet . . . The cork handle is dry to touch . . . The sun stings his back . . . The feel of fur, soft and silky.

TASTE

Sugary-sweet bubble gum . . . The bite of salt spray . . . The rich foam of beer . . . Savoring the meaty taste of spareribs.

Through the use of descriptive language, the task will be to make the reader "see," not to tell the reader what you think. Try to keep in mind that there is a difference between using writing to "think about" or "respond to" an experience and using writing to capture the sensory detail of an experience. Each use has an important place, and the two cannot be cleanly separated, but for this assignment we'll be asking you to concentrate on gathering sensory detail.

Here's how student-writer Tom Rolf collected his observations at the end of a pier near his home. As you read Tom's prewrite, keep in mind that Tom uses a form of listing to collect the details of the events he observes. But before studying Tom's prewritten draft, read his comments about beginning the assignment:

I had finished all the homework for my other classes and decided to tackle English. The task seemed easy enough — merely spend thirty minutes collecting specific details of something I observed. I decided to go to one of my favorite spots, the end of a nearby pier. It was late. I felt lonely. And since I was paying more attention to the scene than usual, everything seemed a little bit mysterious, perhaps even spooky.

Now let's examine Tom's prewritten draft:

– Midnight on the pier. At night the pier looks like a heap of bones. Whale bones or the remains of some prehistoric creature. The backbone rising above the sea. I liked the thought of walking on the spine of some monster; leaving the land behind; moving beyond the edge of the earth.

– Deserted. Near the end of the pier. The fishing shop deserted, haunted, a sign that read "BAIT" . . . Peeling . . . unreadable graffiti scrawled on walls.

– Usually there are several fishermen huddled in groups. Sipping coffee; bundled in coats; smoking. Tonight there is a single fisherman at the end. He stands beneath the only lamp that isn't burned out. He holds his pole; baseball cap tilted forward; jacket collar up; one foot on the lower railing.

– The night is moonless and clear. The stars shine . . . silver flames . . . sequins against black velvet. In the distance, the harbor light marking the harbor opening twinkles. Within, the harbor homes worth millions, safe from the sea, eons away from me.

– The fisherman bends down and baits his hook. Carefully. Slowly. He stands up again and casts the line beyond the lamplight. The reel whirrs. Then a splash. Silence. He lifts his foot to the railing once more. Leans forward; rests his elbows on the top rung.

– A bait boat. A hundred yards or more off to the right. The engine rumbling. The lights that attract fish bright and blazing from the water's surface. Ghostly . . . a white-hot spirit rising from the sea.

– The sea beneath the planks moves. I sense the rise and fall of the sea . . . alive, breathing . . . heaving . . . awakening. Is the creature returning to life? The ocean seems like a hungry beast . . . hunting for prey, devouring, dangerous. No, mysterious. The splash of water against the pilings. The night empty. The boat pulling farther away.

– I feel alone.

Before beginning your own prewrite (see Writing Task, p. 14), we want to offer a few guidelines for you to follow.

Resist Self-Criticism

Notice how Tom frees himself of critical concerns by paying little if any attention to arranging words into sentences and sentences into paragraphs. He generates an expanded list, gathering raw material into raw form. Because he relaxes his critical intellect, he sees the external details and connects some of them with images. For instance, to help capture the quality of the night he compares it to black velvet and the stars to silver sequins. He also indicates that the blazing lights of the bait boat remind him of a spirit rising from the sea. In a strict sense, the sky is not velvet and the stars are not sequins nor is there a spirit rising from the sea, but Tom's intuition makes the connections. Often writers will reach for comparisons of this sort to put themselves on a common ground with their readers. These comparisons help a reader experience what the writer experienced. So if you have associations or make connections like these, don't criticize them; put them in the prewritten draft and later you might use them in the rough draft, or you might drop them, depending on their appropriateness.

Focus Your Prewriting

Notice that Tom concentrates on his observations while at the end of the pier, but that elements of the scene around the pier — the movement of the sea, the bait boat — come into play. He does not, however, include what he experiences walking to the pier or everything he was thinking. He selects, keeps his focus on specific details related to what he observes, and records the detail he selects in specific language.

Use Simple Language

Also notice that Tom uses simple words. Simple does not mean simplistic or oversimplified; simple words are basic, not complicated or complex. You probably know all the words in Tom's draft. Notice too that many of Tom's words, mainly stressing sight and sound, are concrete — words that call up images of what can be seen, heard, touched, smelled, and tasted. Often, concrete words are the ones most common in your vocabulary. With them you can build a solid description. (See Word Choice, p. 382.)

Avoid Judgments

Notice how Tom sticks to gathering the externals of the experience. He does not record what he thinks about the experience. For instance, if he had written his judgments about the fisherman, he might have included some comments such as the ones italicized below:

> Tonight there is a single fisherman at the end. He stands beneath the only lamp that isn't burned out. He holds his pole; baseball cap tilted forward; jacket collar up; one foot on the lower railing. *He must be a lonely person to come out here by himself at night. Probably likes to escape his home or doesn't have any friends.*

For this prewrite we'll ask you to stay with collecting the externals and not to make any judgments about the experience.

What does all this add up to? Well, prewriting is building an expanded list to get your writing started. The prewrite represents a first draft: maybe an awkward first draft, but one that will give you enough detail to shape into a rough draft — the second step in the process.

WRITING TASK

Take a walk around your neighborhood, across campus, or through the library, a market, shopping center, or park and look for something to describe. When that something catches your interest, sit down and record the details. Act like a detached reporter neutrally collecting the raw stuff of the experience.

A word of caution: Resist the temptation to do this task from memory to avoid writing a something-interesting-happened-to-me-last-week piece. We're asking that you set out to record something fresh. If you record a memory, you'll end up writing a narrative — a story — that will lack the specific detail this task requires. So take our best advice: Accept the challenge and take the thirty or forty minutes to do an on-the-spot prewrite.

Remember:

1. Concentrate on an experience you observe.
2. While engaged in prewriting, avoid making critical judgments about grammar, syntax, punctuation, and spelling.
3. Like an objective reporter, capture the external details of the experience, not what you think about the experience.
4. Use simple, concrete language, language of the senses.
5. Select details that will help the reader "see" the experience.

Rough Draft

Now that you have completed the prewriting phase, it's time to shape your prewritten draft into a rough draft. The rough draft stage involves shifting the mind from the intuitive into the intellectual. To make the shift, you will have to face a whole new set of problems.

The first problem has to do with shaping the rough draft. If your prewritten draft is anything like the observations Tom Rolf made on the pier, it is composed of concrete description and creative inspiration — all scribbled in fragments and ragged sentences. In contrast, the rough draft is the first step toward bringing order to the random collection of detail. Not complete order — you still need the creative instinct to fill in the gaps — but enough to give the details shape.

Establish a Purpose

We want you to begin shaping your rough draft by setting a limit on its length. Write it in 250 to 300 words. If you have several pages of notes, meeting this limit might be difficult. But it just means that you, like most writers, will have to select the outstanding details to develop in your rough draft. One way to make this selection is to decide what you wish to communicate to your reader about the experience — perhaps a mood or feeling — in other words, decide what your purpose is to be. Once you have a purpose in mind, you can then select and develop the details from your prewritten draft that will help you convey that purpose. This also means that you will abandon other details you have collected because they might not advance your purpose.

Create a Beginning, Middle, and End

While writing the rough draft try to create a sense of roundness: The rough draft should have a beginning, a middle, and an end. Unfortunately, as with most aspects of writing, there is no magic formula for writing a rounded piece. We suggest you start by writing a sentence or two leading readers into the experience without their needing to know anything that came before. The beginning sentence or two will also convey your general purpose, although in a descriptive piece, such as the one you will be writing, you need not make a direct statement of purpose as you would in more expository paragraphs. (See Using a Topic Sentence, p. 51.) You can then move into the middle of the piece by developing a sequence of sentences that grow from the lead. The middle will be the bulk of the piece. As you write, you will be constantly referring to the prewritten draft as a source of detail you need to build the sentences. In fact, before you begin your rough draft you might rearrange the material in the prewritten draft in rough outline form to give you a better sense of the direction the rough draft will take.

There are several common and logical ways to arrange written material so that a reader can follow it. Time arrangement is probably the most common. A writer will often use time arrangement in narration to tell a story or to explain a process — that is, to give directions on how to do something. In time arrangement the writer begins with the first event or step and ends with the last one.

For material that does not fall into a clear time scheme, a writer may use space aggrangement, especially in descriptive writing, arranging the visual material from west to east, left to right, high to low, near to far, far to near, or whatever seems appropriate for a particular piece of writing.

A writer can also arrange material in order of climax, selecting the most dramatic part of the piece and holding it back until the end. For this arrangement the writer would begin with the least important details and arrange the rest of the material in increasing importance, and then close the piece by showcasing the most dramatic part.

Other arrangements are possible — such as ordering from general to particular or from particular to general — or any combination of them. An important consideration in structuring a piece of writing is that the material be arranged in a clear fashion so readers can follow it.

Finally, you can close the piece where the middle sequence seems to end naturally. And here's where you have to rely on sensitivity. Endings often have a great deal to do with feelings. On the one hand, someone once compared a good ending with the feeling one has after hearing a box click shut. On the other hand, an ending may have the effect of a door slamming. One student writer of ours remarked that she often tried to link the end of her descriptive pieces with the lead, like a snake biting its own tail.

Shape the Sentences

Besides arranging the detail, developing it, and shaping the overall structure of your descriptive piece, you must also shape the sentences. When you did your prewritten draft, you recorded the experience on the fly, in phrases or rough sentences. While writing the rough draft, you should shape the phrases into complete sentences. To write in complete sentences at this point does not mean to fret over grammar, syntax (the way sentences are constructed), punctuation, and spelling. It only means that you should be aware of them without getting yourself bogged down. If you remember that in most writing assignments the rough draft will be for your eyes only, you may be able to find the balance between being aware of and getting mired in concerns over writing correctly. Also remember that there are still two more phases in the composing process: (1) editing and revising and (2) polishing a final draft.

Before showing you Tom Rolf's rough draft, we want to remind you of two points we discussed in Prewriting. First, when you write your rough draft, try to use simple, concrete language. There's no need to be fancy with words. Second, select part of your prewritten draft to emphasize — that is, to "showcase." Remember we suggested that you find an experience and concentrate on it for your prewriting. This experience may be the part you wish to showcase, the highlight of your descriptive piece. To display that part, you will build the rest of your description around it, perhaps leading up to it and dramatizing it more than other elements in your description.

Writing the Rough Draft

Let's see how Tom Rolf used his prewrite to create a rough draft. First, read what Tom has to say about the process:

> Writing the rough draft was not as easy as my writing instructor said it would be. At first I thought I merely needed to start at the beginning and describe my observations in complete sentences as I had recorded them. But then I learned that I needed to try to create a dominant impression, some mood or feeling — a purpose. I also needed to select the central details, especially the ones — at least to my way of thinking — that captured my imagination, after all this was to be my piece of writing, right? Finally, and this was the hardest part for me to accept, I had to rearrange the details and exclude a great deal.
>
> I began by re-reading my prewritten material and remembering that I felt lonely and kind of empty from having studied all afternoon and evening when I would have rather been with friends, so I guess this colored my mood. Also when I re-read the material I sensed a certain mystery about the pier, an "eeriness," which seemed odd to me because I had walked the pier many times at night. I decided to try to communicate these feelings in my rough draft. I also became interested in the fisherman — the lone fisherman — the methodical way he baited the hook and the care he took casting out his line, all in the dim light from the lamppost. I imagined he was gathering his thoughts while fishing the way I was gathering my thoughts while walking. In any case, as my writing instructor advised me, I decided to start writing with the idea that the meaning of all this would come clear in the process. I began by rearranging my prewritten material in a more orderly fashion; I had scribbled it so hastily that it was nearly unreadable. At this point, I was not as interesested in including all the detail as I was in arranging the material. My new arrangement looked like the following:

> Basic arrangement: climatic, journey to the end of the pier, showcasing the fisherman at the climax.
>
> 1. Opening: reason for walk — to collect my thoughts — everything seemed mysterious!
> 2. Descriptive points
>   Prehistoric image — bones
>   Fishermen — coats, caps, huddled together near deserted bait shop

Bait shop — haunted, peeling paint, graffiti
Ocean moving beneath the pier — swells, splashing
Dark, no moon, stars like sequins on black velvet
Bait boat — light blazing, looks like a jewel — diamond —
   or ghost/spirit — white hot
Fisherman (showcase) alone, baiting hook, casting pole,
   spinning reel (humming) splashing sinker
3. Close — ? need to figure this out . . . darkness? splash?

Now study Tom's rough draft to see how he shaped it from the raw material collected on his list. Notice also that he added some material he recalled from memory and embellished other material by sharpening and dramatizing the details. Finally, while writing the rough draft, Tom skipped lines in order to have plenty of space for the third phase of the composing process — that is, space to edit and to revise.

Tom's Rough Draft

I walked from my apartment to the beachfront. It feels good to walk to the end of the pier late after you finish your homework. It's a reward for me, empty, time to gather my thoughts. Often the pier seems mysterious. At night the pier looks like a heap of bones. It looks like the bones of some prehistoric creature. The pier at night is usually empty with only a few fishermen wrapped in heavy coats, watch caps pulled down over their ears. They gather near the deserted bait shop that seems haunted with graffiti scrawled on its peeling walls. On the pier I sensed the motion of the ocean. The swells were very rough, rising and falling, and I could hear them splashing against the wooden pilings. There was no moon tonight, but there were stars that shined like beautiful sequins on black velvet. I saw a bait boat with its lights shining. The boat looked like a jewel glowing

against the black sea or like a white-hot ghost rising

from the water. At the end of the pier I saw a man who

interested me. He was alone and fishing. He stood at the

very end of the pier beneath a dully lit lamppost. He bent

over a bucket, putting bait on a hook. He finished and

stood up. He lifted his fishing pole and guided it way

back over his head and arched his back before he tossed

the line into the water. The hum of his line spinning

from the reel sang in the night. Then I heard the sinker

splash into the water.

Indeed, this is a very rough draft with many awkward spots. That's okay. The purpose of the rough draft is to shape the material, not to make it perfect.

Now let's examine Tom Rolf's rough draft by comparing it to his prewritten draft. First, Tom had to limit his piece to fewer than 300 words; that limitation forced him to be selective. To be selective means to decide not only what to include in a written piece but also what to exclude. Notice, for instance, that Tom excluded such observations as the distant harbor lights, the wealthy homes within the harbor, and the actions of the lone fisherman after casting his line ("He lifts his foot to the railing once more. Leans forward; rests his elbows on the top rung.").

Why did Tom exclude these details and not others? Since writers make their own choices — often by intuition — the answers may be hard to come by. One reason might have something to do with Tom's general intent, though Tom had still not completely formulated his final intent — that is, he started the rough draft by trying to communicate the mysterious or eerie characteristics of the pier. The comparison to a heap of prehistoric bones, the motion of the ocean, the moonless night with shining stars, the ghostly boat all seem to suggest that intent.

And, finally, the writer might have excluded some details because they seemed inappropriate. For instance, again the reference to the wealthy homes does not advance Tom's intent. Also, to compare the ocean to a hungry beast hunting for prey would not bring to a reader's mind the kind of life Tom senses beneath the pier; moreover, when thoughtfully considered, the ebb and flow of tides and rise and fall of swells when compared with the stalking of a panther, leopard, or lion do not make much sense.

It's easy to see that the process of selection is important whether you do it with the general purpose or with the appropriateness of the details in mind.

Tom also arranged his description with a rough beginning, middle, and end. He opens with sentences that suggest his purpose — that is, to present the details of his observations on the pier and to capture the mysterious or eerie quality of the experience. Tom then develops a sequence of descriptive sentences to advance his purpose, selecting those details which he thought would do the job. Tom also showcases the lone fisherman at the end of his rough draft by describing his actions in careful detail. He ends with the sound of the sinker splashing in the water, thus indicating the completion of his journey to the end of the pier.

Tom has also kept his language simple. He uses concrete words that create a picture of his experience, such words as "the pier looks like a heap of bones," "fishermen wrapped in heavy coats, watch caps pulled down over their ears," "I sensed the motion of the ocean, the swells rising and falling . . . splashing against the wooden pilings," "stars that shined like sequins on black velvet," and so on. Tom also transforms the fragments of the prewritten draft into complete sentences — "At night the pier looks like a heap of bones. It looks like the bones of some prehistoric creature" — although at times the sentences are ragged and need revision. For instance, the sentences just quoted above would read more smoothly if combined and slightly embellished, "At night the pier looks like the bones of some prehistoric creature heaped near the shore." But, and this is an important point for you to remember, this is still a rough draft. Tom, like you will do with your rough drafts, will smooth out the raggedness when he revises and edits the whole piece.

WRITING TASK

Using your prewritten draft as a starting point, write a rough draft in no more than 300 words. We suggest you leave plenty of space between the lines — that is, skip lines — so that you'll have room to cross out and add words and phrases when you edit and revise your rough draft during the next step in the composing process.

Remember:

1. **Review your prewritten material and establish a general purpose.**
2. **Try to discover something in your prewritten material that would be interesting to showcase and perhaps embellish it.**
3. **If necessary, rearrange your prewritten material in order to create a clear structure for your piece.**
4. **Write your rough draft in complete sentences, yet keep in mind that rough drafts are usually "for your eyes only," which should free you from being overly concerned about perfection.**

Although we have given you a great deal to consider while writing a rough draft, keep in mind that your goal is not perfection: There are still two more stages in the composing process.

Editing and Revising

The time to begin the editing and revising process is when you have a suitable rough draft in hand — a piece drawn from the prewritten draft that you believe adequately covers the experience you are trying to convey. No doubt you have been struggling to make your experience meaningful to yourself, trying to find and get a grip on what you are trying to describe. Mainly, up to this point, you have been writing to please yourself. Now you must begin to consider your audience — that is, to more actively imagine a reader looking over your shoulder. We are not suggesting that you allow the imaginary reader to loom above your work like some insistent taskmaster, but that when you begin to edit and revise we want to encourage you to keep in mind that your descriptive piece will be read by another person. Thinking about the reader will help you decide about what to include, the language you use, and how your final paper will be organized. More importantly, as a writer you will want to be clear and convincing while avoiding the risks of being misunderstood. In the next phase, writing the final draft, the reader will play a more important role.

While editing and revising, you must muster your intellectual skills to evaluate your work. Under these circumstances evaluation does not involve deciding whether your work is good or bad. Instead, it involves deciding whether or not your work is as vigorous and concise as you can make it. No sentence should have any unnecessary words; no paragraph, any unnecessary sentences. This is not to suggest that all sentences are to be simple or short, but only that the piece is to be as concise as possible.

(See Clutter, p. 304; Editing and Revising, p. 333; Numbed Language, p. 348; Word Choice, p. 382.)

Although individual writers develop their own approaches to the editing and revising process, we offer the following guidelines and illustrations to get you started.

Establish a Point of View

Decide what point of view will rule your piece. In the task that involved writing a note (Chapter 1), the point of view probably came naturally. Notes are usually written in the first-person singular — "I" — and addressed to the reader in the second person — "you." By using the "I" point of view you wrote as a participant in the process. Whenever writing about first-hand experience, as you will be in these early tasks, the use of first person is appropriate. For some subjects, however, you will need to keep a more impersonal point of view by avoiding the first person altogether. You will sometimes be writing as a detached observer who stands some distance away from the reader and the material. The impersonal point of view is appropriate when the subject needs to be treated in a neutral way — in history, for instance, scientific writing, or news reporting. Whether personal or impersonal, the subject usually determines the point of view. The concept to remember here is that the point of view needs to be consistent throughout the piece. For instance, Tom Rolf used the "I" point of view throughout most of his rough draft, but once he mistakenly shifted to "you." When he revises his rough draft, he, like every writer, will have to make his point of view consistent. If the point of view is not consistent, your reader may become confused and lose patience with your writing. (See Point of View, p. 360.)

Keep the Verb Tense Consistent

Another conscious choice you must make when editing and revising is selecting the principal verb tense. In practice the choice is simple. Most writing is done in the past tense: "I *sat* on the bench and *watched* the men while they *were jogging* around the track." But some writers decide to record experience in the present tense: "I *am* on the bench *watching* the men while they *jog* around the track."

Since the present tense often sounds awkward when used as the principal tense in a lengthy piece, we suggest you use the past tense. However, the present tense is not necessarily improper. What is improper is to shift from the principal tense to another without having a purpose for the shift: I *sat* on the bench and *watched* the men while they *jog* around the track. Just *watching* them *makes* me *feel* tired." Notice how the writer has shifted the principal tense from past — *sat* and *watched* — to present — *jog, makes, feel.* This mistaken shift is awkward and confusing to the reader. You keep track of your verb tense when you edit and revise to help your reader move easily through your description.

We don't want to give you the impression, however, that it is always awkward to shift verb tenses. In fact, often you must shift tense. Remember, verb tenses show time — past, present, and future. Sometimes you will need to glance backward and forward when writing: "It *had been* four years since I last *visited* my former high school, and after only a few minutes on campus, I *realized* that I *would never be able* to recapture the feeling of my school days." In this sentence the shifts are natural and controlled. The writer is aware of them but keeps the principal tense — in the example the past tense, *visited, realized* — consistent.

Delete Empty Words

The first words to delete are the empty, meaningless ones: *lovely, pretty, beautiful, good, great, terrific,* and others that lack specific qualities. Also cross out words that you may have added for emphasis: *very, quite, rather, really,* and *so.* Words of this sort carry over into writing from speech habits. When spoken, they add vocal emphasis to intensify a point or feeling. But writing is different from speaking. Writers intensify by being concise and by using concrete detail. Consider, for instance, what the writer actually expresses in the following sentence:

> The very lovely woman with a rather pretty smile walked down the beautiful lane.

Begin by asking yourself what a "very lovely woman" looks like. Or a "rather pretty smile." Or a "beautiful lane." *Very, lovely, pretty,* and *beautiful* fail to give a clear picture of what the writer experienced. These words suggest only a good feeling about seeing the woman; they have no content. Like a child's coloring book, they function as blank spaces for readers to fill in their private perceptions.

For beginning writers, empty words can be deceptive. They can deceive writers into believing they have said something when they haven't. By crossing out such words, a writer can get a better look at the content of the sentence.

> The woman with a smile walked down the lane.

Not much content. And when written more concisely,

> Smiling, the woman walked down the lane.

the sentence seems to say less.

Now, there is an advantage to this kind of editing. It gives the writer a chance to revise — to return to the prewritten draft or to memory and select more concrete details to add to the work. After revision, the sentence might read like this:

> Smiling, the thin woman with flowing blond hair walked down the lane edged with blooming geraniums.

Now the sentence creates a clearer picture of what the writer experienced. The writer has included details the reader can visualize.

Tighten Sentences

There is more to editing and revising than deleting empty words and rebuilding with concrete details. The writer must also tighten the sentences by combining loosely arranged sentences, deleting words that repeat the content of other words, and replacing weak and general verbs with stronger, more accurate ones. As an illustration, let's examine part of a rough draft that sets out to describe an autumn day:

> As soon as I walked outside I knew fall had come. Clouds came in from the west and filled the afternoon with dark shadows. The wind blew around the leaves. They were dead and dry and made a scraping sound against the pavement. Children walking home from school were bundled in heavy coats, and many of them had scarves wrapped around their necks.

The opening sentence sets up a clear purpose. It also leads the reader into sentences that detail the writer's sudden awareness that fall has arrived. That's good, for setting purposes and leading readers into passages are what opening sentences should do. But notice how the descriptive flow is interrupted by the fourth sentence:

> They [the leaves] were dead and dry and made a scraping sound against the pavement.

As you can see, the details relate to the writer's description of fall, but the piece seems to come to a momentary standstill because the focus shifts to the leaves. The sentence could be cut out, but no writer wants to lose good detail. Rather than cutting it, the writer can combine it with the preceding one. So instead of retaining

> The wind blew around the leaves. They were dead and dry and made a scraping sound against the pavement.

he could revise it to read

> The wind blew around the dead and dry leaves that scraped against the pavement.

The piece is now concise and reads smoothly:

> As soon as I walked outside I knew fall had come. Clouds came in from the west and filled the afternoon with dark shadows. The wind blew around the dead and dry leaves that scraped against the pavement. Children walking home from school were bundled in heavy coats, and many of them had scarves wrapped around their necks.

This doesn't end the process of editing and revising, though. It only helps the writer see where other changes need to be made. He might continue by working on the part he just rebuilt:

> The wind blew around the dead and dry leaves that scraped against the pavement.

Consider the words *dead* and *dry:* each has within it the idea of the other — a dead leaf is dry and a dry leaf is dead. There is no reason to use both. Now, consider *wind,* the verb *blew,* and the preposition *around,* which follows *blew.* Also consider the phrase *that scraped against the pavement:* a nice image appealing to the reader's sense of sound, but the wording is sloppy. By pausing to examine these words, the writer will realize that wind has the idea of blowing in it. After all, what does wind do if not blow? *Around,* which is used to buttress *blew,* might even be misread. Certainly the wind does blow around leaves, but it also blows around corners, which is not the same thing. A solution to the sloppy wording lies in the phrase *that scraped against the pavement.* From it the writer can lift the verb *scraped* and revise the sentence to read:

> The wind scraped the dead leaves against the pavement.

Keeping in mind the need to delete unnecessary words along with words that repeat the content of other words, combining weak sentences, and substituting accurate verbs for weak or inaccurate ones, a writer might produce an edited and revised version like this:

stepped
As soon as I ~~walked~~ outside I knew fall had come.

blew
Clouds ~~came~~ in from the west and filled the afternoon   *"Blew" is more accurate than "came."*

with dark shadows. The wind scraped dead leaves against   *A shadow is dark. No need to say "dark."*

the pavement. Children walking home from school ~~were~~   *"Wore" easily replaces the wordy "were bundled in." Also makes the sentence active.*

wore
~~bundled in~~ heavy coats, and many ~~of them~~ had scarves

"Of them" is unnecessary.

wrapped around their necks.

The edited and revised piece now reads:

> As soon as I stepped outside I knew fall had come. Clouds blew in from the west and filled the afternoon with shadows. The wind scraped dead leaves against the pavement. Children walking home from school wore heavy coats, and many had scarves wrapped around their necks.

On rereading the revised draft, the writer might think the sentence "The wind scraped dead leaves against the pavement" might be more effective if *against* were changed to *along*. The change would give the piece a little more movement:

> The wind scraped dead leaves *along* the pavement.

Well, the tinkering has to stop somewhere. Otherwise, papers would never get turned in.

Completing the Revision

The way to start editing and revising is with a pencil in hand and the rough draft before you. Begin by reading aloud at a much slower pace than normal to see and hear whether any words or phrases can be deleted without loss of meaning or emphasis. Draw a line through the words and phrases you wish to delete; but don't totally obscure them, for later they may remind you of detail to add when you are working on the final draft. In the margins and the spaces between the lines write in any additional detail you wish to add.

Now before studying Tom Rolf's edited and revised description, read his comments on the editing and revising process.

When editing and revising I thought I would merely be polishing my rough draft, so I was surprised how much I was still involved in creating what it was that I struggled to illustrate. There was much that I liked about my rough draft — especially the image of the pier looking like a heap of prehistoric bones . . . but that image really was not part of my observation because it was how I felt about the pier before I even began my observations. Also, the rough draft didn't create the sense of mystery I felt or even the stronger sense of being alone. Actually, after rereading the rough draft, I decided that the idea of feeling alone interested me more than the mystery of the place, so I decided to stress that a little more.

What follows is Tom's edited and revised draft with his comments on the process printed in the margin. We suggest you first study how he deleted and added detail by reading through the piece, then reread it along with Tom's explanations.

Tom's Edited and Revised Draft

Tom's Rough Draft

~~I walked from~~ *Last night I walked to* my apartment to the beachfront. It

the end of the pier. I like to ~~feels~~ good ~~to walk to the end of the pier late after~~ *(you)*

visit the pier to collect my ~~finish~~ *(your)* homework. ~~It's a reward for me, empty, time~~

thoughts. ~~to gather my thoughts. Often~~ *the* pier seem*ed* mysterious.

(shifted point of view)

and I felt very much alone.
~~At night the pier looks like a heap of bones. It looks like the~~

~~bones of some prehistoric creature. The pier at night is~~

~~usually empty with only a few fishermen wrapped in heavy~~

~~coats, watch caps pulled down over their ears.~~

These changes tighten up my opening. I had too much unnecessary information and had shifted point of view.

I deleted "Often" because I was only describing one particular night. I added "I felt very much alone" because "aloneness" was part of the impression I wanted to create. I knew, however, that words like "very" were on the teacher's "hit list."

On reexamination, although it hurt to cut all this description, I felt this detail didn't serve my purpose and might even misguide the reader.

~~They gather near the deserted bait shop that seems~~

Beneath

~~haunted with graffiti scrawled on its peeling walls.~~ On ^

sea ○

the pier I sensed the motion of the ~~ocean.~~ The swells

"*Beneath the pier*" *is more accurate, and* "*sea*" *seems more specific than* "*ocean*."

were ~~very~~ rough, rising and falling, and I could hear

them splashing against the ~~wooden~~ pilings. There was

"*Very*" *is empty and* "*wooden*" *is unnecessary.*

no moon, ~~tonight,~~ but ~~there were~~ stars ~~that~~ shined like

single

~~beautiful~~ sequins on black velvet. I saw a ^ bait boat with

spot lights blazing ○   *white-hot*   *ed*

~~its lights shining.~~ The boat ~~looked~~ like a jewel, glowing

against the black sea, ~~or like a white-hot ghost rising~~

"*Tonight*" *is unnecessary since I had already established that it was night in the opening sentence. I also tightened this sentence by deleting the unnecessary* "*there were*" *and* "*that.*" *I deleted* "*beautiful*" *because it is an empty word.*

~~from the water.~~ At the end of the pier I saw a man, ~~who~~

I felt I had overdescribed the boat, so I deleted the ghostly image but used "*white-hot.*" *I also embellished the description by adding* "*spotlights blazing.*" *I added* "*single*" *to remind the reader of the feeling of being alone.*

~~interested me. He was~~ alone and fishing. He stood ~~at the~~

~~very end of the pier~~ beneath a ~~dully lit~~ lamppost. He bent

Here again I tried to intensify my description by deleting unnecessary words.

He worked the hook into the squid's back and then

squid

over a bucket, putting ~~bait~~ on a hook. ~~He finished and stood~~ ○

~~up.~~ He lifted his ~~fishing~~ pole, ~~and~~ guided it ~~way back~~ over his

casting

head, and arched his back before ~~he tossed~~ the line ~~into~~

"*Squid*" *is more concrete than* "*bait,*" *and I used it because I thought the reader could more easily visualize the experience. I expanded the baiting process in an attempt to more directly involve the reader. I deleted* "*up*" *because if someone stands, he stands* "*up.*" *I deleted* "*fishing*" *because the reader already knows the man is using a fishing pole. I also deleted some other unnecessary words and used* "*casting*" *in place of* "*tossing*" *because it more accurately describes what the fisherman was doing.*

hummed   *until*

~~the water.~~ The ~~hum of his~~ line ~~spinning~~ from the reel, ~~sang~~

~~in the night. Then~~ I heard the sinker splash into the water.

The last sentences needed to be combined; "*hummed*" *suggests* "*sang*" *and* "*night*" *was repetitious.*

After completing the editing and revising phase, Tom Rolf made the following comments: "To look at my revised draft can be misleading. It may seem that I made these changes all at once — that I did them while working my way through the rough draft the first time. Actually, for me editing and revising just doesn't work that way. I need to read and reread. I often try out words and different sentence arrangements on scratch paper before making a change."

WRITING TASK

Edit and revise your rough draft. With pencil in hand and rough draft before you, begin to reread and write the changes between the lines and in the margins as illustrated in the example of the two joggers. As you edit and revise your piece, you may notice that it becomes substantially shorter. Don't worry about that. Instead, work toward thoroughly editing and revising this draft.

Remember:

1. Delete empty words and add concrete detail where you find it necessary.
2. Tighten your sentences by combining loose sentences, by deleting words that repeat the meaning of other words, and by replacing weak and general verbs with more accurate ones. (See *to be,* p. 309.)
3. Be prepared to reread your description several times aloud, testing new words and phrases to see if they improve your piece.

Final Draft

When all the editing and revising is done that can be done on the rough draft, one step still remains — the final draft. In many respects the final draft is another revision.

At this point you probably have a piece of writing that looks like a Jackson Pollock painting — you know, the kind with dribbles and streaks across the canvas. A scribbled appearance is typical of edited drafts with revisions penciled between lines and in margins. Professional writers have been known to tape or staple additional strips or sheets of paper to the sides of their rough drafts to accommodate extensive revisions. You may want to try that technique when you are editing and revising future assignments. In the meantime, you are now ready to start your final draft. The final draft continues the revision process. We suggest you begin it by thinking about your readers.

Act as a Reader

During the early phases of the composing process, we briefly mentioned the reader during editing and revising. While completing the final draft, however, you must imagine your reader as a major part of the process. You must remember that whether you are writing for an instructor, your friends and peers, or an audience beyond your campus, your work is going to be read by someone other than yourself. The final stage of the composing process — the final draft — is the time to consider the reader's expectations seriously, which will help you write more clearly.

If you have not identified a specific reader, as you would do for a note to a friend or a report for a college committee, then you must act as your own reader. This is a neat trick that requires you to separate your self from your work and examine the work as if you had not been its author. You begin by reading your edited and revised manuscript aloud. You include all the revisions — that is, you drop from the reading all that you have crossed out and include all that you have added. While reading, ask yourself some simple questions:

Do the opening sentences guide a reader to what follows?
Do the sentences seem logically connected and flow smoothly from beginning to end?
Does the description end in a satisfying way?

And finally,

Would a reader unfamiliar with the information or experience understand the description?

To perform like a vigilant reader is tough, demanding that you step from your skin into another's.

Before going on to an illustration of Tom Rolf's final draft, we want to mention two concepts that will help you keep a reader on the right track. One is the use of transitions and the other is tone.

Use Transitions

The use of transitional techniques helps you hold a reader's attention. Although there are many techniques a writer can use to connect sentences, one way to do it is through overt transitions — words and phrases that guide a reader from point to point. Without adequate transitions, papers seem to skip about, letting a reader's attention stray. As a writer, your goal is to keep your readers with you. You must not allow them to stray, so use transitions to smooth their way from beginning to end. (See Coherence, p. 312.)

Consider the Tone

Tone is a very complicated part of writing, but if you begin by thinking of it as the voice in which you wish to address a reader, you have started to master its complexity. You might approach a reader in a casual or chatty voice or in a more reserved or formal voice. Either is acceptable. In fact, any tone is acceptable as long as it fits the subject. For instance, to write about the crash of a Boeing 707 in the breezy voice of a sports journalist would be inappropriate. It would also be inappropriate to write about Woody Allen's humor in the deadened tone of a government pamphlet. These voices just would not fit the subjects. (See Tone, p. 376.)

Writing the Final Draft

To prepare to write a final draft, you must examine the edited and revised draft to see if there are any further changes you wish to make. As you examine the draft, imagine you are a reader who is unfamiliar with the material. Ask yourself questions as you read: Are there confusing parts? Do the sentences flow together? Can the words be made more concrete and accurate? Is the arrangement easy to follow?

Before examining Tom Rolf's final draft, let's reread the edited and revised draft with the penciled notations integrated and the deletions left out. As you reread it, keep in mind what we have just said about asking questions.

Tom Rolf's Edited and Revised Draft

Last night I walked to the end of the pier. I like to

visit the pier to collect my thoughts. The pier seemed

mysterious, and I felt very much alone. Beneath the pier

I sensed the motion of the sea. The swells were rough,

rising and falling, and I could hear them splashing
against the pilings. There was no moon but stars shined
like sequins on black velvet. I saw a single bait boat with
spotlights blazing. The boat, like a white-hot jewel,
glowed against the black sea. At the end of the pier I
saw a man, alone and fishing. He stood beneath a
lamppost. He bent over a bucket, putting a squid on a
hook. He worked the hook into the squid's back and then
stood. He lifted his pole, guided it over his head, and
arched his back before casting the line. The line hummed
from the reel until I heard the sinker splash into the
water.

It doesn't take much reader vigilance to see some of the flaws in Tom's description. But cutting out unnecessary words and description through editing and revising will help you see the flaws in your work also.

Keep in mind, too, that writing a final draft doesn't merely involve copying the edited and revised draft with the changes integrated and transitions added. Often you will need to rework your sentences so that they flow more smoothly together and you might sharpen your language in order to make your description more dramatic. The completed final draft should also be completely polished — that is, it should be free of errors in punctuation, grammar, and syntax.

Finally, even though the final revision is mainly an intellectual process, the act of doing it often stirs the creative part of a writer's mind. Forgotten details or new comparisons may appear in your awareness. They shouldn't be shut out. If they fit and add to the description, you may work them into your manuscript.

Before reviewing Tom Rolf's final draft, read what he has to say about creating it.

I still wasn't completely happy with my revised draft, although much of it I liked — the image of the stars and the blazing spotlights that made the bait boat look like a jewel. But I felt the opening needed improvement and that many of the sentences still needed tightening and seemed choppy to read, especially the section describing the fisherman. Worse, though, is that the whole description didn't quite create the mood I sensed — the mystery.

Still, I felt the description was interesting, and I was still captured by the idea that I was a lone walker trying to catch my thoughts like the lone fisherman was trying to catch fish. Then I had the thought that I was a "night walker" and he was a "night fisherman," casting into the darkness, which to me suggests casting into the unknown.

For the final draft I decided to smooth out the description and to concentrate on the fisherman even more — especially his baiting the hook and casting his line, which now reminded me of a ritual or a dance movement. I decided to capture these thoughts without editorializing — that is, without directly saying what I was feeling. I also decided to write in an objective, almost detached, tone, which I felt would let the description create a mood for the reader.

Before you study Tom's final draft, we want to suggest a way for you to proceed. First, reread his edited and revised draft on page 31. Then read the final draft that follows here. As you read, note the changes Tom made. Then, after the first reading of the final draft, reread it and, as you work through it, study Tom's comments in the margin, which will help you understand why he made certain changes.

Tom Rolf's Final Draft

Last night I walked alone to the end of the pier to collect my thoughts. The night seemed mysterious.

I combined the first three sentences to create a smoother opening. I added "alone" in the first sentence and kept "The night seemed mysterious" to give the reader a sense of my purpose. Making these changes also allowed me to delete "very much" — empty words, as my instructor claims.

Beneath my feet I sensed the motion of the sea, the swells rising and falling, heaving against the pilings.

I felt the next two sentences were choppy so I combined them and tried to create a "sealike" rhythm. I changed "Beneath the pier" to "Beneath my feet" because "feet" seemed more concrete and I hoped it would appeal more directly to the reader's senses.

Overhead there was no moon, but the stars glistened like

I added the transition "overhead" to direct the reader, and I changed "shined" to "glistened" and added "stitched" because I thought . . . well, I'm not sure why; I just think it makes a stronger image for the reader.

sequins stitched to black velvet. In the distance, I saw a

bait boat with its spotlights blazing. The boat, like a

white-hot jewel, glowed against the black sea. By the

"In the distance" is another transitional phrase I added to lead the reader. I dropped "single" because I felt it was unnecessary. At this point I realized how much contrast there was between light and darkness — bright stars/black velvet sky, blazing spotlights/black sea. I liked the contrast.

lamppost that marked the end of the pier, I saw a figure

move. It was a lone night fisherman bent over a bucket.

He held a hook in one hand and a small squid in the

other. Slowly, meditatively, he worked the hook into the

squid's back, and then he stood. With the pole held

overhead, he began to cast: his body near the rail, one

foot forward, arching back and whipping the pole, the

line humming from the reel. I saw the silver sinker sail

beyond the lamplight and heard it splash somewhere in

the darkness.

I worked very hard to improve the fisherman section, as you can see if you compare the final draft with the edited and revised draft. First, I used a clear transition to locate the reader, "By the lamppost that marked the end of the pier" (I used lamppost because I wanted the fisherman to be in the light, which would help the reader understand how I could see what he was doing). Then I wanted to reveal the fisherman slowly, so I identify him as a "figure" that moved. Then I make his image a little clearer for the reader, "a lone night fisherman," hoping to tease my reader's curiosity. I figured the use of "slowly, meditatively" would create for the reader the sense of care the fisherman took in baiting the hook. I then tried very hard "to paint" a picture of the act of casting.

I liked ending with the word "darkness" because it suggests the unknown sea in which the man fishes and circles back to the opening sentence, "Last night I walked alone . . . to collect my thoughts."

As Tom Rolf's experience clearly shows, the act of writing can become a mysterious activity. Although we can talk about using concrete language, writing in complete sentences, placing punctuation marks properly, arranging the material in a logical order, and creating a consistent point of view, verb tense, and tone, the final work becomes more than the guidelines you use to finish it. Writers are alchemists of words and images. They shape new realities from base materials. Therefore, at some point explanation fails — the act cannot be defined. But it can be illustrated. We suggest you study the illustrations in detail, while appreciating that there is more to writing than can be explained.

WRITING TASK

After examining your edited and revised draft as your own vigilant reader, write the final draft.

Remember:

1. Arrange your description logically.
2. Add transitions to guide the reader's attention.
3. Add and drop details when appropriate to do so.

Polishing Your Work

Often the final draft is the last version you will have to write before turning in your work. But sometimes you will need to write a polished draft. Preparing the polished draft involves rereading to check for sentence fragments, comma splices and run-on sentences, and punctuation errors, all of which are discussed in the Index for Writers. Also check that the principal verb tense, point of view, and tone are consistent. Finally, use a dictionary to check your spelling. If you spot any errors, correct them and recopy your paper, integrating your corrections. A polished draft is just what the term *polished* suggests — a piece that represents your best effort at communicating a point while using correct writing conventions.

3 RESPONDING TO EXPERIENCE

In the last series of tasks, you worked with description. You stuck closely to what you observed and avoided writing about what you thought or felt. The next writing task will ask you to integrate what you think or feel about an experience with a description of the experience. In other words, we want you to *respond* to an experience.

Support Generalizations with Specific Detail

Successful writing is a mixture of generalization and specific detail, but beginning writers tend to overgeneralize by offering their judgments or feelings — their responses — without including enough detail to show a reader why they respond as they do.

The tendency to write in general language is a habit carried over into writing from speaking. In our typical conversations there is little need to specifically describe the details behind our judgments. A listener who wants to hear them will ask. For instance, consider a general statement a friend of yours might make: "It was great at the beach yesterday." You might nod your head and agree, saying, "Wish I'd been there." End of conversation. On the other hand, your curiosity might be aroused enough to start asking questions.

"What do you mean by *great?*" you ask, a frown crossing your brow.

"Hot. The sun was out and there was a lot of action," he answers, his face lighting up with the memory.

"Action? What kind of action?"

"Well," he says, rubbing his chin, "there was a grueling volleyball match between the Daytona Beach and Miami champs. The surf was up — about four feet. And the water was in the sixties."

Depending on the extent of your interest, the questioning might go on. But somewhere you would probably stop and agree that the day was great. The flat assertion might not have convinced you, but the specifics would. Whenever you write, remember nothing so exhausts readers as being led through a bog of general assertions that go unsupported by specifics — like this:

> It was beautiful at the beach yesterday. The weather was terrific. The shore was filled with plenty of action. The waves were great, and the water was the best it's been in months.

On the other hand, if you keep in mind that readers, unlike listeners, lack the right of cross-examination, and if you mix your responses — your thoughts, feelings, judgments, conclusions, assertions, whatever you wish to call them — with the specific details they're based on, readers will move through your work with ease. To write meaningfully, then, you must give readers specific details behind your general responses so that they can make up their own minds about the experience. If the beach conversation had been put in written form, a final draft fleshed out with more detail might have looked like this:

> Yesterday I went to the beach. By eight the sun, like a huge arc light, had burned through the morning haze. The surf, which had been flat for three days, stayed smooth as glass, and the swells reached four feet before breaking in even lines. The water was in the sixties, so warm I didn't need a wet suit. That afternoon about three, two championship volleyball teams held a playoff. Miami had a six-foot-four giant with a spike that hit the sand like a Nike missile. But one scruffy Daytona player kept digging it out. The game lasted for over an hour until Daytona finally caved in. The day was great.

Except for the first and last lines, which carry the writer's responses, the entire piece is made up of specific details. In writing it's never enough just to state your response to an experience; you must also include the specifics behind it.

Use Listing or Clustering to Gather Material from Memory

As your writing assignments become more complex, you'll find that you need to collect more and more material in prewritten form. Either creating an expanded list or clustering your ideas will help you generate enough material to develop a solid rough draft by activating dormant memories. As you compile a memory list, for instance, one notation will lead to another in a series of associations you didn't know existed in your mind.

One way to begin a memory list is to focus your thinking on a subject by writing it at the top of a page. Sit quietly and let your mind drift back to the experience, recording everything that comes to you — descriptive details, names, dates, bits of dialogue, feelings, and such. As you develop the list, try to keep the flow going. Don't reject any items; even a weak idea may lead to better material. Later you can decide which ideas to exclude and which to expand and include in your rough draft. But if you edit your list too soon, you may inhibit the flow of ideas.

The following memory list was written by a student who wanted to recapture a childhood visit to a convalescent home where her grandmother was a patient. As she composed the list she included as much specific detail as she could recall while noting her inner responses — that is, her thoughts and feelings.

Visit to The Palms

- 10 years old. I was mystified. Didn't know what one was — a convalescent home, that is. But I left with a childhood fear of being old.
- Two shabby palm trees out front. The buildings were pink stucco, though I didn't know what stucco was then.
- Old people everywhere. In wheelchairs sitting around the foyer. They seemed strange to my ten-year-old mind. Some babbled to themselves. Some slept, their heads bobbing forward and back. One woman stared at the stained ceiling and tapped her foot as if she were keeping time to music. Maybe the music was in her head, maybe in her soul.
- Smells: Urine. Disinfectant — Lysol? Everything was stuffy, no air. Felt I was suffocating.
- Walking down the hall. More people mumbling. One man who looked out of place, dressed in shirt and slacks, a full head of gray hair, seemed to be comfortable but kept yelling "Help! Help!" Attendants in white walked by him, paying no attention.
- Confused. Why do people come here? Who wants to live like this? I didn't think of them as "people."
- My grandmother. Withered, shrunken, crippled — she had had a stroke. Seeing her made me realize they were all people because I remembered her as a younger, a different person.
- I remember seeing a photograph of her holding my mother and standing next to my grandfather. Then I didn't un-

derstand, but now I realize their smiles said how much in love they were.

– I have a snapshot of her much older — my grandfather had died by then — standing with my mother who was pregnant with me. How odd.

– Another photograph of the three of us when I was about seven. All of us squinting into the sun as if straining to see into the future. Her future took her to The Palms — where is mine taking me?

Composing a memory list, such as the one above, is an effective prewriting activity, but many writers prefer to arrange their memories in clusters because they find that clustering makes finding relations between ideas and details easier. To compile material through clustering, place the topic in the center of a page and circle it. Then as you recall your memories, arrange them around the central topic or in secondary clusters of similar ideas or details.

Sometimes clustering takes place in stages. You might begin by developing a general cluster of the dominant memories that come to you. Then you can return to the cluster and add details and other thoughts to refine the experience.

One writer used clustering to recapture the experience of a trip to Safari Land, an open-space animal park. Initially he clustered the experience as shown below.

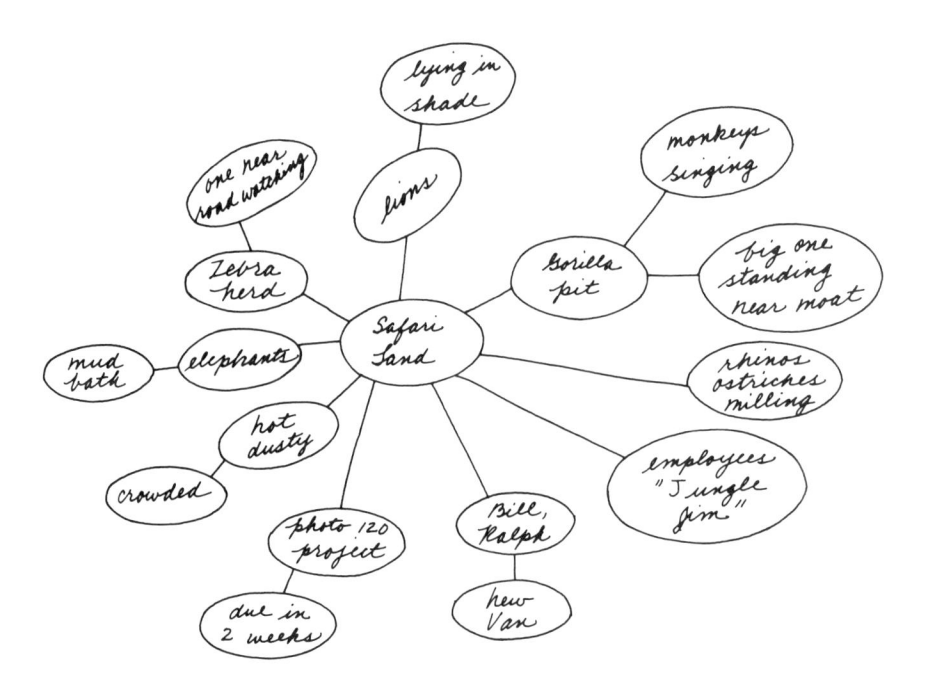

Once he had recaptured the dominant memories, he reviewed the cluster, probed his memory, and added more details and thoughts. A portion of his expanded cluster looked like this:

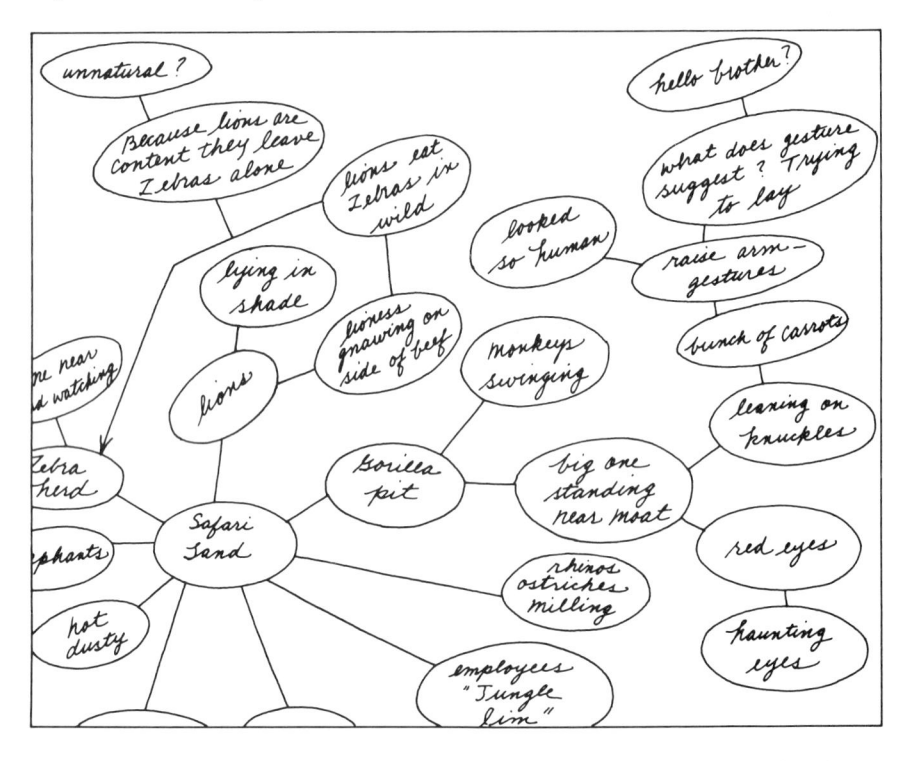

By creating a list or a cluster you will often discover a meaning in an experience that you hadn't realized was there. For instance, while composing a cluster of memories related to his trip to Safari Land, the writer made the ironic discovery that he is much like the wild animals that have been tamed because all their desires are taken care of. He planned to organize his paper around that response.

Use a Response to Organize the Description

Use your response to the experience to organize your description. Your description will be composed mainly of specific detail, but the response will let readers know how you feel or what you think about the experience. The abundance of details will help them see why you respond as you do.

A key tactic for this task is to select details that lead the reader to the same response you had. For instance, in the brief piece above, the writer included only the details that supported his response "It was a great day." He didn't describe the frustration he might have felt while searching for a parking place or standing in line for a hamburger. Instead, he selected details that supported his purpose: the heat, surf, warm water, and volleyball match. There is a specific reason for including these details: to trigger a specific response in a reader.

Not all writing of this sort needs to be as simple as the beach description. Using specific details to reflect an inner response can work in very subtle ways. A writer can use them to suggest a deep personal meaning in an experience that could never be captured by direct statement. Writing of this kind is rich in implication and requires a great deal of concentration on the part of the reader. All the more important for the writer to pay close attention to the arrangement of specifics. The following is the final draft of the Safari Land paper. Notice how the writer organized his description around a particular response. Also notice that he deleted much of the detail included in the memory cluster because it didn't fit his purpose.

Last week while touring Safari Land, I had the thought that many of us live like contented beasts. While we were driving through the gate decorated with jungle trimmings, a friend tapped me on the shoulder and pointed to a sign: "Keep your windows rolled up. Don't feed the animals." He laughed and said, "Wait till a lion eats your new van," before passing an open box of chicken to another friend sitting in the backseat. I joined the procession of cars that twisted along the narrow road toward the hills. Soon we came to a herd of elephants prancing and rolling in a muddy pond. Nearby a man in a tattered safari costume stood by a jeep filling the pond from a hose attached to a hydrant. Some fifty yards beyond, a pride of lions sprawled under a tree, one swishing its tail, others sleeping. And not far from them a lioness gnawed the remains of a side of beef. Within

The writer opens with a general response.

Details of friends eating create a connection with animals eating.

Notice that the description of the elephants, lions, and zebras shows that they are unnaturally contented.

that lioness's easy spring, a herd of zebras grazed on busted bales of hay as if blind to the age-old knowledge that lions live on zebra flesh. A strange world, where creatures that once filled my exotic dreams are tamed by having their desires met with water hoses, hunks of meat, and bales of hay. Then I heard someone mumble through a mouthful of chicken, "Look!" Ahead, circled by a moat, was an island full of apes. Gibbons and chimps swung from rings. Gorillas leaned forward on their knuckles, watching the passing cars. Maneuvering around a Ford, I pulled to one side and stopped. One bull gorilla caught my eye. He lumbered forward, held back by the moat's edge. I raised my camera, my lens tapping against the window glass. My shutter clicked. As if he heard, he lifted a hairy arm and held out a fist filled with bunches of carrots. I clicked again, while he curled the fist back to his chest. Was he gesturing at me to join him? Did he believe all that separated us was the moat and glass? He continued to stare, the red eyes carrying a language that cannot be spoken. I glanced away, surveying the van that now seemed like a cage: the plush carpet, the padded dash, and, sharing it, my two friends who munched away at chicken wings and legs. I glanced back at the staring creature and understood his gesture. It named me brother with desires as small as any beast's.

The writer integrates a response to help the reader understand what he's trying to show.

Notice how the writer showcases the gorilla pit and then concentrates on one gorilla, describing its actions in dramatic terms.

The writer uses questions to reflect his responses.

The writer ends with a responsive interpretation of the gorilla's action. The ending echoes the beginning.

You may have noticed that this piece is thick with specific detail. But did you see that the writer carefully selected those specifics to support the general response that suggests that he, like the creatures in Safari Land, is a captive of his own desires?

After the lead that gets the piece under way, the writer describes the elephants, lions, zebras, and apes as contented creatures that have given up their natural urges in this "strange world, where creatures . . . are tamed by having their desires met. . . ." His response deepens and grows into personal insight when he encounters the gesturing bull gorilla with the massive fist filled with carrots. Of course, the beast isn't attempting to communicate what the writer feels; the writer simply responds to its gesture in this way. He interprets it.

Did you also notice that even the details that might seem unnecessary at first glance serve a purpose? The new van, for instance, functions as a desire that makes the writer captive. His chicken-eating friends may be looked at as contented animals, his companions in captivity. The point is that this writer has selected specific details in an attempt to trigger in the reader a response similar to his own.

Before going on to the next example, we want to mention something about the arrangement of the Safari Land piece. It's constructed in a climactic sequence. The word *climactic* comes from the word *climax* — the point of greatest intensity that ends a series. To arrange a piece in climactic order is to put the most significant part last. Climactic order is an effective way to arrange a paper that deals with personal insights.

Take a look at the next example. Notice how the student blends his inner responses with the specific details he has associated with them. Since he's dealing with personal insight, he arranges the piece so that the climactic point comes at the end. First read the selection through without studying the marginal comments. Then reread it along with the commentary for a more thorough understanding.

While walking through the supermarket last night, I became uneasy about my life. I had just come from home where I had seen the evening news. There had been a report of earthquake destruction in Central America. The report featured a film of a city that collapsed. It showed lost children roaming through the ruins and men and	*The general lead introduces the main elements. It gives the reader some direction.* *"The report featured" begins the concrete description of the report's specifics that relate to the writer's feelings.*

women in shock, sitting in the rubble of their homes. It

showed heaps of bodies waiting to be cremated. A

reporter's voice commented on possible starvation and

epidemic. The whole thing hit me hard. I thought about
"The whole thing hit me hard" begins a sequence of the writer's inner responses.

the emptiness the survivors must feel and about how

they must feel about the future. But life, my life, couldn't

stop. My refrigerator and cupboards were empty; I had to
"My refrigerator and cupboards were empty" prepares the reader for the next phase and ties back to "But life, my life, couldn't stop."

work the next day, and there were places to go and

people to meet, as the saying goes. So an hour later I
"So an hour later" is an overt transition into the next supermarket phase.

was pushing a cart through Ralph's, but I still didn't feel

good. Something was eating away at me. I hurried to
The writer continues to blend in feelings — "I still didn't feel good. Something was eating away at me" — while generating a realistic description of the market.

stock up on groceries for the week — some oranges,

apples, a head of lettuce, juice, milk, a chicken, and a

pound of beef. I began to notice other people shopping

around me: some together, chatting and smiling, and

some alone, lifting items from shelves and comparing

prices. I pushed the cart toward the checkout stand,

trying to understand the feeling that seemed to be
The phrase "trying to understand the feeling" reminds the reader of the main issue and nudges toward the climax.

deepening in me. Just foolishness, I thought. I must have
"I must have become lost in my thoughts" begins the display of the shopper and starving child that crystallize the writer's personal insight.

become lost in my thoughts, for my cart slammed into

another shopper's. I glanced at her. Her eyes sparkled at

my folly. Her tan skin seemed golden, and each eyebrow

was perfectly shaped. But then over her shoulder I saw a

poster advertising a charity. The photograph of a

half-naked child holding an empty bowl, the eyes

pleading, seemed to leap at me. At that moment the

images from the news rose up in my mind — the ruined

homes, lost children, starvation — and I felt anger and

frustration as I realized how helpless I was, and how

spoiled.

The writer closes with his insight and reminds the reader of details mentioned earlier, thus creating a sense of roundness.

As a closing illustration, we offer the beginning paragraph of *Murmurs of Earth* by astronomer-writer Carl Sagan. Notice how Sagan has arranged the paragraph. He begins with a general lead that establishes the scene and sets up the middle. He follows with specific details from the experience and ends with his response. Aside from the arrangement, also notice Sagan's shift in point of view from "I" to "you" and back again. The shift is intentional. It's an attempt to create an impression that the reader is seeing what Sagan saw. Sagan tries to put the reader in the scene. (We suggest you avoid shifts of this sort, however, until you have mastered point of view; see Point of View, p. 360.)

In 1939, before my fifth birthday, my parents took me to the New York World's Fair. It exhibited wonders. Lightning was made to crackle, blue and fearsome, between two metal spheres. A sign read "Hear light! See sound!" and it turned out that, sure enough, such things were possible. There were buildings devoted to strange cultures and faraway lands of whose very existence I had been totally ignorant. The centerpiece of that World's Fair was the Trylon and Perisphere, a stately, tapering tower and a building-sized sphere in which was something called "The World of Tomorrow." You walked on a high-railed ramp and below you, in miniature, was an exquisitely detailed model of the future — graceful aerial skyways filled with streamlined automobiles and happy citizens purposefully intent on some futuristic business, the nature of which was difficult to divine from the perspective of my limited experience and abbreviated stature. But one message was clearly communicated: there were other cultures and there would be future times.

WRITING TASK

In 350 to 400 words describe a meaningful experience. The experience, which may be from the distant or near past, should be one that holds some interest for you, one that brought some insight or new awareness that you can communicate to a reader. To begin, compose a memory list or cluster that includes both inner responses and specific details.

A word of caution: Don't choose a long-term relationship to describe. Relationships are much too complex for such a brief assignment. You might, however, pick just one incident from a complex relationship. Choose a date, an argument, or a chance meeting — an event that embodies the meaning of the relationship.

Remember:

1. Use listing or clustering to compose a prewritten draft.
2. Use a general response to organize your paper.
3. Write a rough draft based on the list or cluster that illustrates your responses with plenty of specific detail.
4. Try to get your reader to visualize the experience.
5. Arrange your material climactically, showcasing the most dramatic part at the end.
6. When you write the final draft, imagine a reader looking over your shoulder to help you shape your paper coherently.

PART TWO

WRITING TASKS

Part Two presents a variety of tasks designed to teach principles of good writing. They range from short paragraphs that emphasize patterns of organization to longer, more complicated essays, and from personal, subjective pieces to more objective ones. Some are accompanied by many examples and thorough discussions that we hope will guide you through the possible pitfalls of the tasks. Others have a minimum of explanation and illustration. Some of the tasks impose structures; some are more open to personal approaches.

How should you approach this part? That depends on the skill you already have. There's no reason for you to start at the beginning and go to the end. Instead, your teacher will guide you through a sequence of tasks to help develop your writing strengths.

4 PARAGRAPH STRUCTURE

Part One contained writing tasks designed to teach you a composing process we hope you will use for all your writing assignments. You practiced the four steps of that process — prewriting, rough draft, editing and revising, and final draft — with assignments that demanded few decisions about organization. We suspect you found it easy to arrange the content you selected from your prewritten lists or clusters because the material fell neatly in chronological or spatial order. But the tasks in the following sections require more conscious choices about structure. In that respect they are typical of the writing you will be expected to do in other courses. Some of the tasks require only one paragraph; some can be better handled in two or three paragraphs; still others will require longer, multiparagraph essays. In any case, as in all prose, the paragraph is the fundamental unit of organization.

Of course paragraphs come in a great variety. In an essay a writer may use one kind of paragraph to introduce the subject and other kinds to develop different portions of the main idea, to summarize evidence presented or arguments made up to a certain part of the essay, to provide a transition between major parts of the essay, or to conclude the essay. If dialogue is included in the paper, paragraphing is used to indicate a change of speaker. The point is that paragraphing is put to a variety of uses in prose writing.

The pages that follow in this chapter, though, focus attention on the most frequently used, the most basic kind of paragraphs — those intended to present one part of an essay's central point, in other words, the paragraphs that serve as major building blocks in the body of an essay. (See Deductive Essay, pp. 139–172.)

A well-structured paragraph consists of several sentences that discuss a single idea. A paragraph can stand alone as a brief work, but usually a paragraph functions as part of a longer piece of writing. Successful paragraphs, regardless of differences in plan and content, share three characteristics:

1. Unity. All of the sentences in the paragraph contribute to the same idea.
2. Coherence. The thought proceeds logically from sentence to sentence.
3. Adequate development. The paragraph contains enough information to convey the idea in a reasonably thorough manner.

By studying the following paragraph you can see how John Brooks applies the principles of good paragraph structure. Brooks develops a single idea — in this case, that the invention of the telephone has had numerous effects on our lives. He maintains unity by making every sentence relate to the single idea. He achieves coherence by repeating parallel patterns, such as *by bringing, by joining, by so doing,* and *it has.* And he fully develops his idea by listing eight effects or probable effects the telephone has had on our lives.

What has the telephone done to us, or for us in the hundred years of its existence? A few effects suggest themselves at once. It has saved lives by getting rapid word of illness, injury, or famine from remote places. By joining with the elevator to make possible the multistory residence or office building, it has made possible — for better or worse — the modern city. By bringing about a quantum leap in the speed and ease with which information moves from place to place, it has greatly accelerated the rate of scientific and technological change and growth in industry. Beyond doubt it has crippled if not killed the ancient art of letter writing. It has made living alone possible for persons with normal

The opening question identifies the single idea Brooks will develop.

The topic is developed by presenting a variety of effects.

social impulses; by so doing, it has played a role in one

of the greatest social changes of this century, the

breakup of the multigenerational household. It has made

the waging of war chillingly more efficient than

formerly. Perhaps (though not provably) it has

prevented wars that might have arisen out of

international misunderstanding caused by written

communication. Or perhaps — again not provably — by

magnifying and extending irrational personal conflicts

based on voice contact, it has caused wars. Certainly it

has extended the scope of human conflicts, since it

impartially disseminates the useful knowledge of

scientists and the babble of bores, the affection of the

affectionate and the malice of the malicious.

Using a Topic Sentence

Frequently a writer uses a topic sentence to announce the content of a paragraph to a reader. In the paragraph above about the effects of the telephone, the topic sentence is really a question, "What has the telephone done to us, or for us, in the hundred years of its existence?" Starting with such a question implies that the paragraph that follows will supply some answers, which of course it does. Brooks chose a question, though he could as easily have announced his subject with a statement. A question is just one possible variation to be used occasionally but not usually. Most topic sentences are statements:

> The invention of the telephone has influenced the way we live in innumerable ways, some less obvious than others.

> Few people know it's possible, and fewer still ever do it, but one way to get a week or two of real rest is to become a paying guest at your local monastery.

> Travelers apparently appreciate the increased security precautions being taken at international airports.

Not every paragraph has a topic sentence, it's true, but before you decide to do without one, consider how useful a topic sentence can be for both the reader and the writer.

For the reader, a topic sentence states the idea of the paragraph (usually at or near the beginning) so he or she knows immediately what the more specific sentences of the paragraph add up to. Imagine the burden you place on your reader if you give several examples, but never say directly what the examples have in common.

For the writer, a good topic sentence serves as a reminder of the boundaries of the paragraph, thereby helping her or him to stick to the point and develop a unified paragraph. Once you have a clear topic sentence, you will find it easier to complete the paragraph. If you find it difficult to write a topic sentence, perhaps you need to think more about your content. Or you may want to write the other sentences of the paragraph first and phrase the topic sentence later.

You may be wondering how you know when you have a "good" topic sentence. "Good" of course is a relative word. It isn't so much that some topic sentences are "bad" and others "good." What you include in your topic sentence depends on your material and how you decide to organize it. The topic sentence cannot be considered in isolation from the other sentences in the paragraph. Without attempting to draw that line between good and bad, though, it is possible to predict what kinds of sentences might make it easier for you to write a successful paragraph.

Keep in mind that a topic sentence should have three characteristics:

1. It includes a subject and a controlling idea.
2. It is limited enough to be developed in one paragraph.
3. It lends itself to development.

The topic sentence "Good listeners not only hear what is said, but also understand nonverbal messages" has these characteristics. It has a subject, "listeners," and a controlling idea, "understand nonverbal messages." It is reasonably limited in scope. The writer has not staked out the entire territory of listening skills. And while it may be true that an expert could write several hundred pages on nonverbal messages, it is also true that a fairly satisfactory discussion could be presented in a paragraph. Finally, the sentence lends itself to development. The writer could follow with examples of such messages and interpret them for the reader. That, in fact, is what a reader will probably be expecting after reading this first sentence.

In contrast the topic sentence "Nonverbal language is interesting" is less focused and therefore it is less clear just what information should follow. Besides that, the tone has changed. The first sentence promises information; the second merely states an attitude. The reader doesn't know what's coming and may be thinking, "Oh, yeah! Not to me!"

How about this sentence: "The guinea pig is a member of the rat family"? You probably noticed right away that this sentence does not meet the third characteristic above. It does not lend itself to further development. It may be a useful fact to know and it could be followed by other facts about guinea pigs, but where is the controlling idea to bring these facts together? Without a controlling idea, any number of unrelated facts could be included and in any order. In short, this example is not a topic sentence at all — just a fact.

As you write topic sentences, ask yourself if they have the three characteristics we have been discussing. For example:

Topic Sentence: The English 320 class is filled with aspiring writers.

Subject?	English 320 class
Controlling Idea?	Filled with aspiring writers
Limited?	Yes
Development	Examples of individuals and their aspirations or discussion about the contests entered, prizes won, etc.

Topic Sentence: At the Compu-Graf convention visitors tested the latest computer graphics software.

Subject?	Visitors at Compu-Graf convention
Controlling Idea?	Tested latest computer software
Limited?	Yes
Development?	Description of testing facilities and/or the latest programs.

Topic Sentence: Students interested in a career in landscape architecture often visit the Randolph Nursery to see the miniature replicas of the world's most famous gardens.

Subject?	Students of landscape architecture
Controlling Idea?	Often visit Randolph Nursery
Limited?	Yes

Development?	We'll have trouble here. The controlling idea — often visit — does not lend itself to development very well. It seems to require a list of the times visited — not a very interesting content. Probably the writer intends to describe the miniature gardens. If so, the sentence should be rephrased to make the gardens the subject.
Topic Sentence Rephrased:	Randolph Nursery's miniature replicas of the world's most famous gardens are a valuable resource for landscape architecture students.

Now the subject is the gardens, the controlling idea is their value as a resource for landscape architecture students, and the development can include description and a discussion of what can be learned by visiting the gardens.

Placing the Topic Sentence

As we have said, writers generally place the topic sentence at the beginning of a paragraph as in the following paragraph from Norman MacKinzie's *Dreams and Dreaming*.

> *The public interest in dream oddities never flags.* Only a few years ago, an English newspaper regularly published the dreams of a man who forecast the results of horse races, and there are frequent press reports of cases in which it is claimed that a lost person or stolen object has been recovered by following the clues given in dreams. There was a famous example of this in 1932, when the small son of Colonel Lindbergh, the famous American flyer, was kidnapped: newspaper readers were asked to submit any dreams that might help to find the baby. Hundreds were studied, but less than a dozen bore any resemblance to all the facts. After Goya's portrait of the Duke of Wellington was stolen from the National Gallery in London in 1961, eager dreamers claimed to have "solved" the crime. In 1958, even the American Atomic Energy Commission considered a proposal that it should employ dream clairvoyants to predict where Soviet bombs might fall in the event of war!

Sometimes the controlling idea of a topic sentence is refined by one or two sentences that follow it, as in the following example:

> *It is rare to find people who actually like to be single and want to stay that way. What one finds more frequently are men and women who say they* adore *being single but who spend most of their nonworking time looking for some kind of sexual or romantic attachment.* Tony, for example, has a certain image of life with a woman. It includes fidelity, marriage, domesticity. But until he finds the particular woman with whom he can have total communication he won't give up his freedom. He has had several almost-major involvements in the past years. But each time he started measuring the current woman against his mental image. Reality never quite matched the ideal: the woman was too thin; they didn't really have that much in common — there were always objections. And he'd begin to long for his single days again. The last time this had happened, the woman found someone else. And he continued on his rounds of the single life. After a time Tony watched the woman get more and more involved with her new man. He began to rethink his relationship with her. She was actually more intelligent, prettier, and more sexually exciting than he had realized. She would not have been a bad person to spend a life with. He even talked to her about that prospect, but she was too attached to her new beau and they were thinking of living together.
>
> — Suzanne Gordon

Although placing a topic sentence at the beginning of a paragraph is sound practice, and we strongly advise you to follow that practice in formal assignments, a writer will sometimes place it in another part of the paragraph or, if the controlling idea can be clearly understood from the discussion, leave it out entirely.

Robin Roberts in this paragraph from *Newsweek* places the topic sentence at the end as a conclusion to be drawn from the details that come before it.

> If you watch a Little League game, in most cases the pitchers are the most mature. They throw harder, and if they throw strikes very few batters can hit the ball. Consequently, it makes good baseball sense for most hitters to take the pitch. Don't swing. Hope for a walk. That could be a player's instruction for four years. The fun is in hitting the ball; the coach says don't swing. That may be sound baseball, but it does nothing to help a

young player develop his hitting. *What would seem like a basic training ground for baseball often turns out to be a program of negative thoughts that only retards a young player.*

If a writer chooses to leave out the topic sentence, then the controlling idea must clearly emerge from the paragraph's details. Philosopher Bertrand Russell leaves out the topic sentence in the following paragraph that describes the role of the subconscious in his writing process.

Very gradually I have discovered ways of writing with a minimum of worry and anxiety. When I was young each fresh piece of serious work used to seem to me for a time — perhaps a long time — to be beyond my powers. I would fret myself into a nervous state from fear that it was never going to come right. I would make one unsatisfying attempt after another, and in the end have to discard them all. At last I found that such fumbling attempts were a waste of time. It appeared that after first contemplating a book on some subject, and after giving serious preliminary attention to it, I needed a period of subconscious incubation which could not be hurried and was if anything impeded by deliberate thinking. Sometimes I would find, after a time, that I had made a mistake, and that I could not write the book I had had in mind. But often I was more fortunate. Having, by a time of very intense concentration, planted the problem in my subconscious, it would germinate underground until, suddenly, the solution emerged with blinding clarity, so that it only remained to write down what had appeared as if in a revelation.

Although Russell starts off with a general statement that effectively takes the reader into the paragraph and names the subject — "writing" — the controlling idea is never stated.

Closing with a Clincher

Often when a writer begins a paragraph with a topic sentence, he or she will end with a clincher — a sentence or two that restates the controlling idea in different words, summarizes the discussion, or offers the writer's personal response to the material. In the following paragraph from "Take Your College in Stride," William Carleton ends his comparison of professors and books with a clincher that restates his controlling idea.

As sources of ideas, professors simply cannot compete with books. Books can be found to fit almost every need, temper, or interest. Books can be read when you are in the mood; they do not have to be taken in periodic doses. Books are both more personal and more impersonal than professors. Books have an inner confidence which individuals seldom show; they rarely have to be on the defensive. Books can afford to be bold and courageous and exploratory; they do not have to be so careful of boards of trustees, colleagues, and community opinion. Books are infinitely diverse; they run the gamut of human activity. Books can be found to express every point of view; if you want a different point of view, you can read a different book. (Incidentally, this is the closest approximation to objectivity you are likely ever to get in humanistic and social studies.) Even your professor is at his best when he writes books and articles; the teaching performance rarely equals the written effort.

Developing a Paragraph

How long should a paragraph be? Paragraph length depends on many things: the complexity of the idea, the method of development, the length of adjacent paragraphs if it is part of a longer work, and the age, knowledge, interest, and educational background of its intended audience. Most important, a paragraph should be developed enough to do justice to the controlling idea expressed in the topic sentence.

Short paragraphs are easier to read, but a paper consisting of two- or three-sentence paragraphs may make the entire effort seem immature and underdeveloped. Long paragraphs seem more intellectual and weighty, but too many of them may discourage a reader and make the subject appear more difficult and intricate than it actually is.

The best approach, really, is not to worry much about paragraph length. Instead, concentrate on fully developing the controlling idea in your topic sentence by including enough specific supporting information to avoid skimpy, immature paragraphs, such as the one that follows.

A number of curious experiences occur at the onset of sleep. A person just about to go to sleep may experience an odd physical sensation, the most common of which is the sense of floating or falling. A nearly universal occurrence at the beginning of sleep (although not everyone recalls it) is a sudden jerk of the body. The onset of sleep is not gradual at all. It happens in an instant.

Obviously, the above paragraph suffers from underdevelopment. The writer needs to add more specific information and concrete details to develop the topic sentence adequately. Now study the original paragraph as Peter Farb wrote it. Notice how the addition of information and specific details turns an underdeveloped paragraph into a fully developed one.

> A number of curious experiences occur at the onset of sleep. A person just about to go to sleep may experience an electric shock, a flash of light, or a crash of thunder — but the most common sensation is that of floating or falling, which is why "falling asleep" is a scientifically valid description. A nearly universal occurrence at the beginning of sleep (although not everyone recalls it) is a sudden, uncoordinated jerk of the head, the limbs, or even the entire body. Most people tend to think of going to sleep as a slow slippage into oblivion, but the onset of sleep is not gradual at all. It happens in an instant. One moment the individual is awake, the next moment not.

When you find that you have written an underdeveloped paragraph, there is no need to moan and wring your hands. Instead, use prewriting techniques to generate more detail — that is, develop another list or create a new cluster. You can then integrate the detail into a revised version of your paragraph.

Achieving Unity

A paragraph is unified when all the sentences clearly relate to the controlling idea expressed in the topic sentence. Read Lael Morgan's paragraph from "Let the Eskimos Hunt" to see how the supporting information and details relate the idea that many people oppose hunting even where animal populations are dangerously large.

Many Americans mindlessly oppose hunting, even in cases where animal populations are dangerously high. In some areas of Alaska, wolves have become so prolific they are running out of hunting ground and prey heavily on moose, deer, and occasionally dogs. In the past, game managers curbed wolf populations by trapping and aerial

Topic sentence

Establishes that some areas are overpopulated

hunting without wiping out the species. Still, whenever

they propose to do this nowadays, they receive tens of

thousands of letters in protest. Growing deer populations

in parts of California threaten to starve themselves out.

Sea-otter colonies, burgeoning along the Pacific coast, are

fast running out of fodder, too, as well as putting

commercial fishermen out of business.

Charges that some people oppose even sensibly controlled hunting

Shows the dangers of uncontrolled animal population growth

Now read the following paragraph for unity problems. As you read, identify the supporting sentences to see if they relate to the controlling idea in the topic sentence.

> [1]Attending this college may be unexpectedly dangerous. [2]Last week in the parking lot my friend Bill accidentally bumped the side of a pickup. [3]Just as he was finishing a note to leave on the windshield, the owner came up, scowled at the grapefruit-size dent, then punched Bill in the nose. [4]He then drove off without looking back or taking Bill's name and address. [5]At least Bill didn't have to pay for the damage. [6]Three days ago a bicyclist wearing portable radio earphones plowed into a psychology instructor, and both went sprawling over the walkway. [7]Yesterday, in the zoology lab, a four-foot snake slipped from its cage. [8]No one noticed until it struck at one student, sending four others into shock. [9]Then the lab technician came in, snatched up the snake, and stuffed it back into the cage. [10]No one plans to sue the college, but those students have a good case if any of them would press it.

No doubt you'll agree that in the following sentences the writer strays from the controlling idea that the college campus may be an unexpectedly dangerous place.

> [4]He then drove off without looking back or taking Bill's name and address.
> [5]At least Bill didn't have to pay for the damage.
> [9]Then the lab technician came in, snatched up the snake, and stuffed it back into the cage.
> [10]No one plans to sue the college, but those students have a good case if any of them would press it.

Each of these sentences gives additional information about the incidents, but they digress from the controlling point. While revising the paragraph for unity, the writer will delete some details and subordinate other details so that each sentence clearly relates to the controlling idea in the topic sentence. (See Subordination, p. 374.) Revised, the paragraph reads as follows:

Attending this college may be unexpectedly   *Topic sentence*

dangerous. Last week in the parking lot my friend Bill

accidentally bumped the side of a pickup. Just as he was

finishing a note to leave on the windshield, the owner   *Integrated details*

came up, scowled at the grapefruit-size dent, then

punched Bill in the nose before driving off without

taking Bill's name and address. Three days ago a bicyclist   *Sentence 5 deleted*

wearing portable radio earphones plowed into a

psychology instructor, and both went sprawling over the

walkway. Yesterday in the zoology lab a four-foot snake   *Integrated details*

slipped from its cage. No one noticed until it struck at

one student, sending four others into shock before the

lab technician came in, snatched up the snake, and

stuffed it back into the cage.   *Sentence 10 deleted*

Maintaining Coherence

A paragraph is coherent when the sentences proceed logically from one to the other. Generally, a writer achieves coherence in one of four ways:

1. By arranging the supporting information in a logical order, such as time order, space order, order of climax, specific-to-general order, or general-to-specific order
2. By using transitional words and phrases to guide the reader overtly
3. By repeating key words and phrases
4. By using parallel structure

When a paragraph is incoherent, a flaw you should guard against, it reads as if the sentences are disconnected, making the reader feel that he or she must leap from thought to thought. (See Coherence, p. 312.)

Study the following paragraph by Laurence Perrine about the psychological differences between ghost and horror stories and great literary works that evoke horror. Notice how Perrine maintains coherence by contrasting details, arranging them in general-to-specific order, and how he uses parallel structure to emphasize the contrast. Also notice how he uses transitional phrases and restates key ideas.

Most of us enjoy the gooseflesh and the tingle along the spine produced by the successful ghost story. There is something agreeable in letting our blood be chilled by bats in the moonlight, guttering candles, creaking doors, eerie shadows, piercing screams, inexplicable bloodstains, and weird noises. But the terror aroused by tricks and external "machinery" is a far cry from the terror evoked by some terrifying treatment of the human situation. The horror we experience in watching the Werewolf or Dracula or Frankenstein is far less significant than that we get from watching the bloody ambition of Macbeth or the jealousy of Othello. In the first, terror is the end-product; in the second, it is the natural accompaniment of a powerful revelation of life. In the first, we are always aware of a basic unreality; in the second, reality is terrifying.

This sentence restates in more concrete language the thought expressed in the opening sentence.

Perrine has placed the topic sentence in the middle of the paragraph.

This sentence is arranged in a parallel fashion.

Perrine arranges the closing sentences with contrasting parallel clauses and uses transitional phrases to guide the reader.

Remember, whether you develop a paragraph by contrast, as Perrine does in the preceding example, or whether you use some other method discussed in the following chapters, you must make your sentences proceed logically from beginning to end — you must maintain coherence.

(WRITING TASK)

Write a paragraph that reflects the principles of well-written paragraphs as discussed in this chapter. Feel free to use your own subject or use one of the following three assignments.

1. The following topic sentences are either too general or too factual. Revise one of them to make it an effective topic sentence and to reflect your own experiences and interests. After composing a prewritten draft, write a well-structured paragraph that supports the controlling idea of the revised sentence.
   a. Hollywood films have both good and bad features.
   b. Vandalism is a problem in urban, suburban, and rural areas.
   c. People must assume responsibility for their actions.
   d. Consumer complaint departments are busy in department stores.
   e. Everyone believes that travel is educational.
   f. Grading policies are different for different classes.
   g. Going to college is expensive.
   h. Dieting is the world's fastest-growing sport.
   i. Part-time jobs teach high school students important lessons.
   j. Computers may or may not be tomorrow's teachers.
2. Read the following paragraph, from "How TV Violence Damages Your Children" by Victor B. Cline, which concentrates on the relation between televised violence and real-life violence.

> Much of the research that has led to the conclusion that TV and movie violence could cause aggressive behavior in some children has stemmed from the work in the area of imitative learning or modeling which, reduced to its simplest expression, might be termed "monkey see, monkey do." Research by Stanford psychologist Albert Bandura has shown that even brief exposure to novel aggressive behavior *on a one-time basis* can be repeated in free play by as high as 88 percent of the young children seeing it on TV. Dr. Bandura also demonstrated that even a single viewing of a novel aggressive act could be recalled and produced by children six months later, without any intervening exposure. Earlier studies have es-

timated that the average child between the ages of 5 and 15 will witness, during this 10-year period, the violent destruction of more than 13,400 fellow humans. This means that through several hours of TV-watching, a child may see more violence than the average adult experiences in a lifetime. Killing is as common as taking a walk, a gun more natural than an umbrella. Children are thus taught to take pride in force and violence and to feel ashamed of ordinary sympathy.

Do some televised programs and movies teach children to take pride in force and violence as Cline suggests? Perhaps they do and perhaps they don't — you can't be certain. You can be certain of what you observe, though, and perhaps you've seen children imitating televised events and situations in their free play.

Write a paragraph that concentrates on the relation of televised violence to children's play. Whereas Cline deals generally with the problem, you are to deal specifically with it — that is, you are to write from your own observations. Begin by composing a topic sentence that states something to the effect that children model televised violence. Use specific information based on your observations of children, such as a younger brother or sister, neighbors, or schoolchildren. You might even include specific information from your childhood experiences with modeling violent events or situations you had seen televised. To get your paragraph started, compose a prewritten draft of your subject and use it as the basis for your paragraph.

3. Write a paragraph on "stars," any kind of stars — night stars, movie stars, football, baseball, tennis stars, the little gold stars teachers did or didn't stick to the tops of your school papers, even five-star generals. Set your imagination free (how about "starry eyed"?). Begin with a cluster by drawing a circle in the center of a clean sheet of paper and writing "stars" in it. The only restriction is that your final paragraph must embody the principles of a well-written paragraph as we've discussed them in this chapter.

Remember:

1. Begin the composing with prewriting.

2. Organize your paragraph by using a topic sentence that announces the subject and controlling idea, is limited, and lends itself to development.
3. Be sure your paragraph is fully developed.
4. Check to see if it is unified.
5. Be sure it is coherent by applying transitional techniques.

5 EXAMPLES

An excellent way to develop a topic sentence is through examples, because an example can convert facts and assertions into concrete pictures that stick in a reader's mind. Writers generally use two kinds of examples: specific and typical.

Typical Examples

Typical examples, as opposed to specific examples, are timeless and general (but not overgeneral and vague). Writers often compose typical examples by generalizing from experiences gathered from many specific observations.

Roxanne Arnold, reporting the results of a poll taken among state lottery players, offers typical examples of the strategies that habitual players adopt to increase their chances of winning. She starts with a general introductory sentence about lottery players being a "varied lot," follows with a topic sentence that limits her attention to the "peculiar strategies and gimmicks" players use, and develops her paragraph with several examples of typical behavior.

As might be expected, the poll revealed lottery players to be a varied lot. Much like the eccentric handicappers found at race tracks, they have their own

Topic sentence limits the subject and suggests examples will follow.

peculiar strategies and gimmicks for bringing them luck.

For the most fatalistic among them, superstition governs how, when and where to scratch off the latex-covered tickets. There are sweeping, single-motion scratchers, others who savor the suspense of uncovering the tickets square by square. Some pick their patterns randomly and others scratch the same sequence ticket after ticket. There are players who buy in threes, some who buy in fours or fives. There are players who carry lucky pen knives or favorite coins and others who call in pinch hitters to do their scratching for them. There are pools of players. In offices, factories and businesses, workers are teaming up in lottery clubs of 10 and 20, banking on the notion that bigger purchases improve the odds. But no matter what tactic they use, nearly all the lottery die-hards have the same aim. That is to win, and to win big.

Typical examples of scratch-off strategies and buying patterns.

Clincher sentence ends the paragraph.

The examples Arnold uses are typical; that is, they are repeated time after time by a variety of people.

Now study the following paragraph by cultural anthropologist Edward T. Hall. Hall uses typical examples to generalize about human reactions when the sense of personal space is violated.

People are very sensitive to any intrusion into their spatial bubble. If someone stands too close to you, your first instinct is to back up. If that's not possible, you lean away and pull yourself in, tensing your muscles. If the intruder doesn't respond to these body signals, you

Hall opens with a topic sentence.

He composes typical examples from specific observations to support the topic sentence.

may then try to protect yourself, using a briefcase, umbrella or raincoat. Women — especially when traveling alone — often plant their pocketbook in such a way that no one can get very close to them. As a last resort, you may move to another spot and position yourself behind a desk or a chair that provides screening. Everyone tries to adjust the space around himself in a way that's comfortable for him; most often, he does this unconsciously.

He closes with a clincher.

Hall's typical examples come from his experiences observing specific human behavior. His training and keen observations give him the authority to generalize in this fashion. Although making general observations about typical human behavior is beyond your authority, you can generalize about your personal observations and experience. In the following example a student writer uses typical examples to illustrate her view of some coffee and detergent commercials.

Many coffee and detergent commercials present degrading images of housewives. Loyal but fearful, the typical housewife in these commercials seems to live in terror of failing to serve her husband a good cup of coffee or get his laundry clean. Coffee commercials often show the husband sipping a cup of her latest brew. Disappointed by the taste, he complains, usually in front of a neighbor. Humiliated publicly, the housewife listens to the neighbor's advice: "Use Brand X, it has robust flavor!" Many detergent commercials create a

The writer opens with a topic sentence.

She adds a sentence that further develops the topic sentence.

A typical example develops one part of the topic sentence.

similarly degrading image. The typical housewife in these commercials faces public humiliation when she fails in her efforts to get her husband's shirts clean. "Ring around the collar! Ring around the collar!" her husband's colleagues whisper among themselves. Moreover, her laundry must look as white, feel as soft, and smell as fresh as the neighbor's, or the entire neighborhood will be sure to break out in song about her failure. Do housewives become as distraught as their harassed counterparts on television? I doubt it. Certainly housewives, and everyone else for that matter, realize that a ring around the collar is not going to strangle anyone and that brewing a weak cup of coffee is not grounds for divorce. To create commercial images of housewives who appear to think of nothing else is to degrade housewives in general.

She uses a transitional sentence to lead the reader into the second typical example, which develops another part of the topic sentence.

The writer adds some closing thoughts and ends with a clincher sentence.

Now consider a paragraph from psychologist Erich Fromm. Notice that the examples Fromm uses differ from the other illustrations we've presented in this section. They are not grounded in observation or research. They are logical generalizations about human behavior. Fromm uses them not as factual information but to impress his reader with the idea that people with different attitudes will view an experience differently.

What is, for example, the attitude of different people toward a forest? A painter who has gone there to paint, the owner of the forest who wishes to evaluate his business prospects, an officer who is interested in the tactical problem of defending the area, a hiker who wants to enjoy himself — each of them will have an entirely different concept of the forest because a different aspect is significant to each one. The painter's experience will be one of form and color; the businessman's of size, number, and age of trees; the officer's of visibility and protection; the hiker's of trails and motion. While they can all agree to the abstract statement that they can stand at the edge of the forest, the different kinds of activity they are set to accomplish will determine their experience of "seeing a forest."

Though Fromm's paragraph is structurally complicated — instead of arranging his examples one after the other he mixes them throughout — still he follows the method of developing his point with typical examples.

Specific Examples

In contrast to typical examples, which are composed by generalizing from extensive observation, specific examples capture a single, unique experience. Study the following whimsical paragraph that captures the writer's baby-sitting experiences with his cousin Tommy. He supports his topic sentence with three specific examples, each of which is a unique event.

Whenever I baby-sit my little cousin Tommy, his zany behavior makes me a nervous wreck. Once when I was baby-sitting him, he climbed out of a second-story window onto the roof of the garage and hid behind the air-conditioning unit while I frantically searched the entire house. About a month ago, he made an "experimental cake," using the kitchen floor for his mixing bowl. It took me a frantic hour to erase all the traces of paprika, Jell-O, and flour before his parents returned. While I was nervously scrubbing up the mess, he was jumping from chair to couch and back to chair in the living room, chattering something about UFOs.

Topic sentence that prepares the reader for examples of Tommy's behavior and its nerve-racking effect.

Example 1: Notice the overt transition "Once" that guides the reader into the example. Also notice "frantically," which links back to "nervous wreck" in the topic sentence.

Example 2: The phrase "About a month ago" signals the reader that a new example is coming. The idea of being nervous is picked up in the word "frantic" and in the writer's rush to clean up the mess before Tommy's parents return.

The episode that shook me up the most, though, took

place on a cold, rainy night in December. Tommy had

gone to bed — or so I thought — and the only sounds

were the splashing rain and crackling fire. I dozed in an

easy chair in front of the fireplace, slipping deeper and

deeper into a Tommyless world of quiet and peace.

Wham! An earthquake? A bomb? World War III? As my

heart floated down from my throat, I discovered what I

should have known all along. It was only Tommy. I

found him lying in a grinning heap near the stairs

surrounded by pots and pans. He had decided it would be

best to make his next cake in his room.

Example 3: This is the longest and most dramatic example. The writer uses an entire sentence to serve as a transition and to set the scene for what follows. He mixes in a great deal of concrete detail and uses dramatic questions to help keep the reader interested.

These three specific examples are vivid. They are clear. After reading them you should understand the meaning of this writer's topic sentence, for he has carefully crafted his examples to create an impression. And the examples are interesting, too. They dramatize the vague and abstract. Examples hold the reader's attention.

The examples that reveal Tommy's behavior are short narratives. But writers often shape examples in other ways. Sometimes they use them to capture exact moments of experience, like snapshots that freeze a moment in time. These verbal snapshots, when appropriate for a subject, help a reader see the point.

Jane van Lawick-Goodall uses short, visual examples to illustrate the social behavior of chimpanzees she has studied in Tanzania. This paragraph from one of her books illustrates the technique of presenting examples like photographs in an album. As you read, notice the stress Goodall puts on visualizing experiences. Although she uses few overt transitions, notice how she guides the reader into each of the first four examples by beginning them with "I saw" and "I watched." She varies the openings of the last two sentences after she has set the pattern in the reader's mind.

While many details of their [the chimpanzees'] social behavior were hidden from me by the foliage, I did get occasional fascinating glimpses. I saw one female, newly arrived in a group, hurry up to a big male and hold her hand toward him. Almost regally he reached out, clasped her hand in his, drew it toward him, and kissed it with his lips. I saw two adult males embrace each other in greeting. I saw youngsters having wild games through the treetops, chasing around after each other or jumping again and again, one after the other, from a branch to a springy bough below. I watched small infants dangling happily by themselves for minutes on end, patting at their toes with one hand, rotating gently from side to side. Once two tiny infants pulled on opposite ends of a twig in a gentle tug-of-war. Often during the heat of midday or after a long spell of feeding, I saw two or more adults grooming each other, carefully looking through the hair of their companions.

For this particular paragraph the verbal snapshots are effective. These visual examples communicate more than a lengthy discussion would. You might also notice how Goodall varies the lengths of the examples. The shortest is only ten words; the longest, divided into two sentences, is forty-one. In order, they are the longest first; then the shortest; next two of middle length; then one that is quite short; then one of middle length as a close. We aren't suggesting you follow this pattern, but we are suggesting that variety in the length of examples adds to the pleasure of reading the paragraph. Whenever you use several examples in a paragraph, vary their lengths. Variety will help keep your reader interested.

Not all paragraphs developed by specific examples are as visual as Goodall's. Often writers use examples that can be characterized as incidents or events. The following student writer uses three specific incidents as examples to illustrate a relationship between a particular film and a murder.

Is there a direct relationship between murder in Hollywood films and murder in real life? No one knows for sure, but after the opening of a film about street gangs called The Warriors, rival gangs clashed in or near some theaters. In Palm Springs during an intermission in the showing of The Warriors, some members of a Fontana motorcycle gang made several sexual comments

The writer opens with a question to hook the reader's interest.

The topic sentence suggests a link between films and real acts of violence.

Example 1. Notice how the writer introduces each example with a clear transition that names the city where the event took place.

to a local girl. The Family, a rival gang, came to her

rescue. Violence exploded. A member of the Blue Coats

killed a nineteen-year-old member of the Family with a

Saturday night special. In Oxnard, two gangs clashed on   *Example 2.*

opening night of The Warriors. When people crowded

into the lobby someone, yet to be identified, stabbed an

eighteen-year-old to death. In Boston several gang   *Example 3.*

members leaving a theater featuring The Warriors

taunted a sixteen-year-old boy with a line from the

script. A brawl broke out. Someone used a knife. Six

hours later the boy was dead.

One effect of specific examples is that they are convincing. They convince in a way that no abstract discussion ever could. But when you use isolated examples such as the ones relating gang violence to films, you must remember that they are not "proof." Their value lies in their emotional impact.

Combining Typical and Specific Examples

Writers often combine typical and specific examples. Sometimes they combine examples in a single paragraph, but at other times they arrange them in separate paragraphs to avoid writing excessively long paragraphs. The following two paragraphs combine typical and specific examples to make a single point about education.

Lower-division courses are far from the ideal of   *The opening sentence serves as the topic*
                                                                 sentence.
education. Generally, an ideal education requires

interaction with teachers and other students. When a   *The writer creates a typical example to*
                                                                 illustrate what an ideal education should
student has difficulty understanding a mathematical   *embody.*

concept, scientific principle, or literary work, he or she

must have the opportunity to meet with an experienced

teacher, one who has spent years not only learning a subject but also communicating with students. When a student encounters new ideas in lectures or reading, he or she must have the opportunity to explore them in teacher-guided discussions, not just in rap sessions over coffee in the cafeteria.

During my freshman year, only one of my classes was small enough to permit interaction with students and the teacher, a sprightly woman who loved literature. Each session was devoted to a discussion of a single literary work. One session that dealt with Waiting for Godot turned into a heated debate about the meaning of human activity. She directed the discussion with questions, helping us understand our positions. Out of the discussion came a series of unanswered questions that became the basis for a writing assignment that she individually reviewed with each of us during her office hours. This kind of education is ideal, but it happens only when classes are small enough to allow for person-to-person instruction. It cannot happen in large lecture classes where many students see only the teacher's tiny figure beyond a sea of heads.

This second topic sentence links clearly to the first while indicating that a specific example follows.

A specific example illustrates the writer's experience with ideal education.

The closing sentences serve as a clincher statement.

In this illustration, typical and specific examples work well together. If the writer had presented only what he considers the typical aspects of an ideal education, the example would have been too vague. But by including a specific example, he gives the reader a concrete illustration of what he believes is necessary to achieve an ideal education. He organizes each paragraph around linking topic sentences.

WRITING TASK

Write a paragraph that uses examples to support a topic sentence. You can develop your paragraph by composing generalized observations, representative facts, brief narratives, verbal snapshots, or brief incidents, as illustrated in this chapter.

As always, we suggest that you select your own topic, but in case you become stumped, we present the following list of suggestions.

1. Observations of behavior in one of the following:
   elevators
   buses
   medical offices
   a nursery school
   classrooms (student/teacher behavior at the start/end of class)
2. Attitudes about the following:
   cruelty to animals
   safety in nuclear plants
   dying rivers/forests/deserts
   reclaimed rivers/forests/deserts
3. Experiences with the following groups:

parents	politicians
teachers	advertisers
students	artists
salespersons	police
waitresses/waiters	civil servants
mechanics	doctors

Perhaps you would like to write two paragraphs related to a single topic. If so, try the following writing task.

In popular magazines such as *Psychology Today, People,* and *Time* or *Newsweek,* study several ads for similar products manufactured by different companies — beer, vodka, whiskey, cigarettes, or cars of comparable price, for example. Determine the common elements, which might include the uses of language and images, that the advertisements use to sell the products. Once you have identified some common elements, list them as a means of prewriting. Next compose a topic sentence that communicates the idea that some companies selling familiar products use similar techniques in their advertisements. Finally, support the topic sentence by using typical and specific examples in your paragraphs. Be sure to develop a linking topic sentence for the second paragraph. You might follow a pattern such as the following.

Paragraph Number 1	Topic sentence
	Typical examples

Paragraph Number 2	Second topic sentence linking to the first one
	Specific example
	Clincher statement

Remember:

1. Develop the material through prewriting.
2. Compose a limited topic sentence.
3. Write a rough draft that arranges your examples in an effective pattern and ends with a clincher.
4. Write a final draft with clear transitions between examples.

6 CATALOGUING

Cataloguing a great many details is an effective pattern you might use to develop a paragraph. A detailed catalogue serves as a way to thrust a reader into the middle of an experience. Often a writer announces a catalogue in a topic sentence that leads readers to expect descriptive details. Then the writer follows with a main clause that sets the pattern in motion and often ends with a colon. The catalogue, which is never made up of main clauses that could stand alone as sentences, follows the colon. The writer of the following example does just that. As you read this short paragraph, notice how the elements of the catalogue follow the colon.

Last summer I attended an out-of-doors concert that erupted into a riot. From where I sat on a distant grass-covered knoll, I watched the participants, like insane characters in a movie scene, attack each other: a guitarist smashing a microphone against a fan's head, a herd of drunks hurling beer bottles at the dodging musicians, a group of girls dressed in punk rock styles shaking their fists and shouting for blood, and club-waving security guards wading into the crowd as innocent bystanders scurried for shelter. The whole time,

The topic sentence sets the time and event the writer plans to describe.

The next sentence is the core of the pattern. It sets the visual quality of the piece and introduces the catalogue: (1) guitarist smashing a fan, (2) drunks hurling bottles, (3) girls shaking their fists and shouting, (4) club-waving guards, (5) bystanders scurrying.

I thought, This is insane, this is insane, while overhead a police helicopter buzzed and in the distance sirens wailed.

The writer closes with a clincher that states his personal response while mixing it with auditory details.

How can readers fail to get involved in this pattern? Tugging at their emotions and pulling at their senses, the rapid presentation of concrete details demands attention.

Not all catalogues are this emotionally gripping. Sometimes writers use them to tantalize their readers. Catalogues of this sort generate expectations and promise excitement. Paul Theroux uses this technique in a paragraph in *The Great Railway Bazaar,* a book that describes his trip by train across Asia. Theroux uses two catalogues in a single paragraph. The first — which begins "Anything is possible" — creates the atmosphere of the train. The second — which begins "It was my intention" — catalogues the various railroads Theroux will ride during his journey. As you read, notice how Theroux uses a colon to set up each catalogue.

Then Asia was out the window, and I was carried through it on these eastbound expresses marveling as much at the bazaar within the train as the ones we whistled past. Anything is possible on a train: a great meal, a binge, a visit from card players, an intrigue, a good night's sleep, and strangers' monologues framed like Russian short stories. It was my intention to board every train that chugged into view from Victoria Station in London to Tokyo Central: to take a branch line to Simla, the spur through the Khyber Pass, and the chord line that links Indian Railways with those in Ceylon; the Mandalay Express, the Malaysian Golden Arrow, the locals in Vietnam, and the trains with bewitching names, the Orient Express, the North Star, the Trans-Siberian.

The topic sentence sets the paragraph in motion.

First catalogue

Second catalogue

Besides generating excitement and building expectations in a reader, a writer can also use the cataloguing pattern to present a great deal of information in a condensed form. Barbara W. Tuchman uses this technique in *A Distant Mirror* to give her readers an impression of the fourteenth century's understanding of distant places. One of the problems a writer faces when arranging catalogues of this sort (or any sort, for that matter) is how to present the details in an orderly fashion. Tuchman solves the problem by first introducing the catalogue with a colon, then beginning each major element with a key word and following it with one or more descriptive details. The key words are *forests, horned pygmies, brahmins, men, cyclopeans, monoceros, Amazons, panthers, trees,* and *snakes.* As you read, study how Tuchman has followed this plan. (See Parallelism p. 357.)

> Faraway lands, however — India, Persia, and beyond — were seen through a gauze of fabulous fairy tales revealing an occasional nugget of reality: forests so high they touch the clouds, horned pygmies who move in herds and grow old in seven years, brahmins who kill themselves on funeral pyres, men with dogs' heads and six toes, "cyclopeans" with only one eye and one foot who move as fast as the wind, the "monoceros" which can be caught only when it sleeps in the lap of a virgin, Amazons whose tears are of silver, panthers who practice the caesarean operation with their own claws, trees whose leaves supply wool, snakes 300 feet long, snakes with precious stones for eyes, snakes who so love music that for prudence they stop up one ear with their tail.

So far we have used illustrations by writers who have arranged their catalogues into single sentences. This is the most common practice. But often writers catalogue a series of questions. Later in her book, Tuchman uses this pattern to make her readers aware of the kinds of mysterious questions the fourteenth-century mind puzzled over.

> For all the explanations, the earth and its phenomena were full of mysteries: What happens to fire when it goes out? Why are there different colors of skin among men? Why do the sun's rays darken a man's skin but bleach white linen? How do souls make their way to the next world? Where lies the soul? What causes madness? Medieval people felt surrounded by puzzles, yet because God was there they were willing to acknowledge that causes are hidden, that man cannot know why all things are as they are; "they are as God pleases."

As we said, cataloguing is a quick way to involve your readers. It's a device — nothing more — to thrust them into an experience. Its underlying effect is made not through logic but through bombardment.

WRITING TASK

Write a paragraph built on the cataloguing pattern. Be sure to write a topic sentence that prepares the reader for the catalogue and to follow with a sentence that sets the catalogue in motion. Remember, a catalogue can deal with almost any subject, but its main purpose is to quickly involve your reader; therefore, you must work to create a strong impression with the material you select. To get you started, here are a few suggestions. Keep in mind that you can shape them to your own purposes.

1. Take a walk down Main Street. Visit some part of the town where you live and record an extended list of physical details you feel convey the dominant feeling of the area. Build the list into a paragraph according to the cataloguing pattern.
2. Visit a store. Walk through a department, hardware, liquor, shoe, drug, or dime store. Or sit around a pool hall, beauty parlor, bar, cafeteria, library, or street corner. Wherever you visit, record your impressions, then develop them in a paragraph according to the cataloguing pattern.
3. Sit on a rock. Go to a park, grove of trees, lake, hilltop, bird sanctuary, or empty football field. Record your impressions and build them into a catalogue.
4. Review your life. Reread some journal entries that focus on your life. Build a paragraph by cataloguing the high or the low points — the peaks and the valleys. Or if questions about your life come to you, build a paragraph out of them.
5. Capture an experience. Record the dominant impressions of an experience you've had, then build the impressions into a catalogue.

Try to be as vivid as possible when composing your catalogue because you want the reader to become involved. The key thought behind this pattern is bombardment. Bombard your reader with vivid details.

Remember:

1. Begin with a topic sentence.
2. Introduce your catalogue with a main clause that ends with a colon.
3. Be sure the elements of the catalogue that follow the colon are not main clauses that can stand alone.
4. End with a clincher.

7 ANECDOTE

An anecdote is a brief story that illustrates a point or a person's character. Simple enough. But unlike other patterns we've discussed, anecdotes seldom make direct statements. They suggest rather than declare; they need to be interpreted, never accepted at face value.

Use an Anecdote to Reveal Character

Time magazine used the following anecdote to introduce a piece about Pete Rose's pride in his baseball ability.

> The plane carrying the Cincinnati Reds bucked and yawed through a storm front, scattering drinks and scrambling stomachs. Peter Edward Rose, the irrepressibly proud captain of the Reds, used the moment to tease a teammate whose fear of flying far exceeded opposing pitchers' fears of his bat. "We're going down!" Rose shouted. Then the punchline. "We're going down, and I have a .300 lifetime average to take with me!"

Brief as it is, this anecdote shows something about Rose's humor, pride, and enthusiasm. In other words, it does what some anecdotes are supposed to do: It reveals character.

The example also illustrates some other aspects of anecdote writing. The opening line — "The plane carrying the Cincinnati Reds bucked and yawed through a storm front, scattering drinks and scrambling stomachs" — sets the stage for the story through description. Many anecdotes require stage setting, but don't get lost in description when writing an anecdote; its purpose is to add reality and help the reader visualize the incident. This anecdote also includes some dialogue. Often anecdotes do. And, finally, the Rose anecdote works indirectly. Only two words serve as straight comments on Rose's character: "irrepressibly proud." The whole anecdote, then, needs to be interpreted to reveal parts of Rose's character. So keep in mind that anecdotes often involve description and dialogue and often work indirectly.

James Phelan uses an anecdote in *Howard Hughes: The Hidden Years* to reveal Hughes' capricious character and the fear his whims stimulated in his attendants.

> During Howard Hughes' years of seclusion in the Desert Inn in Las Vegas, he would demand the same meal every day for lengthy stretches. At one point, according to his long-time aide, Gordon Margulis, he was having two scoops of Baskin-Robbins' banana-nut ice cream with every meal, so his staff kept it constantly on hand.
>
> One day, when the supply needed to be replenished, it was learned that the flavor had been discontinued. Hughes' staff panicked. Someone telephoned the Baskin-Robbins office in California and asked them to make a special batch of banana-nut. They agreed to make up the smallest batch they could on special order — 350 gallons. "We still had a few scoops of the old banana-nut when the new banana-nut arrived," says Margulis, "so we felt all set for the rest of Hughes' lifetime."
>
> When the ice cream was served to Hughes the next day, however, he ate it and declared: "That's great ice cream, but it's time for a change. From now on, I want French Vanilla."

The Hughes anecdote is part of a much longer work. This is usually the case with anecdote. Phelan uses it as a quick means to reveal Hughes' character. Speed and impact give it punch. Punch, or surprise, as opposed to reasoned discourse, is characteristic of most anecdotes. The punch may merely generate a belly laugh, such as the banana-nut ice cream caper. Or it may tug at a deeper emotional awareness.

Use an Anecdote to Make a Point

In *Desert Solitaire* Edward Abbey uses an anecdote to make a point about the plight of Navajos living in a world that has little respect for their heritage.

It will not be easy. It will not be easy for the

Navajos to forget that once upon a time, only a

generation ago, they were horsemen, nomads, keepers of

flocks, painters in sand, weavers of wool, artists in

Abbey begins setting up the anecdote by calling to the reader's mind what the Navajos once were.

silver, dancers, singers of the Yei-bie-chei. But they will have to forget, or at least learn to be ashamed of these old things and to bring them out only for the amusement of tourists.

Notice how he uses a catalogue to work in a great deal of detail.

A difficult transitional period. Tough on people. For instance, consider an unfortunate accident which took place only a week ago here in Arches country. Parallel to the highway north of Moab is a railway, a spur line to the potash mines. At one point close to this road this railway cuts through a hill. The cut is about three hundred feet deep, blasted through solid rock with sides that are as perpendicular as the walls of a building. One afternoon two young Indians — Navajos? Apaches? beardless Utes? — in a perverted Plymouth came hurtling down the highway, veered suddenly to the right, whizzed through a fence and plunged straight down like helldivers into the Big Cut. Investigating the wreckage we found only the broken bodies, the broken bottles, the stain and smell of Tokay, and a couple of cardboard suitcases exploded open and revealing their former owners' worldly goods — dirty socks, some underwear, a copy of True West magazine, a comb, three new cowboy shirts from J. C. Penney's, a carton of Marlboro cigarettes. But nowhere did we see any conchos of silver, any buffalo robes, any bows, arrows, medicine pouch or drums.

Some Indians.

"For instance, consider an unfortunate accident" announces the anecdote.

Abbey gives some background information that leads up to the incident.

Now he moves directly into the story.

Abbey catalogues the contents of the wreckage to show the reader what today's young Navajos possess: a sharp contrast to the proud possessions of former Navajos. At this point the contrast becomes even more direct — the dreams of drugstore cowboys juxtaposed against the reality of the past.

Abbey closes with an ironic comment — "Some Indians" — to show what an insensitive white man's response might be.

The pride of the ancient Navajo has been bartered for the cheap goods of modern society. That may be one way to look at these paragraphs. Or perhaps the criticism goes much deeper. Modern America has sold the goods and the dreams the goods represent to the Indians, thus diminishing their lives. Beyond that, just as the Navajo are diminished, so too are we diminished by the same forces that have driven these Indian boys to the fantasies of Tokay and *True West.*

Do we go too far? But remember that anecdote speaks indirectly. When you read one you must prowl through it to get the point. When you write one, you must shape it for a reader to get the point.

WRITING TASK

Write an anecdote that reveals character or makes a point about a social issue. Keep in mind that anecdotes suggest rather than declare the writer's concern. They also involve some descriptive stage setting so that the reader can visualize the experience. And, most important, they end with some punch that drives the point home.

If you have been doing Daily Writing as described in Part Three of this book, we suggest you reread some of your entries. They may suggest an anecdote to you, especially your entries in Chapter 31, Portraits and Relationships.

If you choose to write an anecdote that illustrates a social concern, be sure to stick to a particular case that suggests the larger issue, as Abbey does in his anecdote of the Navajo youths. For instance, if you're concerned over the health care of the infirm, you might select a particular case from a local convalescent home as the focus for your anecdote. If you're concerned about the behavior of authorities, parents, students or politicians, choose for your focus a particular case from your experience.

Remember:

1. Anecdotes suggest rather than directly state a point.
2. They involve stage setting.
3. They usually involve dialogue.

8 SHORT COMPARISON AND CONTRAST

"My dad's a better baseball player than your dad!"
"Did anyone ever say you look just like Dustin Hoffman?"
"It's a good movie, but I like the book better."
"Get your hair cut — you look like a wild animal."
"Men are all alike."
These bits of imaginary conversation are all examples of comparisons or contrasts. We're sure you've heard such comments many times in your life.

Comparison points out similarities; contrast points out differences. Both are common patterns for communicating information and ideas. They are used not only in conversation but in all forms of writing — essays, research projects, examinations, reports, and so on.

Sometimes a comparison or contrast pattern will be a brief part of a longer work and come at the end of it, such as this illustration from a paper on inflation.

> Modern computers are fast, accurate and able to do a wide variety of programmed tasks, but they still lack the flexibility of the human brain.

Often, though, a comparison-and-contrast pattern will take up at least a paragraph and sometimes extend for several paragraphs.

Combining Comparison and Contrast

Whenever you arrange two things for discussion, you'll almost always be comparing and contrasting them. Keep in mind, though, that for this pattern to be effective, the subjects must be members of the same group. For instance, one writer might effectively compare and contrast a bee with a snake because both are living creatures. Another writer might effectively compare and contrast a bee with a helicopter because both are things that fly. But we doubt that any writer could effectively compare and contrast a helicopter with a snake no matter what the purpose. So when you employ this pattern, we suggest you make sure your subjects are clearly related.

Read the following paragraph that a student wrote as part of a museum report and that combines both comparison and contrast. There are a few techniques we'd like you to watch for as you read:

1. Notice how the writer presents both subjects — elephants and mastodons — in the topic sentence.
2. Examine how the writer uses the topic sentence to lead readers into a comparison-and-contrast pattern.
3. Watch for the brief phrases that remind readers of the comparing and contrasting process: "Like the modern elephant" and "Unlike the elephant."
4. Notice the sentence that pivots the paragraph and moves it from pointing out similarities to pointing out differences between the two beasts.

After you've read the paragraph, we suggest you reread it along with the comments in the margin so that you can more firmly grasp the pattern.

When I first saw the reproduction of the prehistoric mastodon, I thought of elephants I had seen in circuses and zoos. Like the modern elephant, the mastodon is large, with legs that remind me of sturdy tree trunks. The ancient beast had large, floppy ears and a long trunk which he could use as a tool for gathering food. But after a closer look, I saw some major differences between the

The topic sentence sets up the two elements to be compared and contrasted — mastodon and elephant.

Brief presentation of the similarities between the two creatures

"But after a closer look . . ." serves as a pivotal sentence to guide the reader into the contrast section.

modern elephant and the prehistoric mastodon. The
mastodon's tusks grew longer and curved upward at a
sharper angle. Unlike the elephant with its thick, almost
hairless hide, the mastodon was matted with long, thick
hair. And although the mastodon was large, it was not
as tremendous in size as its modern descendant.

Brief presentation of the differences between the two creatures

The final sentence reminds the reader of the two elements presented.

As a final comment on this paragraph, we'd like to point out the writer's use of concrete details to develop the comparison-and-contrast pattern — sturdy legs, floppy ears, curving tusks, hairless hide, and long, thick hair. No matter what patterns you employ, try to include concrete detail.

Comparing

Comparing and contrasting two subjects does not always take place in the same paragraph. Sometimes a writer will devote a paragraph to one or the other. Read the following illustration in which the writer compares fat to thin people. The writer begins by linking the comparison to her father but quickly shifts to overweight people in general. Her paragraph is an appeal to see beyond surface differences to the deeper similarities among all people. (If we were talking about examples here, we would point out that this writer selects typical details that all human beings share.)

My father is fat, but he, like all fat people, is similar
in significant ways to thinner human beings. Fat people
have eyes that see and ears that hear and tongues that
speak. Too often, like most people, they see rejection,
hear ridicule, and speak self-deprecatingly. Fat people
work, play, serve their country, and, like everyone else,
they bleed when wounded. With age their skin wrinkles
and their hair grays. In the end they must face the

The topic sentence leads the reader to expect a comparison.

The series of concrete details link fat people with all other humans.

Notice how "like most people" helps keep the reader focused on the writer's intent.

The phrase "like everyone else" also helps keep the reader focused.

terrible void that everyone must face — death. No matter

what their size, they are human, as human as all

humans. Why, then, are they berated for being

overweight?

After linking fat people to the common fate of death, the writer ends with a question that implies a purpose for the comparison.

We hope you see that comparison paragraphs offer little organizational difficulty. Once you have selected the subjects, you simply go through the ways in which the two are similar. We suggest, though, that you pay close attention to the order in which you discuss the similarities. Save the most dramatic for last.

There are two basic ways of developing paragraphs by contrast: the block pattern and the point-by-point pattern.

Contrasting in Blocks

The block pattern is quite simple. First you sketch the outstanding points of one subject; then you sketch the outstanding points of the other. You always end with a comment that brings the two subjects into focus. This pattern is easy to organize if the subjects are not too complex.

Read the following illustration that contrasts the "negative addict" with the "positive addict." As you read, notice how the writer swings from one section to the other with the phrase "In contrast." He also sets up the closing comments with the phrase "In any case."

The word addict is usually used in a negative way,

but when used in a positive fashion, it has a different

significance. A negative addict may be someone who

smokes until his breath grows weak and raspy and his

lungs decay. At a greater extreme, he may be a person

hooked on heroin, alcohol, or gambling — or on any

compulsion that so dominates his life that it threatens

both his existence and the existence of his loved ones. In

contrast, a positive addict may be addicted to jogging,

swimming, or meditating — activities that sustain his

health and help him live vigorously. He may be addicted

Although the two subjects are not clearly identified in the topic sentence, the writer gives the reader a clear idea of what to expect.

The first block presents details related to the negative addict.

The phrase "In contrast" announces the movement into the second block, which presents details of the positive addict.

to diary keeping, spending up to two hours a day writing
down his experiences and thoughts. Some claim that
concentrated reading may be a positive addiction that
helps the reader sustain intellectual involvement with
his own growth and his society. In any case, unlike the

The phrase "In any case" announces that the two subjects will be brought together to close the paragraph.

negative addict who seems bent on destroying himself
and those around him, the positive addict perpetuates his
life and becomes a better person through his compulsion.

Contrasting Point by Point

Whenever a subject is complicated and writers need to contrast several differences, they will usually use the point-by-point pattern. The reason is simple. Point-by-point development holds a reader's attention when the material gets complex. But writers face one difficulty when using this pattern. They must avoid the monotony of repeating such phrases as "in contrast to" or "on the other hand." In the block pattern these kinds of phrases sparingly scattered throughout a piece serve as guides; in the point method, if a writer frequently uses them they become tiresome.

Writers don't want to tire their readers. They will, therefore, weed from their work all unnecessary transitional phrases. They will then arrange their sentences so that their readers can clearly see the shift from one subject to the other. Often they will mix their sentence structures by using semicolons to both link and set off contrasting points.

Study Gilbert Highet's contrast of early Greek teachers called sophists with their rival teacher Socrates. Notice how Highet counterpoints one difference with another. Also notice how he arranges his sentence structure so that the beginning of each independent clause clearly identifies the subject he's presenting.

To some of his contemporaries Socrates looked like a sophist; but he distrusted and opposed the sophists wherever possible. They toured the whole Greek world; Socrates stayed in Athens, talking to his fellow-citizens. They made carefully prepared continuous speeches; he

The topic sentence opens with some background information before suggesting the contrast between Socrates and the sophists.

The first few differences are organized by the semicolon.

only asked questions. They took rich fees for their

teaching; he refused regular payment, living and dying

poor. They were elegantly dressed, turned out like

As the differences become more complex, the writer divides the details into sentences. This detailing also adds structural variety to the paragraph.

film-stars on a personal appearance tour, with

secretaries and personal servants and elaborate

advertising. Socrates wore the workingman's clothes,

bare feet and a smock — in fact, he had been a

stonemason and carver by trade, and came from a

working-class family. They spoke in specially prepared

The writer returns to the semicolon structure.

lecture halls; he talked to people at street-corners and in

the gymnasium, where every afternoon the young men

exercised, and the old men talked, while they all

sunbathed. He fitted in so well there that he sometimes

The writer leaves the contrast to develop Socrates more fully, thus accentuating his method as superior to the sophists'.

compared himself to the athletic coach, who does not

run or wrestle, but teaches others how to run and

wrestle better; Socrates said he trained people to think.

Lastly, the sophists said they knew everything and were

He closes by bringing the sophists back into the process and suggesting that Socrates is superior.

ready to explain it. Socrates said he knew nothing and

was trying to find out.

Structurally, Highet's paragraph is quite simple, yet he effectively works in a great deal of detail about the sophists and Socrates. Of course, his sympathies are clear: He applauds Socrates while making the sophists look like egocentric materialists. Unless you are required to write an objective report, we recommend that you also make your attitudes clear to the reader.

WRITING TASK ═══════════════════════════════

Write a short comparison or contrast paragraph. You may choose to develop your paragraph around the similarities of your subjects or around their differences according to the block or point-by-point pattern. For this task we recommend that you stick to one pattern and not try to mix the two.

When you begin your comparison or contrast paragraph, be sure to start with a prewritten draft with your subjects as the focus. Then, after you've determined what the topic sentence will be, select from your prewrite those details that fit your purpose and arrange them in a list that reflects it. For instance, Highet might have built his contrast of the sophists with Socrates from a list such as this:

Sophists	*Socrates*
traveled the entire Greek world	stayed in Athens, teaching fellow citizens
gave lectures and speeches	asked questions — no formal speeches
accepted high fees	accepted no fees, died poor
like film stars on tour, had secretaries, servants, fine clothes	wore workingman's clothes; went around with bare feet; from a working family; once a stonecarver
talked in lecture halls	talked in public places where men of all kinds gathered — especially the gymnasium; thought of himself as a coach training people to think
claimed to know everything	claimed to know nothing

When you phrase a topic sentence for this task, be sure it clearly announces a comparison or contrast pattern. It is also good practice to identify the two subjects you will discuss, and, if you are not writing an objective report, your attitude toward them. For example, reexamine the topic sentences from three previous illustrations.

My father is fat, but he, like all fat people, is similar in significant ways to thinner human beings.

The word *addict* is usually used in a negative way, but when used in a positive fashion, it has a different significance.

To some of his contemporaries Socrates looked like a sophist; but he distrusted and opposed the sophists wherever possible.

Here are a few more to consider:

> Although *Return of the Jedi* takes place "long ago in a galaxy far away," most American moviegoers will recognize it as just another Western in disguise.

> After visiting Richard Gere several times last summer, I was intrigued by the difference between the private man and the public image.

> The difference between the old America and the new America is reflected in the two national sports: baseball and football.

> All cacti are succulents, but not all succulents are cacti.

> In practice both coaches stress fundamentals and conditioning, but on the sidelines during the game, Burns is a tiger while Stevens is a pussycat.

All of these topic sentences point clearly to comparison or contrast. They all specify the two subjects the writer will discuss, limit the territory the writer will cover, and often suggest an attitude. That's what we want you to do with your topic sentence.

Here are some possible subjects.

1. Compare or contrast two films you liked or disliked.
2. Compare or contrast two houses or apartments you have lived in.
3. Compare or contrast two teaching styles or teachers.
4. Compare or contrast two outstanding athletes who play the same position.
5. Compare or contrast two dress styles.

While growing up you might have experienced conflicting images of yourself. Perhaps you were "Daddy's little angel" and "Mommy's little devil," or perhaps you are viewed one way by your peers and another by your parents. In any case, you may have been seen in different ways by different people. Select two people who viewed you in conflicting ways and use their views as the basis for a comparison-and-contrast paragraph.

Remember:

1. Use prewriting to generate the raw material for your paragraph.
2. Compose the topic sentence and sort the prewritten material into categories that fit your purpose.
3. Write the paragraph according to sound comparison-and-contrast principles.
4. Be sure to include clear transitions that guide the reader.

As with all writing tasks in this section, feel free to select your own subjects to compare or contrast.

9 EXTENDED COMPARISON AND CONTRAST

As we have said, comparison-and-contrast patterns often extend beyond a single paragraph. After all, within this pattern writers develop two or more subjects, an act that may require more space than most readable paragraphs contain. Moreover, writers sometimes mix comparison with contrast, as in the piece that both compares and contrasts mastodon with elephant. Unlike the mastodon/elephant illustration, the mixing may demand more than a single paragraph to adequately develop the subjects.

As an illustration of an extended comparison and contrast, study the following student piece. The writer develops the similarities and differences in his grandfathers. We suggest that you notice how he presents the similarities in the first paragraph and then follows with the differences arranged in blocks. Unlike the author of the block pattern illustrated in the last section, this writer divides his blocks into two paragraphs and links them with the connecting phrase "On the other hand." There's a reason for doing it — the blocks are long; better to make the reader's way easier by separating them.

In several general ways my grandfathers were similar. Both immigrated to America from Europe to escape military service. Peace-loving men, they were determined to leave petty national quarrels behind. Both settled first in New York City, married American girls, and then moved to Nebraska to raise their families in	*The topic sentence sets up the comparison.* *The first part deals with the similarity of the peace-loving immigrants.* *This part groups several similarities. Notice how the writer introduces his points with "Both" and "They."*

94

the open spaces of the Midwest. They shared a belief in

the simple life: hard work, thrift, honesty, and church on

Sunday. They also shared the disappointment of seeing

sons return to Europe to fight in a war that they felt

was "none of our business." Fortunately, the sons

survived and raised their families too, bringing warmth

and joy to my grandfathers' old age.

Sharing so much, they were so different in

personality. Grandfather Spender was aloof and serious.

He loved to read and to spend his evenings writing long

entries in a diary. Our visits to his house were brief and

quiet. Sometimes he would read a passage in German

aloud while we children stared uncomprehendingly at

his eyes filling with tears. I never knew him well, but I

admired him and secretly sympathized with what I

understood to be a homesickness for his native Germany.

On the other hand, visits to Grandpa Kaluski's

house were always noisy. Most of the noise was provided

by Grandpa Kaluski himself, who loved to play the

accordion while we kids did our best to polka on the

packed dirt of the backyard. Always jovial and proud to

be an American, he never, within my hearing at least,

mentioned Poland or indicated any interest in Polish

things — except the polka. We used to take long walks

together through the fields, sharing secrets, singing

songs, and making plans for my future. When he died I

felt a loneliness I had never before experienced.

They shared simple values.

They also shared the sorrow of war touching their lives indirectly and the joy of their son's surviving to raise families.

The topic sentence unifies the next two paragraphs by setting up the differences in personality. Obviously, these differences could not be structured in a point-by-point pattern.

"On the other hand" clearly identifies this paragraph as an extension of the preceding one.

By the way, did you notice how smoothly the writer works in the difference in nationality? He doesn't hold it up as a major difference but keeps to his focus — the differences in personality.

No matter what the length of an extended comparison and contrast, the structural principles don't vary significantly, as the grandfathers piece illustrates.

Writers tend to handle comparisons in one fashion — by combining the subjects. This is the most natural and efficient way to do it. Notice how inefficient it would have been for the writer of the last illustration to present his grandfathers' similarities in blocks.

> My grandfather Spender immigrated to America to escape military service in Germany. He was a peace-loving man, determined to avoid petty national quarrels. He settled first in New York City, married an American girl, and then moved to Nebraska to raise his family in the open spaces of the Midwest. He believed in the simple life: hard work, thrift, honesty, and church on Sunday. The biggest disappointment of his life was seeing his son return to Europe to fight in a war that was "none of our business." Fortunately, his son survived and raised a family, too, bringing warmth and joy to my grandfather's old age.
>
> My grandfather Kaluski came here to avoid military service, too. Just like Grandpa Spender he settled in New York City first, married an American girl, and moved to the wide open spaces of Nebraska to raise his family. He, too, believed in the value of a simple life. He also saw a son return to Europe to fight. His son also survived and gave him many grandchildren.

No matter how the writer tries to avoid it by changing the wording here and there, the piece sounds repetitious and trite. All the power is spent in the first block. Comparison tends to bring things closer to each other, so we suggest you always go with the natural tendency to combine similarities.

Writers tend to structure short and relatively general contrasts in blocks and long and relatively specific contrasts by points. Contrast usually separates things — puts one thing here, the other over there. In the second paragraph about the two grandfathers, the writer deals with the general subject of their personalities, but he discusses different activities for each one. Consequently, he arranges the information in the block pattern. On the other hand, if his focus had been more specific, he might have structured his paragraphs point by point.

> Grandfather Spender was slender, built like a whip-thin birch; Grandfather Kaluski was massive, built like a deep-rooted oak. Grandfather Spender would spend hours in solitude with his fingers curled around a pen, writing in his diary; Grandfather

Kaluski would surround himself with us children and move his beefy fingers over accordion keys, bellowing for us to polka. . . .

And so on.

For further study we offer two more extended pieces, both developed by contrast. The first writer uses the block pattern, the second the point-by-point method. When reading the first one, we suggest you notice that the two blocks have similar content but that the writer emphasizes the general nature of her subjects; consequently, there's no need to use the point-by-point method. Also notice how she displays her attitude. Unlike an objective report, a personal piece of this sort benefits from the personal tone.

I've lived in only two communities in California, hating both, but for different reasons. Each has its own logic, I suppose, but this little girl from the Midwest would prefer a place less extreme in lifestyle than either Sand Point or the Peaks.

The topic sentence indicates discussion of differences and the attitude of the writer.

The second sentence explains the reason for the writer's hate — lifestyles are too extreme.

Sand Point is a tourist-hating hangout for the locals. The attitude of the area is loose and casual. The motto of the Sandy kids is "Have a good time." And they do. There are never-ending parties, lots of drugs, and surfing all day long. Their only educational goal is a semester or two at the local community college. Only the adults in this area are employed. Most of them are Democrats, unmarried, living together in low-cost housing. Cops patrol the Point intensively, and it's not unusual to find fugitives hiding beneath Mustangs and Falcons or escaping through a yard.

Block of information about Sand Point

The only evidence of law enforcement you see at the Peaks is an occasional security guard informing someone

Block of information about the Peaks, contrasting it with Sand Point

that his Mercedes or Porsche is parked in the wrong

place. The whole environment revolves around stuffy

money and finding new ways to show it off. High-class

young adults here jog daily on the greenbelts wearing

their John Kloss sweats, and they are never caught

without Virginia Slims at invitation-only parties. An Ivy

League college is their future, sorority and frat all the

way. Kids from the Peaks earn play money at Marie

Callendar's during dull summers. Their fathers are car

dealers and their mothers contribute time to charities,

eat lunch at quaint, expensive restaurants, and shop at

Neiman-Marcus or I. Magnin. These Republican families

have everything, including a mistress for Daddy.

In the space of an hour last week I saw a Porsche

in the Peaks and a beat-up Edsel in Sand Point both

sporting a "Save the American Dream" bumper sticker. If

these are examples of the American Dream, count me

out.

Concluding sentences bring the two places together and reject both, reminding the reader of the introduction.

In the following illustration the writer focuses on his past high school experience. In the first paragraph the writer briefly gives his topic and attitude. In the second paragraph, he presents the differences between his old, condemned campus and the new one built to replace it. In the third paragraph, he presents the differences in faculty attitudes that developed after moving to the new campus. If the writer had used the block pattern, his piece would have been much longer. But since he is interested in developing parallel elements, he uses the point-by-point method.

In the first paragraph, notice how the writer announces in the topic sentence his plan to structure his material around three points: safety, versatility, and pleasantness of the environment. He then fills in each point with contrasting details.

Before writing the second paragraph from a prewritten draft, he shaped a list that looked like this:

Old Campus	*New Campus*
SAFETY	
made of brick	reinforced concrete
built in 1903	just built
earthquake hazard	earthquake safe
wooden stairs	concrete stairs
loose banisters	metal railings
exit into crowded halls	exit into outside
VERSATILITY	
auditorium condemned	TV studio
one gymnasium	little theater
	two gymnasiums
cramped rooms	outdoor amphitheater
PLEASANTNESS	
bell tower	uniform appearance
brick walls	chain-link fence
tree-lined entryway	near street
windows that opened	no windows

Once the bare details of the list were established, the writer still faced a major task — to present the material in an interesting way. He avoids monotony by varying his details within each main point.

Unlike the second paragraph, the third follows a simple development that briefly lays out three differences in faculty behavior since moving to the new campus. As you read the piece, notice how the writer weaves the details together and swings from one point to the other.

A couple of years ago in high school I learned progress isn't so hot. Redwood High School got a new campus that was safer and more versatile than the old campus, but for all its faults the old place is a more pleasant campus to attend.

The old brick buildings, built in 1903, were an earthquake hazard, officials claimed, so they were

Besides giving some background, the first sentence sets the writer's general concern and attitude — "progress isn't so hot."

The second sentence serves as the topic sentence — it sets down the three main differences to be developed.

replaced with new buildings of reinforced concrete designed to withstand all but the most severe shocks. The new buildings have concrete stairs with metal railings instead of creaky wooden stairs with dangerously loose banisters. All the new rooms now empty into a concrete quad instead of into crowded hallways where panic could be a serious problem in case of a tremor.

The writer begins the discussion with safety. Notice how the contrasting details all reflect safety concern.

The new campus is more versatile with its TV studio, little theater, two large gymnasiums, and outdoor amphitheater for assemblies and pep rallies. The old school had a boxy, cold auditorium, which had been condemned long before the rest of the buildings, one tiny gym, and plain, cramped classrooms, which were constantly being remodeled to keep up with educational trends.

The writer presents versatility as point 2. As with safety, the contrasting details reflect the point.

These new features are fine, but I miss the bell tower, the brick walls, the tree-lined entryway, and windows that really opened. In the new buildings there are no windows at all, and the buildings, set near the street behind a chain-link fence, are finished with a uniform, flat-topped, smooth-surfaced beige monotony that makes the whole place seem more like a maximum-security prison than a school.

He goes to point 3 — the pleasant environment of the old campus. Notice the shift. While the new campus seems safer and more versatile, the writer clearly appreciated the old campus more.

I guess I'm pretty young to be talking about the old days, but after moving to the new buildings I felt less human.

He closes the paragraph in a way that reflects his human concern over progress — the last sentence circles back to the first.

More important, there were changes in the faculty's human attitudes. Before moving into the modern

To start paragraph 3 he picks up "human" to aid the transition from one paragraph to the other while laying down his topic — the change in faculty attitude.

buildings, the teachers used to dress casually, often the women in slacks, blouses, and sweaters and the men in jeans, polo shirts, and tennis shoes. After making the move, as if attending a formal occasion, the women began to show up in snappy dresses and high heels; the men in suits and white shirts with ties knotted around their necks.

Point 1 deals with faculty attitude toward dress.

Before the move classes were informal. Teachers would often set aside their notes to share personal experiences related to whatever subject they were covering. After the move local educators began to see our new school as a showcase, so we had hundreds of visitors tramping through our classrooms. All these outsiders seemed to have made our teachers nervous; consequently, they became more formal in their lessons.

Point 2 deals with faculty attitude toward class organization.

Finally, in the old days the best teachers used to hang around after school. They would lounge on the grass under the sycamores and talk with students about social issues or their subjects.

Point 3 deals with after-school faculty-student encounters.

Once in the new buildings, when the last bell rang they, like almost all the students, bolted for the doors as if escaping into freedom.

The closing sentence ties back to the closing sentence of the last paragraph — the school has become a prison.

Now that you've had several examples to consider, it's time to write.

WRITING TASK

Write an extended comparison-and-contrast piece. Since this work is to be more than a single paragraph, we suggest you select subjects that will allow you to show both similarities and differences.

Here are some suggested subjects. You don't need to use them, but they may help you get started. If they don't work for you, feel free to develop your own. Compare and contrast:

1. your life with the life of someone you envy
2. your current life with the life you led several years ago
3. an effective with an ineffective teacher, boss, or parent
4. two performers of the same type — comedians, musicians, singers, actors, actresses
5. your public with your private self
6. two paintings of a similar subject by two different artists
7. your values or preferences with someone else's values or preferences — a friend, a parent, a public figure
8. two films of the same genre — two thrillers, two musicals, two comedies, whatever
9. your goals in life now with your goals in the past
10. two magazines devoted to the same interest — sports, collecting, computers, sewing

Remember:

1. Develop an extended list of similarities and differences.
2. Use the list as an aid in structuring your paper.
3. Compose a topic sentence that clearly announces your subject and a comparison-and-contrast pattern.
4. Write your paper according to fundamental comparison-and-contrast techniques.

10 ANALOGY

Earlier we said that to write an effective comparison (as well as an effective contrast) pattern, you need to use two subjects from a common group. Analogy is a special kind of comparison that works only when you compare subjects from different groups. In other words, unlike ordinary comparisons that present the similarities of two things very much alike, an analogy presents similarities between things basically different. An analogy, therefore, is figurative, not literal.

Often analogy is used to explain descriptively, functioning as part of a larger pattern. Read the following paragraph from surgeon Richard Selzer's collection of essays *Mortal Lessons*. Selzer begins with a quick comparison between a scalpel and the bow of a cello. He then compares the way a scalpel cuts to the movement of a slender fish.

> One holds the knife as one holds the bow of a cello or tulip — by the stem. Not palmed nor gripped nor grasped, but lightly, with the tips of the fingers. The knife is not for pressing. It is for drawing across the field of skin. Like a slender fish, it waits, at the ready, then, go! It darts, followed by a fine wake of red. The flesh parts, falling away to yellow globules of fat. Even though I've used it so many times, I still marvel at its power — cold, gleaming, silent. More, I am still struck with a kind of dread that it is I in whose hand the blade travels, that my hand is its vehicle, that yet again this terrible steel-bellied thing and I have conspired for a most unnatural purpose, the laying open of the body of a human being.

The main purpose of analogy is to explain. Sometimes it serves descriptive purposes; then it is closer to metaphor. Selzer's paragraph skirts description. To a slight degree it serves explanation by comparing the known to the unknown — the scalpel's handle to a cello bow or tulip stem and the moving blade to a slender fish. His analogy helps the reader feel and see the scalpel at work.

Usually analogies are more elaborate and functional, less descriptive and lyrical. Often a writer will bring one into a work to illustrate an abstract idea. Julian Jaynes uses analogy in this fashion when trying to explain just how limited human consciousness is. He compares the conscious mind to a flashlight searching in a dark room for an unlighted object.

> Consciousness is a much smaller part of our mental life than we are conscious of. How simple that is to say; how difficult to appreciate! It is like asking a flashlight in a dark room to search around for something that does not have any light shining upon it. The flashlight, since there is light in whatever direction it turns, would have to conclude that there is light everywhere. And so consciousness can seem to pervade all mentality when actually it does not.

By comparing the abstract to specific, concrete, seeable things, a writer can make an abstract concept a little clearer. The same is true of complicated experiences.

A writer might, for instance, decide to communicate the complicated thrill of a love affair. How? Well, the writer might do it by comparing it to a roller coaster ride — by using analogy. Although a love affair and a roller coaster ride are totally different experiences, they do share some general characteristics. Both have moments of heightened anticipation and exhilaration. Both capture a person's full attention. Both provide occasional surprises. And both, perhaps, end too soon. An analogy that is used to explain a complicated experience of this sort would be much longer than the above examples. A writer would develop it in a special pattern by introducing the subjects in the topic sentence.

The following illustration represents such a pattern. In it the writer compares getting a college education to a trip through a car wash. She sets up her subjects in the topic sentence. She then gives a brief description of the aspects of the car-washing experience that she wants to develop in her comparison. Next, she weaves together the experience of being a student with that of a car being scrubbed. Note that she doesn't try to describe every detail of the car-washing experience but instead selects only what she needs to make the connections between the two experiences — no more. We want to stress the importance of selecting appropriate details when writing anything, but especially when writing an analogy. If you include too much description, you may sidetrack your reader.

Like a trip through a car wash, a college education is an unveiling experience. The car arrives, its brilliance dimmed by layers of dust accumulated on the road. Sprayed and brushed repeatedly as it moves down the line, the car begins to regain its true color. So too a student enters the educational process, his potential hidden by inexperience and misconceptions about the world. He may resist at first, but gradually the repeated immersions in course work and the buffeting of his professors will begin to have an effect. He will discover previously unsuspected talents and interests; he will begin to view the world differently; he will become more tolerant of others as he learns of the complexity of human affairs. If he is lucky he will find two or three teachers who seem to speak directly to him, who have the skill and patience to put the final, polishing touches on his education, just as a small group of wash boys clean up the last specks of dirt on an automobile. If all goes well, what emerges from the process is a person better equipped to serve as an example to those who still labor under their private accumulations of ignorance and prejudice.

The topic sentence presents two subjects and clearly leads the reader to expect an analogy.

Two sentences about the car wash set up the comparison.

The writer compares the educational process to previous statements about the car wash.

Second similarity between education and car wash

As you can see from the illustration, analogy differs from ordinary comparison in that the writer focuses more on one subject than the other. She uses the car wash merely to get the reader thinking about a college education in a certain way.

We want to pass on a word of caution here. It's a mistake to carry an analogy too far. If the writer had extended the car wash analogy by comparing the preliminary vacuuming of the car to a college orientation course and a wax job to upper-division art courses (or any other courses, for that matter) the paragraph would have become ridiculous. Remember, the value of analogy lies in its power to suggest. It helps a writer lead the reader to experience something in a different way.

Now, let's examine another pattern built on analogy. Unlike the last illustration, this one relies on suggestion more than on direct comparison. This paragraph, from Donald Hall's essay "Four Kinds of Reading," compares certain kinds of reading to a narcotizing experience. The paragraph comes after others that discuss reading for information, literary experience, and intellectual awareness. As you read, notice the way Hall suggests the relation between reading and narcotics by using such words as *narcotic, opium, daydream, drug, addict,* and *trip.*

> But most reading which is praised for itself is neither literary nor intellectual. It is narcotic. Novels, stories and biographies — historical sagas, monthly regurgitations of book clubs — are the opium of the suburbs. The drug is not harmful except to the addict himself, and is no more injurious to him than Johnny Carson or a bridge club, but it is nothing to be proud of. This reading is the automated daydream, the mild trip of the housewife and the tired businessman, interested not in experience and feeling but in turning off the possibilities of experience and feeling. Great literature, if we read it well, opens us up to the world, and makes us more sensitive to it, as if we acquired eyes that could see through things and ears that could hear smaller sounds. But by narcotic reading, one can reduce great literature to the level of *The Valley of the Dolls.* One can read *Anna Karenina* passively and inattentively, and float down the river of lethargy as if one were reading a confession magazine: "I Spurned My Husband for a Count."

Sometimes analogies, especially those that attempt to suggest more than they state, just don't work. Often an analogy can be flat, confused, and indirectly comic — usually because the writer hasn't thought through the comparison. So be on guard. Make sure your analogies are appropriate for your subject.

Where can we send you to look for analogies? The answer is simple — into your imagination. When you begin to look at one experience and see another, you are on the track of analogy. You will be starting to make figurative comparisons.

Usually, a short descriptive comparison, such as a simile or metaphor, unexpectedly falls like a ripe jewel onto the page. How can a writer plan such descriptive phrases as "With fingers the size of sausages he plucked the wallet from her purse" or "I touched her paper skin and thought of a snake"? Somehow, as though by inspiration, the mind generates them during the writing process.

Unlike a single descriptive simile or metaphor, an analogy can be thought out. Suppose you wish to talk about personal growth. You realize that physical growth can be clearly seen and charted but that inner growth is evanescent. It exists but cannot be held. It cannot even be fixed in the mind because, like smoke, its shape keeps changing. After a time, your rambling thought begins to shape itself into a topic sentence — "Personal growth is much like the movement of smoke." You've seen one thing in another. You have an analogy.

As a closing illustration of analogy, study the following paragraph. In it James Thurber compares editor Harold Ross of *The New Yorker* magazine to a skilled mechanic.

Having a manuscript under Ross's scrutiny was like putting your car in the hands of a skilled mechanic, not an automotive engineer with a bachelor of science degree, but a guy who knows what makes a motor go, and sputter, and wheeze, and sometimes come to a dead stop; a man with an ear for the faintest body squeak as well as the loudest engine rattle.

Thurber immediately introduces the comparison of Ross to a skilled mechanic.

He develops analogy by describing the skilled mechanic's sensitivity to automobiles, for Ross is skilled in a similar way in his work.

When you first gazed, appalled, upon an uncorrected proof of one of your stories or articles, each margin had a thicket of queries and complaints — one writer got a hundred and forty-four on one profile.

He shifts to Ross's handiwork.

It was as though you beheld the works of your car spread all over the garage floor, and the job of getting the thing together again and making it work seemed impossible. Then you realized that Ross

Thurber returns to the analogy, this time comparing a writer's corrected manuscript to a dismantled car.

was trying to make your Model T or old Stutz Bearcat

into a Cadillac or Rolls-Royce. He was at work with the

tools of his unflagging perfectionism, and, after an

exchange of growls or snarls, you set to work to join

him in his enterprise.

Did you notice that Thurber used many words and phrases associated with automobiles? *Sputter, wheeze, come to a dead stop, body squeak,* and *engine rattle* are just a few. These words and phrases help keep the comparison before the reader. They serve as the thread that runs through the analogy and holds it together. Whenever you write an analogy, we suggest you use words and phrases associated with your subject as Thurber does with his.

WRITING TASK

One problem in assigning an analogy task is that an analogy usually leaps to mind while a writer is deep in the process of expressing thought. Because of the spontaneous nature of analogy, we don't want to stifle your creative expression with too much direction.

If, however, you need a nudge for training purposes, consider comparing one of the following with an idea, person, experience, or process. We suggest you begin prewriting by developing four or five sentences that state how your subjects are similar.

a flowing river	a merry-go-round
the changing seasons	the phases of the moon
the passage of the sun	the changing tide
a spider web	running long distances
walking through a desert	mountain climbing
a tornado	a dark tunnel
a bird of prey	a slot machine
a crap game	ripening fruit
an unweeded garden	a cluttered room
a poker hand	a game of solitaire

Remember:

The term to which you compare an idea or experience is not the subject of your piece. For instance, when Selzer writes, "One holds the knife as one holds the bow of a cello or tulip — by the stem," he is not writing about a cello or tulip stem, he is writing about the process of surgery that starts with the proper handling of a scalpel. Be sure not to lose sight of your true subject.

11 CLASSIFICATION

Human beings love to classify. We speak of lyric poetry and dramatic poetry; farces, comedies, and tragedies; economy cars, sports cars, and luxury cars; and, all too often, the good guys and the bad guys.

A music teacher may classify students according to their voices: soprano, mezzo-soprano, alto, tenor, baritone, and bass. A political science teacher may classify the same students according to their political leanings: radicals, liberals, conservatives, reactionaries, and maybe even confused. The registrar, for statistical purposes, may classify them according to sex, age, major, grade point average, city or county of origin, or future educational plans. A female student may be content just to classify males: dreamy, attractive, passable, and no thanks.

The point is that any subject can be classified in a number of ways depending on the writer's point of view and purpose in writing.

Establishing Categories for Classification

When writers classify, they use at least three categories; otherwise, they would be skirting comparison and contrast. They approach the subject they plan to classify by creating their own categories or by using ready-made categories. For example, the student who wrote the following paragraphs, which are part of a larger paper on off-beat hobbyists, creates her own categories to classify comic book collectors. She begins with a standard opening for classification pieces by clearly announcing the categories she slips her collectors into.

Other fascinating off-beat hobbyists are comic book collectors. These collectors, whether sixteen or sixty, at first glance seem to be a bushy-haired, disheveled, absentminded, and disorganized lot. But after close examination you'll find their habits put them into one of four major groups: the Antiquarians, Mercenaries, Idolators, and Compulsive Completers. You'll be able to find all these types rummaging through pile after pile of unsorted, secondhand comics in magazine marts scattered from New York to Los Angeles.

The opening sentence includes a transition from the preceding paragraph and announces the subject of "comic book collectors."

These sentences supply background and a general description of collectors while establishing four categories.

The Antiquarian cares only for age value; subject matter is of no concern. He's looking for a 1933 Funnies on Parade from the days when men were men and comics were comics. To the Mercenary, value is all-important. Certain numbers and titles ring a bell in his cash-register brain and start him furtively checking through a half dozen price sheets. A pristine first edition of Action Comics (value: $4000) would suit him just fine. The Idolator couldn't care less about age or value. He's looking for favorites: a Sheena, a Flash Gordon, or another Incredible Hulk. Hiding in a corner, reading those he can't afford to buy, he'll be the last one out of the mart at night and the first one back in the morning. The most frustrated collector is the Compulsive Completer. He'll examine and reject thousands of comics in his search for a badly needed Felix the Cat to

In this paragraph the writer presents the four kinds of collectors along with supporting details. Notice how she introduces each type by using her label in the first sentence of each section.

complete a year's set or the one <u>Howdy Doody</u> missing
from his collection. But no matter what the reason for

collecting, these hobbyists share a common trait: They

love the thrill of the hunt.

She closes the piece by identifying a common trait — all love the thrill of the hunt.

The writer of the preceding example wasn't just handed her classes; she created them. She then created labels to identify them for the reader.

Working with existing classes may be tougher than finding new ones. The writer is obligated to offer some new insights into the groups, not merely to pass on well-chewed information. For instance, in the following example from *Blood and Money,* Thomas Thompson spends a paragraph describing the different classes of surgeons. To make his material fresh, he describes each group according to its general personal characteristics, thus giving the reader a new way of looking at the people who might be plunging scalpels into their flesh.

Among those who train students to become doctors, it is said that surgeons find their niche in accordance with their personal characteristics. The orthopedic surgeon is medicine's carpenter — up to his elbows in plaster of Paris — and tradition holds that he is a gruff, slapdash sort of man whose labor is in a very physical area of healing. Away from the hospital, the orthopedists are often hunters, boaters, outdoorsmen.

The neurosurgeon, classically, does not get too involved with his patients. Or, for that matter, with anybody. They are cool men, blunted, rarely gregarious.

Heart surgeons are thundering egotists, star performers in a dazzling operating theater packed with assistants, nurses, paramedics, and a battery of futuristic equipment which could seemingly lift the room into outer space. These are men who relish drama, who live life on the edge of the precipice.

And the plastic surgeon? He is, by nature, a man of art, and temperament, and sensitivity. "We are the artists who deal in beauty lost, or beauty that never was," said one plastic man at a national convention. "Our stitches are hidden, and so are our emotions."

Unlike the author of the first classification example, Thompson doesn't use the opening sentences to list the classes he'll be describing.

There is no need to; most readers are familiar with orthopedic surgeons, neurosurgeons, and heart and plastic surgeons.

Arranging a Classification

The arrangement of a classification piece is quite simple. A writer will present the categories in the order that seems most appropriate. We do want to make one hard rule about classification arrangement: Always give the name of the class in the first sentence that starts the group description. The name will help you keep the reader on the right track by announcing that a shift from one group to another will be taking place.

You face one danger here. Often a classification piece will get boring if you merely tick off one category after another. How do you avoid boring your readers? Create some variety. For instance, Thompson begins his first three group descriptions with "The orthopedic surgeon," "The neurosurgeon," and "Heart surgeons." After these three standard openings the reader might react with a ho hum. But Thompson anticipates this response, so he varies the last opening by beginning with a question: "And the plastic surgeon?" It's not a spectacular tactic, but it serves to nudge a drowsing reader. It's unexpected.

Now study the following example that classifies high school basketball fans. Since the writer creates his own categories, he mentions them in the opening to let the reader know what to expect. As you read, notice how clearly he arranges the classes: He presents one group with its description, then the next, and the next.

A high school coach I used to know insisted there were three kinds of basketball fans: Friends, Romans, and Countrymen. He was well aware that for Mark Antony, who used these words to address his fellow Romans after Julius Caesar had been assassinated, the terms were just three ways of addressing the same people. But for Pete Munson they represented distinct groups. Friends were the majority of fans. They loved to watch the game, didn't know much about it, never criticized the coaching, supported the team in victory or defeat, and ate a lot of popcorn. Nice guys. No problem. It was the Romans he had to watch out for. Aggressive, raucous, even vicious, they knew that the game was being staged by a dumb coach, incompetent or possibly corrupt officials, and greedy but inept players. What's more, they told everyone about it — loud and clear:

"Let Smith play, Munson!"

"Hey, Homer, how much you get paid?"

"Point hog! You had an open man!"

After an hour of such abuse, my friend would seek the solace of a glass of beer and a small group of Countrymen. Countrymen were other coaches. They knew Munson was working miracles with poor material; they understood his strategy; they sympathized with his decision to bench the uncooperative Smith. And for the rest of the evening, at least, they helped him forget the Roman words he feared most: "We come to bury Munson, not to praise him."

Obviously, this classification piece is based on personal experience. It represents the view of one man — Coach Munson — and may not fit anyone else's experience. That's fine: The writer is attempting to give the reader Munson's point of view regarding fans, not suggesting that every high school coach would describe fans the way Munson does.

Grouping and Sorting Classes

You can think of classification as another word for grouping or sorting. You have a large number of instances, too many to discuss individually, and you group, sort, or classify them into a small number of classes according to some principle of similarity that is meaningful for your paper.

It's very much like sorting the mail. When you drop a letter into the slot at the post office, you take the first classification step yourself by dropping your letter in the out-of-town slot instead of the local one. A mail clerk going through the out-of-town mail conducts further classification as he sorts the letters into bags labeled New England, Middle Atlantic, South Atlantic, Midwest, South, Southwest, Northwest, and Pacific Coast. When a bag of letters arrives at a New England depot, it is further sorted by zip code and later still by street address. Only then does the name of the individual addressee become important.

When you want to arrange some information in a classification pattern, you must sort its components into meaningful groups. *Meaningful* is the key word. Consider our post office analogy. For the first clerk to decide to classify the letters alphabetically would not have been to sort them meaningfully. Such a sorting would produce stacks of bags labeled A, B, C, and so on through Z. This system would not serve the post office's purpose of passing mail from senders to receivers. A meaningful classification would be for the clerk to sort the mail by destination, not by alphabet.

In a different situation, the destination of a letter may not be the best way to classify it. Consider the needs of someone in business who receives bundles of mail daily — requests for charitable donations, advertisements, business reports, invitations, demands for business actions, and notes from old friends. Whether formally or informally, the executive will classify the day's mail according to the importance of each letter, perhaps arranging it in categories such as immediate response, eventual response, information only, and junk. Given the executive's situation, these would be meaningful classes.

Once you have your meaningful classes spotted, you need to be sure they're equally general. It wouldn't make much sense to classify bundles of mail headed for the East under the labels New England, Middle Atlantic, Southeast, and Boston. These classes are not equally general. The first three are regions. Boston is a city — in fact, part of New England. Would Thomas Thompson have made much sense if he had classified surgeons under orthopedic surgeons, neurosurgeons, heart surgeons, plastic surgeons, and surgeons in training? Of course not.

Your classes should also be inclusive — they should cover the territory reasonably well. If the postal clerks had forgotten to label a bag Midwest, their system would not cover the territory of the United States. If you classify religions in America by referring only to Catholics, Baptists, Methodists, and Christian Scientists, you have not covered the territory. Of course the word *reasonably* has to operate here. Perhaps your paper can't include every specific instance, and if you think you've covered the territory and someone says, "Hey, how about the Poseidon freaks?" you may be justified in dismissing that person as a crackpot. If you want to avoid leaving yourself open to criticism, you may have to resort to changing your subject to major religions in America and then define the term *major* as you see it. Realistically, such problems won't crop up too often, and if you avoid major omissions, most readers will accept the fact that you are characterizing prominent classes, which most cases fall into rather logically. Your classes should be exclusive, too, with no overlapping. If the postal clerks have drawn their boundaries well, there will be no doubt that a particular letter belongs in the Middle Atlantic and not the Southeast bag. If you are classifying television programs and you decide to group them as children's, Westerns, situation comedies, and educational, your classes are not exclusive. A children's program could be a Western or educational. The problem here is in the method of arriving at the classes. Children's is a class arrived at according to age; Westerns and situation comedies are classes arrived at according to content; educational is a class arrived at according to purpose. You can't mix methods of classification without confusing your reader.

Hold the following four principles in mind while thinking through a classification piece.

1. Develop meaningful classes.
2. Shape them at the same general level.
3. Make sure they cover the territory by keeping them inclusive.
4. Make sure they don't overlap by keeping them exclusive.

WRITING TASK ═══════════════════════════════════════

Write a piece developed by classification. Since virtually any subject can be organized into classes, whatever interests you will probably work. A key to getting off to a good start is your selection of classes. Avoid the obvious and the superficial. Don't classify salespeople into the successful and unsuccessful or cars into luxury and economy classes. Such classifications and others like them don't merit your attention or your reader's. They're too obvious.

Here are some general subject areas you might consider classifying. Keep in mind that they need to be focused — that is your job.

teachers	vacations
jobs	restaurants
department stores	boutiques
students	athletes
coaches	lies
police officers	movies
books	disguises
TV programs	sports fans
playgrounds	affairs
dates	lovers
doctors	nurses

If these don't work for you, you may want to use one of the following questions to lead you into classification.

1. What are the ways to obtain knowledge?
2. What are the ways to manipulate others?
3. What are the ways to bring joy to others?
4. What are the ways to make big money?
5. What are the ways to stop smoking?
6. What are the ways to get a person to say yes?
7. What are the ways to live without working?
8. What are the ways to cook a good anything?

Remember:

1. Divide your subject into at least three groups.

2. If you develop your own categories and labels, announce them at the beginning of your paragraph.
3. Develop meaningful categories that don't overlap.
4. Keep your reader interested and avoid merely ticking off one category after another.

12 DEFINITION

When speaking, many of us toss away words like a gambler throwing quarters at a Las Vegas slot machine. But when writing, most of us try to use words precisely. We live with the knowledge (maybe even the fear) that on a sheet of paper our words can be examined — studied in context and explored in a dictionary; whereas in speech we relax with the knowledge that words melt like cotton candy on a warm tongue.

Trying to use words precisely can be a gut-wrenching business. Some words are so much a part of a specialized vocabulary that only certain occupational or recreational groups know them. Some are used so infrequently that few readers know what they mean. Some are so slippery that people understand them differently. But when you write, you have to struggle to be precise — painfully precise — in overcoming the specialized, the infrequent, the slippery word. Sometimes that means defining, briefly or extensively, any key word you use to make sure the reader understands what you mean.

Brief Definitions

A brief definition will usually do for an obscure or specialized word. A synonym, a short phrase, a brief comparison — that's all you need.

> *Synonym:* When my uncle returned from abroad, he gave each of us a grego, which is a jacket.

> *Short phrase:* Some historians suggest that the American government during the last century conducted an unofficial pogrom, an organized massacre of helpless people, against Indians confined to reservations.

Comparison: Thallium, a metallic element resembling lead, is rare.

When you give a brief description, always try to work it into the flow of your piece. Don't stop the movement, announce the word's meaning, then pick up the march. Also avoid misusing *when* and *where* in definitions. Don't write something like this:

Gregarious is when people flock or herd together.

Or this:

Gregarious is where people flock or herd together.

Gregarious is neither a time nor a place — it's a mode of social behavior.

Extended Definitions

Brief definitions are easy enough. The real difficulty comes with extended definitions of abstract or general words, words such as *freedom, love, prejudice, equality, delinquence,* or *patriotism.* Words such as these have become so slippery you must define them. Usually the definition will be extended — a paragraph or more — so that your reader will have a clear idea of what such a word means to you. To write an extended definition you can

1. use synonyms
2. give examples
3. discuss the word's origin
4. develop comparisons or analogies
5. tell what the word is not
6. create an anecdote to show the word in action

As you will notice, many of these items (examples, anecdote, comparisons, and analogies) are methods of development studied in earlier chapters. We don't suggest you try to use all these techniques in any single definition. We listed them to give you an idea of the possibilities.

Now let's take a look at an extended definition of *patriotism.* The writer starts with a topic sentence that suggests a broad meaning. He then spends four sentences exploring what patriotism isn't. He follows with examples — brief ones — of patriotic behavior. He then spends a sentence on the origins of the word before moving into a comparison with parental love. He finishes the paragraph by reminding the reader of his opening thought, thus indicating he has covered the territory.

True patriotism is wishing your country well. It does not require chest thumping, flag waving, fiery speeches, or parades. We use the word incorrectly when we confine it to ostentatious acts. It is not boasting, but service; not hatred, but love; not loud, but quiet. Quiet, loving service is what a patriot has to offer. The voter who puts public welfare above private greed is practicing patriotism. The person who expresses his opinion on local, state, and national problems; who dares to criticize elected representatives; whose personal behavior serves as a prod to the conscience of others is practicing patriotism. Those who do these things do so because they care about their country. We get the word patriot from the Latin for "fellow countryman," a term suggesting a loving relationship that is at the heart of patriotic behavior. One's love for his fellow countrymen and therefore his country is not unlike parents' love for their children. Parents want their children to realize their potential, to grow, to become better. They invest time and effort to this end. They support their children through rough times, but they also demand certain standards of behavior. It would be a poor parent who said, "My child, right or wrong," if that phrase is intended to convey an unthinking support of whatever the child wants to do. By the same token the phrase "My country, right or wrong" should not be accepted blindly as a patriotic

This opening sentence clearly suggests that a definition will follow.

The following four sentences tell what patriotism isn't. Since patriotism is such an abstract concept, the writer tries to give his definition life with image-producing phrases: chest thumping, flag waving, fiery speeches, and so on.

Because definitions tend to be inclusive, examples tend to be impressionistic and general, as these are. The last sentence in this series comes back to the central point: wishing your country well.

Here the writer dips into etymology — word history — to set up the comparison that follows.

This comparison further illustrates what patriotism means to the writer.

position. Wishing your country well is harder and more

complicated than blind loyalty.

The clincher sentence recalls the introduction and closes the paragraph.

Do you agree with this definition? Perhaps not. But agreement isn't what this writer is after. Instead he seeks understanding. There is no doubt that you have a strong impression of what he means by *patriotism.*

Extended definitions can be purely personal or they can be largely objective. A personal definition, like the preceding one, explains how a writer is using the term — "Never mind what other people think *patriotism* means; it means this to me." Such a strategy is useful if your purpose is to get a reader to see a word in a different light or if you are discussing your understanding of the term. Everyone knows, for instance, what *prejudice* means: "prejudging without adequate information." But to a six-year-old, *prejudice* may mean waiting at a candy counter until all the adults are served. It may mean not counting as a real person, tolerated rather than truly listened to. It may mean being discriminated against on the basis of size.

An objective definition, on the other hand, seeks general agreement. It's the kind of definition that applies in all cases at all times. This requires detailing. The word *democracy* means "rule by the people." At this level, most people can agree with the definition without further discussion. But two opposing political forces may need to reach a more detailed agreement if they are to talk together productively. For example, who are the people? Everyone? Voters? Only those over twenty-one? A ruling class that claims to speak in the name of all? It would be meaningless to discuss the value of "democratic elections" without a comprehensive definition of *democracy.* Objective definitions, therefore, should spell out the details.

Now let's examine an objective definition to give you an idea of how to go about writing one. One dictionary definition of *plagiarism* is "to steal someone else's ideas or words and pass them off as one's own."

As you define a term in your paper, you may wish to see what a dictionary's definition is, but don't quote the dictionary in your paper ("as the . . . says . . ."). Instead make the word yours; discuss it as you see it and as you want your reader to understand it. The dictionary definition of *plagiarism* is clear, as far as it goes, but a more extended objective definition gives the reader a better understanding of plagiarism and how it happens.

Plagiarism is taking the words or ideas of another and pretending they are yours. It is a serious literary crime, a form of dishonesty that, if discovered, carries heavy penalties. There are two kinds of plagiarism, the intentional and the unintentional. Intentional plagiarism is an act of either defiance or desperation. The defiant student sees no reason to learn about photosynthesis (for example) himself, and so he "rewrites" an article or textbook entry and brazenly submits it to the instructor as his own work. The desperate student probably agrees that the subject is worth knowing about, but he's neglected his studies too long. In panic he also turns in someone else's work, throwing in a few misspellings for authenticity. More often plagiarism is unintentional, a product of ignorance. The student is required to write on a subject he is not expert on. The instructor knows this and expects the student to turn to other written sources for information. Unfortunately, those other sources phrase things so well that the student cannot see any alternative ways of organizing the material. Instead of making the information his and then expressing what he has learned, he produces a patchwork piece of alternating amateur and professional sentences and paragraphs. He's not proud of it, but what can he do? Well, fortunately, there are many things he can do. And in the process of following the tips presented below, he

The topic sentence is a capsule definition.

Next the writer amplifies on the capsule definition.

Then he divides the term into two kinds.

He divides the first kind into two subparts.

He explains one subpart.

He explains the other subpart.

The writer discusses the second kind of plagiarism.

The final sentences lead to the rest of the paper, discussing ways to avoid plagiarism.

will not only learn his subject well, he will avoid the

embarrassment of being charged with plagiarism.

An extended definition such as this is often used as just a part, usually of a longer paper and usually comes near the beginning. In a paper discussing the skill of bullfighting, for example, it may be useful to have a definition of the term *adorno*. Briefly, it means a kind of flowery theatricality by which the bullfighter shows domination over the bull. But an extended definition giving examples of *adorno* in practice would be helpful for the reader of such a paper.

You may also have noticed that these writers have used other patterns in their definitions. The writer who defined *patriotism* used examples and comparison. The writer who defined *plagiarism* used classification. Keep in mind that patterns seldom appear in pure form. They get mixed together. And nowhere do they get more mixed than in defining terms. So when you write an extended definition, stay on your toes; use good horse sense. If you don't know what horse sense is, read the following extended definition by writer Earl Rudolph.

Horse sense is a judgment which reflects sound thinking. It is not a blind jump into a decision which may lead to ruin. Horse sense is not a hasty conclusion which prompts action causing deep regret later. In other words, horse sense is common sense. Anyone possessing this common sense would know better than to wear bathing trunks outdoors in December. He certainly would regret this action while recuperating from pneumonia. A sensible casting machine operator will turn off his machine before he attempts to retrieve a die which has fallen into the mechanism. A thoughtful homeowner carries liability insurance to avoid being sued by someone injured on his property. These people all use

The topic sentence puts the term into a general class. The two sentences that follow tell what it is not.

Next Rudolph gives a synonym.

Then he gives three examples.

Then he makes a summary statement about the examples.

horse sense or common sense in making important

decisions almost every day of their lives. | We see then   *Rudolph's clincher sentence returns to*
                                             first statement.

that horse sense or common sense often requires sound

thinking.

There's always a limit to how far a definition can go. We're sure you could sit down and list many more examples of horse sense than Rudolph does. But remember, in definition your goal is to give the reader a clear understanding of the term. That calls for personal judgment. When you've nailed down the term, stop.

WRITING TASK

Write an extended personal definition of a word or phrase. Develop your definition with several of the techniques discussed earlier: Use synonyms, give examples, discuss the word's origin, develop comparisons, tell what the word is not, create an anecdote to show the word in action.

Let your definition reflect your thinking; do not merely tell what everyone already knows. And don't rely on or quote the definition given in a dictionary. You may wish to consult the dictionary, but only for your own information. You may also wish to investigate the word's origin in an etymological dictionary, but develop your own fresh comparisons, examples, analogies, or anecdotes.

The list below includes formal and informal language. Many of the words have more than one form, and you may use whatever form you wish or even more than one form in the same paper. For example, you could define *glamour, glamorous, glamorize,* or all three.

You may, of course, select a word not on the list. Often currently used slang expressions make good subjects for definition papers.

glamour	guerrilla
harassment	scholar
luck	negligent
beauty	whoopee
glutton	highbrow
abundance	mickey-mouse
heyday	funny

finicky   confidence
dedication   shoddy
gobbledygook   phoney
fiasco   clever
ambition   hocus-pocus
greenhorn   ghetto
funky   tragedy
tyranny   comedy

Remember:

1. You're writing a definition that not only explains how the word is generally used but also explains your understanding of the word.
2. Develop your definition by using patterns such as example, comparison and contrast, analogy, anecdote, and classification.

13 CAUSE AND EFFECT

An eight-year-old bursts through the screen door, tears running down his cheeks, hand clasped over his nose with a few droplets of blood squeezing between the finger cracks. Dad puts down the dish towel and turns from the sink with an "I'm an understanding poppa" look on his face.

"Sandra hit me," the boy cries. "Right in the nose."

Dad begins to wipe away the droplets and tears. The screen door flies open again. The sister storms into the kitchen and shouts, "He threw the baseball at me."

"She tried to horn in on our game. She can't hit."

"I can hit better than you. Look at your nose."

And on and on and on.

At one level this drama illustrates normal child behavior. At another it illustrates cause-and-effect relationships.

We begin the drama with a clear effect — the bloody nose. We then fall back to a cause — a right cross. At first it all seems simple. We probe deeper: right cross to nose caused by brother tossing baseball at sister.

Hmmmmmm!

The plot thickens: tossed baseball caused by sister trying to join the game.

Here we stop, for we want only to give you an idea of what cause-and-effect patterns involve, not probe the roots of sibling rivalry.

When writers explain why something happened or what could possibly happen or the results of something happening, they are dealing in cause and effect.

Why did Sandra punch her brother? Does violence broadcast on TV stimulate violence on the street? Has the women's liberation movement changed college programs? Why do so many Americans revere John Wayne? These are all questions that would lead you into using a cause-and-effect pattern.

A cause-and-effect piece may cover only causes or only effects or both. When the effect is clear, you won't need to spend much time discussing it, but you will need to explore its causes. For instance, statistics indicate that teenage suicide is increasing. If you were to write about the problem, you wouldn't need to spend much space substantiating the fact. You would spend a great deal of space discussing why — the causes.

Sometimes a cause will be clear. Most readers would generally agree that children spend more time watching television than they spend in school. No need to prove it. Plenty of surveys already have. But if you were writing about children spending more time before a TV screen than in school, you would need to discuss what it might mean — that is, the possible effects.

Consider the following example. The writer assumes that her readers will not dispute the existence of a women's liberation movement. So instead of documenting the fact, she gets right to its effects on her college campus. She uses a basic pattern. First she presents the liberation movement as a basic cause of the changes. Next she details the obvious effects.

The fallout from the women's liberation movement has settled on our campus and produced changes in both student body and curriculum.	*The topic sentence indicates the effect in broad terms.*
In the last few years over a thousand women, newly liberated or trying hard, have enrolled in classes to launch academic careers, prepare for new vocations, or seek self-fulfillment. The historical male majority on campus has given way to this inundation, and the balance is tipping more every year. Our typical student is now a twenty-six-year-old female.	*The writer introduces effect 1.*
No longer the husband hunters of yesterday, these women are dedicated and serious students. Their presence has led to the development of new courses and the revision of some old ones. Many courses now give	*This sentence provides transition between effect 1 and effect 2.* *Effect 2 begins.*

equal time to the contributions that innovative women

have made to the fields of science, literature, and

philosophy. Teachers have developed new courses in

female sexuality and women writers. Our campus has a

women's center and a new women's studies department.

Effect 2 has four subparts.

Women even have their own athletic teams — not

powder-puff imitations of male teams, but the real stuff,

complete with leagues, spectators, and championships.

The clincher sentence shows women making inroads in the most male-dominated area of campus life.

Often causes and effects are classified as immediate and ultimate — those that are most apparent and those that underlie them. This writer presented the immediately apparent effects of women's liberation: changes in student population, curriculum, and the athletic program. She could have probed more deeply: changes in male roles as related to female roles, in student government, in relationships between older and younger women. But her intent was not to give the ultimate effects but only to present some immediate ones. The depth to which a writer goes always depends on the subject and how thorough the writer wishes to be. Getting to the ultimate causes or effects requires a greater effort than getting to the immediate ones. It takes more space than a short piece offers, because a writer will usually have to establish a foundation for the analysis.

In *The Seasons of a Man's Life*, a study that deals with the psychological development of men, Daniel J. Levenson establishes a solid base before presenting some ultimate results that stem from internal conflict some men experience during the middle years. Halfway through the book Levenson explains the concept of Young/Old polarity — the problems men must confront as they move from youth to old age — and the Dream — the aspirations that motivate men in their youth. He then shows how the Young/Old polarity and the Dream might create conflict between middle-aged men and young adults.

At around 40 a man is deeply involved in the

Young/Old polarity. This developmental process has a

powerful effect upon his relationships with his offspring

and with young adults generally. When his own aging

Levenson spends two sentences to introduce his topic and focus — the effect of relationships with young adults.

He begins to detail the effects.

weighs heavily upon him, their exuberant vitality is more likely to arouse his envy and resentment than his delight and forbearance. He may be preoccupied with grievances against his own parents for damage, real or imagined, that they have inflicted upon him at different ages. These preoccupations make him less appreciative of the (often similar) grievances his offspring direct toward him.

If he feels he has lost or betrayed his own early Dream, he may find it hard to give his wholehearted support and blessing to the Dreams of young adults. When his offspring show signs of failure or confusion in pursuing their adult goals, he is afraid that their lives will turn out as badly as his own. Yet, when they do well, he may resent their success. Anxiety and guilt may undermine his efforts to be helpful and lead him instead to be nagging and vindictive.

The second paragraph begins with the topic of the Dream and focuses on its role in the conflict.

Levenson begins to detail the effects.

Levenson has gone much deeper than immediate gripes a middle-aged man might have with young adults; he explores the ultimate reasons buried deep in the male psyche.

We don't want to give you the impression that cause-and-effect patterns always deal with objective material, as the last two examples have. They don't. Cause and effect play an important part in self-analysis. The writer of the following example uses totally subjective material. He charts the effects the women's liberation movement has had on his life. As you read, notice that the writer builds his piece through examples taken from personal experience.

I'm not sure I like the effects that the women's liberation movement has caused in my life. Equal pay for equal work is fair enough, but the more subtle changes

The opening sentence clearly states the topic and personal focus.

Sentence 2 shows that the writer is interested in exploring attitudes, not issues.

in women's attitudes toward men really bug me. I don't
like being asked for a date, for one thing. Some weeks
ago a girl in my philosophy class stopped me to ask if I
would attend a Rolling Stones concert with her. My God!
I didn't know what to do! Ordinarily, I'd go to a Stones
concert with Dracula. But I was too dumb to accept on
the spot, so I blushed and stammered out some stupid
excuse. The whole scene made me uncomfortable. Then
the service station I go to hired a female gas pumper. It
embarrassed me to have her check my oil and to tell me
I needed air in my front tires. I quit going there. I know
there's no reason to feel she shouldn't be doing the job,
but it made me feel inadequate somehow. The other day I
opened the door to the library for a girl who was just
behind me. She went through all right, but she gave me
an awful dirty look as if to say, "I can do it myself, jerk!"
I was just trying to be polite, but I guess I insulted her
sense of independence. Every day I see examples of
women becoming more aggressive and independent as a
result of the liberation movement, and while it's easy to
agree with the idea behind it, it's hard for this
male-person to accept these changes.

Example 1: a brief narrative to illustrate effect 1

Example 2: another specific example that mixes details — "change my oil" and "air in the front tire" — with responses — "It embarrassed me" and "made me feel inadequate"

Example 3: the writer continues to use vivid details in specific examples.

He closes with a clincher that restates his agreement with the issues while keeping his personal reservations.

When writing a cause-and-effect piece, we suggest that in the beginning sentence you include *cause* or *effect* or other words that let the reader know what pattern to expect. In the topic sentence of the last paragraph, the writer used both *cause* and *effect*: "I'm not sure I like the effects the women's liberation movement has caused in my life."

Although many words can guide a reader into the pattern, some writers start with a question that begins with *what* or *why*.

In the next example a writer explores the reasons people jog in southern California. She begins by asking why. Since people jog for a variety of reasons, she carefully qualifies each one she offers, thus avoiding the claim that any single cause drives all joggers to the streets. Qualifying causes in this fashion is an important technique to learn, for sometimes you will be faced with a clear effect but have only probable causes. When this is the case, qualify them.

Why is jogging becoming a popular activity in southern California? Perhaps because we live in a youth-oriented culture, and those moving into middle life jog in a desperate effort to keep what nature is tearing from them. Others may jog to be part of "the scene," just as some people go to discos to be part of that scene. Or perhaps the cause is much deeper. Some jogging enthusiasts claim that extended periods of running can lead the jogger into meditative trances with all the benefits of quiet sitting. They see themselves as innovators in the tradition of "moving meditation," such as that practiced by Sufi whirling dervishes. Still others claim they jog merely to stay fit by burning off extra servings of cream pie, chocolate cake, ice cream, and jelly rolls.

The opening question clearly leads the reader to expect causes.

Qualifying words and phrases such as "perhaps," "others may," "some," and "others claim" clearly indicate the writer isn't claiming that people jog for all these reasons.

We will close with another example from a writer's personal experience. Too often when learning this pattern, writers feel they need to deal with earthshaking subjects — the causes of the energy crisis, the effects of nuclear proliferation, the causes and effects of terrorism. But to say anything meaningful about earthshaking subjects requires expertise. You probably don't have it yet. To write about earthshaking subjects, therefore, would mean you had to pass on common information from *Time, Newsweek,* or the "NBC Nightly News." So when learning this pattern, try to stay with personal experience, as this writer does.

When my team, the Astros, won the summer softball championship a few years ago, I took a lot of sour grapes guff from my friends on other teams. They said we were just lucky or they accused our coach of stacking the team with the best talent. I guess there's a certain amount of luck in winning so much — we were undefeated in twenty-four games — but luck can't explain it all, and as for talent, we had some pretty ordinary players, really, including me. I think our secret was our short, intense, and infrequent practice sessions. We only practiced for an hour just before each game, never on other days. It doesn't seem like much, but it put us in the right mood to play well. By game time other teams were tired from daily practice but we were starved for action. We practiced hard. Bunting, sliding, throwing, and fielding. Although we were known for our hitting, we never had regular batting practice. Our coach said it was too boring for everyone but the guy batting. When we took the infield just before game time we concentrated hard on running the patterns smoothly. A good infield warmup is a thing of beauty in itself and puts you in a good mood to play. A lot of coaches wouldn't agree with this approach, but I think it was the cause for our success. After all, we won every single game!

The writer begins with some background information. He also rejects some immediate causes — luck and team stacking.

This is the focusing sentence that presents the cause — short, intense, and infrequent practice sessions.

The writer presents the details of the session.

The clincher reminds the reader of the focus — the cause of the Astros' success.

Not earthshaking, but the writer uses a basic cause-and-effect pattern. When the time comes to write about earthshaking events, he'll be ready.

WRITING TASK

Write a piece patterned on a cause or effect structure. Depending on the subject, you can choose to explore immediate or ultimate causes or effects. If your subject is complex enough you might want to explore both the causes and the effects. As a way of getting started, you can use any of the following leads. But, as always, you can create your own subject.

1. Write a piece about the causes/effects of a personal experience that moved you emotionally.
2. Write a piece that presents the causes/effects of one of your strong interests.
3. Write a piece that presents the effects of an outside event, movement, or institution on your life.
4. Write a piece that presents the causes behind a family, institutional, or social custom.
5. Write a piece that presents the possible effects of a particular choice you must make.

Remember:

1. Limit your subject; keep to what you know.
2. Announce in the opening sentence that you are writing a cause or effect piece.
3. Know whether you are dealing with ultimate or immediate effects.

14 DESCRIPTION

You've already had some experience with descriptive writing in Getting Started. We've emphasized the value of embedding bits of description in all but the most scientifically objective pieces. Descriptive details will bring life to classifications, comparisons, contrasts, examples — indeed, descriptive details will make all patterns you use more vivid. Moreover, when a descriptive paragraph is mixed with other patterns, it can tug powerfully on the reader's attention. Writers who use description effectively evoke scenes, people, situations, and actions by involving their readers' senses and experiences. But unlike development by examples, comparison and contrast, classification, or analogy, descriptions aren't always cast in traditional structures. Writing effective description, therefore, often depends on cunning. Of course, to be cunning the writer must be tuned to what the paper needs and what readers can follow.

Use Description to Dramatize Experience

A pedestrian piece of prose can be elevated to a more vivid reading experience through a paragraph of description. In the piece that follows, a student who is also a police officer includes a paragraph of dramatic description in a paper that deals with the psychological requirements of the deadening routine of a detective. She begins by relating clichéd views of what it takes. Then she develops a descriptive paragraph by using typical details from a detective's work life. As you read the illustration, note how the descriptive paragraph paints a vivid picture of the routine work of a detective and seems to flow from the opening paragraph.

To be a police investigator a person must meet some tough requirements. He must stay alert, keep calm under pressure, and perform his job fairly. These are general requirements — the kind of requirements every citizen would expect every cop to meet, somewhat like the Boy Scout motto, "Be prepared." But there's a much tougher requirement. Anyone who wants to be a detective must consider it to be the spine of his work. It has to do with the courage to meet the tedious, unglamorous day-to-day activities every detective faces.

In a year a detective is required to spend hundreds of hours in routine work behind a government-gray desk under the glare of fluorescent lights. He'll dial thousands of telephone numbers until a callus grows on his index finger. He'll get thousands of busy signals and few answers for his trouble. He'll spend hours filling out reports and sitting in courtrooms waiting to testify. Often he'll see the criminals he has described in his reports sent home by the court he sits in. In a year he'll spend endless hours driving crowded streets during a steamy summer and frigid winter. He'll eat pounds of hamburger, salami, and bologna for lunches and wash it all down with enough coffee to kill ten normal kidneys. The odds are he'll never be shot at, but he'll probably get spit on and cursed. No doubt some violent drunk or strung-out junkie will retch on his shoes. A dramatic life — no. Moreover, keep in mind how hard it is to stay alert, calm, and fair in the face of this kind of psychological torture.

The writer continues her essay by exploring the psychological effects of this kind of tedious routine. She develops most of the paper through objective research that supports her points. But without a descriptive paragraph that paints the detective's routine, the information would not have much impact.

The illustration raises an obvious question. Is the description a true one? Yes and no.

It isn't true if you read it as objective information. Not every detective eats pounds of hamburger, salami, and bologna during a year of lunches. Not every detective gets spit on.

But if you read it for the writer's emotional intent, the paragraph is true. The writer wants to generate a feeling in the reader. She's not claiming to be objective. She's clearly biased. She has a point of view and uses a dramatic description to involve her readers in it. She is writing subjectively, not objectively. So, from an inner perspective — from the writer's emotional viewpoint — the illustration reflects a general truth. Moreover, within the context of the entire essay, it is effective.

Use Description to Dramatize the Abstract

Most writing draws from our creative juices, but description seems to draw the most. To use description effectively, you must be supple enough in your writing to turn details to your writing needs. Nowhere is this more difficult than in attempting to describe the abstract — that level of experience almost impossible to communicate. One way to do it is through analogy. Another, perhaps one that wears better on readers, is to find descriptive details strong enough to make readers see and feel the abstraction.

Michael Herr does it in *Dispatches,* a collection of personal essays about the Vietnam War. Through the use of concrete description he makes the reader feel how sensitive one becomes to sound while in a jungle filled with enemies. Before going on, think for a moment about how you would describe the abstract experience of straining to hear sounds in a world gone silent. Then study Herr's paragraph to see how he does it.

> There were times during the night when all the jungle sounds would stop at once. There was no dwindling down or fading away, it was all gone in a single instant as though some signal had been transmitted out to the life; bats, birds, snakes, monkeys, insects, picking up on a frequency that a thousand years in the jungle might condition you to receive, but leaving you as it was to wonder what you weren't hearing now, straining for sound, one piece of information. I had heard it before in other jungles, the Amazon and the Philippines, but those jungles were "secure," there wasn't much chance that hundreds of Viet Cong were coming and going, moving and waiting, living out there just to do you harm. The thought of that one could turn any sudden silence into a space that you'd fill with everything you thought was quiet in you, it could even put you on the approach to clairvoyance. You thought you heard impossible things: damp roots breathing, fruit sweating, fervid bug action, the heartbeat of tiny animals.

Like the police officer's piece, this illustration is subjective. Herr uses as much experience as he needs to make the reader feel the threatening silence. He draws from the past — "I had heard it before in other jungles" — and relates the past to the present he describes. He even flies into imagination to illustrate how the strain of listening leads one to hear the impossible, "damp roots breathing, fruit sweating, fervid bug action, and the heartbeat of tiny animals." Herr touches another abstraction: fear — the fear of being caught unaware by an enemy that moves through the silence.

Use Concrete Language in Description

Whatever is being described, the writer must use concrete language and specific detail. Without them writers cannot lead their readers to see and feel what they have in mind. Consider the following portion of an essay by Flannery O'Connor describing the way her peacocks greet visitors to her home. Her use of specific detail allows us to accurately visualize the scene.

> The peacock himself is a careful and dignified investigator. Visitors to our place, instead of being barked at by dogs rushing from under the porch, are squalled at by peacocks whose blue necks and crested heads pop up from behind tufts of grass, peer out of bushes, and crane downward from the roof of the house, where the bird has flown, perhaps for the view. One of mine stepped from under the shrubbery one day and came forward to inspect a carful of people who had driven up to buy a calf. An old man and five or six white-haired, bare-footed children were piling out the back of the automobile as the bird approached. Catching sight of him they stopped in their tracks and stared, plainly hacked to find this superior figure blocking their path. There was silence as the bird regarded them, his head drawn back at its most majestic angle, his folded train glittering behind him in the sunlight.

Use Description in Reports

Sometimes descriptive paragraphs are absolutely necessary for a paper to be effective. This is often the case with reports that involve close observation. For a psychology class one student was asked to visit a preschool and select a child for a day's observation. Then she was to describe the child at school and draw some conclusions about how well the school's program was meeting the child's needs. The whole project took ten paragraphs. Having explained the program in the first paragraph, the writer devoted the second to a description of the child and his behavior.

> At first glance John seems to be a typical four-year-old: scruffy sun-bleached hair, a few freckles, worn cords, short-sleeved shirt, and tattered tennis shoes on his feet. But behind his boyish appearance, he seems to be a loner. During the first fifteen-minute class session, he was the only child who did not raise his hand to answer a question or share an experience. He was attentive at first but soon lost interest. Once he reached out a

finger to poke a boy in front, then stopped, perhaps thinking better of it. Finally, his thumb went into his mouth. As soon as the class broke up, he headed for the monkey bars, where he climbed to the highest rung and sat, his eyes staring toward the distant hill. No one tried to approach him; the other children, most of whom chased around the play yard, seemed to respect his wish for privacy. Later, when the class regrouped for story time, John didn't show as much interest as he had during the sharing session. He seemed more interested in tracing the cracks in the wall than in listening to *Frog and Toad Are Friends.*

One last word about description. Often when beginning writers have little to say, their eyes will reach into the mind's landscapes and return with chunks of description. They'll then glue them onto their papers. This practice just won't do. Whenever you include a full paragraph of description in an essay, be sure it has a clear purpose. Description is not batting to be stuffed into assignments.

WRITING TASK

Write a description that evokes a scene, a person, a situation, or an action. Keep in mind that an effective description works to create a predetermined response in a reader. For instance, if you were to write about a teacher you see as absentminded, you would select details that reflect absentmindedness. Remember, too, that description often works indirectly. Don't tell readers; show them. If you decide to describe an action, avoid telling a complete story.

15 DEDUCTIVE ESSAY

If you are able to develop a paragraph with examples, catalogues, comparisons, contrasts, and so on, you'll probably have little trouble writing a deductive essay of several paragraphs.

An essay is a nonfiction composition about a limited topic. It analyzes or interprets information in a personal way. This does not mean that an essay is *about* the writer. It could be, but usually it is not. Rather, the sense of personal involvement comes from the writer's thoughts, insights, and values being used in an analysis or interpretation of a topic.

The deductive essay begins with an introduction, generally one paragraph long, but occasionally more. The purpose of the introduction is to arouse readers' interest and prepare for the discussion to follow. It contains a central point (sometimes called the *thesis statement* or *controlling idea*) that sets the boundaries of the essay just as a topic sentence sets the boundaries of a paragraph.

The introduction is followed by a discussion several paragraphs long. Each paragraph includes a topic sentence and develops a subpoint of the central point in a detailed, thorough manner. The paragraphs are linked by clear transitions, smoothing the way for readers to follow the ideas.

The essay ends with a conclusion that often restates the central point and provides a sense of completion to the essay. A typical essay for a college class is between 500 and 750 words, but the length is most appropriately determined by the complexity of the idea and the amount of detailed discussion necessary to support the idea sufficiently.

A simple diagram of a typical deductive essay looks like this:

Introduction

Opening statement that leads to central point
Central point

Discussion section composed of several paragraphs. The number varies according to content.

Topic sentence
Development of topic sentence

Topic sentence
Development of topic sentence

Topic sentence
Development of topic sentence

Topic sentence
Development of topic sentence

Conclusion | Thesis restated/Closing comments |

Please don't get the idea that an essay needs to be as mechanical as the figure might indicate. It doesn't. But we want you to understand that simple essays have the same basic structure. How well writers use the structure depends on their skills.

With the diagram in mind, study the following essay written by Judy Robinson for a composition class. We suggest that you read the essay through once; then read it a second time along with the marginal notes.

Changing Nature's Work

A recent issue of Los Angeles Monthly magazine carried the following advertisement headlines: "Trust Your Face . . . Only to a Specialist"; "Re-create Your Ears"; "Porcelain Made Her Smile"; and "Get a Preview of Your Coming Attraction." Other advertisements offer "in office correction of wrinkles," "chin and cheek augmentation," "hair transplants and scalp reduction," and new "eye contours." Facial improvement seems to be an important value in Southern California.

First paragraph presents striking facts to get readers' interest.

Do not assume, however, that these advertisements are addressed only to the rich and famous. Los Angeles

Second paragraph shows that interest in facial improvement is common.

<u>Monthly</u> is a mass-circulation magazine, not a snobbish publication for screen idols and starlets. No doubt at this moment numerous executives, secretaries, salespersons, bankers, teachers — people just like our friends and neighbors — are counting the days until they can afford down payments on new self-images.

If you are asking yourself, "How did we ever become so involved in facial appearance?" then maybe you need a little history lesson. The truth is that humans have never been satisfied with nature's work. They have always — everywhere — made temporary or permanent changes in the color, shape, and features of their heads and faces.

Central point: interest in facial changes is universal.

Much of the human effort to alter nature's handiwork has been done in the pursuit of beauty or style. Humans have created an assortment of simple alterations to enhance the face and head: cosmetics, hair-styles, hair dyes, wigs, neck and ear ornaments, and hats, which both sexes have used to frame the face. Early Greek women, for example, created elaborate hairstyles and frequently dyed their hair bright red, blue, or yellow. By the time of Elizabeth I in England, men were dying their beards orange and carefully curling one lock of hair over their foreheads. Perhaps the most outlandish long-hair fashion was reached in the courts of eighteenth century Europe. There it became fashionable for court ladies to attach their hair to a decorated frame

Topic sentence for first subpoint.

List of typical facial alterations.

Two brief examples from the past.

Extended example from the past.

extending several feet above their heads. Such ladies

slept in chairs and had to kneel when traveling in a

carriage. Today we may consider such a fashion foolish,

but imagine the warm glow of satisfaction the owner of

such a structure felt when she first revealed it at a royal

ball. Currently, punk trends seem to be returning to the   *Current example.*

ancient traditions of using dramatic color and shape to

decorate facial appearance, an activity that should not

surprise anyone who understands the historical human

interest in changing nature's work.

Another common method humans have used to   *Topic sentence for second subpoint.*

redesign nature's work is skull-shaping. If you had been

a member of Egyptian, Greek, or Roman royalty living

centuries ago, you might have had your head reshaped at

birth. A baby's skull is soft and pliable and can easily be

reshaped during the first few weeks of life. The shaping   *Description of skull-shaping process.*

can be done by applying pressure on the forehead until

the desired shape is achieved. The custom was

widespread. Social anthropologists, for instance, point to

sculptures of Princess Nefertiti, and other daughters of

Egyptian rulers, that clearly show severely deformed,   *Two brief examples from the past.*

elongated skulls as evidence of skull shaping. But ancient

Egyptian, Greek, and Roman cultures were not the only

ones practicing skull shaping. Some American Indians

tied boards to an infant's head in front and in back and

gradually tightened the cords connecting the boards,

shaping a flatter, more oval, skull. Does head shaping

sound grotesque? Is it any more grotesque than to have a nose carved into a new shape by a surgeon's scalpel — all in the name of beauty? This is exactly what many Americans are doing today.

Reference to similar activities today.

But not all facial and head alterations were done solely out of vanity, that is, to create a beautiful self-image. Other alterations, while still decorative, served more complex purposes.

Transitional paragraph moves paper from changes for beauty to changes for more complex reasons.

One common facial alteration is scarring, a drastic method of redesigning nature's work and communicating complex messages. Primitive societies create facial scars in intricate patterns that are not only decorative but also convey religious dedication, commemorate rites of passage, identify a person as a member of a particular group or cast, indicate rank or feats of valor, or simply record events in a person's life.

Topic sentence for third subpoint.

Catalogue of reasons for scarring.

No doubt you have seen Hollywood films about World War I or II. A stock character in most of these films is the German officer who has a welted scar on his cheek. The scar is not merely a Hollywood ploy to identify a villain, but is calculated to identify a former member of a student fencing cult. In pre–World War II Germany, a prominent dueling scar symbolized courage and prestige. Indeed, a dueling scar created what we might today call a macho image. Even now, a facial scar such as the German dueling scar, though earned unintentionally, may be considered attractive as an

Extended example.

emblem of masculine strength or an indication of an

adventurous life. Consider, for example, the scarred chin

of Harrison Ford, who played the romantic heroes Han

Solo and Indiana Jones in the films Star Wars and

Raiders of the Lost Ark.

    More than likely you have seen issues of National

Geographic magazine featuring primitive cultures whose

members have beaded tattoos on their faces. Well,

tattooing may well be the most common and complex

means of facial alteration. Besides tattooing decorative

geometrical patterns on faces, primitive societies also

tattoo images of animals and insects. These images,

primitives believe, endow the wearer with the creature's

power. A bat, for example, might improve a person's

ability to move around at night, while a scorpion might

protect one from insect bites.

    Besides their magical power, facial tattoos, like

scars, have been widely used as marks of identification

and achievement. A tribal mark on the forehead may be

useful in wartime to prevent the accidental killing of the

wrong warrior; rank and wealth can be indicated by the

nature and complexity of a tattoo; criminals can be

identified, achievements recognized, historical events

commemorated, and a record kept of the number of

enemies killed or children born. In some groups, the

absence of a facial tattoo may even identify an unmarried

female or a male who has not yet achieved adulthood.

Current example.

Second sentence is topic sentence for fourth subpoint.

Example of belief in power of tattoos.

Catalogue of uses for tattoos.

Some people also believe that tattoos have a mysterious
sexual attraction. At one time Ainu women in Japan
exaggerated the apparent size of their lips with tattoos
stretching from cheek to cheek, and Maori tribesmen of
New Zealand tattooed intricate, scroll-like designs on
their faces to communicate their masculinity. Perhaps
the psychic power of the tattoo — if not the facial
tattoo — still exists. Who has not seen members of the
American armed forces with dragons tattooed on their
forearms or hearts on their shoulders?

Another use of tattoos: sexual attraction.

Current example of tattoos.

And so the conventions of the past live on in the
present. Although, historically, facial changes have been
made for many reasons, the belief that beauty promises
happiness seems to dictate most of the changes we
Americans make, both temporary and permanent. The
successful pursuit of the current norms of beauty may
bring subtle inner changes too. In that sense, beauty is
more than skin deep. Humans are the only animals that
create their own beauty. That is our good fortune.

*Conclusion recalls introduction and states
author's approval of the custom.*

Now that you've studied the diagram and a short deductive essay, let's
look at the steps Judy worked through to complete this final draft. We
have divided the process of writing an essay into steps for purposes of
instruction. But the step-by-step process we describe is not as rigid in
practice as it might seem in print. You will frequently move back and
forth between steps as you explore the possibilities of your topic, experiment with content and organization, and decide on the final phrasing of
sentences and paragraphs.

Getting Started

Selecting a Subject

You will write your best essays on subjects you already know something about, so look first at your own interests and experiences. Your educational interests, your work, or your leisure activities may suggest a subject. Think back on recent conversations you have had with friends and family members. Examine your ideas about topics in the news, your reactions to a book, a movie, or a television show. Explore your imagination. Make a list of possibilities. If you make a long enough list, you should be able to find a few subjects that you could write about.

Judy Robinson, the writer of the preceding essay, described her search for a subject as follows:

> I have always had an interest in the people of other places and other times. In junior high school, whenever the class visited a museum, I would spend most of my day wandering through the scenes devoted to the everyday life of cavemen, South Pacific islanders, African tribes, and the ancient Greeks and Romans. I tried to imagine what the people in these scenes were thinking or what they were saying to each other. More recently I have taken two anthropology classes, so whenever I've been assigned an essay, I've always considered writing about other cultures. Usually I don't, because I think I don't have enough information. This time, though, my anthropology class had just finished a unit on body alterations and decorations — using bones and other objects to reform ears and lips, binding the feet of females, dying hair, scarring the body and the face, tattooing — all kinds of fascinating techniques humans have used to alter their physical appearances. I decided to write from the information I had received in class.

Narrowing the Subject

> I knew I couldn't include all the information from class. The unit had taken three weeks and I had many pages of notes. I considered writing about just one group of people at a particular time in history, but my notes weren't complete enough for that. One of the things that had struck me during the lectures was the parallels I could see between different cultures and my own. We don't do exactly the same things they did, but we haven't lost interest in changing or decorating our bodies either. I wanted to include some comment on that fact. After thinking about it

more I decided to narrow my subject to facial changes because I thought this was where the parallels were most obvious.

Some writers are fearful about narrowing a subject because they believe that the broader the subject, the more they will have to say about it. But the opposite is true. A writer can find more informative and interesting things to say about a narrow subject such as "three types of facial alterations and decorations" than about a more general topic, "body alterations through the ages." A narrow subject allows, even forces, a writer to use specific supporting material, and specific information is always more interesting than general statements. Judy's decision to narrow her subject was a step in the right direction. Her topic would become even narrower after she had collected the details she needed to write her paper.

Prewriting

Judy's next task was to use prewriting techniques to generate ideas and specific details. She used a combination of methods you have already practiced — clustering and making lists. She began with a simple cluster that included information about tattoos, scars, skull shaping, and hairstyles. She made a list of specific details for each of these areas. If you need to review information about clustering and list making, see pages 37–40.

Planning the Essay

Phrasing a Central Point

After Judy felt she had enough material to draw on for her essay, she turned her attention to phrasing a central point.

A central point serves the same purpose for an essay that a topic sentence does for a paragraph — it states and imposes limits on a narrowed topic. The central point, stated in one or two sentences, appears in the introduction to a deductive essay, usually at the end. Sometimes a central point also indicates the subparts of the topic or suggests the method of essay development to be used.

We should perhaps mention that the methods of development that you have been practicing in earlier writing tasks are all applicable in one way or another to a deductive essay. For example, an essay may have a paragraph devoted to definition, another to a catalogue, others to comparison and contrast or a cause-and-effect relationship or examples. Or the dominant method of development might be classification while the individual paragraphs are developed with examples, analogies, anecdotes, and descriptions. In other words, an essay is built by selecting a variety of methods appropriate to your content.

A central point, sometimes called a thesis sentence, is a generalization that indicates the main idea of the paper. It is the idea that all the later paragraphs support, argue for, or illustrate. It should be broad enough to serve as an umbrella for everything in the essay, while at the same time providing a focus. It other words, it should clearly stake out the territory of the essay.

Because a central point guides both the reader and the writer, it should be phrased carefully. You may find it necessary to revise the sentence containing the central point several times until you are satisfied that it clearly indicates what your content will be. It is probably a good idea to do this early in your planning so your have a clear idea in your own mind of where the paper is going. Even then, you will probably find yourself changing the wording of the central point from time to time as your essay develops.

Judy Robinson wrote several versions of her central point before she was satisfied:

My first central point was too broad and probably misleading:

History is full of examples of people making changes in their facial appearances.

I could see right away that this sentence promised a paper much bigger than the one I planned. It seemed to include all history. Even more importantly, it implied that I would be giving examples of individual people. I saw my paper as a brief introduction to the subject and I just wanted to give some examples of facial changes from different times and different places to spark interest in the reader. I tried again:

Throughout the world people have used various means of altering their facial appearances.

This sentence put the focus on "means" instead of "individuals," so that was an improvement. It also seemed a little less all-inclusive to me, but it was still vague and it sounded flat and uninteresting. I wanted a sentence that would give a sharper picture of the content to come. As I reviewed my notes, I noticed that some of the items on my lists were permanent changes and some were only temporary. I thought my central point should include that distinction too.

Human beings have always made temporary or permanent changes in the color, shape, and features of their heads and faces.

I liked this sentence better. The word "always" included today, so I could comment on present-day parallels; I had included the words "temporary and permanent" to describe the changes; and the addition of "color, shape, and feature" made the whole sentence less vague. I decided this was good enough for now, though I knew I would probably change the final wording when I wrote my introduction.

No matter how thoroughly you work at sharpening a central point, you may find that you need to change it again after you have done more planning of your essay or after you have started writing the paper. When Judy wrote the final draft of her essay, she changed her central point one more time, this time stating it in two sentences coming at the end of her introduction.

The truth is that humans have never been satisfied with nature's work. They have always — everywhere — made temporary or permanent changes in the color, shape, and features of their heads and faces.

The first sentence serves as a lead-in, answering, in a way, the question, "How did we ever become so involved in appearance?" In the second sentence, the addition of the word "everywhere," set off by dashes, makes the statement more emphatic. Let's quickly review the steps Judy has taken so far:

1. She thought about her interests and her recent learning and chose a subject — body alterations in different cultures.
2. She narrowed the subject to a topic she could handle in a single essay — facial alterations at different times and different places.
3. She made a prewriting cluster and followed that with prewriting lists of information taken from her notes about tattoos, scars, skull shaping, and hairstyles.
4. She phrased a tentative statement of her central point.

Deciding on Purpose and Audience

At this point Judy needed to consider what the purpose of her essay would be. Every essay should have a dominant purpose: to inform, to entertain, or to persuade. Of course, an informative essay can have entertaining moments, and an entertaining essay can inform or persuade. But one purpose will be dominant. Deciding on a purpose is easy and nearly automatic — the content you are planning to present usually suggests the purpose immediately. Nevertheless, it's a good idea to make a conscious decision because then you will be less likely to mix purposes inappropriately.

Judy told us,

> I knew that my subject wouldn't be entirely new to my readers. Everyone has seen tattoos and pictures of facial scars, but I hoped that some of my information would be new, and I wanted to point out some parallels between other cultures and our own. I wouldn't be trying to persuade anyone to do anything, of course. I hoped that my readers would find some of the material entertaining, but my main purpose would be to inform.
>
> I also decided that my audience would be fellow students. I'm not an expert in the field, or even an anthropology major, so I wouldn't pretend to be writing for a professional group. I don't have the vocabulary, for one thing. I thought that fellow students would have about the same familiarity with the subject that I had before my exposure to more information in class. With this audience I could assume some things (for example, I wouldn't have to explain what a tattoo is), and we would share a common vocabulary.

The audience you address will influence choices you make about content and vocabulary when writing an essay. It is essential, therefore, that before you move too far into the planning of an essay, you should determine the audience.

Making a Preliminary Plan

Judy's next step was to sketch out a plan for her essay by selecting items from her prewriting lists and arranging them in an appropriate order. Her preliminary plan for "Changing Nature's Work" looked like this:

Central Point	Human beings have always made temporary or permanent changes in the color, shape, and features of their heads and faces.
Subpoint 1	Hairstyles are one common way of achieving beauty and style. – Greek women dyed their hair bright colors: red, blue, or yellow.

— Men in Elizabethan England dyed their beards orange and curled one lock of hair over their foreheads.

— In eighteenth century Europe, court ladies attached their hair to decorated frames several feet long. They had to sleep in chairs and kneel in carriages.

— Present-day punks use color and shape too.

Subpoint 2

Another common method of changing nature is skull-shaping.

— Egyptian, Greek, and Roman royalty reshaped the skulls of infants by applying pressure on the forehead.

— American Indians tied boards to infant's skulls and tightened the cords to make the skull flatter and more oval.

— We don't do that, but we do have surgeons reshape eyes, noses, and eyes. And we spend thousands on orthodontists, at least partially to have a better-shaped mouth.

Subpoint 3

A more drastic method is scarring of the face.

— Primitive societies sometimes carved fancy patterns on their faces to identify themselves, commemorate rites of passage or other events, or as a sign of religious dedication.

— Student fencing cults in Germany valued scars for the masculinity they indicated.

— We are sometimes attracted to scars too — for example, Harrison Ford in *Star Wars* and *Raiders of the Lost Ark.*

Subpoint 4

One of the most common ways of facial alteration is tattooing.

— Primitive tribes tattooed themselves with geometric patterns and other marks for identification, to indicate rank, to identify criminals, to commemorate historical events, and to keep records (like the notches on a gun).

>   — Tattoos are sometimes held to be magical — a bat tattoo might help one move at night, or a scorpion tattoo might ward off insects.
>   — Tattoos are sometimes thought to make a person sexually attractive.
>   The Ainu women in Japan enlarged their lips with tattoos.
>   Maori in New Zealand believed beautiful facial designs indicated masculinity.
>   — American servicemen (and others, too) often tattoo dragons, roses, and hearts on their bodies, though not usually on their faces.

Conclusion   Our pursuit of beauty today is part of a universal tradition.

The form your planning takes is up to you. Some writers construct very specific outlines, delineating subpoints and sub-subpoints until they have listed every item to be included. Others list main subpoints only and informally jot down some ideas under each one. Some outline in complete sentences. No matter how you go about it, have a plan — that's the message.

Because your plan should grow from your material and purpose, we don't want to lay down rigid rules, but you should keep in mind one general principle: Start strong and finish strong. You have to have some good content early to keep readers interested. And the most emphatic position in an essay is near the end. (The same is true to a lesser extent of sentences and paragraphs.) In practical terms, unless you have a good reason to do otherwise, keep the material with the most impact for the end, and present the next-strongest early. Weaker or less interesting material, assuming it is important to include, should come somewhere in the middle. This strategy will prevent your essay from trailing off at the end.

Writing the First Draft

Now would be a good time for you to reread Judy's essay on pages 141–146 to see how she worked the material from her plan into her essay. Of course she reworded the items as she shaped her sentences and paragraphs. She wrote a three-paragraph introduction that carefully leads to her central point. She treated her first and second subpoints in a single paragraph each, but she used two paragraphs for her third subpoint, scarring, and for her fourth subpoint, tattooing, because the content seemed to naturally divide that way. She created a short transition paragraph, number 6, to move smoothly from alterations done for beauty and style to those done for more complex purposes. You will also note that she left out some material and rearranged the order of some examples. Finally she wrote a conclusion linking the examples from the past to the present, as she had done for each subpoint earlier.

Introduction

Now, with a clear, though possibly tentative, central point and a plan for presenting subpoints and supporting material, you are ready to begin writing an introduction. For most of your papers one paragraph of introduction will probably be sufficient, although several paragraphs are sometimes appropriate.

Effective introductions do more than offer writers a chance to clear their throats — they are more than a series of aimless, dull comments. They focus papers by presenting central points in ways that draw in readers. Here is a brief list of some traditional introductory techniques:

1. descriptions of personal experience that allow the reader to identify with the writer
2. statements of striking facts or statistics that surprise the reader
3. a provocative quotation or interesting question
4. a definition, but not one merely taken from a dictionary
5. a glance at an opposing argument or attack on a commonly held opinion
6. an anecdote or narrative closely related to the topic

Any one of these is a fine way to begin a deductive essay if it fits your subject (see Introductions in the Index for Writers for illustrations of the various forms an introduction can take). We want to make one strong suggestion: Always end the introduction with the central point.

The introduction to "Changing Nature's Work" actually takes three brief paragraphs. The first paragraph begins with a few striking facts: advertisment headlines and quotations all relating to facial alterations. The second paragraph points out how common the interest in such alterations is. The third paragraph connects this present-day interest to similar interests in the past and presents the central point:

> A recent issue of *Los Angeles Monthly* magazine carried the following advertisement headlines: "Trust Your Face . . . Only to a Specialist"; "Re-create Your Ears"; "Porcelain Made Her Smile"; and "Get a Preview of Your Coming Attraction." Other advertisements offer "in office correction of wrinkles,"

"chin and cheek augmentation," "hair transplants and scalp reduction," and new "eye contours." Facial improvement seems to be an important value in Southern California.

Do not assume, however, that these advertisements are addressed only to the rich and famous. *Los Angeles Monthly* is a mass-circulation magazine, not a snobbish publication for screen idols and starlets. No doubt at this moment numerous executives, secretaries, salespersons, bankers, teachers — people just like our friends and neighbors — are counting the days until they can afford down payments on new self-images.

If you are asking yourself, "How did we ever become so involved in facial appearance?" then maybe you need a little history lesson. *The truth is that humans have never been satisfied with nature's work. They have always—everywhere—made temporary or permanent changes in the color, shape, and features of their heads and faces.*

Judy explains,

In addition to presenting examples of facial changes in my paper, I knew I wanted to connect the historical information with present-day interest in the same thing. I puzzled awhile about how to do this and decided I should start with some examples from the present and work toward the central point. I thought I would begin with some comments about tattooing because that is still fairly common. But one day I was just leafing through *Los Angeles Monthly* and there were all those advertisements — there must have been two dozen at least! I started jotting down the text of the more interesting ones and I knew I could use a few of these items for my examples from the present. I felt they were striking enough to get attention right away. After I wrote that first paragraph, I didn't feel comfortable just jumping to my central point. I needed a bridge between those advertisements and my point, that the concern for facial changes is apparently universal. So I wrote a second paragraph arguing that the interest in cosmetic surgery is widespread. My introduction moves logically, I think. It says: Look at this (paragraph 1)! That's really not uncommon (paragraph 2). In fact, that's universal (paragraph 3), and I can give you many examples.

Here's another example of an introduction, developed in a different way. This paragraph opens with a general contrast, develops the contrast by using a catalogue of images, then closes with two sentences that clarify the central point. (The complete text of this student essay begins on page 162.)

> Members of my generation have grown up during a time when the majority of Americans have lived in relative comfort. Nevertheless, we have all seen photographs of the Great American Depression of the 1930s: images of anonymous men in dark suits and tweed caps selling apples on street corners; hollow-cheeked women cuddling infants in front of clapboard shacks; crowds milling before factory gates; hoboes gathered around campfires and eating from tin cans; Model T Fords loaded with chairs, tables, mattresses, and boxes of clothes crawling along desert highways toward the Pacific. These dreadful memories, perserved in history books, seem totally grim. *But beside the dreadful memories, there are positive aspects to the Depression that haven't been preserved in history books. These memories are carried by people who suffered yet lived through the thirties.*

An introduction of this sort acts somewhat as a funnel — it begins big and narrows at the bottom. The funnel method is a good way to start a deductive essay. By using it you will put the central point of your essay clearly before your readers just before they begin to read the discussion part of your paper. A diagram of the funnel method looks like this:

```
general subject introduced
  becoming more specific
         narrowed
            to

     the central point
```

Whatever method you use in your introduction, keep in mind what you are introducing: the content of the essay. Whatever you say in the introduction must relate to what follows. Some writers prefer to write the discussion section of an essay first. They say the introduction is easier to write when they know exactly what will follow it. You may wish to follow their advice. Or you may wish to write the introduction first and be prepared to go back and change it if the discussion section takes some unexpected twists.

Discussion

Once you've completed the introduction to your essay, move on to the discussion. If you can write paragraphs with topic sentences, you should have no trouble putting together a discussion of a central point. If you haven't already done so in the planning stage, the first step you should take in writing the discussion is to turn the subpoints into topic sentences. You will then develop these topic sentences in separate paragraphs by expanding the ideas and details you listed in your plan. Feel free to develop the subpoints by using examples, catalogues, comparisons, contrasts, causes and effects, classifications, or any combination of methods. In other words, develop the discussion in any way that fits the material. The writer of "Changing Nature's Work" developed the essay's central point mainly through examples, but we want to stress that different central points require different strategies.

Here are some comments Judy Robinson made about writing the discussion section of her essay:

> As I started to write the discussion section, I looked back at my prewriting lists and my essay plan. Each subpoint of my plan contained several examples from the past and at least one from the present. It seemed natural, therefore, to begin each subpoint with a topic sentence, give examples from the past, and end the paragraph with a present-day example. I worked through each subpoint the same way. Of course I had to phrase the sentences and make each paragraph coherent, but the concerns for organization and unity had been pretty well taken care of in the essay plan. I think repeating the same pattern for each subpoint, even though the material for each was different, helped give the whole paper coherence.
>
> When I reached my third subpoint — a more drastic method is scarring the face — I decided to present the content in two paragraphs, one for the past and one for the present, because in this case I had more to say about the present than I did in the earlier subpoints. This material seemed to deserve a paragraph of its own. I also devoted two paragraphs to subpoint 4 — one of the most common ways of facial alteration is tattooing — because I had a lot of content to cover.
>
> As I reread my discussion paragraphs, I felt the movement from subpoint 2 to subpoint 3 was too abrupt. At first I tried rewriting the topic sentence for subpoint 3, but finally decided I needed to write a brief transition paragraph because the first two subpoints emphasized changes made for beauty and style while the last two, though still related to beauty, were really more complex. I think the addition of that transition paragraph helped smooth the way for my readers.

The main difference between writing individual paragraphs and writing a complete essay has to do with the need to use transitions to link all the paragraphs in a discussion. In a short paper, transitional markers are usually combined with topic sentences and are often achieved by a single word or short phrase, usually a key word repeated from the central point. But sometimes in the third or fourth paragraph a writer will restate the central point to remind readers of the essay's purpose.

We suggest you reread "Changing Nature's Work" to see how Judy used transitions to link the essay's paragraphs. But to give you an idea, notice the repetition of key words or synonyms for key words carried from the central point to the topic sentences.

Central point as stated in the final two sentences of the introduction:

> The truth is that *humans* have never been satisfied with *Nature's work*. They have always — everywhere — made temporary or permanent *changes* in the color, shape, and features of their heads and faces.

Topic sentence of subpoint 1:

> Much of the *human* effort to *alter nature's handiwork* has been done in the pursuit of beauty and style.

Topic sentence of subpoint 2:

> Another common method *humans* have used to *redesign nature's work* is skull-shaping.

Notice too how the transition paragraph (paragraph 6) picks up key words from the earlier subpoint topic sentences:

> But not all facial and head *alterations* were done solely out of vanity, that is, to create a *beautiful* self-image. Other *alterations*, while still decorative, served more complex purposes.

And then how the topic sentences for subpoints 3 and 4 pick up key words from both the central point and the transitional paragraph:

Topic sentence of subpoint 3:

> One common *facial alteration* is scarring, a drastic method of *redesigning nature's work* and communicating *complex* messages.

Topic sentence of subpoint 4:

> Well, tattooing may well be the most common and *complex* means of *facial alteration*.

These are not the only transitional techniques working between paragraphs, but by repeating key words Judy keeps the essay's point before the readers.

Conclusion

Finally a successful essay should conclude, not just stop. Conclusions and introductions are important; they stand out as the first and last contact you'll have with the readers. While an introduction serves to hook readers and to present the paper's focus, a conclusion completes the focus and may echo the central and supporting points, along with their applications.

In other than descriptive and process writing, an essay's conclusion usually is contained in a paragraph separate from the discussion. There are several standard ways to develop concluding paragraphs. For instance, an effective conclusion can

1. offer an answer to a question, a solution to a problem, or the result of behavior raised in the introduction and explored in the discussion; or point out that there is no clear answer, solution, or result, thus showing the issue's complexity
2. present a quotation, especially one that amplifies the central point or varies another quotation already presented in the introduction
3. relate a relevant anecdote that the reader will be likely to remember and that echoes the central point
4. rephrase the central and supporting points, followed by a closing sentence or two to turn the readers' minds back to the paper

"When I wrote my conclusion," Judy says, "I wanted to repeat the technique I had used for developing each subpoint — ending with a comment about the present. Doing so satisfied my sense of wholeness and balance. I also wanted to end on a note of approval. I think the pursuit of beauty and keeping up with fashions is fun and I know that when I am pleased with my appearance, I'm happy inside, too. I think that's a human trait and I approve of it."

As you can see, Judy's conclusion looks back to her introduction. It also expresses her approval of the whole process:

> And so the conventions of the past live on in the present. Although, historically, facial changes have been made for many reasons, the belief that beauty promises happiness seems to dictate most of the changes we Americans make, both temporary and permanent. The successful pursuit of the current norms of

beauty may bring subtle inner changes too. In that sense, beauty is more than skin deep. Humans are the only animals that create their own beauty. That is our good fortune.

A word of caution: The conclusion must grow from the paper; it should not open a new subject by raising questions not explored in the discussion. Also keep in mind that the tone should be consistent with the rest of the essay. (See Conclusions in the Index for Writers for some specific examples.)

Titles

Once you've got the introduction, discussion, and conclusion written, all that's left is the title. Judy's title, "Changing Nature's Work," is taken directly from the end of her fourth paragraph. It's also a phrase that she used throughout the essay in slightly different wordings. There's only one general principle behind titles: Keep them simple.

But whatever you do, don't title an essay "Assignment 13." The title should suggest the essay's content, not the sequence of the course. And don't underline or put quotation marks around your own title. If you use part of a quotation or the title of another work as part of your title, however, use quotation marks or underlining, whichever is appropriate for that part.

Revising the First Draft

If you set your essay aside for a few days before you revise, you will be more objective in your evaluation and better able to see its strengths and weaknesses. But if you cannot delay the revision, you must still try to approach the paper from the point of view of a reader. Review the paper slowly, concentrating on its overall clarity. Try doing this while reading aloud. It will help you find confused or inconsistent areas. For this first reading, ask yourself the following questions:

1. Is the central point stated clearly? Does it indicate the scope and direction of the paper?
2. Is the paper unified? Does every sentence and paragraph have a clear relation to the thesis?
3. Are the vocabulary and content appropriate for the chosen audience?
4. Is the paper organized logically and effectively?

If you need to make changes, make them and then read the paper again, concentrating on smaller elements by asking yourself the following questions:

1. Are the paragraphs developed with sufficient detail and explanation?
2. Does the paper move smoothly from paragraph to paragraph — that is, is the paper coherent?
3. Is the introduction interesting and to the point? Does it lead naturally to the statement of the central point? Does the concluding paragraph bring the paper to a satisfactory close without being unduly repetitious or introducing a new subject?

During a third reading you should concentrate on even smaller elements. As you do, try reading the essay backward sentence by sentence. By reading each sentence out of context, you may find it easier to answer the following:

1. Are the sentences clear, grammatical, and free from sentence errors?
2. Is the paper consistent with the conventions of punctuation and mechanics?
3. Do the words convey the intended meaning? Are they spelled correctly?

If all this sounds like a lot of work, it is. But excellence is not born in first drafts. It is achieved through thoughtful and painstaking revision.

Essays for Further Study

A second student example, a deductive essay written by Elaine Kubo, follows. Elaine's assignment required that she select a subject of historical and national significance. She was to develop a 750- to 1000-word essay about the subject from a "personal" perspective. Elaine selected the Great American Depression of the 1930s, a period of severe economic disruption. Before studying Elaine's deductive essay, read her comments about the assignment and also study her comments printed in the margin.

Deciding to write about the Depression wasn't easy. First I thought I would write about the Vietnam War but I had nothing personal to say. There were other subjects I considered — the 60s Free Speech Movement, the Watergate scandal during the Nixon Presidency, the assassination of John Kennedy, even some recent terrorist activities — but I couldn't find what my instructor called the "personal angle." While browsing through my daily writing entries, I came across a reference to the Depression. I had always been struck by how my grandparents said the

Depression, which they lived through, was a frightening period of their lives because of the economic uncertainity. But I also remembered their wonderful stories about the strengths that the Depression experience brought out in them. Their experience along with my parents' experiences as children during that time gave me the personal angle I needed.

Because of all the information I had, the main problem I faced was finding a focus and drafting a central point. I decided to approach the Depression by recognizing that it was a dreadful time for many Americans — who could deny that — but that there were personal sagas worth telling that didn't get put in history books, the kind of stories my family told. This was the start of my focus, but I needed at least three subpoints. After some brainstorming, I decided I could categorize the stories under subpoints that reflected determination, dignity, and sense of community.

Working with family stories caused another problem. I would mostly have to develop my essay through narrative examples. I had, therefore, to summarize the stories without putting in unnecessary detail, and I had to find representative examples, ones that reflected broad experience without being overly general. With all this in mind I began to make lists and to "sketch" the paper before writing the rough draft.

The Thirties: A Personal History

Members of my generation have grown up during a time when the majority of Americans have lived in relative comfort. Nevertheless, we have all seen photographs of the Great American Depression of the 1930s: images of anonymous men in dark suits and tweed caps selling apples on street corners; hollow-cheeked women cuddling infants in front of clapboard shacks; crowds milling before factory gates; hoboes gathered around campfires and eating from tin cans; Model T Fords loaded with chairs, tables, mattresses, and boxes of clothes crawling along desert

My introductory paragraph was the hardest to write. First I wanted to establish my perspective — that is, I was a person who had not experienced the Depression. Then I wanted to show my readers that I recognized how terrible the Depression was for most Americans. Here's where I got the idea to use a catalogue [see Cataloguing, p. 76] of Depression photographs that most everyone would have seen. This gave me a chance to recreate the Depression experience in my readers' imaginations. I wanted to make the images vivid, so I used some specific detail in each one. The opening then sets up a contrast with what I have to say about the Depression experience. The last two sentences embody my central point.

highways toward the Pacific. These dreadful memories, preserved in history books, seem totally grim. But besides the dreadful memories, there are positive aspects of the Depression that haven't been preserved in history books. These memories are carried by people who suffered yet lived through the thirties.

One positive aspect of the thirties my grandparents remember was the determination to overcome adversity it stirred in them. Like many Kansas farmers in the early thirties, they were suffering from the country's sudden economic collapse, but they still had land and raised some crops. Then nature turned against them. Unrelenting winds swept across the plains, destroying crops and swirling away the topsoil. A drought came with the wind and destroyed any chance they might have had to grow a crop. Finally, the bank demanded payment on the farm's mortgage. They couldn't scrape together the money, so they lost the farm. But if economic collapse and a senseless act of nature destroyed them financially, these events toughened their will to overcome adversity. They moved to a small Kansas town. Days, my grandfather worked as a clerk in his uncle's store; nights, he studied law. My grandmother, who had taught before marrying, worked at the local school. By 1938 my grandfather had passed the state examination allowing him to practice law. By the end of World War II my grandmother was school superintendent.

I worked in a key phrase — positive aspects — which I repeat in every topic sentence to help my readers recognize that a new subpoint is being introduced.

Paragraph 2 introduces my first subpoint — that the Depression experience helped my grandparents become determined to overcome adversity. Although I use my grandparents as an example, I also try to show that they represent many people who lived during that time.

This is probably the paragraph I rewrote the most. I wanted to create some drama; that is, life went from bad to worse, but through personal determination life got better. I actually saw this paragraph as a tribute to human courage as embodied in my grandparents.

I know there were many less fortunate than my grandparents, many who were fighting poverty all those years, but some people who lived through the thirties remember poverty as being different then. It seems that another positive aspect of the Depression was that people could be poor without losing personal dignity. My mother has a childhood memory of a gray-haired man who knocked at the kitchen door one day and asked to do some work in return for a meal. Her father refused to allow him to work, but invited him to join the family for a lunch of soup and biscuits. After the meal he whittled little wooden birds for all the kids. My mother says that the whole family gave him the respect they would give any successful artist now. My retired neighbor knew out-of-luck businessmen and bankrupt investors who sold flowers on street corners and caddied at golf courses without losing a sense of personal dignity. Can you imagine such things today? Perhaps because there were so many people broke and hungry, it wasn't considered a failure not to have a regular job. People respected each other anyway.

Another positive aspect some people experienced during the thirties was the sense of community it created in them. Many people carry stories about grocers who supplied out-of-luck neighbors with food on credit and charged no interest. Others talk about going to wedding showers without enough money to buy a nice

I open paragraph 3 with a transitional sentence that reminds my readers of the central point. The second sentence is the topic sentence that sets up the second subpoint — "that people could be poor without losing personal dignity." I decided to use one specific example and one typical example to support my subpoint — one from my mother's childhood and one from a neighbor's experience. Since the example in my second paragraph was so long, I wrote shorter ones to create some variety for my readers.

I round off the third paragraph with a clincher written as a question, and then I answer the question in an attempt to show the difference between today's values and Depression values.

The opening sentence of the fourth paragraph presents my subpoint — that for some people the Depression experience created a sense of community. To create variety and move my readers along I created three one-sentence examples of community. Then I use a transitional sentence that begins "But perhaps the most startling example . . ." to set up the most dramatic of my examples. I actually considered making this example a separate paragraph because it is so long; then the topic sentence would have been developed in two short paragraphs instead of one long one.

gift and the guests all digging into their pockets and pooling their change to buy a community gift for the bride. My aunt remembers over a hundred people turning out to help repair a neighbor's house that had partly burned down. But perhaps the most startling example of the sense of community I've heard comes from my friend's family experience. Her grandparents were forced to move from the countryside to Boston, where they rented a one-bedroom apartment. At the time, my friend's grandmother was seven months pregnant and started having labor pains. A doctor, selected at random from the phone book, came over immediately, completed a quick examination, then called for hot water. He delivered a healthy, six-pound girl. A week later the new parents got a bill for $7.32, the cost of home delivery. Since the move and rent had taken all their money, they couldn't pay. But when other people living in the building — all of whom had been complete strangers to them until the baby was born — heard of the couple's plight, they chipped in pennies, nickels, dimes, and quarters. They sent the fee to the doctor. Less than three days later, the doctor drove up with a backseat full of groceries. He said his nurse had sent the bill by mistake, so he used the payment to buy groceries for them. At one time I might have seen this aspect of the Depression as an act of charity; now I see it as an act of community.

I end the paragraph with a clincher and distinguished the sense of community from charity, which I felt was an important distinction to make.

Indeed, the historian's portrayal of the Depression as a grim time for Americans is accurate, but we must remember that a personal history that doesn't get into books parallels the social upheaval we've read about. It's the history carried in the minds of people who endured through that time. Often those memories have some positive aspects.

In my concluding paragraph I merely restate my central idea by reasserting that the historical view of the Depression is accurate but that another kind of history exists in the memories of people who lived through it.

Finally, we would like you to examine a brief essay by a professional writer, Norman Cousins. Editor of the *Saturday Review* for over thirty years and now Professor of Medical Humanities at UCLA, Mr. Cousins has written widely in the fields of literature, the arts, and politics. This essay, actually one of his columns from the *Saturday Review,* is an argument for a renewed emphasis on the liberal arts in colleges and universities. As you read it, note the variety of methods of paragraph development he uses, among them cataloguing, examples, cause and effect, and comparison and contrast. You will notice Cousins uses "we" to refer to himself in the first paragraph. Editors (as well as monarchs, judges, and others) sometimes use "we" to reflect the fact that they are speaking for an institution or a group larger than themselves. Cousins uses it because his words express the editorial viewpoint of the *Saturday Review.*

How to Make People Smaller than They Are

Three months ago in this space we wrote about the costly retreat from the humanities on all the levels of American education. Since that time, we have had occasion to visit a number of campuses and have been troubled to find that the general situation is even more serious than we had thought. It has become apparent to us that one of the biggest problems confronting American education today is the increasing vocationalization of our colleges and universities.

Cousins begins with a reference to an earlier column apparently protesting too little emphasis on the humanities in education.

He stresses the seriousness of the problem and tells what colleges and universities are becoming, implying they should be something else.

Throughout the country, schools are under pressure to become job-training centers and employment agencies.

The pressure comes mainly from two sources. One is the growing determination of many citizens to reduce taxes — understandable and even commendable in itself, but irrational and irresponsible when connected to the reduction or dismantling of vital public services. The second source of pressure comes from parents and students who tend to scorn courses of study that do not teach people how to become attractive to employers in a rapidly tightening job market.

Paragraph 2 identifies the causes of the problem: the tax revolt and the belief that courses of study should lead directly to employability.

It is absurd to believe that the development of skills does not also require the systematic development of the human mind. Education is being measured more by the size of the benefits the individual can extract from society than by the extent to which the individual can come into possession of his or her full powers. The result is that the life-giving juices are in danger of being drained out of education.

Cousins asserts that employability alone is not the proper measure of education, a view which leads to his central point: "that the life-giving juices are in danger of being drained out of education."

Emphasis on "practicalities" is being characterized by the subordination of words to numbers. History is seen not as essential experience to be transmitted to new generations, but as abstractions that carry dank odors. Art is regarded as something that calls for indulgence or patronage and that has no place among the practical realities. Political science is viewed more as a specialized subject for people who want to go into politics than as

Paragraph 4 describes the effects this thinking has had on attitudes toward history, art, political science, and literature and philosophy courses.

The words "dank odors," "indulgence and patronage," "specialized subject," "add-ons," and "intellectual adornments" characterize these disciplines in a negative way. The deliberate exaggeration of these characterizations shows Cousins' disgust with this attitude.

an opportunity for citizens to develop a knowledgeable

relationship with the systems by which human societies

are governed. Finally, literature and philosophy are

assigned the role of add-ons — intellectual adornments

that have nothing to do with "genuine" education.

Instead of trying to shrink the liberal arts, the

American people ought to be putting pressure on colleges

and universities to increase the ratio of the humanities

to the sciences. Most serious studies of medical-school

curricula in recent years have called attention to the

stark gaps in the liberal education of medical students.

The experts agree that the schools shouldn't leave it up

to students to close those gaps.

In contrast to the preceding paragraph, Cousins states what he thinks the public should be asking for.

He mentions studies to support his view.

The irony of the emphasis being placed on careers is

that nothing is more valuable for anyone who has a

professional or vocational education than to be able to

deal with abstractions or complexities, or to feel

comfortable with subtleties of thought or language, or to

think sequentially. The doctor who knows only disease is

at a disadvantage alongside the doctor who knows at

least as much about people as he does about pathological

organisms. The lawyer who argues in court from a

narrow legal base is no match for the lawyer who can

connect legal precedents to historical experience and

who employs wide-ranging intellectual resources. The

business executive whose competence in general

management is bolstered by an artistic ability to deal

The paragraph begins with an argument for the study of humanities: their value on the job.

He supports this argument with brief contrasts between those who have a humanities education and those who don't in the fields of medicine, law, business, and technology.

with people is of prime value to his company. For the

technologist, the engineering of consent can be just as

important as the engineering of moving parts. In all

these respects, the liberal arts have much to offer. Just

in terms of career preparation, therefore, a student is

shortchanging himself by shortcutting the humanities.

    But even if it could be demonstrated that the

humanities contribute nothing directly to a job, they

would still be an essential part of the educational

equipment of any person who wants to come to terms

with life. The humanities would be expendable only if

human beings didn't have to make decisions that affect

their lives and the lives of others; if the human past

never existed or had nothing to tell us about the present;

if thought processes were irrelevant to the achievement

of purpose; if creativity was beyond the human mind and

had nothing to do with the joy of living; if human

relationships were random aspects of life; if human

beings never had to cope with panic or pain, or if they

never had to anticipate the connection between cause

and effect; if all the mysteries of mind and nature were

fully plumbed; and if no special demands arose from the

accident of being born a human being instead of a hen or

a hog.

    Finally, there would be no good reason to eliminate

the humanities if a free society were not absolutely

dependent on a functioning citizenry. If the main

The paragraph begins with another argument for the humanities: they enhance understanding of human life.

"The humanities would be expendable only if . . . " introduces a long catalogue of human situations in which an education in the humanities would be important.

Again, the paragraph begins with an argument for the humanities: they develop a "functioning citizenry."

purpose of a university is job training, then the underlying philosophy of our government has little meaning. The debates that went into the making of American society concerned not just institutions or governing principles but the capacity of humans to sustain those institutions. Whatever the disagreements were over other issues at the American Constitutional Convention, the fundamental question sensed by everyone, a question that lay over the entire assembly, was whether the people themselves would understand what it meant to hold the ultimate power of society, and whether they had enough of a sense of history and destiny to know where they had been and where they ought to be going.

He raises the question, Can the people be trusted with the "ultimate power of society"?

Jefferson was prouder of having been the founder of the University of Virginia than of having been President of the United States. He knew that the educated and developed mind was the best assurance that a political system could be made to work — a system based on the informed consent of the governed. If this idea fails, then all the saved tax dollars in the world will not be enough to prevent the nation from turning on itself.

In his conclusion he emphasizes the value of education with a reference to Thomas Jefferson and connects the study of the humanities with the survival of a free society.

One Last Thought

We have very limited intentions for this task. We've tried to give you only the most basic elements of the deductive essay. We're a little fearful that you'll approach the writing of a short deductive essay rigidly. That would be a mistake because within the general framework we've presented, approaches to the deductive essay are as varied as the people who write them. As a writer you have to find the voice and method of development that fit the idea, emotion, knowledge, and experience you wish to communicate. Your choices will vary with your subject matter and your attitude toward it. The more you write, the more choices you will see as possibilities. It's the real challenge writing offers. Enjoy it.

WRITING TASK

Select a subject you feel personally involved in either because you hold strong opinions about it or because it has touched your life directly. Once you have your subject, write an essay of five or more paragraphs exploring it. You can go about this task in one of two ways. You can take each step to your instructor for review, or you can work through the steps on your own. In either case, we advise you to follow this procedure:

1. Select a broad subject and narrow it until you have a topic that can be treated with specific content in a single essay.
2. Do prewriting exercises to develop ideas and specific details.
3. Phrase a tentative central point that states the topic, limits it, and either implies a method of development or indicates the subparts of the topic.
4. Organize a plan on a separate sheet of paper. Include the central point and subpoints that will make up the discussion paragraphs. Fill in brief phrases to remind yourself what material you will use in the development of the subpoints.
5. Once you have a plan, write an introductory paragraph that presents the central point in the closing sentences. Remember, the introduction should serve a purpose by giving the reader important information related to the central point. Also remember that the central point you started with may need to be reshaped to fit into the introduction.
6. Once the introduction is completed, shape the subpoints into topic sentences and develop the discussion section of your essay. You should have several discussion paragraphs, each built around a subpoint cast in a topic sentence. Also be sure to use clear transitions linking your paragraphs.

7. After you've completed the discussion section, write a conclusion that restates the central point and adequately closes the essay.
8. Write a title — a simple one. Don't put quotation marks around it or underline it.
9. Reread your entire essay several times, making revisions and corrections as necessary.

16 INDUCTIVE ESSAY

The inductive essay moves from specific detail to a generalized central point presented in the final paragraph. It therefore differs structurally from a deductive essay, which starts with an introduction that presents a central point, moves through a discussion consisting of several paragraphs that present subparts of the central point, and ends with a conclusion that often restates the central point.

Sometimes you won't want to reveal your central point in the opening paragraph. You may want to save it for the end so that it will have more impact. Or you may want to develop two sides of an argument before revealing your own position. In either case the inductive essay will serve the purpose.

The inductive essay is often used to present personal insights. By presenting personal experience and responding to it you inductively lead a reader to a central point — an ah ha! experience.

From the diagram of an inductive essay on page 174 you can see that the inductive essay gives the writer a great deal of freedom, but if a writer doesn't have a firm grip on the form, he or she might go astray by failing to link the discussion paragraphs to the central idea that appears in the conclusion.

By this time you must be painfully aware of the process of mixing concrete details with personal responses. (See Responding to Experience, p. 36.) You are also aware of the importance of using transitional techniques to help guide the reader. But you probably aren't as aware of the need to integrate background information into your work, yet more than likely you have been doing so.

Background information functions as the mortar that holds together much of the writing you do. Through the use of background informa-

Discussion: Paragraphs can be developed by examples, catalogues, anecdotes, comparison and contrast, analogy, classification, causes and effects, definitions, or description and narration

Conclusion: Clearly states the writer's attitude and states the central point

tion you supply readers the information necessary to follow the train of your thought. In other words, background information establishes the situation for readers. This is especially important in writing that deals with personal experience and is specifically true in constructing personal inductive essays.

Now let's examine an inductive essay in which the writer presents a personal insight. Student writer Tom Stevens uses the pattern in the diagram, with one exception — he adds a brief opening that announces his general subject — "growth" — to orient readers. As you read Tom's essay, notice how he works background information into his paragraphs. Also notice the following:

1. Tom announces his general subject — "growth" — without stating it in the form of a central idea.
2. Tom's discussion paragraphs detail separate but thematically related experiences that lead up to and support his central point as it appears in the conclusion.
3. The conclusions clearly states Tom's attitude toward the subject and the central point.
4. Tom uses a quotation as another way to suggest his concern about growth.

What follows is Tom's inductive essay. We suggest that you read it through, then reread it along with the marginal comments.

Growth

I have been becoming more aware lately of just how much meaning is summed up in the commonplace word growth.

Notice how Tom's lead gives the reader the general subject without stating it as a central idea.

After spending August working as a counselor at a YMCA camp in the Sierra Nevada, I headed home to Orange County. Since the thought of a trip through Los Angeles always depresses me, calling up visions of housing tracts pasted together and of jammed freeways that lead to the city's concrete heart where gray towers spear into the afternoon pall, I decided to take the longer but more scenic route north of L.A. and over the Cajon Pass. I was in for a surprise. When I crossed the last ridge just before sunset and began the descent to the

Tom's opening sentence in the first paragraph gives some background to help orient the reader.

"Since the thought of" gives a response to past experience and backs it up with specific details.

"I was in for a surprise" prepares the reader for the specific details that follow in the next few sentences.

coastal plain, I saw that the fields of crops and citrus I remembered having been there had vanished. In their place were housing projects, shopping centers, gas stations, trailer parks, and schoolyards. The whole scene reminded me of a huge bowl heaped with junk and covered over with a layer of haze thick as gauze. I felt I was entering a nightmare. Certainly all this growth couldn't have happened in a single month, but then I remembered I had not traveled this particular route for almost ten years. I wanted to escape the numbing scene, so I stepped on the gas pedal and pointed my VW toward the city of Irvine and my home.

"The whole scene reminded me" begins a response shaped in an image that suggests all the clutter and pollution Tom has associated with L.A.

"Certainly all this growth" gives the background of the writer's thought. Using the key word "growth" is important here. Tom wants the reader to associate it with building.

"I wanted to escape" begins another of Tom's responses.

Irvine is a new city being slowly carved from a massive cattle ranch, according to the designs of a master plan. I can remember my parents saying they had moved to Irvine because it would never have the growth that came to Los Angeles. The morning after I returned home, I was up early. It's my habit to jog just after sunup. I set out on my usual run: an easy jog to a nearby field, then a harder run across a mile of open space to the high school where I usually do four leisurely laps around the track, and then I head for home along a road that takes me to the crest of a hill and down a path that leads to my back gate. At the field I saw that things had changed. All along its perimeter builders had terraced the hillsides and poured concrete slabs for housing foundations. Ahead, adjacent to the

Notice how this paragraph and the preceding paragraph are linked by "Irvine."

The opening sentence of this paragraph supplies the reader with more background.

"The morning after . . ." set up the next sequence that begins with background information related to Tom's usual run. If he didn't present this information here, he would have to work it in later.

Even though much of this is background, Tom works in specific details.

"At the field" sets up the specifics that follow.

Notice how Tom uses guiding words like "along" and "ahead."

school, they had framed eight apartment buildings. I did

four spiritless laps with my view of the field and hills

glutted by the new construction; then I started up the

road to the hill's crest. I grew sad as I ran. Just one

month earlier, wildflowers, rabbits, squirrels, sparrows,

meadowlarks, and ground owls thrived in the field along

the road. Now, the builders had scraped the field clean of

vegetation. I saw no life. I did see heavy bulldozers and

earthmovers, like the gorged offspring of ancient

mastodons, standing in the fields. At the hill top, I

paused to catch my breath. Below, in the northern half

of the city, I saw where builders had cleared other fields

for construction and had sawed down whole eucalyptus

stands that once protected orange groves from harsh

winds. I couldn't get over the thought that all this

leveling had happened in a single month. I felt as if I

were in the presence of a demonic force whose power I

couldn't grasp. It had changed the old growth of flowers,

trees, and wildlife into the new growth of houses,

apartments, and shopping centers.

That afternoon, while driving to campus, I passed

more construction in the part of Irvine set aside as the

industrial center. Here, the growth seemed to move

upward rather than outward. I drove through the

awesome shadows of multistoried buildings with the

afternoon sun flashing through the steel skeletons rising

in what had once been strawberry fields. I had seen it all

This section includes background information mixed with a great deal of detail. Tom contrasts the hills and fields as they were with how they are. Notice how "now" is used to guide the reader from past to present.

Here Tom shapes a response into an image by comparing the machines to prehistoric creatures.

Tom continues to document the "growth" he sees.

He moves from the concrete details to his inner responses.

Here Tom brings out the idea that the old growth of living things has been replaced by a new growth.

"That afternoon" shows that time has passed and introduces the new sequence of experiences related to observing growth.

"I had seen" presents more background information and pulls together the experiences Tom has been recording.

before — this part of the city had been under

development for years — but after my experiences driving

back from the Sierras and jogging through my

neighborhood, the growth took on a new meaning. The

thoughts from Joni Mitchell's "Big Yellow Taxi" came to

me. I had heard the song often, but this time its thought

seemed to capture what I was thinking. I recalled the

words "they paved paradise and put up a parking lot."

He brings in a quotation. Notice that he gives all the important information related to it — the name of the song and the vocalist. He also places it near the end of the essay because it serves to bring his thoughts together.

    Maybe southern California or Orange County or the

city of Irvine fails as an example of paradise, but it

seems to me that each field and hillside no matter where

it is holds a little bit of paradise. All this new growth

was bringing me a sense of loss — not just for my

neighborhood but for all neighborhoods that are giving

up their bits of paradise to more housing tracts,

shopping centers, and industrial complexes. And, finally,

the question comes to me: Just as the unchecked growth

of vines will destroy smaller plants by blocking out the

sun, won't the unchecked growth of buildings smother

people who must live in their shadow?

Notice how Tom refers to the song by bringing out the idea of paradise.

The entire paragraph provides a showcase for Tom's insight. He closes by raising a question about the dangers of unchecked growth. But notice how he has tied it to other communities, thus linking his insight to the experience of others.

The final question embodies the central point.

WRITING TASK

    Write an inductive essay according to the information we've given in this section. Begin by selecting an insight from your experience with which others might identify. Then select a quotation from an article, book, poem, song, lecture, or from Responding to Quotations (p. 215) that reflects your personal observation.

Next, prewrite the essay by developing an extended list or cluster of experiences that you associate with your insight. Using the list, develop a rough draft. Write an opening paragraph that announces the general subject of your entire essay and a conclusion that provides a showcase for your insight and central point. Tom Stevens arranged his discussion around a drive from the Sierra Nevada, a morning jog, and a drive to campus. If you search, you will probably find some simple dividing points for your essay.

As for the quotation, we suggest you place it near the end. It will then serve as a logical lead to the final insight, and it will also follow the details and responses you've accumulated to that point; therefore, it will have more psychological impact on the reader. To integrate the quotation into your essay, be sure to mention its source — both the person and place it comes from. (For more information on using quotations see Quotations in the Index for Writers.)

17 ASSOCIATIONAL ESSAY

By this time you would probably have little trouble arranging a paper covering the advantages and disadvantages of a particular job, the effects of the energy shortage on your campus, the process of preparing for an overseas journey, or the reasons for supporting one political candidate over another. This kind of material lends itself to organization reports and traditional essays.

But what of personal growth? What of insight that comes from life's disruptions and joys? How do writers go about exploring feelings involved in ending a relationship, losing a friend, becoming an adult, seeking truth? How do writers deal with feelings about succeeding, failing, aging, and dying. How do writers share insights that come from experiences such as these? They put them in reports, right?

Not likely. Separating, growing, seeking, failing, succeeding, aging, dying — this is the stuff of emotion. More often than not, these subjects can't be handled in formal patterns, but can be handled through less direct means. That's the function of the associational essay. This pattern offers the means to explore elusive areas of experience — that is, a way to search through life's nooks and crannies to see what experience has stored there.

This exploration usually involves the intuitive rather than the intellectual part of the mind, for the explorer abandons logical constraints in order to make more creative connections between separate memories drawn from personal experience. These memories often span a writer's life history by associating bits and pieces from the past and present that connect to a subject. Associational essays, then, tend to reflect the flow of psychological time instead of the procession of chronological time.

They often begin with an event or a thought important to the writer's current life, then skip to memories that connect with the present, hop forward to the not-so-distant past to make other connections before returning to the present. They may leap ahead, just as everyone's thought does, to construct a possible future. Sometimes they even include dreams and fantasies, hopes and fears, and, at times, philosophical musings.

At this point you probably sense that the writing of an associational essay requires a more creative touch than the writing of standard patterns. It does. The fact that it does presents a problem. As with most creative forms, the associational essay follows no clear pattern; therefore, we can't give you hard-and-fast rules. What we can do is give you some general guidelines.

Begin by recalling an experience that holds a great deal of emotion for you and that has brought some insight about yourself. Don't worry about whether the experience will seem earthshaking to your readers. Often the slightest experience, while appearing to be ordinary to others, may hold tremendous emotional energy for you. It's your job to show the emotion of the experience to the readers.

Once you've identified the experience and insight, draw together a list by associating memories you connect with the experience. In this prewriting phase, you shouldn't waste time evaluating the associations, you should only record them — no judgment, just writing.

After collecting the raw material, you need to shape the whole essay. Like all finished writing, the associational essay has a beginning, a middle, and an end. But unlike the deductive essay, the beginning of an associational essay merely suggests where the essay is headed. It never sets down a controlling idea.

The middle of the associational essay weaves together memories connected with the central experience, but the bulk of the details will come from the past. The paragraphs, though less organized than traditional patterns, should begin with sentences that give readers a sense of order. Never let readers stumble in disordered associations, but guide them each step of the way.

The end of the essay reveals the insight you've gained from the experience. This revelation, however, should be suggested, not flatly stated as the moral of your experience. Such suggestion is often hard to achieve. To make writing the conclusion easier, we suggest you use an image or thought that circles back into the essay and indirectly captures the point.

One last thought: Since the strength of an associational essay comes through the power of suggestion, the method of development is suggestive description. But before you can use description to suggest, you must have a clear understanding of what you want the reader to feel — a sense of loss; the pain of separation; the joy of discovery; the fear or acceptance of success, failure, aging, death. Once you have a clear understanding of your intent, you can select descriptive details that suggest the feeling. Often you may go through several drafts before you know exactly what it is you're after — that's the nature of creative writing — but before you write the final draft, you should have an exact understanding of what you're doing.

By way of illustration, we offer the following associational essay. Larry Swanson, the writer, relates an experience he had returning to the home and neighborhood where he was born and raised. His parents have moved to a new house, and his former home is to be destroyed. He uses the experience to indirectly communicate his feelings about change and to share an insight that comes to him through the encounter. As you read, notice that Larry never flatly states a moral or a controlling idea; rather he suggests his feelings by describing early memories he associates with growing up in the old neighborhood. The use of suggestion creates subtle suspense and prepares readers for the final insight.

First read Larry's opening comment on the essay; then read the entire essay. Finally, reread the essay with Larry's marginal comments.

My goal for this essay was very clear — I wanted to communicate what "home" and "change" means to me. By "home" I mean all those deep feelings, often confused feelings, that seem to be located just below consciousness. By "change" I mean a sense of loss and separation. I began developing the essay from various daily writing entries. These were bits and pieces of memories I had recorded in the Past Life and Portraits and Relationships chapters. Of course, the daily writing entries were incomplete in themselves; I had to polish and add information to make everything fit. There is one experience I very much liked about writing this essay, a discovery I made while doing the final draft: The use of Allie, Allie Oxen Free in the closing section. In children's games of hide and seek, the phrase means the players can come "home" safely, but in the essay it means that childhood is over.

Allie, Allie Oxen Free

In the middle of my freshman year in college I returned to my hometown to visit the old neighborhood. It was the last time I could go home. Home — the word has a deep meaning for me.

I use the opening sentence to set up the event that will organize the essay and to suggest the direction. I repeat "home" followed by a dash and a short comment on its personal meaning to stress its importance.

Driven out by a severe drought, my parents came from the cornfields of Nebraska to the house where they lived for thirty-five years. I was born in the back bedroom because, as my mother said, "there just wasn't enough time to get to a hospital." My earliest memories center on playing in that house: pushing trucks over the hardwood floors, my pajama knees mopping up the morning dust; rummaging through my mother's pan drawers and banging them on the linoleum; and hiding behind the overstuffed couch whenever I was called for lunch. The backyard seemed to stretch the length of a football field and was the place I would chase my older brother and sisters until I fell down, breathless and sweating. Before I started grammar school, I knew all the neighborhood's marvelous places: the avocado tree where my friends and I used to climb to an ancient tree house that had been built by children before us, the park where the old-timers would sit on benches and laugh at our wild games, the abandoned garage where we used to spy at the neighborhood through knotholes.

Here I needed to supply some background that shows my family's connection with the house and neighborhood.

I felt I had to catalogue a series of memory experiences I associated with the house and neighborhood so that the reader would feel what I was feeling. I arranged them chronologically — from childhood to starting school.

All that came back to me as I drove to pick up my parents for a final visit. You see, my home and the surrounding two blocks were to be destroyed. The City Council, those faceless champions of change, had condemned the neighborhood and planned to replace it with a civic center.

I conceived this paragraph as a bridge. It gives more background and expresses my attitude toward destructive change done in the name of progress. I remembered that social critic Lewis Mumford once said that "Progress does not necessarily mean improvement."

As I turned onto the street where my parents had bought a tract home, I saw my father, a little stooped since retiring after years of hard labor, standing before the recently seeded lawn that was beginning to sprout slivers of grass. In work boots, khaki trousers, and plaid shirt, which had become faded and thin from too much sun and too many washings, he didn't seem to belong to the stucco house packed with all the modern conveniences I knew my parents had avoided most of their lives. I pulled to the curb and he climbed in.

In this brief portrait of my father, I wanted to create the feeling that he was out of place in this new environment. Also I wanted to create a contrast: my father who once grew corn in vast fields has been reduced to growing grass and forced into a life of modern conveniences.

"Where's Mom?" I asked.

"Not coming," he said. "Let's go."

That was all he had to say to make me understand that Mom didn't want to make a final visit to the old place and to make me realize I didn't either.

I should say I have never written dialogue before. What I learned is that dialogue that works needs to be shaped. You just can't write down what people say. You must "arrange" it, strip it to the essentials. I'm also trying to enlarge the portrait of my father for my reader.

As we drove, he filled his pipe, lit it, and began puffing — the smoke carrying the smell of Sugar Barrel, a smell I will always associate with him. We chatted about nothing important. "How're classes?" he asked and I answered routinely, knowing that neither of us wanted to say much about losing our home. Then we were on the old street, and the memories seemed to rise in my blood.

I first saw the store the Hungarian couple used to run. The advertisements were peeling off the walls, the windows had been boarded up, and the screen door dangled stiffly from one hinge — empty, abandoned. But I

These next three paragraphs come from revised daily writing entries. I added detail and polished the entries. I begin each paragraph with a clear opening sentence to orient my reader. I try to create a contrast between past and

remembered how I once spent summer afternoons sitting in front of it and playing Monopoly with my friends or chess with old man Jefferson, a retired sailor. The car seats we used to lounge on were still there, but the stuffing had been torn out and only the springs remained.

Then we passed Mr. Salling's house. Tall and bony, Salling was the neighborhood's mysterious figure. The few times I saw him in the sunlight he wore a gray suit and had gray hair and skin. But more often I saw him moving behind the curtains where he paced the darkened parlor or rocked in a creaky chair. I was told he had been "that way" since "losing his wife." He wanted only to be left alone. One morning I learned that he had "left" the night before. I never heard of him again.

We drove past the vacant lot that had been the scene of many of my childhood joys. Each Independence Day the neighborhood fathers would set up a fireworks display and thrill us kids for hours. In the spring we held war games there. Costumed in makeshift army uniforms and wearing plastic helmets and carrying plastic rifles, we dodged through the tall grass and dove into foxholes, shouting "TATATATATA, Gotcha! C'mon you're dead!" During the summer, the lot served as the center for our nightly game of hide-and-seek. As my father and I drove past, I imagined hearing Billy Kieler's voice, the loudest and most melodic among us, echoing

present, to suggest death in the Mr. Salling paragraph and to highlight loss through change, especially in the part that refers to Billy.

throughout the neighborhood, "ALLIE, ALLIE OXEN

FREE! ALLIE, ALLIE OXEN FREE!" Billy was the first of

my childhood friends to move away. How much had his

life changed, I wondered. Yes, how much?

Then we were in front of our old wood-frame home.

My father climbed from the car. I looked straight ahead.

"Coming?" he asked. But before I knew I had made a

decision, I said no. I turned in time to see him walk the

five steps up to the front porch, unlock the door, and

step inside. No, I just could not bring myself to see the

house empty, abandoned.

Not going into the house reflects my reluctance to making the journey that I expressed in the opening. I hope the words "empty" and "abandoned" echo the statement about the store.

I sat staring at the front lawn and recalled how I

had spent hundreds of Saturday mornings mowing the

grass, trimming the hedges, and hoeing around the rose

bushes. I had hated to spend my Saturday mornings in

such labor since I hadn't inherited my dad's love of

growing and caring for things. Now the grass was brown

and the hedges and rose bushes were dying and I missed

the unvarying routine those secure Saturday mornings

brought.

In this paragraph I weave past with present. I'm trying to suggest my desire for things to stay the same — but, of course, I know they can't.

In a few moments Dad was returning, lugging a

heavy toolbox in each hand. I saw he breathed a little

heavy. I went to help him.

"Hard going?" I asked.

"It's the last time for me," he said as we hefted the

boxes into the car.

I use this exchange with my father to set up the final insight.

At first I didn't make the connection between his

words and mine. I had referred to the difficulty he had

carrying the boxes. He referred to much more. He

referred to the illusion I wished to keep. I glanced up the

street to the vacant lot and wished I could hear those

comforting words that meant everything was okay, that

the game was over and I could return home: ALLIE,

ALLIE OXEN FREE!

I wanted to create a sense of loss — very complicated loss — loss of youth, home, neighborhood, and loss through death. I wanted to suggest that life is not a game, unlike the childhood games I've mentioned. Everyone must accept change. There is no Allie, Allie Oxen Free in life.

Did you notice how muted Larry's essay seems, yet how it still communicates a great deal of emotion? He patiently develops the scene and memories through description that suggests a deeper meaning than he reveals. When he does comment, he doesn't shout; he comments in a quiet way. After rereading the essay Larry said, "Now Allie, Allie Oxen Free" seems to be about growing up, about becoming an adult."

WRITING TASK

Write an associational essay. We recommend the following procedure:

1. **Select an event that means a great deal to you and that brought you some personal insight.**
2. **Use your journal to trigger memories you associate with the experience. Collect the raw material in extended lists.**
3. **Decide what you wish to communicate to readers. Use it as the essay's guiding principle.**
4. **Write the essay by beginning with the main experience. Follow with a development of the experience while weaving in the associations you've collected.**
5. **Round off the essay by stating or implying how you feel or what you've learned from the experience.**

Remember, the primary method of development should be description. You will need to work in some background information and responses, but the main intent is to suggest the meaning of the experience, not to explain it.

18 GIVING DIRECTIONS

Giving directions is a practical kind of writing that everyone uses sometime. You may, for example, want to explain how to get to a particular place, how to perform an experiment, how to assemble a kit, or how to create a craft project.

Giving directions demands special attention to clarity: The assumption of such writing is that your reader will actually follow your directions. Basically, you'll be saying "Follow me," so write clearly. If you don't, your reader will get lost.

Select a subject you know well. You'll have to present a sequence of steps and comment on them, so write about something you have done yourself.

Select a narrow subject so you can handle it thoroughly. "How to sew" wouldn't do, but "How to make a wall hanging from a piece of discarded sheet" would. On the other hand, avoid subjects that are easily reduced to recipes.

Once you have selected a suitable subject, organization is easy; most procedures naturally fall into a chronological order of steps. As you work through these steps, though, keep the following practical points in mind.

1. Early in the paper, specify the materials needed so your reader can have them ready before he or she begins the process:

   For this project you will need 30 feet of number 10 wire and a pair of ordinary household pliers.

2. Make comments and add details on some steps to avoid being monotonous and to help your reader visualize the process:

> Press down three or four times on the silver squirter marked "chocolate" so that dark, sticky syrup slips down the sides of the glass to the bottom.

3. Give some reasons for some steps:

> Clip the design to the tracing paper to avoid those little shifts that destroy accuracy.

4. Define special terms as you go:

> The needle must oscillate — swing to and fro freely. If it does not, loosen the screw at the bottom of the dial.

5. Finally, include comments about what not to do:

> Don't tighten any bolts until all have been attached loosely, or the framework will slip out of alignment.

The introduction and conclusion should be brief. At the beginning, specify the process you are writing about and perhaps comment on the reason for doing it, its level of difficulty, or the overall approach you will present. At the end, a sentence or two to signal a close is all you need.

Before writing your own paper, examine the following directions given by Delia Ephron:

How to Cut off Your Jeans

It seems like the easiest thing to do. Then you do it and somehow one leg comes out shorter than the other. This time you're going to do it right.

A brief introduction gives reasons for following the directions.

The trick is this: cut one leg first, then match the second one to it. Never cut off both legs at the same time and never cut jeans while wearing them.

The writer presents an overview of the process and tells what not to do.

You will need one pair of used jeans, scissors, ruler and a felt-tip pen (like a Pentel).

Specifies materials needed

Put on the jeans and look in the mirror. With the pen, mark one leg an eyeballed two inches above the knee if you want Bermuda shorts, four inches above the knee for short shorts.   *Step 1*

Take off the jeans, lay them flat on a table, and cut off the leg even with the mark. Don't worry if your cutting is a little crooked. You can correct it later.   *Step 2. Comment*

Put the jeans back on and look in the mirror. Now you are going to find the length that is you. Experiment by turning under the bottom edge of the cut-off leg and adjusting the material up and down until you find a length you like. You'll know it when you see it, but it's hard to predict ahead of time. It will depend on such things as your taste and the shape of your thigh. When you find the right length, mark it on the cut leg with the pen. Then take off the jeans.   *Sequence of steps with comments*

Lay them flat on a table or the floor. Now here's the important part: Place the ruler <u>perpendicular</u> to the side seam and <u>even</u> with the mark and draw a line across the jeans. The ruler must be perpendicular to get a straight line. Cut the leg carefully along the line through both layers of fabric at the same time.   *A key step presented with cautions*

Now cut the second leg to match the first. Fold the jeans in half along the fly so that the cut-off leg is on top. Make sure the waistband is even all around. Using the ruler and pen, mark the length of the cut leg on the   *End of sequence* uncut one. Cut off the second leg. Align the legs again to

make sure they match.

The cut edges look unfinished now. If you run the   *The writer closes by commenting on the*
final results.

jeans through a washing machine a few times the

material will unravel into a nice fringe.

WRITING TASK

Write a paper giving directions for the successful completion of a specific and limited task. Introduce briefly; specify materials needed; give details, comments, and reasons for the steps; and guide your reader by explaining what not to do when appropriate. When the process is complete, bring the paper to a close in one or two sentences. Remember, since basically you're saying "Follow me," write as clearly as you can so the reader will not get lost.

19 INFORMING AND ADVISING

We're sure you've encountered written attempts to guide you through a step-by-step process to complete a task — preparing a dinner by recipe, putting together a model, developing a photograph, setting the wake-up switch on a new clock radio, connecting the components of a stereo, repairing a flat tire, cleaning a paintbrush, making a pair of shorts from jeans, and so on. (See Giving Directions, pp. 189–192.) This kind of writing usually involves particular procedures laid out in chronological sequence. In other words, it gives directions. The writer's purpose is to march you from point A to point Z without any mishaps. The writer is saying "Follow me, I'll get you there."

Informing and advising is close to giving directions, but the writer who informs and advises intends to give the readers information: how does a bill pass through Congress; how does one successfully interview with a prospective employer; how does one eat a formal dinner; how does a detective get an impression of fingerprints; how does one evaluate a restaurant, college, hotel, novel, marriage prospect; and so on.

Writers who inform and advise will not expect readers *to do* what they're describing but intend instead to satisfy a curiosity or to give advice and guidelines that cannot be applied in any procedural way. For instance, a paper that gives directions about changing a flat tire would have clear steps toward successfully doing the job, whereas a paper that informs about evaluating a college could be approached from many angles.

When you write an informing and advising paper, you must be interesting as well as informative. This allows you a chance to use several patterns to make the paper interesting — vivid description, specific and informational examples, comparisons, contrasts, definition, anecdotes to make a strong point, and even analogy to make the strange familiar.

We can suggest no single way to arrange an informing and advising paper; you need to stay on your toes and keep up with the needs of your subject. An informing and advising paper does, however, tend to fall into the same general pattern as the deductive essay — that is, it has an introduction, which is brief and usually interest catching or dramatic; several paragraphs in the discussion; and a conclusion. You won't need to worry about a central point because your contract with readers is clear: You're going to give them some advice and information.

For an impression of how such a paper might develop, read the following excerpt from Roberta Ridgely's *The Tijuana, Mexicali, Ensenada Shopping, Restaurant and Entertainment Guide, Olé.* Ridgely informs and advises her readers about eating at the open stalls of Tijuana and Ensenada and passes on some general dining and drinking guidelines for them to follow. As you read, notice how Ridgely weaves together description, which creates a picture of the experience, with information and advice. She also defines some Mexican terms, uses narrative examples, and tells general anecdotes. She includes numbered guidelines, characteristic of informing and advising papers but not always necessary. And note this, too: Ridgely has clearly identified her readers — first-time tourists visiting Tijuana and Ensenada, Mexico.

Eat, Drink and Be Careful

In the days of taco carts on Revolucion, Tijuana's tourist avenue, I eschewed chewing their wares. I've never eaten from a Tijuana clam cart. Nor have I bought a street vendor's churro (pastry fried in deep fat), thought by some to be a best buy. (I wonder if it isn't just a bargain in cholesterol.)

This brief introduction sets the piece in motion.

Ridgely assumes her readers will know what tacos are but defines the less familiar "churro." Then she generally suggests caution when eating at open stalls.

In Ensenada, however, I once let the then-director of the Chamber of Commerce direct me to a particular clam cart in that seafood wonderland. As a sweet sea breeze swept the street corner, fresh clams were pried open before my eyes and seasoned with fresh lime juice, sherry, and a zinger of chili. Served up in a plastic cup, the concoction was ambrosial. I supported that cart

Paragraph 2 gives an exception to the cautionary advice but suggests that you know what you are doing when you eat seafood.

Ridgely develops this point through a narrative example, packing it with plenty of vivid description.

many seasons, perhaps spurred on by gringos who not infrequently crowded around to ask, "You're not going to eat that stuff RAW?"

Since the agricultural products of Mexico so often find their way unsuspected to our tables, it seems foolish not to partake of her bounty. About two years ago I threw caution to the winds one sweltering day when a hot santana was blowing and I was parched. As my car turned a corner near Tijuana's downtown park, I saw a boy and his mother selling plastic cups piled high with spears of melon, papaya, cucumber, pineapple, with or without a sprinkle of chili powder. I gratefully sated my thirst, and suffered no ill effects whatsoever. These fruits have since become so popular they're sold on the main tourist drag, where thousands of visitors succumb as I did.

In paragraph 3 Ridgely shifts to agricultural products and zeros in on the fruit stands. Again using vivid detail she develops a narrative example, the point of which is that fruit is generally okay to eat. Through the description Ridgely shows how the fruit might be served.

Oh, the summer of '74! It will linger in memory as the advent of the luscious mango peeled and sculpted to look like an artichoke formed of orange sherbet. Firmly impaled on a stick, it can be eaten with or without chili sprinkle. This is a delicacy of mainland Mexico but never before had it penetrated Tijuana's Av. Revolucion or Ensenada's Blvd. Lopez Mateos. I bought the sticks all summer (the price finally settled at 40¢ in Tijuana). It was either that or a cold beer. If you're tempted, always peer closely at the mango to verify that the fruit still glistens moistly. Then you'll know it's freshly peeled and

In paragraph 4 Ridgely narrows her focus to the mango. She describes the way it should be served and gives some information about where to get it and the price. She also advises her readers about identifying a good mango and demanding a fresh one.

wondrously juicy. If the mangos look dry, demand

"Fresco!" and the vendor probably will sigh and peel one

just for you. . . .

　　If you wish to follow my personal rules (unscientific

but I think sensible) for staying well in La Frontera,

then you will:

1. Frequent the better restaurants. . . . There you're sure

   to be served bottled water. Even if there is nothing

   terribly wrong with local water, bottled water says

   something for the quality of the restaurant, don't you

   agree?

2. Never drink from a faucet, unless you're staying

   at a hotel or resort that has put in its own

   water-purification plant. All the other reliable

   inns will keep a filled water pitcher in your

   room.

3. If you're not used to highly seasoned food, don't

   plunge into it. Anywhere in this world unfamiliar

   cuisine can put you off your feet for a few days. Go

   easy. Some estimable Mexican dishes are almost

   bland. Basque and Spanish food is even more so.

   Many tourist-oriented restaurants deliberately serve

   food which from a Mexican point of view is

   underseasoned. You're expected to use your own

   discretion.

4. Understand Mexican hot sauce and the art of applying

   it.

In this section Ridgely gives some general guidelines for dining and drinking.

Ridgely develops point 4 in detail, which suggests that Mexican hot sauce may be a real danger to tourists.

In the last century and during part of this one, at the mineral-springs resorts which were the foundation of California tourism, local yokels often played a cruel joke on naive Easterners, who were served sulphur water disguised as chicken soup.

These days Californians often hear about another mean joke: Patrons of Mexican restaurants look on poker-faced, the story goes, as an innocent, assuming the little dish on his table to be some sort of cold soup (maybe that gazpacho he's heard about), downs it with a gulp. What he's swallowed, of course, is salsa picante — hot sauce. It will take him some time to put out his fire.

Salsa picante, if not sitting on your restaurant table, will be brought to you. It comes in several confusing varieties, all loosely called Salsa. To my mind the best (and the easiest to learn to like) has tomatoes and other fresh ingredients such as cilantro and onion chopped in, adding a fresh wild taste to mitigate some of the hot. This is known as Salsa Ranchera.

There are other varieties. If you find yourself in something less than an A-rated restaurant, beware of a variety that looks like pure Tabasco. Because they think it's sort of self-embalming, the proprietors of these joints often let it sit around for days till it gets kind of scummy.

Were I a newcomer to Mexico's snappy and satisfying cuisine, I'd eat no hot sauce the first day. The

In paragraphs 6 and 7 Ridgely develops a general anecdote to make her point — actually, she develops two in a comparative way. The result (implied) of drinking sulphur water and eating too much salsa picante would be the same — several hours in the hotel restroom.

Ridgely follows with some concrete information about salsa and advises which is the best.

She ends with some solid advice cast in a loose procedural form.

second day I'd treat it as if it were radioactive,

experimenting with a microscopic amount on the tip of a

spoon and distributing it as widely as possible in one of

my servings. But eventually I would try it, for this is a

taste which grows on you and can add immeasurably to

the spice of Mexican cookery.

How does one eat in a border town? Now you know enough to avoid the greasy food like tacos and churros served in open stalls and have some information about selecting clams and fruit, along with general advice for dining and drinking. If you were a tourist headed for the Baja border, this information and advice would come in handy.

A final comment on the point of view in Ridgely's essay. She writes in the first-person "I" because she comes to the information from personal experience. But if she had written from research, she would probably have used an objective viewpoint. Keep that in mind. When you participate in an experience, write from the "I"; when you are an observer or researcher, write from an objective stance.

WRITING TASK

Write a paper that informs and advises your readers about a subject that falls within your expertise. Keep in mind that this paper is not to give a procedure for readers to follow in a step-by-step fashion but should cover the problems and situations readers might encounter within a territory new to them. Your paper will guide readers by anticipating any difficulties they might face and by offering guidelines to handle them.

Remember:

1. **Pick a subject that will capture readers' interest.**
2. **Use plenty of concrete detail.**
3. **Use a variety of paragraph patterns, such as examples, catalogues, anecdote, comparison and contrast, analogy, and such.**
4. **If appropriate, use a numbering system to arrange the guidelines.**

20 OUTSIDE REPORT

In classes other than English, you may be asked to write reports on places you visit. The kind of place will depend on the class — perhaps tide pools for marine biology, museums or galleries for art history, child-care centers for developmental psychology, or even night spots for social anthropology. Generally, although outside reports deal with different kinds of experiences, your instructors will want you to communicate both your observations and your interpretations.

The obligation to observe and interpret seems clear enough, but sometimes beginning writers go astray when doing outside reports. Some seem to believe their only obligation is to fill up two or three pages that generally describe what they saw and did — a kind of let-me-tell-you-what-I-did-last-Saturday paper. They may include details of what they observed, but they leave the meaning of the observations to the imagination. This is shoddy practice and will usually be rewarded with a low grade.

An effective outside report includes not only a writer's observations but also an interpretation of them — that is, not merely a record of what was seen but also the meaning of what was seen. But how? you may ask. Simple. By applying some of what you've learned in the class through lectures, discussions, and readings. An outside report is another means for you to demonstrate and apply the knowledge you've acquired during the semester.

For example, imagine for a moment that you're taking a sociology class. You've been studying nonverbal behavior as it can be observed in public settings. For a final project, you've been asked to write an outside report based on personal experience with nonverbal behavior. You decide to study waiters and waitresses in a local restaurant. Fine. Probably a good choice. You go to the restaurant and sit in an unobtrusive spot that gives you a clear view of most of the tables and the counter. You select two or three subjects to study. You record every significant gesture, body stance, facial expression. You leave with a notebook full of raw material, much more than you'll need for the full report. At home you sift through the material and organize it into rough form. Now you're ready to write. When you write the paper, you not only describe your observations but also interpret their meaning based on information you've gained from a study of nonverbal behavior. This final step of responding to the material from an informed viewpoint is what the instructor will be looking for when evaluating your paper.

Now study the following paragraph. It is a discussion paragraph taken from a report generated by the sociology assignment. As you read, notice how the writer mixes interpretation with observations. Although the paragraph is developed mainly through concrete description, the bits of interpretation focus the details.

> I noticed that the waiter would nonverbally expose his interest in young female customers and his disinterest in middle-aged female ones. I watched him wait on two women in their early twenties. When he took their orders, he leaned forward and glanced with them at the menus as if he were acting as a friendly advisor. After collecting the menus, he paused for a moment to chat, although neither one's facial expression showed much interest in what he was saying. While he talked and the women sipped from their water glasses, he dangled the menus at his side as if to suggest that he was ready to receive their interest. Later, when he waited on three older women, perhaps in their late thirties, he stood erect, like a private during a military inspection, and hardly looked at them as he wrote on an order pad. He didn't lean forward or try to start a conversation, even though the women seemed friendly. When one called him back to request another item, he stood with the menus held before him as if they served as a protective barrier.

The topic sentence sets up the interpretation of this writer's observations — the waiter nonverbally exposes his interest and disinterest. The writer then details his observations to support his interpretations. He slips in fragments of interpretation, such as "acting as a friendly advisor," "ready to receive their interest," and "the menus held before him as if they served as a protective barrier" — which help focus the details. This is an effective paragraph that not only reports what the writer saw but also demonstrates some understanding of nonverbal expression.

Sometimes you may be assigned to do an outside report that doesn't require a specific application of what you've learned during a class.

Instead it may involve appreciation. No matter, because your obligations are the same: you must deliver a detailed rendering of your observations and your responses to them. The difference is that your responses will be more subjective — they will come out of personal awareness rather than out of a body of knowledge you've mastered.

The following paragraph is taken from an outside report on a photography exhibit. After giving a general description of the exhibit and the background of the photographer, the writer presents her responses to particular works. She begins this discussion paragraph with a topic sentence that identifies a quality of one photograph, then follows with a detailed description before presenting her response to it.

> Harold Chan's photograph "Night Wood" has a haunting quality. Fog rolls through the pines, but the fog looks more like steam. Leaning against a tree, a man dressed in black and wearing a white mask stares directly at the observer. With fog swirling around him, he seems ghostly, perhaps demonic. I thought of nightmare images. I felt pinned by his round black eyes. I felt almost as if I had been caught in a horrible dream and was unable to awaken. It seems that Chan is depicting the strange forces that exist in the mind's forests where the sleeper may helplessly stumble.

This writer has carefully combined her observations with responses. Concrete description helps the reader see the experience, but the interpretation of the experience helps focus the piece.

There will be two distinct phases in writing an outside report. First, you'll set out to prewrite the report the way you would any task. You collect the raw material to use in the final draft by capturing concrete details and your responses to the experience. This note taking is an active part of the assignment. Don't try to write a report from memory. Such reports usually turn out inaccurate and dull.

After you've made your visit and collected notes, you begin the second phase — the actual writing. Begin by sifting through your material. Reread your notes. Reflect on what you've recorded. Is there anything to add? Do you see a general shape? Is there an outstanding point you might use to organize your report?

The general structure of an outside report is much like that of a deductive essay. Begin with an introduction that gives the instructor some background information and presents a central point. In this case the central point will capture the general point of your paper — the conclusion you've drawn from the experience. For instance, the report from which we took the first example has this central point:

> Waiters and waitresses expose their attitudes toward customers through nonverbal behavior.

The report from which the second example came has this central point:

> Harold Chan's black-and-white photographs have a haunting theme.

Once you've decided on a central point, you will be able to cut excess detail from your paper and focus your thought.

With the central point chosen and the introduction written, you need merely to organize the remaining material into a discussion. Remember, be sure to include not only detail but your interpretation of the detail. Keep in mind, too, that the discussion paragraphs can be built on any of the patterns you've mastered — development by example, comparison, contrast, analogy, classification, and so on.

The conclusion of an outside report is usually short, perhaps a brief reminder of the central point or a further observation that grows out of the experience and relates to the class you've been writing it for.

A final thought. When you write an outside report, don't spend any time telling your instructor why you went where you went. Don't include information that isn't related to the experience itself.

WRITING TASK

We suggest you select a report that would be appropriate for one of your other classes. If you have not been assigned an outside report in another class, you might visit an art exhibit, museum, job site, nursery school, or even another college to use for a report.

Remember:

1. Make your visit and compile ample notes that include both details and responses.
2. Develop a central point to organize your material.
3. Write an introduction that gives your instructor any pertinent background information.
4. Write a discussion several paragraphs long giving the particulars of your report. Be sure to combine your observations with interpretation. Keep in mind that this is a chance to show your instructor that you can apply some information you've learned during the course.
5. End the report with a brief conclusion.

21 BOOK REVIEW

In newspapers and magazines, book reviews usually deal with recently published books. Reviewers, therefore, must assume that their audiences don't know the works. They see their role as mainly that of guides — persons who acquaint readers with a book's content and make judgments about its value. Since most reviews are short, ranging anywhere from 750 to 1500 words, a reviewer hasn't the space to comment on every aspect of a particular book but must select the outstanding features or the ones that will hold the greatest interest for the audience. There's a danger here, for if the focus is too narrow, the reviewer is not doing a good job of guiding the prospective readers. The reviewer must tread the middle ground between being too specific and too general.

When writing a book review, you will be treading the same path as the reviewer. You are bound to present some general information, yet you must develop enough specific information to make your report valuable. You will also need to work in your judgments about the quality of the book based on the specifics you select to develop. A big job, but not impossible. Although we can't give you any hard-and-fast rules for writing a book review, we can give you some general guidelines that should serve most of your book reviewing purposes.

1. *Introduction:* Generally, you'll open with an introduction that gives some specific information: title, author's name, type of work, author's general intent (which for a work of nonfiction can usually be expressed in a quotation), and your general attitude about the work.
2. *Overview:* After the introduction, you'll follow with an overview that should be designed to give readers a general feeling for the

book. If the work is fiction, identify the situation; write a brief description of the setting, atmosphere, and historical time; and summarize the plot. If the work is nonfiction, you'll do much the same, but instead of a plot summary, you might present any important background, capture the general movement, and identify the high points of the work. If you are reporting on a collection of essays, you might give the collection's general focus and summarize representative pieces. Keep in mind that all this information should be integrated, not boxed into little compartments. We also suggest that before you begin an overview you ask yourself what your intended readers need to know to decide whether to read the book. Remember, too, that no matter how you go about writing the overview, it should be no longer than a quarter of the length of your entire paper. Your goal is to give readers a feeling for the work, not to rewrite it.

3. *Close examination:* You'll follow the overview with several paragraphs that closely examine important elements in the work. If the work is fiction, you might explore how the writer deals with character, take a closer look at plot elements, or examine theme. You can sometimes handle a nonfiction work similarly: If a person is the focus, you might trace how the author handles his or her life; instead of plot, you might deal with the story line or life history. If the work deals with ideas, however, you'll need to examine the central thought. When you are reviewing a collection of essays, we suggest you select representative pieces and examine them. You might classify, compare, and contrast them according to theme, style, or point of view. Throughout this section, you should quote from the work, but be sure the quotations fit what you are saying about the work.

4. *Evaluation and conclusion:* After talking about some specific elements, you'll move on to evaluate the work and to conclude your paper. Most book reviews present balanced evaluations, the reviewers presenting both the strong and weak points, although in the end a review may tip toward recommending, recommending with qualification, or not recommending the book. Do the same when you evaluate a work. Select several specific examples you believe represent the book's strengths and weaknesses. Don't hedge. Be forthcoming with your judgments, but always support them with examples, usually in the form of quotations. After working your way through the evaluation, you'll be ready to make a recommendation. Is the book of value? Should it be read? If so, by whom — specialists, everyone, children? For what reasons? The recommendation, usually only a few lines, concludes the paper.

Sounds simple, right? If you carefully read the work you've selected for the review, it should be. After all, the overall pattern is clear:

Introduction	Includes the title, author's name, type of work, general intent, your attitude
Overview	Generally acquaints readers with the work
Close examination, usually several paragraphs	A close look at significant elements of the work through analysis and quotations
Evaluation	The weighing of the work's strong and weak points with judgments supported by examples or quotations
Conclusion	The closing recommendation and evaluation

Although the overall pattern of the book review is fairly rigid, what writers do within it is flexible. Consequently, rather than give you a single illustration, we want to present several tips on how you might handle the tough spots.

Introduction

The introduction is a place where many beginning writers stumble. Remember, the introduction should include the title, author's name, type of work, general intent, and your attitude. Fine — no problems here. But too often the information is presented in Dick and Jane prose, something like this:

> This book is titled *The Executioner's Song.* It is written by Norman Mailer. It is a biography of killer Gary Gilmore that covers the time when he was once released from prison until his execution by a firing squad. Norman Mailer writes, "This book does its best to be a factual account of the activities of Gary Gilmore and the men and women associated with him in the period from April 9, 1976, when he was released from the United States Penitentiary at Marion, Illinois, until his execution a little more than nine months later in Utah State Prison." Norman Mailer's account is riveting, though at times he burdens the reader with unnecessary details.

All the important information is here, but the passage is written in such a pedestrian manner that only the most dedicated reader would plow through it. Don't write an introduction in this manner. Instead try to integrate the information into flowing sentences. An obvious way to go about it is to cut the clutter and combine the sentences where you can. In the preceding paragraph, can you see a reason for stating the author, title, and type of work in separate sentences? Does the type of book have to be stated, since the quotation makes its nature clear? A revised version, one that's much more effective, might read like this:

> Norman Mailer's *The Executioner's Song* is "a factual account of the activities of Gary Gilmore and the men and women associated with him in the period from April 9, 1976, when he was released from the United States Penitentiary at Marion, Illinois, until his execution a little more than nine months later in Utah State Prison." Mailer's version of those nine months is riveting, even if he at times burdens the reader with unnecessary details.

The revised introduction not only gets the information to the reader; it flows. Work to get your introduction to flow; integrate the information; don't write Dick and Jane prose. The revised version also sets the principal verb tense for the entire report. Notice that it is written in the present tense: *The Executioner's Song is* "a factual account . . . Mailer's version of those nine months *is* riveting, even if he at times *burdens* the reader." The present tense is the principal tense you should use for book reviews. Also notice that Mailer's full name is only used once. After you've identified the author by his full name, refer to him or her only by the last. Don't use Dr. or Mr. or Mrs. or Ms., either — use only the last name.

Now let's look at another example to see how someone else might handle an introduction to a book review. As you read this paragraph, notice how much information you get about the book in question — but not too much. The writer merely wants to prepare you for what's coming, not overload you with too many specifics.

> "What parents have to learn is how to become a match for their children, wise to their ways and capable of guiding them without letting them run wild or stifling them," claims Rudolf Dreikurs in *Children: The Challenge*. Dreikurs's self-help book offers parents ways to handle problems in child rearing that could improve if not revolutionize the relationships between parents and children.

Overview

Beginning writers sometimes stumble in the overview section because they feel overwhelmed with the task of creating a feeling for a work in such a short space. Aside from a paragraph of summary that captures the highlights of a book, you can also use a catalogue that captures the tone, atmosphere, or setting.

> Mailer creates life as lived in the rural West. In the section called "Western Voices" he evokes people struggling to make a living in gas stations, roadside cafés, movie theaters, small factories, farms, and country stores. It's a world filled with pickup trucks, six-packs, country music, Monday night football, deer hunting, motorcycles, and honky-tonk violence. The city slicker is suspect and the easy buck is hard to come by. The four-wheel drive Blazer, not the sleek Mercedes, is the status symbol. It is a world of macho, not of sophistication.

The catalogue thrusts readers into the scene. Through the multiple listing of particulars, the writer can sweep into a work and give readers a feeling for what it contains. Try it. In the overview a catalogue will help you move in broad steps.

Close Examination

In the section that takes a closer look at the work, be sure to use quotations wherever you can to develop your thought. For instance, one writer of a book report on Dennis McNally's *Desolate Angel, a Biography: Jack Kerouac, the Beat Generation and America* wrote this paragraph to demonstrate one of the work's outstanding elements:

> McNally gives more than a detailed portrait of Kerouac and a historical rendering of the beats. He probes at the creative motivations behind their acts. He points out that Kerouac felt obligated to tell the truth "in all its delicate and hideous glory." He goes on to generalize that other artists of the period, such as musician Charles "Bird" Parker and painter Jackson Pollock, were motivated by similar principles. McNally writes, "Each artist had concluded that in the limbo of war and Cold War, only the most risky commitment to personal creativity and intuition could allow them to transcend the times." It seems that McNally isn't just speaking of artists of this time, but artists of all time.

When possible, let the author speak to your readers through quotations. But remember, you have an obligation to show readers the significance of the quotation. Don't just quote and leave the readers to figure out its significance.

Here's another example from a review of John D. MacDonald's thriller *The Green Ripper*. In this paragraph the writer is trying to illustrate an important aspect of MacDonald's vision:

> Often MacDonald's view of the world seems grim. He creates a society headed for Apocalypse. "All the major currencies will collapse. Trade will cease. Without trade, without the mechanical-scientific apparatus running, the planet won't support its four billion people, or perhaps even half that. . . . There will be fear, hate, anger, death. The new barbarism. There will be plague and poison. And then the new Dark Ages." But keep in mind that a good thriller writer must create the potential for chaos. Would the actions of his hero in a stable world seem worth reading?

Evaluation and Conclusion

You should use quotations not only in the close examination of the work's important elements but also in the evaluation. One writer reporting on Thomas Thompson's *Serpentine* wrote this evaluative paragraph. Notice how the writer has strung fragments of quotations together.

Using several short quotations is often the only way you can support a broad judgment.

> A minor flaw in the book comes from Thompson's flagrant use of clichés in place of more thoughtful prose. He writes, "It was the dead of winter, 1967, and the prison walls were as cold as ice." He refers to Sobhraj's court room chicanery as a "bag of tricks." His girlfriend clung to him "like moss on an oak." Sobhraj tried to pass their tawdry affair off as an "epic romance more poignant than Romeo and Juliet." Trite expressions and clichés such as these mark every other page and blemish an otherwise powerful performance.

At other times you won't be able to support a judgment with quotations. Then you need to fall back on summarizing broad points to shore up the evaluation. In the paragraph that follows the one above, the reviewer of *Serpentine* pulls together some outstanding features of Thompson's central figure to support another evaluative point:

> Much of Thompson's powerful performance comes from his fascinating portrait of Sobhraj as a suave yet grisly nomad full of contradictions. A man without formal education who learned to survive in the rubble of Saigon, along the docks of Marseilles, on the boulevards of Paris, in the marketplaces of Delhi, and in several prisons. Sobhraj mastered ten languages, studied French and Indian law and read thousands of books ranging from thrillers to Eastern philosophy. He was a man moved by some ill-defined dream of material success that sent him blazing across much of Europe, through the Middle East, and into Asia, while he spouted romantic ideals and supported himself by befriending tourists, drugging them, and stealing their valuables. Born a bastard to an Indo-Chinese mother and an Indian father in French-dominated Saigon under Japanese occupation, he was never able to establish permanent connections with either parent. But during the peak of his criminal career, he surrounded himself with hapless travelers he called his "family," then methodically poisoned or bludgeoned them to death and left the bodies smoldering at roadsides, dumped in the jungles, or floating in the surf. A complex portrait, one that should make any traveler to exotic places suspect the stranger's friendly smile and firm handshake.

As for the conclusion, we suggested that it should flow from the evaluation section. Beginning writers sometimes stumble here because they try to say too much. Since by this point the readers will already have a clear idea of your attitude toward the work, you'll usually need to do little more than write two or three lines to tie a recommendation together.

> Thompson's *Serpentine* is for every reader fascinated by the bizarre and criminal. It moves swiftly, and if you don't mind the bumpity-bump of the clichés, then you'll be enthralled roaming much of the world with Thompson as he tracks the life of Charles Sobhraj.

When you write a conclusion to a book review, keep in mind that besides making a recommendation and identifying the potential reader, you should also reflect your opening attitude and evaluation and re-name the work and author.

WRITING TASK

To facilitate this task, your instructor will probably provide a list of books that will be appropriate for you to review. We suggest you take the list to the library or bookstore and browse through several of the books to find one that interests you. After you've made a choice, read the work carefully, noting its interesting aspects. Once you have a solid understanding of the book, use the guidelines in the preceding discussion to write the review.

Remember, in writing the review try to give the reader a broad understanding of the work as well as your evaluation. Finally, arrange your report in this fashion:

1. an introduction that presents the title, author's name, type of work, general intent, and your attitude
2. an overview that acquaints readers with the whole work
3. several paragraphs that examine specific aspects of the work
4. an evaluation that focuses on the work's strengths and weaknesses
5. a conclusion that identifies the potential reader, renames the author and title, and reflects the opening attitude and evaluation

22 PERSONAL ESSAY: CURRENT LIFE

If you've been doing Daily Writing, during the second week you collected raw material from your current life. You began by writing an overview that captured this period's dominant activities, impressions, and fantasies. On the following days of that week, you focused your writing by enlarging individual aspects of your current life. You described where you live, personal possessions, important activities, and special places. You also recorded your personal associations with these aspects of your life. Although roughly written, these entries probably come together as part of an account of who you are. We hope that they serve as a first step in achieving what Henry David Thoreau asks of every writer: "a simple and sincere account of his own life, and not merely what he has heard of other men's lives."

To go beyond the general knowledge you've acquired from family, friends, and society at large — to go beyond what you "have heard of other men's lives" — is to approach a deeper understanding of how you fit into the world, an understanding of who you are and what you want to be. Now, after the entries reflecting your current life have had time to incubate, we suggest you write a polished account of your current life — one that not only communicates the details of this period but that also communicates your personal insights.

WRITING TASK

Write an inductive, associational, or deductive essay that gives an account of your current life. We recommend that you begin by reviewing your Daily Writing entries to stimulate more thoughts. Record your thoughts. As you read and record new thoughts, make a general observation about your recent experience. Shape the generalization into a central idea and use it to select material for your essay. Then, once you've selected the material, use the central idea to organize the paper's development.

Remember, whereas the Daily Writing entries may be rambling, the finished essay should be organized and developed with focused paragraphs. Never set your reader adrift in unfocused material. Your central idea, although not necessarily stated, should be clear to any attentive reader.

23 PERSONAL ESSAY: DREAMS

Sigmund Freud, the founder of psychoanalysis, described dreams as forbidden wishes symbolically disguised to preserve the dreamer's sleep. But Freud drew his conclusions from limited information. He didn't know, as today's researchers know, that virtually all mammals dream. What forbidden wishes, one may wonder, could birds and infants have?

Since Freud's time, researchers have taken a new attitude toward dreams. They reject the notion that a set of standardized interpretations can be applied to them. They maintain that each person creates individual meaning from dream experience. For instance, if ten people were to dream of wandering through a strange city, the dream would have ten different meanings, one for each dreamer.

These contemporary researchers also maintain that dreams serve as bridges between our conscious and unconscious experience. Many researchers maintain that dreams sometimes indicate the dreamer's destiny by pointing out unrecognized aspects of the dreamer or by focusing on another person who embodies the dreamer's potential. Sometimes dreams provide what is missing in the dreamer's waking life — love, friendship, success, adventure, travel, or freedom. Dreams can sometimes serve as a release from tension, pain, fear, or other emotions that can interfere with waking life. Finally, today's researchers point out the practical nature of dreams. Just as dreams have sometimes helped artists and inventors solve problems in their work, they sometimes serve the same purpose in every dreamer's life.

If you've been recording dreams as part of your Daily Writing, then perhaps you've made connections between your dreams and aspects of your waking life. If so, you might like to develop "dreams" as a subject for an essay.

WRITING TASK

Begin by rereading your Daily Writing entries on dreams. Have any dreams given you an insight into your life? Have any offered a solution to a problem you've faced? If so, shape a central point from your observation and use it to develop an essay that deals with your dream experience as related to your waking experience.

24 RESPONDING TO QUOTATIONS

The Writing Tasks given on the next few pages ask you to respond in some fashion to the words of others. Each task begins with one or more quotations expressing an attitude, insight, or personal opinion. You should read the quotations carefully, relate them to your own experience or knowledge, then write an essay responding in some way to this stimulation.

These tasks are open-ended. We are not asking that you agree or disagree with the quotations. Your paper shouldn't be limited to either an answer to or an amplification of the ideas expressed. Rather, you should let your mind speculate about the quotations and see where your thoughts lead.

Perhaps the quotation will arouse emotions, bring to mind nostalgic memories, or lead to philosophical thoughts. Take, for example, a short quotation from the writing of George Santayana: "To me it seems a dreadful indignity to have a soul controlled by geography." How could you respond in writing to this quotation? You would begin, of course, with prewriting — jotting down the thoughts that go through your mind as you read it.

- The old cliché — travel broadens the mind. Is it true? My aunt and uncle's trip to Europe just reinforced all their prejudices against foreign things.
- Haven't traveled much myself, so can't support or deny the cliché from personal experience.
- Why "soul"? More important than the mind, I guess. Harder to pin down than thought. He's not talking about knowledge in the sense of facts and stories to relate, but about something more fundamental, something closer to the self.

- A soul controlled by geography would be a person imprisoned in some fashion — tied down rather than soaring free — missing out on full potential — the fullness of experience.
- Americans are criticized for this — being provincial — not willing to see the value of other ways of life.

> Example — languages. We think everyone should speak English. I've read that this is a problem in our diplomatic relations — not only do our reps not speak the language, they ignore customs too. What do we miss when we travel and can't speak with the people? All we have for the experience is a lot of slides.

- The other word I wonder about is *indignity*. What does it mean here? Being insulted is an indignity, or having pie shoved in your face — not exactly what he means. Here it is more personal — something you do to yourself — a kind of failure to reach potential again.
- Even if we don't travel we can learn about other ways of doing things.

> Example — influx of refugees gives us a chance to relate to another culture, probably in a better way than a whirlwind tour. Trouble is we sit back and wait for them to adopt our ways (and language). How do they manage to study in American colleges?

- The world is becoming Americanized, they say. Coca-Cola in Egypt and McDonald's everywhere. I read that the most successful McDonald's stand is in Japan. And rock music — is that an American export or just a world phenomenon of the times? Is it a way to get beyond the limits of geography?
- Jeans and T-shirts. I saw a picture of a little boy in Cambodia wearing a Butterfinger T-shirt. Where did he get it?

This line of thinking has taken us quite a way away from Santayana's original words, but the journey has suggested any number of possible papers:

- How your aunt and uncle's trip was wasted — what they failed to get out of it
- Where you would like to go and why
- The intangible benefits your own travels have given you
- Your experiences with the language barrier
- Your experiences with people from other countries now settled in your community
- Your failure to learn from newly arrived immigrants
- The good and bad aspects of Americanizing the whole world

It doesn't matter if any of these topics speak directly to what Santayana had in mind. The quotations should be seen as stimuli only. Use them as springboards to your own thinking.

Extended Quotations

This section contains eleven quotations from various sources. Each quotation is followed by a writing task with a series of questions designed to get you into the prewriting portion of the task. We hope the questions will be helpful, but ignore them if you don't need them. In no case should you assume that you should write in direct response to any of these questions. Open up your responses. Allow your mind to wander over the entire landscape of possibilities.

After you have chosen a quotation and done some prewriting exploration as we have suggested, your task is to write an essay of your own design (it may be deductive, inductive, personal, or associational) that grows from your consideration of the quotation and the questions that follow it. In your essay you need not mention the quotation at all unless you find some good reason for doing so. Remember, its purpose is only to stimulate your thinking. If you do mention it, make it an integral part of your essay by quoting it in full or in part and including the name of the author. Do not assume that your readers have read the quotation before.

The quotations themselves tend to be general in phrasing; they are statements of attitudes, insights, or personal opinions. The specifics that support such statements are missing. But your paper should include such specifics. If, for example, you were responding to the Santayana quotation given earlier by writing about the benefits you have gained from your travel experiences, you would not just say they have helped you appreciate the customs of others; you would get specific by giving readers the anecdotes and the individual experiences that illustrate the point.

1. May Sarton

> The reasons for depression are not so interesting as the way one handles it, simply to stay alive. This morning I woke at four and lay awake for an hour or so in a bad state. It is raining again. I got up finally and went about the daily chores, waiting for the sense of doom to lift — and what did it was watering the house plants. Suddenly joy came back because I was fulfilling a simple need, a living one. Dusting never has this effect (and that may be why I am such a poor housekeeper!), but feeding the cats when they are hungry, giving Punch clean water, makes me suddenly feel calm and happy.

>Whatever peace I know rests in the natural world, in feeling
>myself a part of it, even in a small way.

WRITING TASK

Write an essay that grows from your consideration of the quotation
from May Sarton. You may use the following questions as a way of
generating material for your essay.

Does this quotation arouse emotions in you? Do you envy the writer's apparent ability to find joy in such simple things? Do you reject
the idea? Do you have your own ways of fighting depression? How big
a role does the "natural world" play in your daily living? What simple
things bring you peace and calm? Or do you really prefer excitement
and a more hectic pace? Do you have friends or neighbors who might
make interesting studies of either the simple life or the high-pressure
one?

2. e.e. cummings

>to be nobody-but-yourself in a world which is doing its best,
>night and day, to make you everybody else — means to fight the
>hardest battle which any human being can fight

WRITING TASK

Write an essay that grows from your consideration of the quotation
from e. e. cummings. You may use the following questions as a way of
generating material for your essay.

What are some of the victories and defeats you have had in what
cummings describes as the battle to be "nobody-but-yourself"? Are
you still fighting the battle or do you find it more comfortable to be
"everybody else"? In what ways does the world (society, family,
friends, teachers, the media, the government) try to make you like
everybody else?

3. Jeffers, Dostoevski, Montaigne

The following three short quotations each make substantially the
same point. Consider them together.

ROBINSON JEFFERS

I have never been ambitious, but it seemed unpleasant just the same to have accomplished nothing, but exactly nothing, along the only course that permanently interested me. There are times when one forgets for a moment that life's value is life; any further accomplishment is of very little importance comparatively.

FYODOR DOSTOEVSKI

Perhaps the only goal on earth toward which mankind is striving lies in the process of attaining, in other words in life itself, and not in the things to be attained.

MICHEL DE MONTAIGNE

The great and glorious masterpiece of man is to live to the point. All other things — to reign, to hoard, to build — are, at most, but inconsiderable props and appendages.

WRITING TASK

Write an essay that grows from your consideration of the quotations from Robinson Jeffers, Fyodor Dostoevski, and Michel de Montaigne. You may use the following questions as a way of generating material for your essay.

All three of these quotations stress the importance of process (living) over product (accomplishments). How much do we judge others and ourselves on the basis of product? Competitive sports at all levels are one obvious example. Can you think of others? Can you think of times in your life when the experience itself turned out to be more important or worthwhile than the end result? Is the pursuit of a goal as important as the achievement? Or is lack of achievement really failure? How should success in life be measured?

4. Mark Kram

All of this brings us down to marbles, not the argot for brains but the real thing: perfectly round; so smooth; brilliantly colored; as precious to generations of children as any diamond.

Has anyone seen a marble lately? Has anyone seen a marble in the hand of a kid? Most likely the answer is no, for the only things kids carry these days are transistor radios, slices of pizza and tickets to rock concerts. The marble belongs to a time that now seems otherworldly, when trees lined big city blocks as far as the eye could see, when barley soup was supper three times a week, when children had secret places.

WRITING TASK ═══

Write an essay that grows from your consideration of the quotation from Mark Kram. You may use the following questions as a way of generating material for your essay.

Have things changed much since you were a kid? What did you do for fun when you were eight, or ten, or twelve? What did you do finally on "Mommy-there's-nothing-to-do" days? Schoolchildren used to survive the year by moving mysteriously through a cycle of ill-defined seasons — marble season, jacks season, mumblety-peg season, bottle-cap season — all without the aid of any adult direction or organization. Now, even the very young, boys and girls alike, get involved in soccer season, football season, basketball season, baseball season, camping organizations, and "lessons" of all kinds. Old-timers will tell you that something valuable has been lost because of all this organization, carried out under constant adult supervision. What do you think? Should kids be left alone more? Should they be allowed to invent their own activities? Are their lives too scheduled? What's the difference, as you see it, between carrying a bag of marbles and carrying a transistor radio?

═══

5. *John Holt*

From the very beginning of school we make books and reading a constant source of possible failure and public humiliation. When children are little we make them read aloud, before the teacher and other children, so that we can be sure they "know" all the words they are reading. This means that when they don't know a word, they are going to make a mistake, right in front of everyone. Instantly they are made to realize that they have done something wrong. Perhaps some of the other children will begin to wave their hands and say, "Ooooh! O-o-o-o!" Perhaps they will just giggle or nudge each other, or make a face. Perhaps the teacher will say, "Are you sure?" or ask someone else what he thinks. Or perhaps, if the teacher is kindly, she will just smile a sweet, sad smile — often one of the most painful punishments a child can suffer in school. In any case, the child who has made the mistake knows he has made it, and feels foolish, stupid, and ashamed, just as any of us would in his shoes.

WRITING TASK

Write an essay that grows from your consideration of the quotation from John Holt. You may use the following questions as a way of generating material for your essay.

Have you ever felt humiliated in a classroom? By a teacher? By classmates? Can you recall details of the experience and how you felt? Have incidents of this nature influenced how you feel about being in classrooms even now? How *do* you feel about being in classrooms? Comfortable? Uneasy? If allowed your choice, where do you sit? Why? Do you prefer an active or passive role as a student in a classroom? Do you prefer lectures or class discussions? Why? Can you recall particular classes at any level of your schooling that you either looked forward to or dreaded? Can you bring to mind details of the scene and specifics about how you felt while there? Do you agree with John Holt that having students read aloud is a poor teaching method? If you were a teacher at any level of schooling, what would you do differently than your teacher at that level did? Have teachers or have fellow students had more to do with your attitudes and behavior in classes? Have you ever done anything really stupid in class? Can you tell about it without embarrassment? What punishments are the most effective? The least?

6. Alison Lurie

For thousands of years human beings have communicated with one another first in the language of dress. Long before I am near enough to talk to you on the street, in a meeting or at a party, you announce your sex, age, and class to me through what you are wearing — and very possibly give me important information (or misinformation) as to your occupation, origin, personality, opinions, tastes, sexual desires and current mood. I may not be able to put what I observe into words, but I register the information unconsciously; and you simultaneously do the same for me. By the time we meet and converse we have already spoken to each other in an older and more universal tongue.

WRITING TASK

Write an essay that grows from your consideration of the quotation from Alison Lurie. You may use the following questions as a way of generating material for your essay.

What do your clothes reveal about you? Do you make conscious choices designed to say something to others? Do your clothes influence your mood, your behavior? Do you judge others by their clothing? How important are clothes in your life? Do changes in fashion reflect changes in public attitudes or are they just the whims of fashion designers? Would you expect to see changes in fashion in a time of great prosperity? A time of economic difficulty? Wartime?

7. *Joseph L. Braga and Laurie D. Braga*

Whether you die at a young age or when you are older is less important than whether you have fully lived the years you have had. One person may live more in eighteen years than another does in eighty. By living, we do not mean frantically accumulating a range and quality of experience valued in fantasy by others. Rather, we mean finding a sense of peace and strength to deal with life's disappointments and pain while always striving to discover vehicles to make accessible, increase, and sustain the joys and delights of life. One such vehicle is learning to focus on some of the things you have learned to tune out — to notice and take joy in the budding of new leaves in the spring, to wonder at the beauty of the sun rising each morning and setting each night, to take comfort in the smile or touch of another person, to watch with amazement the growth of a child, and to share in children's wonderfully "uncomplexed," enthusiastic, and trusting approach to living. To live.

WRITING TASK

Write an essay that grows from your consideration of the quotation from the Bragas. You may use the following questions as a way of generating material for your essay.

Do you really believe that one person can live more in eighteen years than another in eighty? Is there value in "accumulating a range and quality of experience"? What are your personal "joys and delights of life"? Are there aspects of life that you "tune out" but feel you shouldn't? What are they? What is your definition of "living"? In other words, what is important? What gives you pleasure? What gives you peace and strength?

8. Carl Sagan

Every major power has some widely publicized justification for its procurement and stockpiling of weapons of mass destruction, often including a reptilian reminder of the presumed character and cultural defects of potential enemies (as opposed to us stout fellows), or of the intentions of others, but never ourselves, to conquer the world. Every nation seems to have its set of forbidden possibilities, which its citizenry and adherents must not at any cost be permitted to think seriously about. In the Soviet Union these include capitalism, God, and the surrender of national sovereignty; in the United States, socialism, atheism, and the surrender of national sovereignty. It is the same all over the world.

WRITING TASK

Write an essay that grows from your consideration of the quotation from Carl Sagan. You may use the following questions as a way of generating material for your essay.

Does war become more likely or less likely as nations invent and stockpile new weapons? Is there any way to avoid the kind of confrontations Sagan writes about? Is conflict between nations inevitable? Do you think individuals and citizen groups can influence government defense policy? Or do you feel that individuals are essentially powerless in this situation? How would you justify the defense expenditures of the United States in a debate? How would you argue against those expenditures?

9. Sharon Curtin

I am afraid to grow old — we're all afraid. In fact, the fear of growing old is so great that every aged person is an insult and a threat to the society. They remind us of our own death, that our body won't always remain smooth and responsive, but will some-day betray us by aging, wrinkling, faltering, failing. The ideal way to age would be to grow slowly invisible, gradually disappearing, without causing worry or discomfort to the young. In some ways that does happen. Sitting in a small park across from a nursing home one day, I noticed that the young mothers and their children gathered on one side, and the old people from the home on the other. Whenever a youngster would run over to the "wrong" side, chasing a ball or just trying to cover all the available space, the old people would lean forward and smile. But before any communication could be established, the mother would come over, murmuring embarrassed apologies, and take her child to the "young" side.

WRITING TASK

Write an essay that grows from your consideration of the quotation from Sharon Curtin. You may use the following questions as a way of generating material for your essay.

What are some of the ways our culture separates the old from the young? What are some of the ways we honor old people? What are some of the ways we take away their dignity? Have you ever avoided contact with an old person? Can you explain why? Are you uncomfortable around them? What is the source of the discomfort? Are there old people who are important in your life right now? In what way? Are you afraid of growing old? What do you fear most about it?

10. Morton Hunt

The record of man's inhumanity to man is horrifying, when one compiles it — enslavement, castration, torture, rape, mass slaughter in war after war. But who has compiled the record of man's kindness to man — the trillions of acts of gentleness and goodness, the helping hands, smiles, shared meals, kisses, gifts, healings, rescues? If we were no more than murderous predators, with a freakish lack of inhibition against slaughtering our own species, we would have been at a terrible competitive disadvantage compared with other animals; if this were the central truth of our nature, we would scarcely have survived, multiplied and become the dominant species on earth. Man does have an aggressive instinct, but it is not naturally or inevitably directed to killing his own kind. He is a beast and perhaps at times the cruelest beast of all — but sometimes he is also the kindest beast of all. He is not all good and not perfectable, but he is not all bad and not wholly unchangeable or unimprovable. That is the only basis on which one can hope for him; but it is enough.

WRITING TASK

Write an essay that grows from your consideration of the quotation from Morton Hunt. You may use the following questions as a way of generating material for your essay.

Humans are very critical of humanity. Why is this so? Why are newspapers and newscasts so full of man's inhumanity to man? Why do history textbooks consist largely of records of conflict? Is anything accomplished by all this attention to our failures? Is kindness boring? Why not make a contribution to the record Hunt calls for, "the record of man's kindness to man"? When did you last see an instance of human love freely given? What examples come to mind of people helping other people? Do you know of instances where one human risked his comfort or life for another? Do you recall an incident where you made yourself feel good by showing thoughtfulness to another? How about recording the time your day was brightened by the smile or kind words of someone else? Can you do it? Can you make such a paper interesting? Can you make it real rather than sentimental?

11. Ecclesiastes

To every thing there is a season, and a time to every purpose under the heaven:

A time to be born, and a time to die; a time to plant, and a time to pluck up that which has been planted;

A time to kill, and a time to heal; a time to break down, and a time to build up;

A time to weep, and a time to laugh; a time to mourn, and a time to dance;

A time to cast away stones, and time to gather stones together; a time to embrace, and a time to refrain from embracing;

A time to get, and a time to lose; a time to keep, and a time to cast away;

A time to rend, and time to sew; a time to keep silence, and a time to speak;

A time to love, and a time to hate; a time of war, and a time of peace.

WRITING TASK

Write an essay that grows from your consideration of the quotation from Ecclesiastes. You may use the following questions as a way of generating material for your essay.

What is meant by "time"? What are the contradictions in the quotation? Does the quotation capture aspects of your life? What is the "philosophical attitude" expressed in the quotation? If you find a message in the quotation, what is it? How is the quotation helpful in putting experience in perspective?

Brief Quotations

Following are twenty quotations without comments or questions. Your task is to write an essay using one or more of the quotations as an integral part of your paper. Perhaps the quotation itself will become your title; it may be your first or your last sentence; or it may be quoted elsewhere in your essay. In any case, the essay will be written in illustration of the meaning of the quotation. Notice we said "in illustration." You should not explain the quotation by saying "This quotation by Benjamin Franklin means . . ." Nor should you say "I agree with Somerset Maugham's idea" or "I disagree with Jessica Mitford's statement." These approaches are likely to result in uninteresting papers. Instead, you should describe situations, present information, or discuss your opinions with the intent of rounding out the meaning of the quotation and then use the quotation as a sort of summing up or punch line for your essay.

Some of the quotations here are quite simple and direct; others are more figurative and should not be taken literally. For example, John F. Kennedy's statement "A child miseducated is a child lost" is a simple, direct sentence that starts us thinking about the importance of education. There is no need for interpretation. But when Stephen Leacock says "Personally, I would rather have written *Alice in Wonderland* than the whole *Encyclopaedia Britannica*" he is not talking directly about these works. He is, instead, using them to represent different worlds — one of imagination and wonder and the other of fact and knowledge. In this quotation at least, he sees these worlds in opposition and says, indirectly, that the world of imagination is of more value to him. Kennedy's quotation would lead you to a paper on education. Leacock's quotation could lead you to a much broader range of possibilities. It is more open-ended, more challenging, and therefore, probably, more fun.

Today the real test of power is not capacity to make war but capacity to prevent it.
— Anne O'Hare McCormick

The family you come from isn't as important as the family you're going to have.
— Ring Lardner

This will never be a civilized country until we spend more money for books than we do for chewing gum.
— Elbert Hubbard

Beauty is the promise of happiness.
— Stendhal

The real danger is not that computers will begin to think like men, but that men will begin to think like computers.
— Sydney J. Harris

I like men to behave like men — strong and childish.
— Françoise Sagan

To find a friend one must close one eye — to keep him, two.
— Norman Douglas

The man who strikes first admits that his ideas have given out.
— Chinese proverb

We cannot defend freedom abroad by deserting it at home.
— Edward R. Murrow

We can destroy ourselves by cynicism and disillusion just as effectively as by bombs.
— Kenneth Clark

Intelligent discontent is the mainspring of civilization.
— Eugene V. Debs

The secret of education is respecting the pupil.
— Ralph Waldo Emerson

Science may have found a cure for most evils; but it has found no remedy for the worst of them all — the apathy of human beings.
— Helen Keller

I'd rather have roses on my table than diamonds on my neck.
— Emma Goldman

Man is what he believes.
— Anton Chekhov

Man prefers to believe what he prefers to be true.
— Francis Bacon

A good laugh is sunshine in a house.
— William Makepeace Thackeray

To be wronged is nothing unless you continue to remember it.
— Confucius

Never let a fool kiss you or a kiss fool you.
— Joey Adams

You grow up the day you have the first real laugh — at yourself.
— Ethel Barrymore

We always find something to give us the impression we exist.
— Samuel Beckett

WRITING TASK

Write an essay of your own design illustrating the idea expressed in one of the preceding short quotations.

Remember:

1. **Do not explain the quotation directly or make direct statements agreeing or disagreeing with its message.**
2. **Include the quotation somewhere in your paper, perhaps as a summing up or punch line for your essay.**
3. **As always, be specific. Use details and examples to support your statements.**

PART THREE

DAILY WRITING

This part includes eight week-long units of thirty-minute writing tasks. The writing you do will be free flow, a form of prewriting. Besides giving you regular practice sessions, through the use of daily writing, we're trying to show you that one way to find something to write about is to write. These thirty-minute tasks take no special skill or knowledge. For instance, one week you'll spend the thirty-minute practice sessions writing about your current life. The first thirty minutes you'll describe what's taking place in your life at the moment. For the next sessions you'll write about the contents of your wallet, purse, or medicine cabinet or about interesting activities and places. During the successive weeks, you'll write about such things as past experiences, world events, people you know, even dreams and fantasies — but for no longer than thirty minutes. Besides giving you daily practice at writing, these tasks will provide raw material that you can use as a resource for the formal assignments you'll be doing.

25 KEEPING A JOURNAL

To say it right out, this section is going to ask you to spend some time doing a great deal of writing. If you spend thirty minutes each day writing one or two pages in a notebook, your graded work will get better.

Thirty minutes! Every day?

Yes. A very simple command — *sit down and write* — but one that is hard to meet because many forces compete for attention.

One student journal writer describes her experience with the busy world this way:

> The outside world is so confusing. At times I feel I'm dreaming. I sense I'm in a forest — something from Grimm's fairy tales. I'm lost. It is night. All around me at unexpected moments creatures keep popping up out of the dark, whispering and screaming for my attention. I want to ignore them and find the path out, but some eerie fascination keeps drawing me deeper into the woods.

Like this writer, all of us at times feel the eerie fascination of the marketplace. Its pull is hard to resist. In the thirty minutes most of us spend struggling to fill a blank page, by merely flicking a TV knob we can take a fairy-tale journey across America to see the destruction left by an earthquake, tornado, or torrential rains. In an instant we can be lifted to the Middle East to see the rubble of a village left from a terrorist attack. Carried to Finland we might hear a report on the efforts of the superpowers to avoid a rerun of Hiroshima and Nagasaki. We might see the World Tennis Championship or the World Series or the Academy Awards. We certainly would hear pitches for dog food, beer, cars, deodorants, or headache or hemorrhoid remedies. With all this going on, who has time to practice writing? you might ask. No doubt it would be easier to meditate in a typhoon. Still, to improve your writing you must practice. And practice. And practice.

The practice writing you will be doing is relaxed writing — some call it free writing. When you are doing free writing your work should be unbound, snaring fleeting hunches, half-remembered experiences, and images as soon as the mind shapes them. When you are doing formal writing your work should be more controlled. Formal writing gets reports, essays, and research projects done; free writing helps you train and prepare to write reports, essays, and research projects. When doing free writing, you need not be concerned with grammar, logic, spelling, punctuation — the niceties of writing. Instead, you will work to capture the flow of your thought — limbering the writing muscles as sprinters might limber their legs before a race.

Creative People and Journals

By this point you may have gotten the impression that free writing involves more than meeting a course assignment.

It may.

Without much searching in the library you would find that creative people from all fields have written regularly in diaries, journals, daybooks, and notebooks. For many, the entries not only allowed them to express themselves by keeping a history of their experiences but also fed their life works.

If you take the trouble to search the library, you will find that Leonardo da Vinci, the great Renaissance artist and scientist, kept journal entries about his observations of birds and his theories of flight; and that nineteenth-century French painter Paul Gauguin kept a notebook that captured his memories, dreams, and thoughts on art. You would find that contemporary artist Claes Oldenberg consciously set out to generate his art from his own life and psychology. He developed a "scrapbook" of a fantasy city, and many of the details surface in his current work. Oldenberg has said, "Everything I do is completely original — I made it up when I was a little kid." He began by capturing it all in a notebook.

You would also find that psychologist Carl Jung kept a notebook he called the "Black Book." It numbers five volumes and traces his personal growth in both writing and art. The deep value of keeping a personal notebook is reflected in a comment from his autobiography, *Memories, Dreams, and Reflections:* "All my works, all my creative activity, have come from fantasies and dreams which began in 1912. Everything that I accomplished in later life was already contained in them, although at first only in the form of emotions and images."

And if you continued your search, you would find that modern photographer Edward Weston kept daybooks that chart the details of his life and the growth of his inner self and art; that an educator named John Holt kept a log of his experiences teaching elementary school children; that a young Jewish girl named Anne Frank kept a record of her life while hiding with her family from the Nazis; and that writers such as Gustave Flaubert, Henry James, F. Scott Fitzgerald, Anaïs Nin, Graham Greene, and Albert Camus kept diaries, journals, and notebooks at different times in their lives.

Journal Styles

Often a journal entry will be brief. Something — a gesture, an idea, an observation, or a bit of conversation — will capture the journal keeper's interest and will be recorded. For instance, Graham Greene's African journal published under the title *In Search of a Character* makes several brief entries dated February 10:

> The cows with the elegant snow-white birds — *pique-boeufs,* not egrets — which attend them like guardian angels. The birds are so sleek and smooth that their feathers seem of porcelain. Innumerable butterflies. . . .

> Names of Africans. Henry with a y, Attention, Deo Gratias. . . .

> Men playing mysterious game altering the number of beans that lie in rough troughs on a home-made board. . . .

> A coil of caterpillars brought home by a leper to sell or eat.

And under February 12 Greene briefly notes:

> The water at the bow of the pontoons the colour of burnt sugar.

> A first sentence perhaps: "Each day after breakfast the captain read his breviary in the deck-house." . . .

> The approach to Bakuma and the excitement of Père Henri: "my home."
> "Not your prison?"
> "No. Yonda is my prison."

In other entries Greene, whose fictional characters often face a crisis of faith, becomes more philosophical. Again from the section dated February 10:

> How often people speak of the absurdity of believing that life should exist by God's will on one minute part of the immense universe. There is a parallel absurdity which we are asked to believe, that God chose a tiny colony of a Roman empire in which to be born. Strangely enough two absurdities seem easier to believe than one.

And under March 7 he records:

> Hinduism is a tropical religion: a reaction from indiscriminate slaughter, which only happens in the tropics. For every insect one kills in Europe, one must kill a hundred at least in tropical countries. One kills without thinking — a smear on one's napkin or the pages of one's book.

Greene's fleeting details, observations, and thoughts may not have been of immediate value beyond keeping him in the habit of writing and looking hard and close at himself and life. Yet by regularly making notebook entries while on a journey through Africa, he stored away enough to draw on for a novel he titled *A Burnt-Out Case*.

Of course, not everything that goes into a notebook will find its way into a future work. Indeed, writing daily in a notebook may seem to involve a series of wasted motions. But there is one advantage. The material you collect will have a time to cool off so that later you can come back to it and begin to see how it might be used in another way.

Sometimes the entries will not be as brief as the ones from Greene but instead will be extended impressions recorded with care and in detail. Albert Camus must have made thousands of short and long entries in his notebooks. This excerpt published in *Notebooks: 1935–1942* influenced the shaping of situations and characters in his novel *The Stranger*.

> The old woman who dies in the old people's home. Her friend, the friend she has made over a period of three years, weeps "because she has nothing left." The caretaker of the little mortuary, who is a Parisian and lives at the mortuary with his wife. "Who could have told them that at seventy-four he would end up at an old people's home at Marengo?" His son has a job. They left Paris. The daughter-in-law didn't want them.
>
> Scenes. The old man finally "raised his hand." His son put them in an old people's home. The gravedigger who was one of

the dead woman's friends. They often went to the village together in the evening. The old man who insisted on following the procession to the church and then to the cemetery. Since he is lame, he cannot keep up and walks twenty yards behind. But he knows the country and takes shortcuts that enable him to catch up with the procession several times until he falls behind again.

The Arab nurse who nails down the coffin has a cyst on her nose and wears a permanent bandage.

The dead woman's friends: little old people ridden with fancies. Everything was wonderful in the past. One of them to a neighbor: "Hasn't your daughter written to you?" "No." "She might remember that she does have a mother."

The other has died — as a sign and a warning to them all.

You can see in this passage that Camus has captured an interesting situation, drawn brief portraits of the people there, suggested the setting, recorded snatches of dialogue, and responded to the entire entry by commenting on the fear that may be running through these old people: "The other has died — as a sign and a warning to them all." When he made the entry, he may not have had a hint that the "little old man" would become Perez in *The Stranger* and that the funeral would become the funeral of the central character's mother. How could he have known? This entry along with all the others are scraps from his daily experience. But by keeping them in a notebook, he had them handy when he needed them.

Of course, after an artist becomes successful the critic can analyze his or her notebook entries. Many critics like to do that. But notebook entries are not made for analysis. They are made to sustain the creative person in work and are written without concern for what future critics or the admiring public may think. So, like the artist, when you work in your notebook don't write as if some critic, whether an English teacher, a parent, or a helpful friend, is peeking over your shoulder. In your notebook you have one audience — yourself. If you wish to share your entries, that's your decision, but as a working principle, keep in mind that you're writing for you.

Where to Keep Daily Writing

Perhaps the best place to keep daily writing is in a large notebook. If you use a pocket-sized pad, you will not have room to stretch out; your writing will be cramped; you will quickly fill the pages. Soon you may be toting around several tiny volumes of daily writing — an awkward situation.

You might be tempted to use a calendar book, one of those appointment books that have the days divided into neat squares. While the calendar book may be fine for keeping records of assignments and appointments, it is too limited for free writing. After all, when your thoughts start flowing, how can you contain them in a four-by-six-inch square that represents the space for that day's entry?

Better to use a regular ten-by-eleven-inch three-ring binder. A ringed binder is more effective than a permanently bound book because the binder will give you more flexibility. Flexibility is what you want for your daily writing. You will often find time on your hands, perhaps while riding a bus, waiting for a class to begin, or just sitting in the cafeteria or library. You can use some of this free time to make an entry. If you have been storing your work in a binder, then there is no need to carry it with you. You can write an entry on any sheet of notebook paper. When you return home, all you have to do is snap open the rings and insert the new sheet or sheets.

A permanently bound book lacks this advantage. You must lug it with you. You may also wish to develop a section with a specific focus, adding entries over a period of time. You can do that with a ringed binder; you cannot with a bound book. It is also a good idea to have a section where you keep old papers, written tests, book reviews, and reports — all the writing you do in such classes as history, psychology, sociology, or geology. Often, just as practice writing in the form of a notebook entry becomes the spark to ignite a formal class assignment, an old paper can become the base for future work. A binder makes it easy to save papers that might be reworked. Of course, the choice of a book to work in is yours, and you should feel comfortable with the one you pick.

Guidelines for Practice

To get this practice rolling and to collect material to use in other assignments, in the following sections we have sketched out several weeks of journal exercises. After that you are on your own. Meanwhile, here are some suggestions for working:

1. Keep all your writing in a single book, preferably a three-ring binder. The binder will give you the flexibility you need in shuffling and rearranging your work into sections.
2. Date all entries so that you will have a chronological history of your free-writing progress.
3. Try to set aside a thirty-minute block of time to complete each exercise. Write at least two pages — two authentic pages — but do not bloat the size of your writing to fill the page. If you finish in less than two pages, write something else.

4. Write clearly enough so that you will be able to read the entry when you go back, and leave plenty of space between entries.
5. Always keep in mind that this is practice. Although the material can be reworked if you need it for a formal assignment, in your journal write it once. If you write a line or phrase you do not like, leave it and keep going.
6. Don't be concerned with mechanics. Don't stop to look up words. Don't stop to revise. Instead, write to capture the flow of your thought, the detail of experience.

26 FIRST WEEK: FREE WRITING

You have your notebook. You have set aside some time. You are ready to begin. For the first exercises you will do unfocused writing. The goal here is to write nonstop for at least twenty minutes. Don't stop to think or judge or arrange your thought — just write, letting the words pepper the page.

Some beginning writers get scared when set free. They might say, "I can't get it loose. I just shut my eyes and it's all a blank. No thought — except 'What shall I write about? What shall I write about?' Beyond that there's only a void, a big zero."

The problem is not uncommon with beginning writers, and probably it is not uncommon with professional writers either. But professional writers have learned to live with it, knowing it will pass. So here is what you do: describe your "zero." If you are sitting in a quiet place, notebook open to a fresh sheet, pen ready to start recording, and nothing comes, describe the nothing.

Here is how one student started his unfocused writing:

> I can't think . . . mind's a blank. Eyes closed. See nothing but black . . . something purple, circles expanding in the black — reminds me of a lake I visited in the Cascades. A bowl. What was it? Devil's punch bowl. I tossed a rock as far toward its center as I could. The rings. . . .

Though this entry continues by discussing the circles floating toward shore, it starts off describing the color black many of us might see if our eyes are pressed shut. Then some purple comes in the shape of expanding circles; finally, the writer's mind begins to free-associate — that is, to make loose, spontaneous connections. His mind is becoming less constrained. It is opening up for imaginary flight. If you give yours the same opportunity, it will fly, too.

One goal to keep in mind before you start free writing is to be honest. To be honest does not mean you have to confess or to "come clean," as a detective in a thirties cop film might say. Instead it means to write the truth, the kind of truth with a little *t,* not a big *T.* The little-*t* truth has to do with firsthand experience: the facts of your life, your imagination, your dreams. It is a personal truth, the truth of your life experience. This truth is uniquely yours because it is filtered through your eyes and your mind. In your daily writing, work to corral your unique experience. Remember, too, that you should be less interested in recording your interpretation — the whys behind your experience — and more interested in describing it — herding its details onto the page.

There is another kind of truth to keep in mind while making entries in your notebook — the truth of the words you use. Of course, no words are untruthful in themselves; their falsity depends on how accurately or inaccurately they are used to describe experience. All good writers try to use words accurately by being as concrete and specific as their subjects allow them. But for beginning writers that may be hard.

This is the age of the marketplace, and there is little doubt that marketplace language, the language of advertising, politics, talk shows, and so on has affected our language. All of us have spent too many hours listening to the drone of disc jockeys, TV commentators, politicians, and show business personalities for our language not to be tainted. It is safe to generalize that much of this language, if not downright false in the way it presents experience, is certainly misleading and almost always general and vague. Consider the problem ad writers face in communicating with millions of people. The size and breadth of their audience force them to be vague. They hope that by writing at the most general level they will get buyers in cities, towns, and hamlets across the nation to identify with a product and plunk down the cash to own it. They do not give buyers information; instead they try to give them feelings.

Often, the ad writer's vague language will creep into a beginning writer's prose. The beginning writer may be attempting to express a sincere feeling, but often the words smack of the ad writer's talent for saying very little. (See numbed language, p. 348.)

Here is one student's first attempt at describing a trip to the beach:

> Yesterday I spent a delightful day at the beach. Whenever I feel lost or just want to be with friends I go to the cove and lie on the sand to collect my thoughts. The sky was a New England blue.

Many of my friends were there. I have known some of them since elementary school. To see them makes me feel good. Some were flying kites, some were playing volleyball. Everyone was having a good time. It picks me up to go.

This writer may wish to be sincere, but this piece is general and vague. Not much is being said except that the writer feels good going to the beach whenever he feels "lost." What does "lost" mean? The writer doesn't confront the feeling, but going to the beach will cure the condition because thoughts can be collected and friends are doing it. At the beach everyone has a good time. Consequently, the beach will pick him up. Perhaps the writer did not know he was writing an advertisement. Still, the point here is clear: The sooner you can break the grip the marketplace has on your writing, the sooner you will become a good, honest writer.

Here is part of another brief entry that deals with the beach. This student has tried to capture the detail of the experience in concrete language. In itself the entry may seem unhinged from any point. But for notebook entries the goal is to practice and to collect raw material. This piece is fresh, unlike the first example, because the writer trusts what her eyes, ears, and nose tell her: She focuses on the actual experience, not on what she thinks about it.

Walking across the sand. Hot. The sun eating at my back. The sand so hot I feel it burning through my sandals. Bodies scattered everywhere on towels, some lying, some sitting. All of them young. Only the young come to 39th Street. They grease themselves up, streaks of silver reflecting off the grease coating their arms and backs. The beach has the smell of cocoa butter. The smell mixes with the music from portables.

In seven lines this writer has escaped the influence of the marketplace and packed her work with detail. Besides collecting some specifics she may use in a later piece, she has touched on a theme that could be expanded into a formal work — the contrast between the young and the old. In any case, she is collecting raw material and getting practice doing it.

WRITING TASK

Each day for the next five days write as fast as you can without interruption for thirty minutes. Keep the writing going. Don't stop. If you draw a blank, describe the blank — the zero, the nothing, or the void, whatever you might call it. You may be like many beginning writers and hear a voice that seems to come from some mischievous gnome riding on your shoulder. This critic is never happy with anything you write. It nags at each word and carps over sentences and condemns each paragraph. This tiny creature is a pest. If you have a critical gnome that tells you to give up, don't; there is a way to beat the gnome.

The gnome is a little like a pet. When you most want to do something, it will decide to rub up against your leg or screech or growl. But if you reach down and give it a couple of strokes, the chances are it will curl up in its favorite corner so you can finish your job. So the best way to deal with this pest is to give it a couple of strokes. You stroke it by recording what it says and by giving it credit for having said it. You might do it something like this:

> The grouchy gnome speaks, "You know you can't write. What are you doing it for? If I've told you once, I've told you a thousand times — YOU CAN'T WRITE! Now don't misunderstand me, I'm not saying you're dumb. Maybe you are, maybe you aren't. Who's to judge? BUT WRITE YOU CAN'T! So stop. Go do something you do well. Take a nap!"

If you hear a voice like this and you record it, you may find some new path to your creative depths. After all, in folklore a gnome is reputed to be a creature that lives underground and guards buried gold. Once you get past it you may be free to mine the tunnels of your imagination. In fact, by writing down its chatter you may be led to answer it; then you have a dialogue. Who knows what kind of honest encounter could come from that?

So the message for this week — and for all the weeks of the term — is to write about specific experience in concrete language. Keep writing. Keep the flow going. Remember, you are not working for perfection. You are practicing.

After thirty minutes, stop. Reread the entry; if you have anything to add, add it. As a final check, see if you have dated the entry. You might also want to jot down the day and place: "Monday, September 12, 1987 Library." Now, before you begin; go back and read the guidelines on pages 238–239.

27 SECOND WEEK: CURRENT LIFE

You spent the first week's practice doing unfocused tasks to help you capture bits and pieces of experience. This week will be slightly different. We'll give you more direction, and the exercises will focus on your current life. In the words of Henry David Thoreau, you will begin a "simple and sincere account" of your life. He writes:

> I, on my side, require of every writer, first and last, a simple and sincere account of his own life, and not merely what he has heard of other men's lives; some such account as he would send to his kindred from a distant land; for if he has lived sincerely, it must have been in a distant land to me.

The distant land Thoreau writes of is the land of the mind. Although we often work with common materials, none of us sees, smells, touches, or hears the world as anyone else does. This is what makes each mind a unique landscape.

One writer, a mother who returned to college after a five-year absence, began to chart her immediate life in this fashion:

> I'm in a place where I never seem to get anything done; the laundry, dishes, trips to the market, birthday parties, term papers. Two children with runny noses, skinned knees, and elbows — that damned skateboard — a midnight toothache. Why does it all happen at once? A cosmic question!
>
> The car breaks down; trip to the mechanic's: "Can't do it now, lady. Next Tuesday," he says. Why do I feel so weak around mechanics and hardware and paint salesmen? Real power.

Walk to the bus. Thirty minutes to school. Books dropping, wind, clouds. The rain comes. Cold, cold days.

Everything working against me.

Tuesday rolls around. Phone the mechanic and imagine him leaning back in a chair, puffing a cigar, his feet propped up on my gutted VW engine. He says, "Have it tomorrow morning. How's 'bout nine." He says it not like a question but like a command. He knows he has me trapped. Slam down the receiver and press down a scream — another day on the bus.

"Mommy, can I have a jelly sandwich" — it too is not a question it is a command: "GET ME A JELLY SANDWICH NOW!" Peanut butter, jelly, milk, cookie crumbs, gum balls — all smashed and ground into the floor. Need to scrape it off. Need a chisel.

Must read *Gatsby* by Friday.

Wednesday A.M. Back to the mechanic's: "That's $78.50." More than I had intended to spend. Oil, grease job — you bet, a grease job — brakes, spark plugs, points. "The points, lady, that's what's giving you trouble. That's why it won't start. Ought to have 'em changed at least once every two years." His cheeks, so smoothly shaved look like a barber with a straight razor did it; odd, always think of mechanics as grubby. A cynical smile — small sharp teeth under a lavish mustache. Teeth for chewing into my bankroll, teeth for biting into my time.

I need a vacation! Spring — a fantasy: I see myself flying over snow and landing in Bermuda, lying on some beach. White, white sand. Blue, blue sky. Blue, blue water. With my recent luck, blue, blue sharks. The sharks are in the surf. I'm swimming for the beach. Stroking toward safety. Why do I want a degree? I want leisure. I want escape. I wish I had a harpoon. The college is my white whale.

Overall this is a rough piece of writing, and well it should be. To be rough is the nature of free writing. No one was sitting on the writer's shoulder giving her commands about proper punctuation, spelling, and organization. Those commands come with formal writing, not with practice writing.

The only direction she was given was to write nonstop for thirty minutes about her current life. She does it, not by sitting down and figuring it out but by taking the first step on the exciting journey. She gets into the movement instead of analyzing whether what she writes will be correct. Potters do the same. They thrust their hands into the clay so that they can find out what shapes hide in their imagination. Critics have another method. They stand back and analyze the result to see if it has artistic value. The one group plunges forward and gets the job done; the other sits and calculates. Calculating is an important part of formal writing, but in free writing it can block the work.

So this writer has thrust herself into her life's flow. By groping around, she has captured the chaos and frustration that she feels is running through it by recording those fleeting thoughts and images that seem to swim just below the surface.

Often her catch is surprising. For instance, the encounter with the mechanic begins with a stereotypical image — a cigar-chomping bandit, who pridefully poses with his latest kill. The image then becomes more realistic — a meticulous man, who shaves his cheeks as carefully as a professional barber would. And finally, the image turns surrealistic — a cartoon character, perhaps a giant rabbit, who eats at her bankroll and her time as if they were hunks of lettuce.

And she uses concrete words and phrases from her daily life — not clichés as they might be gleaned from advertising, but language that comes from looking at the particulars of her world. Here are a few words and phrases taken from the lists she compiles:

laundry	jelly
dishes	milk
trips to the market	cookie crumbs
birthday parties	gum balls
term papers	oil
runny noses	grease
skinned knees and elbows	brakes
skateboards	spark plugs
midnight toothache	points
peanut butter	

Concrete words and phrases create a feeling that a work is made from more than straw and air. Snatches of dialogue help make it seem real. People talking to us are part of our daily lives. Shreds of their talk hang in our minds: If lines from a recent conversation come to you while writing nonstop, record them. This writer quotes one line from her child and several from her mechanic:

> "Can't do it now, lady. Next Tuesday. . . . Have it tomorrow morning. How's 'bout nine. . . . That's $78.50. . . . The points, lady, that's what's giving you trouble. That's why it won't start. Ought to have 'em changed at least once every two years."

And she also includes fantasy. When you are practicing writing, your mind may want to drift. If so, follow it by recording where it goes. The writer's fantasy starts in an idyllic setting — "Lying on some beach. White, white sand. Blue, blue sky" — followed by a tug back to her real life — "Blue, blue sharks." Some of a writer's richest images may come from fantasies; be sure to record yours when they appear.

Finally, our writer has uncovered some provocative questions she may wish to explore in more direct ways. "Why do I feel so weak around mechanics and hardware and paint salesmen?" "Why do I want a degree?"

For us to overexplore a single journal entry may be a mistake if you take the entry and our comments about it as a model to emulate. If you ever feel that urge, don't give in to it. We offer the example and comments as possibilities, not as formulas. Don't, like Cinderella's step sisters, try to cram your foot into another's shoe.

WRITING TASK

What follows is a group of five tasks designed to focus your practice. Each exercise will lead you to write something about your current life. In another section you will do exercises designed to lead you into your life history, but in these exercises you are to capture some of the present — the now of your life.

As a reminder, be sure to set aside thirty minutes for uninterrupted writing. Keep the pen moving across the page for the full time, trying to fill at least two pages without worrying about punctuation, grammar, or spelling. Give yourself plenty of space so your entries will not be crowded. Write legibly enough so you will be able to reread the entry. Finally, be sure to date your entry.

One last suggestion. Before you begin to write, relax a moment. Close your eyes or rest your head on the desk top. Feel your breathing. Let the breathing become rhythmical. Sometimes a minute or two of relaxation will let a busy mind clear. It will then be easier to focus and begin.

First Day: This entry is to capture where you are in your life. It might be a good idea to begin with a comment on your general situation as you sense it. For instance, in the example above, the writer begins with a broad comment: "I'm in a place where I never seem to get anything done." She then lets her mind sweep through her recent life. She records the specifics, the bits of dialogue, the frustrations, the questions, the fantasies — everything that comes to her.

You might also keep this thought in mind while you write: There is no reason to worry about whether what you record is true — true in a permanent sense. Indeed, if the woman who wrote the example had done the exercise the following week, the entry might have been completely different. Your goal is to capture the truth of the moment in as much detail as you can.

Now take a moment to relax. With your eyes closed, consider where you are in your life now. When the moment is right, begin to write your entry.

Second Day: In yesterday's entry you described where you are in your current life. Today you are going to continue the process by recording impressions of where you live.

Where you live. If you think about the phrase, it may suggest outlandish possibilities. If you have read enough science fiction, recording impressions of where you live might lead you to the outer reaches of the solar system and back to earth. But if you have a less expansive nature, you might be content to focus on your country, state, county, city, neighborhood, or house. Or if you tend to be nomadic and wish to narrow the focus further, you might describe your van. And these are just the literal possibilities. There are metaphorical ways of looking at "where you live."

If you see yourself as a spirit temporarily housed in a body, where you live — for now — could be inside a bag of skin. But for this assignment, you can skip that kind of metaphysical chin rubbing. Try instead to keep your work simple. This exercise assumes that where you live means your immediate physical surroundings — maybe your room, house, or apartment complex, but certainly nothing larger than your neighborhood.

Keep in mind that your entry need not cover every aspect of where you live. Instead try to capture fleeting impressions and details. Let your mind loose, recording the associations it makes. Perhaps your mind will connect with other places where you have lived; work those details into your entry, but always come back to your immediate surroundings. Remember, be specific. Never let your mind linger for long in general statements such as this:

> I live in a pretty white house with a big lawn and some palm trees near the center of town. I like it here. The neighbors are. . . .

Instead, get to the details and the associations they bring:

My front lawn has gone brown from the drought, but it still has two fat palms about two stories high with drooping limbs. I used to swing on them when I was a kid: Ahhhhhh — Tarzan. People could hear my scream all over town (at least my mom said they could). Ahhhhhhh, ahhh, ahhhhhhhh! But now things are different. I've gotten older and the house. . . .

Be specific. Capture the details. Now, for thirty minutes write about where you live.

Third Day: Today you can begin to take the next step in exploring your current life by making a list of the personal items in your possession. Keep in mind that a list need not be limited to naming individual items but can also include brief descriptions of the items and associations you have with them. To start the writing session you might empty the contents of your wallet or purse on the desk. Arrange the items in whatever way suits you, then begin to study them. Take them in your hand. Read the writing on the ones that have writing. Smell the ones that have smells. Read the numbers on the ones that have numbers. Then, in your own time, begin to record your list. If exploring the contents of your purse or wallet doesn't capture your interest, go to the medicine cabinet or cosmetic table. Follow the same procedure by listing the jars, bottles, tins, and toothbrushes and any associations you have with these items.

As with this week's other entries, this writing session should last for thirty minutes. Be sure to date the entry and to leave yourself plenty of space — don't crowd your entries.

Fourth Day: What are some of the activities you do? You attend classes, read, write papers, take tests; you drive, walk, bike, or ride a bus to school; you sleep and roll out of bed in the morning; you talk with friends, teachers, parents; you may also hold a job. Many activities you do are commonplace; many, many people do them. The fact that people do them doesn't mean they're not important; they are. But you probably need less routine activities that add more meaning or pleasure to your life.

For today's writing you can begin by drawing up a list of activities you do or wish you did, not because you are forced to do them by the necessities of living but because you want to. Then from the list select one or two activities to write about. Record everything that comes to you: how it feels to do it; why you like it; how long you've been doing it. Record the associations you have with it; these might include the different times and places you've done it. While recording the entry, use specific language. This student entry about jogging starts off fuzzy, a way many writers begin, then goes past the general comments to the particulars of the experience:

> I like jogging because it makes me feel good. After I finish jogging, I relax. My body is limber — limber, reminds me of lumber. That's how I start in the mornings, my legs like pieces of lumber — I lumber along. But after I run for a while, I feel limber, like a birch tree in the wind. I like the sound of my feet slapping the asphalt and the sound of breathing deep in my chest. I like to jog on cold mornings. Once there was frost on the grass. I ran across the park. Crunch, crunch, crunch.

Keep in mind that you are still working under the thirty-minute time limit — so work fast. Try not to spend time evaluating your writing; just write. Leave yourself plenty of space between and within entries. Be sure to date the entry at the top.

Fifth Day: Where you are in your life now, the place you live, the items and activities that compose your current life — all these practice entries have helped collect experience that you can begin to use in your formal work. Start looking for opportunities to use them. Now, to conclude this week's daily practice, you will write about special places in your current life.

Once again, start by sitting quietly and letting your thoughts settle. Then begin to randomly list places that come to mind. These special places need not be your favorite spots, ones you associate with pleasure; they may also be places you associate with discomfort, such as a doctor's or dentist's office. Perhaps one or two places on your list will be secret places, spots you may visit for a moment or two when the world seems to be coming down around your shoulders, such as a rock overlooking a field, a window looking out to a yard or street, or a couch in a quiet place in your home.

The list you draw up may include places that are not so special but that you recorded because you listed as many as possible. Whether each place you record is truly a special place is not the point of the listing process. The listing process is to pull out a great deal of material in a short time. For example, here is a part of one student's list of special places:

the mountains: love the cool breezes that hum through the pines

the beach: but not with people — people everywhere, an anthill

restaurants: Salernos — ummmmm! El Torito, but only on Fridays
   between four and six. El Tapito: carnitas, jalapeños, flautas

I like: my shower
   the park in early morning
   sitting in the quad
   my granddad's garage — cans of old paint, rusted tools,
   pipes, bicycle parts, at least a dozen alarm clocks — all waiting to be fixed.

Notice the phrases that follow some of the items on the list. They add the concrete details; often they are lists themselves. This kind of random listing helps writers cover a great deal of territory so that they can find out what might be worth exploring more completely.

Now it is time for you to begin. During this practice session, take the first ten minutes to draw up your list of special places and record some associations you might have with the spots. Then after ten minutes, select one or two to write about more completely. Be sure to practice for the full time.

28 THIRD WEEK: PAST LIFE

Your notebook is beginning to fatten from collecting the scraps of your present life. In many ways your notebook may begin to work like an artist's sketchbook, except your practice is done with words rather than lines and curves. Artists practice figure drawing through a series of quick studies — fast sketches of arms, hands, fingers. They may sketch finger joints and nails. Other parts of the body will fill other pages — stomachs, chests, shoulders, and necks. An artist may have done heads and faces from several angles. No sketch is a finished piece, yet someone who flipped through all the pages would get an impression of a whole body.

The same is true of the entries you have made thus far. If someone were to scan them, though the entries are fragmented — works in progress — he or she would go away with a feeling for the whole. Of course, in the case of your notebook, the parts are not of a figure but of your life. Certainly you have not been consciously composing an autobiography, but only capturing a series of passing impressions and immediate associations that make up your life in motion — a view caught on the run. And finally, like artists working to develop their skill with form, you too have been practicing to become more limber at the writing craft.

During this week's thirty-minute writing sessions, you will practice by continuing to capture experiences from your life. This week's exercises will have a basic difference from previous ones: Instead of dealing with the present you will deal with the past.

If you've watched your mind during the last two weeks of notebook entries, you have seen how it hops around. You may have wanted to keep it on a straight path, but it probably acted like a rabbit erratically skipping, stopping to nibble, then dashing off down a trail. No doubt you have already captured experiences and feelings from your past by following these associations. They are embedded in your previous entries. Do you recall the example used to illustrate the exercise asking you to describe where you live? It began:

> My front lawn has gone brown from the drought, but it still has two fat palms about two stories high with drooping limbs.

After the opening, this writer's mind starts associating. He connects with the past, and for a line or two he's a kid again, swinging from vines like Tarzan.

> I used to swing on them when I was a kid: Ahhhhhh — Tarzan. People could hear my scream all over town (at least my mom said they could). Ahhhhhhh, ahhh, ahhhhhhhh!

He records the association with the past, then he returns to his original intent — to record the details of where he lives.

The point here is that the mind naturally leaps to the past. It acts like a time traveler who is not a prisoner of calendars and clocks. If you link up with past experiences, record them. This kind of practice writing is supposed to rouse associations. Memories and images should be hooking together from all parts of your experience.

Now, in order to keep the work going, this week's exercises will give you a way of nudging your memory so you can capture more details that may be of use to your formal writing. But first, here's how not to do it. Don't sit at your desk with your fingers clutching a pen and in cold blood start hacking out an autobiography. After about three minutes and forty-five seconds you'll feel as if some half-educated surgeon has cut open your skull, taken out your brain, and put it in the freezer.

Better to begin less directly. Better to let the mind do its skipping, nibbling, and dashing away. And then better to use that natural energy to sketch those parts of your past that seem to connect to your current life.

It can be done in two phases: first, by making a list of brief entries that span your life; and second, by taking the entries separately and enlarging them.

WRITING TASK

First Day: Make a series of brief entries in the form of an extended list that spontaneously captures memories from your past. The key word is *spontaneously,* for the goal here is not to capture only the most important events in your life — although they may be on your list — but to let the memories and images from your past come uncalled. Their relative importance to the movement of your life is not your concern. So work to create your list spontaneously and try to record each entry in no more than two or three lines. For example, here is a list of random experiences recorded by photographer Edward Weston in one of his notebooks under the heading "Notes from N.Y., 1922":

> Near the "penny bridge," a few steps from my room (Columbia Heights).
>
> Morning coffee with Jo from the purple cup sister gave me.
>
> The Hurdy Gurdy man who played to our window.
>
> The lone man who wandered by playing a softly quavering flute; 30 years ago. I must have heard the same man in Chicago. "God bless you sir for the money. I surely needed it."
>
> Almost daily I haunted the bridges, Brooklyn or Manhattan. One Sunday I walked over Williamsburg Br. at sunset — then down among the tenements on Rivington Street — memorable night.
>
> Two "specials" from Tina, each with $20.00 enclosed: "knowing that I would need money, that I must see Balieff's *Chauve Souris.*"

You may find deciphering Weston's brief entries impossible. Sure, you can pick up some references to common places, but the experiences behind the entries belong to Weston. Of course, journal keeper Weston does his work for himself without being concerned if a reader can understand the entries. He drops a bucket into his experience and may be surprised at what it holds when he hoists it up. Yet no one else, while the details are in rough form, may even appreciate his catch.

Now here is a list of entries written by a student journal keeper. Like Weston's, these also seem fragmented — written in a personalized code:

> — I remember walking to school on a cold morning. It had rained — puddles covered with thin ice. Mountains with snow.
>
> — Graduating from high school. The speech seemed like hours. Fear. Thought I could never do it.

- Running on the mountain trail. A trip with dad. A cabin. Fishing. Hated the smell on my hands.
- Living in the city. Once a man stopped me on the way to school. "Got a quarter, missy? Give me your lunch money." I ran.
- My first real date. Must have taken three hours to get ready. Spilled a Coke in my lap.
- Flunked geometry — the end of the world. Thought all hell would break loose. Mom shrugged her shoulders. Dad said to take it over.
- Mom and dad divorced. Took me a year before I could say the word.
- Away to school. Mixed feelings. Couldn't wait to get out of the house. Yet scared.
- Bobby K. shot. Remember my mom weeping. Train going across the TV screen. I was 9. Didn't mean much to me.

This writer dips deeply into her past. In fact, the list appears to stretch from early memories to more recent ones. The list also includes the ups and downs of experience. Often when making life history lists of this sort, writers tend to consciously exclude difficult times. But if the mind finds its own course, the list will include both good and bad memories. Finally, notice that the list goes beyond the personal by including a memory of Robert Kennedy's assassination. Although changes, especially traumatic events, may be beyond our control, they still affect our lives. If these kinds of memories come to you, record them. Notice also that the writer quickly ties Kennedy's death to her personal world. That's natural. We see the world from our own situation.

Now, let's go back to see what this writer has done to complete the first step in recording material from her life. Her goal was simple. She had only to sit for a few moments in quiet and let the memories come to the surface. She did it by sending her thought into the past, as far back as she could. Then by letting it move forward across years of memory to the present, she randomly recalled a handful of experiences. She continued to sit quietly for a few more moments. Finally, after the strongest memories, the ones that held her interest, presented themselves, she recorded them in a few lines. She didn't judge if they were the most important. She didn't criticize herself for having any particular memory; she merely listed them on a sheet of paper in enough detail to recall them when rereading at another time.

For this first half-hour session develop a list of memories from your past. Begin by sitting quietly and directing your thought to the past. Then record in two or three lines a half dozen to a dozen of the strongest memories that come to you. They may not be big events in your life, but for the moment they will hold your interest. Be sure to write legibly enough to reread your entries, and leave plenty of space around them. And finally, after you finish the list, reread it and write the dates when the events took place.

Second through Fifth Days: During the rest of this week's writing sessions, you will work by expanding four entries from your list. In a way each memory you've listed is like a doorway to your past. To write a brief entry is to open the door just a crack. To expand the entry is to swing the door open wide. Behind it will be a story or heaps of detail that you may have forgotten. This recalled detail can work as material for other writing. But even if you never use it, the writing practice will aid in limbering your style. The fear of confronting the blank page — if that fear is one of your hobgoblins — will lose some of its witchery.

But before you begin, here's another example that illustrates what you are supposed to be doing. Recall the list used to illustrate the last exercise. One entry dealt with the assassination of Robert Kennedy:

> Bobby K. shot. Remember my mom weeping. Train going across the TV screen. I was 9. Didn't mean much to me.

The writer selected this entry to expand. She sat quietly for thirty minutes and recorded the thoughts that came to her while focusing on the memory.

> March 7, 1978: Bobby K. killed
>
> I was nine then — I didn't know what being nine meant. I didn't know that it was a good time to be alive, a time to play, and laugh, and innocently cry. Crying was something you did when you got hurt or wanted your way. But looking back I can remember sensing the sadness my mother felt when Bobby Kennedy was shot. I didn't know about politics then. I only knew it usually took the TV away from me. Politics and the news. Neither were very much fun for me then. They're not now, either. I remember getting out of bed. My mother was

watching the news and she was crying. I asked her why — I was confused. It was the first time I had seen her cry and I didn't see her cry again until dad left — then they were both crying. She said that a great man had died — she didn't say "was shot" — only that he died. I put the "was shot" in later. I remember being upset at first because I knew to die wasn't good, but then because I was missing the programs I liked to watch — then I think it was Captain Kangaroo or maybe Soupy Sales. How stupid a kid is — no that's not fair, not stupid but innocent. That's the key. Maybe that was my first step out of innocence — the death of Bobby K. and my not knowing what it meant. After that my family began to break up. After that . . . there's a lot of after thats. They all seem to lead to where I am now, at college, and it seems that many, many people like Bobby K., only who are not so well known, are being murdered every day by bombs and bullets and clubs. Sometimes I wish I were nine again. Nine and just cuddled up in front of Captain K. Sometimes I wish I had never learned about Bobby K.

Did you notice how the entry begins with the focus then starts to skip and hop? It moves from the far past to the present and pauses at places in between. The writer doesn't linger with any one thought but records whatever comes to her in relation to the focus.

Each day for the rest of the week, reread the list of memory experiences. Select the one you feel most curious about. Then for thirty minutes expand it by recording whatever comes to mind.

29 FOURTH WEEK: DAILY ACTIVITIES

In this week's writing sessions you will describe daily experiences from the inside or the outside. Feel free to do whichever you wish — or do both.

Though there are a couple of ways of going about it, a description of the day is an exercise close to traditional diary keeping. To do it writers sit down (usually in the evening) and describe the highlights of their experience from the time they crawled out of bed to the time they took up the pen. The danger in this kind of entry is that it can become routine and dull. A typical example might begin like this:

> John called this morning. We talked for two hours about which college he should attend. He went through the entire list — UCLA, U. of Arizona, Berkeley. . . .

And so on.

If this entry were to continue in this fashion, it would give the writer practice — and that's what we want — but it would be lifeless.

Let's take the subject of lifeless writing a bit further. By this time you've probably found that writing comes more easily when your emotion gets involved. Emotion gives prose energy, and when yours comes into play, you may find it tough for the hand holding the pen to keep up with the mind generating the words. You may even feel transported, as if you had leaped into another space. If you reach that state of deep involvement, great. Stick with it. Later, if you wish to integrate a journal entry into a piece of formal writing, you bring in the intellect to prune the overgrown first effort.

The problem you'll be facing in this task is how to pump life into routine entries.

It's easy: Describe them from the inside. Get your emotion involved and expand your entries by including feelings and insights. Describe the emotional nuances, those subtle messages behind so many of your experiences, the ones you may seldom listen to. This is writing from the inside. Here is the preceding entry rewritten, after a routine beginning from the inner perspective.

> John called this morning. We talked for two hours about which college he should attend. He went through the entire list — UCLA, U. of Arizona, Berkeley . . . the list seemed endless. And he had to go through the pluses and minuses of each one. I wanted to scream, to slam down the receiver, to escape. All those thoughts were running through my mind. Then I realized he was truly confused. I listened more carefully. He said things like, "Berkeley has a great name, but that town scares me. I like the campus, but there is something wrong with the feeling there. It's the town. And I don't want to live in a dorm." As I listened, and he went through a similar routine with each school, I realized he was scared. He didn't want to leave home. Then I realized something about myself. I was feeling scared, too. Maybe that's why I wanted off the phone — his fear was tugging at mine. Then I thought, well, why shouldn't we be scared? We were both born here and neither of us has lived anyplace else.

The writer has gone beyond routine practice by recording feelings and insights — the emotional responses that connected him to the entry.

In contrast, outside entries involve describing something you saw that held your attention. To write an outside entry, take the point of view of the detached observer, someone who is not part of the event yet captures it in writing as a photographer might snap a photograph. This kind of exercise is often associated with the professional writer who collects random material for a future work. Whatever you record as a detached observer doesn't need to be earthshaking, but it should be sufficiently interesting to make you pause when you see it. One notebook keeper recorded this entry describing a boy trying to fly a kite:

> *Sitting in the park:* A little boy about six was trying to fly a kite. He was in the center of a grassy area. His father sat nearby, smoking a pipe. The boy carefully laid out about ten feet of kite string. He then lined the kite up at the end. Next, while holding the stick with the excess string wrapped around it, he ran toward the trees, the kite bumping along behind him. Finally, he stopped

and flopped on the ground to rest. A minute or two later he reset the kite and ran back toward his father. Finally, after several runs, the father took the pipe from his mouth and shouted, "There's no wind." The boy was again laying out the string and the now tattered kite. He stopped, turned to his dad and said, "Dad, I run and make wind."

This entry has been done from an objective viewpoint — from the outside. Whether you choose to record daily experiences as an outsider who is merely describing an event or as an insider who includes emotional responses, you will get practice putting experience into words.

WRITING TASK

For this week's thirty-minute practice sessions each day, record highlights of your day or interesting events you observed during the day.

30 FIFTH WEEK: DREAMS AND FANTASIES

This week will take your writing practice into another dimension. So far you've recorded unfocused entries and collected material from your current life and daily experiences. You've also collected memories. Now you'll collect dreams and fantasies.

Dreams offer excellent material for those who say, "Nothing ever happens to me. My life is so uninteresting. I have nothing to write." Well, dreams are often full of excitement. They take dreamers into landscapes and situations they might never be able to imagine while awake. One notebook keeper recorded this dream:

THE CAVE

I found myself in a strange land . . . a combination of wooded mountains and barren desert. All around me were pines, rivers, and lakes — there were even patches of snow. Yet the land was also a desert with volcanic rocks and ancient lava flows. I was walking through pine groves that seemed to be growing out of rock. It was hot, the sun like a desert sun. I came to a stream, and though I wanted to rest, I decided to move on — I felt I had an appointment, although I wasn't sure what kind. I crossed the stream, the cold water swirling around my calves. Soon I left the trees and began to walk across a wasteland, a place that looked like a moonscape. I wanted to turn back — to go to the stream — but I couldn't. I began to climb a hill with a steep grade that ended at the face of a cliff. Rocks kept slipping under my feet. Finally, when I reached the foot of the cliff, I noticed a cave and walked to its entrance. The mouth was so black it looked as if it had been painted on the rocks with tar. I became uneasy. I wanted to go in; after all, I had come this far — or so I thought. But I couldn't bring myself to take the step into the darkness. I woke without entering the cave.

Is a dream seen or felt as intensely as the "real" experiences we record from our day? Though the setting seems to come from a mythic land, the writer's dream is described with all the intensity of a waking experience. She has concentrated on capturing the particulars of her dream journey, attempting to give us as full a picture as her writing skills allow. This picture not only is concrete but includes her feelings.

If you are one of those people who forgets dreams, you can record fantasies. Some people call fantasizing "wool gathering" or "castle building in Spain" or "middle-distance staring" or just plain "daydreaming."

Daydreaming has the quality of "tuning out," of taking a momentary leave of absence by stepping from the realistic world of objects, people, and tasks and into an imaginary space filled with private creations or recreated combinations from daily life — pictures in the mind's eye. Daydreaming! A trip to Araby with tales of a thousand and one nights.

A child dawdling over a math problem who begins to mumble about space creatures and galactic wars, punctuating his thoughts with zooms from passing star ships; the history student who suddenly realizes she has read ten pages and can't recall doing it; the professor who falls into a profound silence while staring at the chalkboard — all are daydreaming. Even Albert Einstein, the scientist who described relativity, daydreamed. He once asked a friend, "Why is it I get my best ideas in the morning while I'm shaving?"

Einstein's question brings up an interesting point. People may need daydreams to allow the mind to relax for ideas to emerge. Most of us have used expressions such as "it came from the blue," "the idea just popped into my head," or "it suddenly hit me." These experiences usually come when the intellect has dropped its guard and the intuition begins to shape itself into the images of the imagination.

Daydreams come in two varieties — brief and extended. Brief daydreams are more like hunches and insights, yet they have the quality of stepping into another space. Whenever you have one, jot it down and add it to your notebook. Extended daydreams, on the other hand, may have recurred during our lives. These are the ones you especially want to record during this week's sessions. They offer more material for practice.

Here's an example of a recurring daydream written by a young man raised in the city:

FLY-FISHING

Ever since I saw a film about Ernest Hemingway's life I have wanted to fly-fish. Not such a big wish, but one that is totally unrelated to my life. I've never even been to the mountains, let alone waded in a stream with hip boots. Still, I have this vision of myself like the guy who played Nick Adams (Nick Adams was supposed to be Hemingway) in the early parts of the film, pulling in a trout. My daydream usually goes something like this:

The scene — early morning. The sun coming through thick pines.

The action — I crawl from my tent, stretch, and breathe deep from the fresh mountain air. The world seems great. I kick a log on the fire, which has been smoldering all night, and toss on some chips. Leaning down, I blow on a few hot embers. The flames flare up. Then I decide to catch some fresh fish for breakfast. I take up the pole that has been leaning against a tree next to my fishing vest.

Of course, the piece continues to the end of the fantasy. One technique this writer uses is to begin with a brief background statement. That's fine. If you decide to record a daydream and you know its background, include it.

WRITING TASK

During your five thirty-minute writing sessions this week, practice by recording dreams and/or fantasies. They need not be current — if you have dreams and fantasies that you recall from different times in your life, record them. While practicing, write as concretely as you can. Include details. Finally, be sure to keep to the task for thirty minutes. If you finish describing a dream or fantasy in less than thirty minutes, write another entry. Perhaps you will want to include your thoughts on the dream or fantasy. Also, after you have made the entry you may want to give it a title. Sometimes dream and fantasy entries have the qualities of brief narration. A title can highlight the main element.

31 SIXTH WEEK: PORTRAITS AND RELATIONSHIPS

Some entries never seem finished. Dreams and fantasies may come neatly packaged with beginnings, middles, and ends, but memories are seldom as tidy as dreams and fantasies. Often, by tugging on a thread of some distant experience you may begin to unravel large parts of your personal history. You record and record and record yet seem unable to reach an end. Thirty minutes pass. Soon you've worked into the early morning — when to stop?

Well, there is no true stopping place — there is only an arbitrary one determined by the thirty-minute time limit or by the feeling that it's comfortable to step out. You see, a journal is as open-ended as life itself. We don't live a life neatly packaged like TV programs. We live an organic process. When we write about it — even for writing practice — we may become involved in its intricacies.

If you're feeling uncomfortable about the open-ended nature of some of your entries, we suggest you return to them and add more detail. Or, as you already may have found to be true, the details you left unrecorded in one entry may surface in another. This week's practice will give you a chance to pick up some of the material you may have left unrecorded, for you will be writing portraits of people in your life.

To begin the portraits we suggest you develop a list of people from your past as well as your present. Keep in mind that these people should hold some significance for you. They should be people you've been emotionally connected to, not people who just casually passed through your life. It is the emotional connection that will fuel these practice entries. Now, a way to develop the list is to return to those parts of your notebook where you collected details from your current life and where you expanded entries from your memory lists. Reread those sections and make a separate list of people who appear in them. Your list should be more than a simple record of names; it should also include some brief comments to locate the people in your life.

For instance, here are three entries from an extended list developed by one student:

> Martha K: See her often. Sometimes we walk down University where the sycamores drop their leaves. No real commitment, just comfortable with her. We sometimes have lunch — introduced me to lox and cream cheese on bagels.
>
> Old Ben: Vietnam. Playing with blocks, Tinkertoys. Fishing at the jetty. Taught me about death.
>
> John C: Three years together on the football team — left and right halfbacks. Everyone called us Heckle and Jeckle. "He's Jeckle," we both once said, while pointing at each other.

Notice that this partial list includes specifics. The writer does not slap a few general comments on the page and leave it at that. If he had, an entry might read like this:

> Martha K: A real swell person. I like to walk and have lunch with her.

But instead the writer has worked in details — "where the sycamores drop their leaves . . . introduced me to lox and cream cheese on bagels" — along with some general words that suggest the quality of the relationship — "No real commitment . . . comfortable." The use of specific detail makes writing come alive.

After developing a list of people, the next step is to select someone from the list to use for your portrait. At first glance a portrait may suggest a physical description, but yours will be much more. Besides physical and personality impressions, you'll include some background information and describe some experiences you've shared with the person. If you are writing a portrait of someone from the past and the entry leads to recent experience that connects to those early points in your life, record those details just as you did in other entries.

So this kind of portrait goes beyond a limited physical rendering; it attempts to show an evolving relationship. Here's a portrait expanded from an entry on the writer's list above:

I can remember playing and learning from a man I used to know as Old Ben. I'm not sure how he came to be called Old Ben, maybe because of his white, white hair that seemed to get blown every which way whenever a breeze came up. And his face was wrinkled and a deep tan from spending a lot of years in the outdoors. His laugh, though, was young. Whenever something pleased him he would laugh at the sky. He had a way of lowering his upper lip when he laughed — I guess to cover his front teeth which were chipped and partly brown, as if rust was slowly taking them over.

When I first met him I was about seven. It was a tough time. My dad flew helicopters for the navy, rescuing downed pilots somewhere off the coast of Vietnam. At that time I couldn't understand what war meant — sure, I saw war films on TV and played combat with neighbor kids, but it was all a game. Because my father was gone, my grandfather used to come to stay with me when my mom had errands to run. That's how I met Old Ben — he came with my grandfather. My grandfather didn't care much for children, or at least that's what I thought then, because he would always sit in an easy chair and read. But Ben was different. He would always want to get down and play with me. He loved to build with Lincoln Logs (I had an old set that belonged to my father) and Tinkertoys. I can remember trying to keep his constructions together from one visit to the next. I would try to copy them; that's how much I liked him. Of course, I would always fail. For some reason I would end up needing a particular piece that would be in the middle of whatever he built. So when I would try to work it free, all the other pieces would cave in around my hand.

Once Old Ben and I went fishing. When I think about him now, I understand — I guess I should say appreciate — how patient he was. Last summer I watched a kid fish with his dad. The boy must have been about the age I was when Ben took me. The boy couldn't let his line stay put — reeling it in, shouting for his dad to put more bait on the hook and then to help him cast it out. His father was trying to fish also, but the demands of his son didn't give him time to do it. Finally, the father got angry. He shouted something at the boy, then reeled in the boy's line and put the pole away. The boy cried, trying to choke back the sobs. Now when Ben took me fishing, he never tried to fish himself, he just sat on a nearby rock and smoked a pipe while giving me simple advice. And once in a while when my line got tangled, he'd get up to help. Whenever I fish I think of Old Ben.

But Ben taught me more than fishing and how to build with

Lincoln Logs and Tinkertoys — he taught me about death. My father was killed in a crash — that's a whole other entry and I don't want to go into it now. Everyone in the family came to our house. I remember some woman, later I found out she was an old cousin, who was somewhere in her seventies, coming out of the crowd and leaning her powdered face to me — I can still smell the perfume — and saying, "It was the Lord's will. Your father is with the Lord."

Later, I asked Ben about what the woman had said. He kind of smiled, keeping the upper lip over his teeth. He said, "That probably made her feel good to believe it." Then I asked him what he thought death was. He said it was up to each person to decide for himself. And the only way to do it was to spend some time studying death.

The idea of studying death hit a curious note in my mind. About three years later I had a chance to do it: Ben gave it to me. He had a stroke and was sent to the hospital to recover. Of course he didn't — the stroke had paralyzed his right side and he couldn't talk. He couldn't even smile because half his face was paralyzed and his lip had a permanent lifeless droop. I used to visit him when my grandfather went. My grandfather would read aloud to Ben, never really noticing what was going on around him. While my granfather was spending his time in books, I looked into Ben's eyes. They always seemed to be staring back at me and asking whether or not I was learning.

Notice that the entry goes back into the writer's life. It connects to some very important parts of his life — the separation from his father and the death of his father. The writer skirts these large concerns by focusing on Ben, but they lie behind most of the entry's detail. If the writer continues to keep a notebook, he will probably describe these experiences. Once you learn to trust free writing, you'll find that notebook entries often lead to the important experiences in your life. Your entries may not go directly to the target, but they get there in their own fashion something like a boomerang tossed in one direction and coming back in another.

Notice also that in this potrait the writer gives more than a physical description and personality sketch of Ben. Certainly these descriptive facts are in the piece, but they speak beyond ordinary description by suggesting the deep relationship developing between the writer and Ben. It is easy to see that Ben becomes a surrogate father by serving as a sometime playmate, teacher, and model. He even becomes a teacher for the final lesson of life — death. The father's death took place un-naturally and at a distance. The writer could only participate in the rituals, which were probably marred by insensitive comments as suggested by the appearance of the aged cousin. Ben's death takes the writer beyond cosmetics.

Finally, notice that there is tension in this portrait — the entry is built on opposition. This is suggested by the implied contrasts between Ben and the grandfather. Although the writer does not develop the difference, in fact may not even be aware that it is developing as he writes, two conflicting views of life emerge. Ben wants to get into the boy's world: to play at building, to show him how to fish, and ultimately to teach him about death. We see the grandfather with his nose poked in a book. He seems uninterested and withdrawn. This kind of natural tension deepens the entry by helping the writer to capture a universal truth.

We may be overevaluating a notebook entry. That's not what practice in a notebook is for. Yet, if you find subjects in your daily writing that capture your interest, return to them with the idea that they can be expanded. Those interests that naturally emerge from practice are valuable to develop the emotion needed to give writing life. This portrait is still rough, as most notebook entries are. But it offers raw material for an original paper.

WRITING TASK

First Day: **Spend your practice time today developing a list of people to use for possible portraits. You can go about doing it in two ways. First, you might draw together a memory list by sitting quietly and allowing your mind to roam throughout your life history. As the names of important persons come to you, jot them down. Another way to draw up a list is by browsing through your previous entries to find references to persons who may be important to you. Put these people on your list. Remember to add brief comments about the relationship and the experiences you've shared with them. In other words, this is to be an extended list, full of detail and observation.**

Second Day through Fifth Day: **Each day select one person from your list. Spend your practice time describing the relationship you've shared with the person. Remember to include more than physical details. Include all that comes to you about the relationship.**

32 SEVENTH WEEK: SOCIAL ISSUES

So far the bulk of your practice writing has been done by focusing on the personal aspects of your life. By concentrating on current activities, dreams, fantasies, memories, and people from your past and present, you were guaranteed subjects you knew well and had strong feelings about. These subjects acted as flywheels to keep your notebook entries moving. You will still be working with personal responses during this week's sessions, but the exercises will have a new twist. They will take you to places located beyond your personal domain.

Although we may wish to escape them, the reality of our lives doesn't let us isolate ourselves from issues of social importance. Questions about such issues as crime, poverty, abortion, ecology, energy, political corruption, industrial chicanery, and international terrorism often take up our emotional and intellectual energy. Since these and many other issues are part of the larger social fabric, we must deal with them, at least on a personal level.

Often these larger-than-our-personal-life issues — these "big issues" — are the ones beginning writers most want to confront in formal assignments. After all, the big issues are the backbone of most academic courses. They dominate sociology, psychology, history, anthropology, and literature. Their dominance may lead beginning writers to feel as if their personal experiences are not important. This attitude could be the reason many students choose to write about the Mafia controlling American politicians instead of vandalism in their own neighborhoods, or to write about the moral implications of abortion instead of the effects of abortions on people they know. Or to write about the American way of death instead of the death of a friend or relative.

Although in short formal papers the big issues are too large to cover, they can give you the opportunity for writing practice. Using them as a center for daily writing gives you a chance to creatively explore your relationship to issues beyond your immediate influence. But first you need to find out what interests you — to identify your social concerns.

The way to begin is to start your first writing session by sitting quietly and making a list of issues beyond your direct influence, the ones that occupy your thoughts or conversations. Don't formulate a position. Don't be overdetailed. Merely jot down a word or two so you'll be reminded of the concern that lies behind the issue. Here's an example of one student's concerns:

> noise
> abortion? not so sure!
> terrorism
> cigarette smokers — all smokers
> language
> whales — ecology
> killing/battering children
> not killing murderers (execution): capital punishment
> trucks

No one told this writer what should be important. Her job was to sit quietly and let some concerns she has about issues beyond her control come to mind. She listed them very quickly. Then after she collected a handful, she took the exercise to the next step.

The next step is to reflect on the issues a little more. The writer returned to the list and recorded in a few phrases the thoughts she had about the entries. Here's what a few of her fleshed-out entries look like:

> Noise: Portable radios blaring at the beach and pools, FM blasting in clothing shops, beauty parlors, restaurants, the cafeteria — everywhere. I can't seem to get away. Like music, all kinds, but when it's played too loudly and blares from third-rate speakers, it isn't music, it's torture. Maybe my focus here is the inconsiderate people who play music in public places.
>
> Abortion: For some reason abortion is on my mind. Have no clear feelings about it. Just confusion. Hasn't touched my life.
>
> Smokers: Tie in with music. Smoking in public places inconsiderate. I feel rage when around a smoker in a restaurant. They can kill themselves, but I don't want them fouling up my air. What about cars? Smog? The smog from cars is killing.
>
> Language: Never thought about language until I took a critical thinking course. Whenever I hear a politician speak, I feel stupid — rather, I used to feel stupid — now I know better.

Many of them use vague, deceptive language to fool the people — and that's me, a people. I want to get on the politicians' cases. And TV also.

Remember, first draw up a brief list, then flesh out each item with your general observations.

Once the list is complete and the observations have been added, you'll select one item at a time to extend. Just as you've done in other journal-keeping tasks, you'll write everything that comes to mind during the practice time. As an illustration, here's an expanded item from the above list. Notice how the writer lets her mind drift with the subject. She includes details from the current news, history, and films.

Terrorism: Should have written it with an exclamation point. But what do I truly know about terrorism? Very little. But to write a notebook entry I don't have to know anything. I just need to feel something about it, and I need to write my feelings.

–A kid in a vacant lot. Several of us. Billy K. had matches and firecrakers. Was near the 4th, hot, hot summer. Billy stuffed a firecracker into an anthill, lit the wick. Boom! The ants began to swarm. Lit several more. Boom! Boom! Boom! Ants going crazy. Then he lit some weeds and began to fry the swarming ants. I watched, yet knew something was wrong with doing what Billy was doing.

–Remember *Experiment in Terror,* film on TV with Glenn Ford as the cop. A heavy breather terrorized a young woman and her sister.

–Films of Nazi Germany concentration camps (the word "concentration" seems out of place, the Nazi politicians/ propagandists). The Uris novel, forget the title. Jews escaping to Israel before it was Israel.

–Middle East, hijackings, assassinations, burning buses, exploding bombs. Death. Red Brigade, kidnapping, S.L.A., Patty Hearst — victim or criminal. What is all this adding up to? My thoughts are expanding but seem so confused. How do I feel about terrorism? Fascinated — sickened.

Somehow it's all mixed in with people wanting change. If change doesn't come, the terrorists attack — beat the opponent to the ground, make a midnight call — "if you value your life" — or blow up a plane or school or movie theater. Stupid. I think of the opening scenes from *The Wild Bunch.* The gang shooting up the town parade. Many slaughtered. The innocent, that's what cuts me. Children or just happy folks, everyday people, destroyed by some crazies who come out of nowhere. Boom! For no real reason.

Glancing at this example you can sense the difficulty the writer has in dealing with a large subject like terrorism. She doesn't have a great deal of information about terrorism, so once she lets her mind go, thoughts of her past come up, associations she has with terrorism from childhood. The childhood memory of terrorizing the ants echoes the sense of helplessness with which the journal entry ends.

WRITING TASK

First Day: **Begin by listing the big issues in your life. Then, once the list is complete, flesh out each item by adding your general observations.**

Second through Fifth Day: **Each day spend your practice period by expanding one item from your list of big issues. Let your mind roam freely. Collect the associations you make with the issue.**

33 EIGHTH WEEK: SELF-REFLECTION

You have been practicing for several weeks by exploring a subject close to you — your life. We hope you are beginning to sense the scope of self-exploration. People, places, memories, feelings, objects, events, books, films, music, dreams, even unharnessed thought — all fall into that vast, partially charted territory called your life. We also hope you have made some discoveries about yourself. One of the side benefits of pursuing daily writing in a notebook is the self-examination that comes with accumulating a record of your life experiences.

If you were to ask around, you would find that educators disagree on what kinds of knowledge people need to learn to get through life. Should they master the classics? Foreign languages? Should they be able to recite math formulas and scientific principles?

The issue becomes more confused when you stumble across scholars and scientists who have not mastered all the important classics and who have forgotten the simple principles of geometry and physics — and are all doing just fine, thank you. But the educator reasons that these are rogues — the talented, the gifted, the intuitive — people who don't fit into the common scheme of things.

So the debate rages. You don't need to listen long to discover two views. The first supports practical education, one that stresses the nuts and bolts of living today. The second supports a more liberal education, one that points to ancient texts as keys for unlocking life's predicaments.

But there is a neutral zone where weighty thinkers can meet and proclaim in a single voice (probably because none of them can build a course around it) that one kind of knowledge is indispensable: self-knowledge, the kind that comes from self-examination. During this last week of daily writing tasks we want to lead you a few steps down the path of self-examination, or, as we prefer to call it, self-reflection.

Self-reflection has nothing to do with parading what you consider to be your hang-ups onto the page. You must have acquaintances who like to lead now-I'm-going-to-tell-you-the-truth-about-you sessions, which are made up of an hour's worth of slander disguised in pseudo-analytical jargon. This is not the kind of reflection we suggest. After all, if insensitive criticism and verbal harassment could lead to a deepening of our self-knowledge, the chances are we would all be perfect. We aren't. And self-slander won't help us gain insight into our lives.

Instead of making a direct assault on yourself, you'll follow a more gentle course by merely rereading your entries and recording any responses or insights you have.

Once, after considering the course of his life, P. D. Ouspensky, an esoteric philosopher, wrote:

> There exist moments in life, separated by long intervals of time, but linked together by their inner content and by a certain singular sensation peculiar to them. Several such moments always recur to my mind together, and I feel then that it is these that have determined the chief trend of my life.

"The chief trend of my life" — a very large phrase that holds some meaning for Ouspensky, but perhaps not for you. Nevertheless, the point is clear. Before he could gain this insight, Ouspensky had to collect his experience, reflect on it, and somehow come to conclusions about where he had been and where he was going. He actively reflected on his life.

Novelist Anaïs Nin, after years of keeping diaries, reflected on her recorded experiences:

> In the early diaries I speak of my feeling that I am playing many roles demanded of woman, which I have been programmed to play. But I know also that there is a part of myself that stands apart from that and wants some other kind of life, some other kinds of authenticity. R. D. Laing [a contemporary psychiatrist] describes this authenticity as a process of constantly peeling off the false selves. You can do this in many ways but you can also do it by looking at it, for there is so much that we *don't* want to look at.

Both Ouspensky and Nin talk about the broad insights self-reflection has brought them, the former of the intuitive threads connecting his experiences, the latter of her awareness of a self behind the social roles she plays and the difficulty in reaching that self.

Reflecting on notebook entries need not always lead to deep insights. Often a thought will come that's related to your current life. Or you may feel as if you have re-experienced what you've already described. You may then want to extend it. After rereading a dream, one student wrote:

> Reread the cave dream. The whole experience came back to me, almost as if I were in the dream again. When I finished I felt I was still standing at the cave's mouth. Afraid, unable to move, just staring into the darkness. This is crazy, I thought, why am I scared of going in there. Then I began to imagine I went in. I told myself there was no reason to be afraid of the unknown. Unknown! The word sounded in my mind like a scream. Unknown! That's what the cave was. So I imagined I walked into the darkness. I had to put my hands in front of my face the cave was so black. I felt my way around a turn and there was a blue light ahead — a soft hazy glow. In a moment I was at the edge of an underground pond — more the size of a lake than a pond. It was beautiful. It seemed to glow. It was worth the journey through the dark. This entire imaginary journey took only a second, but I saw some truth in it. It told me that I'm often too timid when I face something I don't know or understand. Thinking the word "unknown" made me realize I'm frightened of it, but if I move ahead with some caution, it will be okay.

The sequence of this entry is simple. The writer reflects on the dream, which led her to again face the dream dilemma — to enter or not enter the cave. She suddenly realizes what the dream suggests to her — the unknown — then does in fantasy what she was unable to do while dreaming. She finally gains the insight that facing unknowns in her life needn't frighten her.

Whether or not her insight will have any lasting significance is not the point. What's important is that she's looked at a part of her life and come away with a message. She's been engaged in self-reflection.

WRITING TASK

During this final week of directed journal entries, spend each thirty-minute session both rereading previous entries and recording your responses to them. You may reread several entries before you have a response. That's fine. The appropriate way to do this task is the way that works best for you.

34 CONTINUING WORK

We hope the several weeks you've spent in daily writing practice have not only perpetuated some good writing habits but also improved your writing fluency. We also hope you've accumulated a pool of material to draw from and use in more formal assignments. If you use your journal material in this fashion, you'll be in the company of many other writers who have done just that.

If Henry David Thoreau had not kept a journal, would we have the marvelous record of his life at Walden Pond? Any reader who wishes to make the effort can discover how Anaïs Nin's *Diaries* and Albert Camus's *Notebooks* fed their works. Even world statesman Winston Churchill — the man who led the British Empire through its grimmest years during World War II — claimed he was able to write his six-volume history of those years because of wartime diaries and journals.

Of course, it may be hard for you to see yourself as a Thoreau, Nin, Camus, or Churchill. But along with them and others who have kept personal records of their lives and times you may feel the satisfaction that comes with this sort of self-expression. Disclosing the self to the self, telling a private tale held in the heart, charting the soul's inner territory — these may be the deeper values of journal keeping. By this time we hope you've experienced these values.

If you've become interested in this mode of self-expression, you may be just beginning your journal work. Perhaps you've also found a direction. If so, keep writing in whatever way suits you. But if you wish to continue and have no direction, we have some suggestions.

Logs

A log is similar to a diary. It is used less to explore aspects of a life, as you have been doing in this section's writing tasks, and more to record important day-to-day details. It holds one danger: Often a log can become routine and boring to keep up. To avoid a dull routine we suggest you focus your log.

Use one part to keep track of an important activity. Though you may also use the log to record interesting details along with the activity, the primary focus will be on the activity.

What is an important activity? You need to answer that question yourself. One thing is certain. Since you are a student, we assume you value your education. You may, therefore, wish to record your educational progress. Or to be more specific, you may want to record progress in a particular subject area or course.

But more than likely education is not the only important activity you have. You may have several. Exercise, art projects, hobbies, business, a household to run, even relationships with friends and family could be important activities in your life. You must decide for yourself. Keep in mind, too, that your list of important activities also changes over time — one might last no longer than the time it takes to complete a research project, while another, such as mastering a musical instrument, might last for years.

Arnold Bennett, early-twentieth-century novelist, used his journal to log the progress he made while writing *The Old Wives' Tale*. The following selected excerpts from Bennett's journal also include details from his life, especially details of his walking excursions into the French countryside. Study Bennett's entries along with our comments to see how he kept a log.

> *Wednesday, October 9th*
>
> Yesterday I began *The Old Wives' Tale*. I wrote 350 words yesterday afternoon and 900 this morning. I felt less self-conscious than I usually do in beginning a novel. In order to find a clear 3 hours for it every morning I have had to make a timetable, getting out of bed earlier and lunching later. This morning I calculated that I could just walk to the Croix de Montmorin and back in an hour. I nearly did it this morning without trying, in heavy rain. Tomorrow I may do it. A landscape of soaked leaves and thick clouds and rain — nothing else. But I like it.

Did you notice how Bennett also includes his inner responses — "I felt less self-conscious than I usually do in beginning a novel" — and specific physical details from his walk — "A landscape of soaked leaves and thick clouds and rain"?

Read a couple more entries, watching the focus, the inner responses, and the specifics.

Thursday, October 10th

A magnificent October day. I walked 4 miles between 8:30 and 9:30, and then wrote 1,000 words of the novel. This afternoon we penetrated into the forest with our bicycles and without a map! Had to walk miles, got lost gloriously, and at last reached home after 2 hours 40 minutes of labour. Far off, in an unfrequented path, we came across 3 old women sitting in the hedge and discussing mushrooms.

Wednesday, October 16th

I have written 7,000 words of the first chapter of the novel, and am still far from the end of it. Regarding it objectively, I do not see that it is very good, but from the pleasure I take in doing it, it must be.

Nothing but rain. I walked 4 miles in 59 minutes this morning in the rain. And this afternoon I went with Marguerite to Moret in pouring rain. A promenade on a thoroughly bad day in autumn is the next best thing to a promenade on a fine late spring morning. I enjoy it immensely. I enjoy splashing waterproof boots into deep puddles. Now it is dark, and I write this by my desk-lamp (after only 1½ pages my eyes feel fatigue) and it is still raining on the window.

Again, Bennett records his inner responses — "I do not see that it [the novel] is very good, but from the pleasure I take in doing it, it must be." He also makes some observations about the weather and his walk. The closing details relate to his working conditions and add reality to his entry. By embodying inner responses, observations, and some specific details, these entries go beyond a limited log of Bennett's work activity.

He continues this practice:

Monday, October 21st

Today I finished the second chapter of my novel. I seem to be rather uneasy as to its excellence. The date of the first part worries me, as my own recollections don't begin till 10 years later than 1862. However, the effect of the novel will be a cumulative one.

Lately I have been overworking, in spite of all the resolutions to the contrary. I rise at 6:30 or so, and after reading Italian, one hour's walking, etc., I begin on the novel at 9:30 and work till 12:30. Then my afternoons are often taken up with articles. I had meant to keep my afternoons quite free of composition. Nevertheless, my health, thanks to walking 4 miles in an hour each morning, is simply admirable, and I sleep well. But my eyesight is weakening.

And notice in the next selection the opening comments on nineteenth-century novelist Stendhal. Bennett has read Stendhal's journal. He momentarily regrets having taken care, unlike Stendhal, in proper sentence construction when vivid, fragmented impressions would have served him as well. He then follows with a paragraph of fragmented details that capture the rain and forest before he returns to logging the progress of his novel.

Wednesday, October 23rd

In reading Stendhal's unpublished journal in the *Mercure de France*, it seemed to me that in *my* journal I wasted a great deal of time in the proper construction of sentences. Quite unnecessary to do this in recording impressions.

Still much rain. A perfect baptism of damp this morning in the forest, though not actually raining. The forest all yellow and brown. Leaves falling continuously. Horse-chestnuts quite yellow. Sound of water occasionally dislodged from the trees by wind.

I have written over 2,000 words of the third chapter yesterday and today. I planned the chapter perfectly yesterday morning in the forest.

Finally, one last selected illustration:

Saturday, October 26th

The forest is now, for me, at nearly its most beautiful. Another fortnight and the spectacle will be complete. But it is really too close to our doors for us to appreciate it properly. If we had to walk 5 miles instead of 500 yards in order to get into one of these marvelously picturesque glades, we should think we were exceedingly lucky in being only 5 miles off and not 50. On the whole a very wet month, with, on days free from rain, heavy persistent fogs lasting till afternoon. The sound of voices is very clear in the forest in this mushroom weather. I have learnt a little about mushrooms. I have tremendously enjoyed my morning exercise in the mist or rain. But mushrooming only interests me when the sport is good.

In general, slightly too much work. 18,000 words of *Old Wives' Tale* in 2 weeks 4 days.

A work log, a collection of inner responses, observations, and specific details from his walks and the weather — all these make Bennett's entries interesting and vivid. We offer them as illustrations. They can be guides for you to follow if you choose to keep a log of your important activities. Of course, after starting your log, you will find your own way.

Extended Portraits, Imaginary Conversations, Unsent Letters

You may also keep your practice going by writing more portraits. If you've already written portraits of the people collected in your first listing, you might begin a new list and then continue the descriptive process. On the other hand, you may wish to extend the portraits you've already completed.

Since the people you've listed are emotionally important to you, you've probably found that a single portrait for each one doesn't truly capture the relationship. After all, relationships are complex, and to get at that complexity in writing may take several sessions.

In order to do it, we suggest you begin by rereading one of your portrait entries. Then write another descriptive entry. This time you might focus on one aspect of the relationship or on one event you and the other person shared. Keep this up for several sessions, at least until you feel the relationship has been adequately fleshed out. We suggest, as with every entry, that you date these descriptions and that you keep them together in a portrait section. Remember to continue to record memories, physical details, feelings — all the stuff that comes to you while practice writing.

After you've fully described a person and the relationship, try writing an imaginary conversation with the person. These conversations are not necessarily transcriptions of actual conversations nor are they attempts to imagine what the person might say if the person were with you. These conversations are merely you letting yourself record an inner dialogue between yourself and the other person.

Sometimes these conversations will deal with feelings that have never been expressed in the relationship — deep feelings of love or intense concern; anger or gnawing frustration; perhaps even fearful feelings. Other times they might revolve around an issue or event. You may record an imaginary conversation during which you ask for advice or give it.

To begin an imaginary conversation, review your previously written portraits and then write a brief introduction that expresses the reasons for holding the conversation — nothing formal, just a relaxed explanation to set the scene. Next, address the other person in a way that seems natural. Write down what you say and what the other person says in script form — the way a playwright might record dialogue.

What follows is an imaginary conversation between a young man and his uncle. The young man begins with a brief opening statement in order to focus the conversation, then records the dialogue that follows.

> Uncle Pete was always important to me, yet I've never told him how important. I don't know why I haven't. Maybe because I haven't had the chance or maybe because I'm just now beginning to realize how much he means to me.

> *Me:* Well, Pete, I'm in college now. Bet you didn't think I'd get here.
>
> *Pete:* I knew you'd get to where you wanted to go. You were the most determined toad I've ever seen.
>
> *Me:* Toad! You used to always call me toady, ever since you read me *Mr. Toad's Wild Ride,* or is that the name of the Disneyland attraction?
>
> *Pete:* I hope you're not majoring in history. You aren't one for facts. Or at least one for getting them straight.
>
> *Me:* I used to sit on your lap and you'd read. And I can remember thinking of you as my father. I knew you weren't but —
>
> *Pete:* That was when your dad was overseas — Korea. Your mother let me stay there while I got settled in Los Angeles. She is the best sister a man could have.
>
> *Me:* I still remember the stories you used to tell me about the two of you growing up in Vermont. I always wanted a younger sister after hearing them. I wanted to live in the snow, too. You made me feel so good by telling them to me. I guess I felt lonely then and you made me . . .

And so on.

If you decide to continue practice writing by recording imaginary conversations, you may find that they often circle back over the relationship as you've recorded it in the portraits. That's fine. Let them circle. Eventually, they will reach where they set out to go.

If practicing by recording imaginary conversations isn't for you yet you would like to address a significant person in your life, we suggest you write an unsent letter. The purpose is to give yourself a chance to record what you're feeling in another format. There is no need for you to bother with including a formal salutation; just get the letter under way in a fashion with which you feel comfortable. (And don't worry about sending the letter. To send it is not the purpose.)

Here's the start of one student's unsent letter addressed to her roommate:

> Clare: I'm tired of picking up your nightgowns, shoes, stockings, sweaters, skirts, pants, books, papers, pencils, pens — everything. Tired! Tired, Tired, Tired, T-I-R-E-D! DOG TIRED! This isn't working for me, but it must be working for you. You leave messes like an unhousebroken, six-foot pigeon. And I'm not cleaning up your cage anymore. You think I'm your mother, maybe. A mother I'm not. A zookeeper I'm not. What I am is . . .

The content of unsent letters and imaginary conversations comes spontaneously. We suggest, therefore, that you give them plenty of space, recording whatever comes to mind.

Drawings and Photographs

When you first started journal keeping, we said that undirected writing — free writing — is a good way to loosen the writing process. We also said a journal is much like an artist's sketchbook, a place where writers can practice sketching fragments of their lives in words just as artists do with lines. Well, writers sometimes like to draw squiggles and curlicues, perhaps even figures from dreams or caricatures of people from their lives. They often like to decorate the margins of books and note paper.

What do these images mean? Who knows? We know only that to doodle doesn't take much artistic talent. In fact, doodling seems to grow from an urge totally separate from artistic drives. It seems to come from a need to meditate. There is a strange compulsion in some writers to let the hand follow the uncharted direction of the mind and create images in the process.

If you are a writer who finds yourself doodling, fine. Keep it going. Do it on scraps of paper or in the margins of lecture notes. Then paste the doodles into your journal. The next step is to describe them —

describe all that they suggest to you. Ask yourself what the images mean. Explain where they come from. Write your responses under the doodle.

By writing about your drawings, you'll not only be practicing, but you'll also be exploring your inner nature. Here's how one writer responded to her doodles of a snake image:

> This is Mister Snake. To some people he may seem dangerous, but to me he's the source of deep wisdom. Sometimes when I catch myself drawing him I am daydreaming about some problem I face. In many ways drawing him is like talking to a wise man — someone who knows the answer I need. I guess that's a dialogue because my drawing him makes me feel as if I'm having a conversation. He doesn't always give me a straight answer, snakes are like that. They speak with forked tongue. So I have to decipher his message. It is usually very secret, for snakes are secret things. This snake, my old friend, knows many of my life's secrets. He'll never reveal them. Just ask to see.

When this writer set out to write a response to her doodles, she didn't know what would come out; she merely started writing while focusing on her drawing.

A variation of the doodle exercise involves the use of photographs. This exercise can take a couple of forms. You might write a response to a photograph you see in a book or magazine. Or you might write a response to a photograph or photographs from your personal experience. We suggest you paste the photographs into your journal. If that isn't possible, write brief descriptions of the photographs as part of your entries.

What follows is part of a philosophical response to a photographic slide of Salvador Dali's *Persistence of Memory:*

> This morning in art history I saw a slide of a Dali painting. A crazy thing. It was filled with melting pocket watches — pocket watches that looked more real than real watches. These watches were melting in a desert wasteland with some strange trees in the background. One watch had thousands of ants crawling out of it. Another was melting over a strange amoeba-shaped object covered with hair and with a tongue hanging out of an opening.
>
> The painting reminded me of words from an old song: "Time, time, time — what's to become of me. . . ." And I began to wonder about how time worked in my life. Time is a funny thing to be thinking about, but I can't get the thought out of my mind. I wonder how time works. I know I live in time that moves

forward, that is, I was born, I went to grammar school, junior high school, and high school. I know all this education has led to college, but in my mind I can be in all these places at once. Time in my mind seems to melt together.

While this writer chose to write about a photograph of a well-known painting, the following writer chose to record his responses to a series of childhood photographs. Over a period of weeks he spent thirty to forty minutes each day recording his inner responses to pictures of himself as a child and pictures of family members. His response to a photograph of himself as a baby being held by his father starts like this:

When I look at this picture, I feel very strange. I know the man standing next to the birch tree is my father and I know the baby he holds wrapped in a blanket is me. But for some reason I can't emotionally accept the thought. My father seems so young, not any older than I am now, and I find imagining him at my age is difficult.

Did he feel at 22 what I feel?

At that age he had a child — me. It makes me feel he had his life under control. But here I am at 22 without an idea of what I'll be doing four years from now.

My father now, compared to the picture, seems so much older. So changed. Once he was thin, athletic. Now he has a paunch and looks as if he never sees the sun. His hair, once full and wavy, is now thin. His face was smooth, now wrinkled.

At this moment I wonder if somewhere there exists a photograph of him and his father. I wonder if he has ever compared himself to his dad's image. Where does this lead, this photographing, this photographing of fathers and sons?

Where?

Back, back, back. And forward — into the future. The never-ending future. But somehow I feel there's knowledge to be gained from studying these images.

And so on.

The key to responding to images, whether drawings, paintings, or personal photographs, is to avoid trying to figure out what you are going to write before you write it, but instead to focus on the image and just write — write as an artist sketches.

Off Days

Writers have off days — days when the words don't seem to come in the right patterns. That's to be expected. Writing, like any other activity, depends on energy. On some days there are larger supplies than on others. If you have an off day, we suggest you do some simple exercises to keep yourself writing — exercises that don't require much mental effort.

One activity you might do is copy word for word a poem or a piece of professional prose you admire. The copying doesn't require much thought, since all you have to do is make sure you get the right words in the right order. But the copying will help you develop a feel for the English language. Good writers make good teachers. Use them as models.

Another activity you might pursue on an off day is writing random lists. These lists can serve as a kind of doodling with words. Be sure to center them — focus on a single aspect of your life.

To get started, here are a few ideas. List the joys and sorrows of your life and add the details you associate with each up or down experience. You might also center another list around fears — all kinds of fears: childhood fears and adult fears. Try centering on a particular period of your life and make a memory list or try centering on a relationship and make a list of its key events. You could also write a list of trips you've taken or music and books you like. No matter how you center your list, be sure to include some details, and always work in a spontaneous way.

On an off day one writer decided to write a memory list of his senior high school year. Read the first few entries.

> Playing ball: remember the photo in the *Daily Pilot*. Gil pitching the ball to me, the field open all the way to the goal posts. Fumbling. Ugh!
>
> Sally: two dates — wham. In love. Walks on the beach. Empty, empty sands. A month later, tears. Living in Denver.
>
> John: knew John since the 6th grade. Big John — 6′4″. All black hair and white teeth. A friendly bear. Joined the Marines.
>
> Reminds me of: trip to big bear, Big Bear John — must be a connection. First time in the snow. The whole gang staying in Brenda's cabin. Took hours to clean it up. But the snow, white powder that seemed to float down, gently falling and collecting on the window ledges.

On off days this kind of practice will keep your hand moving across the page. You may also find that one entry begins to develop into a longer piece. If that happens, you're no longer having an off day.

PART FOUR

INDEX FOR WRITERS

This book is mainly a collection of tasks designed to teach you the process and structure of good writing. But there's more to say about writing than can be said through the use of tasks. Consequently, we've included this section to give you additional information about basic principles (such as coherence, tone, and point of view) as well as standard conventions (such as punctuation, capitalization, and agreement). We've also included more information about editing and revising and several examples of various kinds of introductions and conclusions that you can use in your essays. All the material is arranged alphabetically for easy reference. Your instructor may guide you to particular entries as you need the information, or you may independently study the information. In either case, you'll be able to demonstrate what you've learned by integrating the knowledge into your work.

INDEX FOR WRITERS

Abbreviations

The best advice we can give you on the use of abbreviations is don't overdo it. What is acceptable is a matter of convention that depends on both subject matter and tone. Technical and medical writing typically includes more abbreviations than general writing. And so does very informal writing — notes, lists, and memoranda, for example. The more informal the writing, the more acceptable it is to abbreviate. But for general writing of the kind you do for most college courses, the list of acceptable abbreviations is rather brief. If in doubt, don't abbreviate. You will seldom be criticized for writing the complete word.

1. Use abbreviations for titles and degrees used with complete proper names.

Mr. Samuel Needham	Gen. Edward Wymer
Mrs. Patricia Sandoval	Thomas Rich, D.D.S.
Ms. Sarah Glidden	Gloria Smith, D.V.M.
Dr. James Heard	James Hanson, M.D.
Prof. Susan Nelson	Bullard Ralph, Jr.
Rev. George L. Butler	Leslie Norman, Ph.D.

Don't abbreviate titles when you write them by themselves; instead spell them out.

The general will arrive by tank at dawn.

not

The gen. will arrive by tank at dawn.

The professor kept dropping the chalk.

not

The prof. kept dropping the chalk.

2. Use abbreviations for well-known companies and agencies. Periods are not needed.

IBM (International Business Machines)

CBS (Columbia Broadcasting Company)

FBI (Federal Bureau of Investigation)

UNESCO (United Nations Educational, Scientific, and Cultural Organization)

If the name is not well known but you plan to use it repeatedly in a fairly long paper, write the full name the first time and show the abbreviation in parentheses. Then use the abbreviation throughout the remainder of the paper.

Dwayne Merry, Ph.D., has taken the first steps toward his goal of establishing the Society for Cultural Interchange (SCI). The SCI will dedicate itself to . . .

3. Use abbreviations with times and dates when the reference may be unclear in your paper.

12:40 a.m. (*or* A.M.)

5:21 p.m. (*or* P.M.)

540 B.C. (B.C. follows the date)

A.D. 2980 (A.D. precedes the date)

If the reference to date and time are clear within the context of your paper, you don't need to include B.C., A.D., a.m., or p.m.

In 1980, the year of my twenty-first birthday, the sky fell dark at 10:05 on the morning of September 21.

4. In general writing, don't abbreviate the following:

Personal names: Robert (*not* Robt.) Johnson

Units of measure: three feet (*not* ft.) long; two inches (*not* in.) high

Names of countries: France (*not* Fr.)

Names of states: Virginia (*not* Virg.)

Names of streets: Longfellow Boulevard (*not* Blvd.); the boulevard (*not* blvd.)

Subjects in school: political science (*not* poli. sci.)

Divisions of a book: seven chapters (*not* ch.); Chapter (*not* Ch.) 3

Days of the week: Sunday (*not* Sun.)

Active and Passive Voice

Good writing is vigorous and direct. In nearly all circumstances, the active voice achieves vigor and directness better than the passive voice.

Active	*Passive*
Jennifer softly squeezed his hand.	His hand was softly squeezed by Jennifer.
Arnie bought a fancy new collar for his dog.	A fancy new collar was bought by Arnie for his dog.
Ruth slammed the ball over the center-field fence.	The ball was slammed over the center-field fence by Ruth.

In all these examples, the second sentence shifts emphasis from the doer (Jennifer, Arnie, Ruth) to the receiver (hand, collar, ball). The receiver actually becomes the subject of the sentence.

As a practical definition, then, we could say that if the subject *performs* the action of the verb, the sentence is in active voice:

> I tripped the mailman.

If the subject *receives* the action of the verb, the sentence is in passive voice:

> The mailman was tripped by me.

More precisely, the passive voice is formed by combining a *to be* verb (*is, was, were, are, am, been, being*) with the past participle form of a transitive verb (for example, *seen, thrown, purchased*):

He is seen.	They are seen.
He was seen.	They were seen.
He has been seen.	They have been seen.
He will have been seen.	They will have been seen.
He is being seen.	They are being seen.
He was being seen.	They were being seen.

There's no need to consult this list or memorize a definition of passive voice, though. Just remember that when the subject of the sentence is the doer of the action you have active voice.

In most situations you should use active voice. Why? For several reasons. Active voice sentences are usually briefer and more economical and therefore more direct:

> Trinkets cluttered the shelves. (4 words)

Many trinkets had been placed on the shelves. (8 words)

Active voice emphasizes the doer of the action and is therefore more specific:

Greg will always remember his years in the army.

Greg's years in the army will always be remembered. (By whom?)

Active voice is more forceful:

Hank pushed Rodney against the locker.

Rodney was pushed against the locker by Hank.

At times, though, the passive voice is legitimate and useful.

Sometimes the doer of the action is obvious or unimportant and the passive voice is appropriate:

He was elected senator five times.

The high-rise apartment building will be completed by June.

When Sanders became president of Farley Motors the decision to seek government contracts had already been made.

Crosswalks should be painted at all intersections.

Sometimes the doer is not known:

The windshield had been smashed and peanut shells had been thrown into the gas tank.

Paxton's Liquor Store was robbed last night.

Sometimes you want to emphasize the receiver of the action:

He was wounded by shrapnel.

My car has been ruined!

The entire block was flattened by the explosion.

But appropriate situations for the use of passive voice occur far less frequently than situations that call for the active voice. Carol Havens in "The Sky's the Limit in a Solar Balloon" writes in active voice, but twice in the following excerpt she uses passive construction.

> When Frederick Eshoo climbed into the gondola of his hot-air balloon and floated aloft over Albuquerque, New Mexico, at dawn, *the only sounds that could be heard were Eshoo's own cheers.* He had good reason for jubilation, beyond the normal exhilaration a hot-air balloonist feels on lifting off. For Eshoo was piloting a unique balloon, his own invention, which rose to an altitude of 12,500 feet and stayed up four hours, 10 minutes and 17 seconds, using the most economical of all fuels — the heat of the sun's rays.

Eshoo, an Iranian paper manufacturer and inventor who claims to be the Middle East's only balloonist, spent more than two years designing the balloon and testing materials that would make it an effective solar collector. He named the balloon Sunstat — a yoking together of the sun and aerostat, the technical term for a hot-air balloon — and he sees it as a harbinger of a new generation of aircraft and space vehicles whose *flight will be powered by the sun.*

The first passive construction — "the only sounds that could be heard were Eshoo's own cheers" — is appropriate because it emphasizes what is heard rather than who hears it. The hearer would be anyone witnessing the event at Albuquerque, but the important thing here is the relative silence of the scene and the personal triumph of the inventor. If the writer had said "none of the observers said a word" the event would appear trivial or the audience hostile. If she had said "he cheered in triumph" the sentence would emphasize the character of the man rather than the awesomeness of the scene.

The second passive construction — "flight will be powered by the sun" — is appropriate because the key idea here is the flight of aircraft and space vehicles, not the behavior of the sun.

The point is that selective use of the passive voice is effective.

And now, before we conclude our discussion of active and passive voices, we are going to yield to the temptation to show you an effective piece of writing that uses the passive voice almost exclusively. The subject matter is brain surgery, and Roy C. Selby, Jr., uses the passive voice to keep the focus on the process itself, excluding mention of either the patient or the surgeon.

> A curved incision was made behind the hairline so it would be concealed when the hair grew back. It extended almost from ear to ear. Plastic clips were applied to the cut edges of the scalp to arrest bleeding. The scalp was folded back to the level of the eyebrows. Incisions were made in the muscle of the right temple, and three sets of holes were drilled near the temple and the top of the head because the tumor had to be approached from directly in front. The drill, powered by nitrogen, was replaced with a fluted steel blade, and the holes were connected. The incised piece of skull was pried loose and held out of the way by a large sponge.

Only one sentence here is in active voice. But don't let the excellence of Selby's paragraph divert your attention from the main point of this section: Use active voice unless there are compelling reasons to believe that passive voice would be more appropriate.

Agreement

Agreement is the correspondence of one word to another in person, number, or gender. A verb must agree with its subject:

> Each day at 5:45 p.m. Harold eats two bags of peanuts. (The verb *eats* and the subject *Harold* agree.)

A pronoun must agree with its antecedent:

> Wallace loaned Houston his camera. (The pronoun *his* agrees with its antecedent *Wallace.*)

Subject/Verb Agreement

Here are some guidelines to review if you have been making errors in subject/verb agreement.

1. Subject and verb should agree even when words intervene.

    > Martha Tanner, who worked as an anthropologist in the Amazon, *has written* a book on South American tribes.

    > Collecting stamps, once his teenage hobby, *dominates* his professional life.

2. Two or more subjects linked by *and* require a plural verb.

    > Corned beef and prime rib *are* his favorite meat dishes.

    > "Cherrylog Road" and "Looking for the Buckhead Boys," no matter how often he reads them, *bring* him great pleasure.

    If the subjects refer to a single person or thing, the verb should be singular.

    > The owner and manager of the store, Mr. Stevens, *decides* who will be hired. (Since the owner and manager is one person, the singular verb *decides* is required.)

    If *each* or *every* precedes a singular subject joined by *and,* use a singular verb.

    > Each tree and each brook *is* important.

    > Every comma and semicolon *is* to be exact.

3. Use a singular verb when two or more singular subjects are linked by *or* or *nor.*

    > Jones or Smith *is* to pick up the package.

    > Neither stroking nor striking *is* likely to change his thinking.

    A problem might arise if you have one subject that is singular and another that is plural. In that event, the verb should agree with the subject it is closest to.

    > Neither Ralph nor the Snows *are* coming.

    > Neither the Snows nor Ralph *is* coming.

4. Use a singular verb with most indefinite pronouns. Pronouns like *anybody, anyone, anything, each, either, everybody, everyone, everything, neither, nobody, no one, one, somebody, someone,* and *something* do not refer to specific persons or things. Most indefinite pronouns are singular in meaning, and you should use singular verbs with them.

> Something *has been nagging* me all week.

> Anyone *is* allowed to use the language lab.

> Someone *is* knocking at the door.

> Everybody *is* getting into the act.

> Everyone in the class *is* reading poetry.

Some indefinite pronouns, however, like *all, any, none,* and *some,* may be either singular or plural. When using them, select the verb form appropriate for the particular situation.

> All the students *are* to bring their lunches. (*All* refers to students.)

> All of the class *is* nervous over the final. (*All* refers to class.)

5. Generally, use a singular verb with a collective noun. Collective nouns are singular in form — *administration, army, audience, class, committee, crowd, faculty, family, government, public, squadron, team,* and so on — but possibly plural in meaning. Most often you'll use a singular verb with a collective noun.

> The committee *stands* firm.

> The class *meets* from three to five each afternoon.

> After dire predictions from sociologists, the family *is* still surviving.

Sometimes you'll need to use a plural verb because you are referring to individual members within a group.

> The committee *have split* into factions.

However, to use a plural verb with a collective noun often sounds awkward. We suggest, therefore, that you rewrite to avoid this kind of awkwardness.

> Committee members *have split* into factions.

6. Use singular verbs with nouns plural in form but singular in meaning.

> Measles *is* one childhood curse.

> Billiards *takes* concentration to play well.

7. Use a singular verb with the title of a work or with a word written as a word when either is used as a subject.

Games People Play is required reading in Psychology 100.

Persons is often misused for *people.*

8. Use singular or plural nouns and verbs — whichever are appropriate — with the expletive *there.*

There *is* only one right answer.

There *are* sixteen right answers.

Pronoun/Antecedent Agreement

Problems with pronoun agreement are easy to clear up. Begin by remembering that the antecedent of a pronoun is the noun or pronoun it refers to. Then remember that a pronoun and its antecedent must match.

John did well on *his* project.

The students did well on *their* projects.

Sometimes sentences are more complicated than these; then the relationship between pronoun and antecedent is harder to trace.

Since the *students* requested the second *test,* I gave *it* to *them.*

Keeping the pronoun/antecedent relationship is usually easy. There are only three places where writers seem to run into trouble.

1. Generally use a singular pronoun with such antecedents as *anyone, each, everybody, none, no one,* and *something.*

Something ominous made *its* presence felt in the mansion.

Each of the women likes *her* teacher.

Everybody on the men's volleyball team gave *his* opinion about the match.

In these examples the gender of the pronouns is clear. But often when you use an indefinite pronoun, the gender won't be clear. Although indefinite pronouns refer to no particular gender, by tradition you would use a masculine pronoun to match an indefinite pronoun.

Everybody in the neighborhood did *his* best to clean up the park.

Clearly the neighborhood would be made up of both males and females, but traditional usage calls for the masculine pronoun, a tradition that unfairly excludes females. Some writers would solve the injustice by using a plural pronoun.

Everybody in the neighborhood did *their* best to clean up the park.

Other writers would use both masculine and feminine pronouns.

Everybody in the neighborhood did *his or her* best to clean up the park.

Even though this is colloquial, it is unacceptable in written form to most authorities. The use of *his* and *her* in this way seems cumbersome. Instead of using either solution, we suggest you substitute a sentence of this sort.

People in the neighborhood did *their* best to clean up the park.

2. Use a plural pronoun with two or more antecedents joined by *and;* use a singular pronoun with two or more singular antecedents joined by *or* or *nor*.

The dog and cat fought until *they* collapsed in the flowerbed.

Beth and her friends enjoyed *their* holiday.

Did either Joe or Tom pay *his* bill?

Neither Jill nor Jan will give up *her* claim.

If one of the antecedents joined by *nor* or *or* is singular and the other is plural, the pronoun should agree with the nearer antecedent.

Neither the speaker nor the respondents made *their* points clear.

3. Use a plural or singular pronoun with a collective noun, depending on whether the collective noun is used in a plural or a collective sense.

The team held *its* yearly awards dinner last night. (*Team* is used as a single unit.)

The committee is trying to explain *its* behavior. (*Committee* serves as a single group.)

The band put away *their* instruments. (*Band* acts as a group of individuals.)

Apostrophe

Errors in the use of the apostrophe are common among beginning writers. But the situation isn't hopeless, because the apostrophe has only three main uses — to show contraction, to show possession, and to form plurals of numbers, symbols, and words.

Contractions

Contraction is a shortening of a word or word group by dropping a letter or syllable. When you form a contraction, you usually join the contracted word to another word and use an apostrophe to show the omission.

it is	it's	you have	you've
you will	you'll	of the clock	o'clock
do not	don't	they are	they're
cannot	can't	you are	you're

Possession

The possessive case shows ownership. Possession may be shown with an *of* phrase — the performance of the troupe — but more often it will be shown by adding an apostrophe and *s* to the word — the troupe's performance. Seems simple, doesn't it? But it's not quite that simple. There are several guidelines you must be aware of when you form the possessive case.

1. Add an apostrophe and *s* to show possession by singular or plural nouns or indefinite pronouns not ending in *s*.

Tom's book	Connie's car	someone's hat
men's club	children's school	

2. Add an apostrophe and *s* to show possession by singular words ending in *s* unless the addition of an *s* makes pronunciation awkward.

the boss's desk	Lois's career
Charles's homework	Moses' life

3. Add only an apostrophe to show possession by plural words ending in *s*.

   the Smiths' car

   the writers' convention

4. Add an apostrophe and *s* to the last word in a compound or word group to show possession by the compound or word group.

   mother-in-law's story

   everyone else's dream

5. Add an apostrophe and *s* to the last word in a word group that has joint possession.

   Tom and Bill's radio

   Flora, Carl, and Hank's family

6. Add an apostrophe and *s* to each word in a group that has individual possession.

   Tom's and Bill's cars

   Flora's, Carl's, and Hank's families

Plural Numbers, Symbols, and Words

Whenever you form the plural of a number, symbol, or word, add an apostrophe and *s*.

   The second graders are learning to count by 3's.

   His name has three *m*'s.

I'm working for straight *A*'s.

He bores me with his *what*'s and *why*'s.

When referring to a decade you may leave out the apostrophe.

The movement flourished in the 1920s.

Never use an apostrophe and *s* with possessive pronouns (*his, hers, ours, its, yours, theirs,* and *whose*). Those words are already possessive.

This cabin is theirs.   *not*   This cabin is their's.

Whose balloon is this?   *not*   Who's balloon is this?

What is its name?   *not*   What is it's name?

Generally, avoid using an apostrophe and *s* to form the possessive of an inanimate object unless using an *of* phrase sounds awkward.

the door of the shed   *not*   the shed's door

However, a word expressing time or amount usually forms the possessive by adding apostrophe and *s* to the singular and only the apostrophe to the plural.

an hour's notice   a day's work

several weeks' time   a dollar's worth

fifty cents' worth   two years' delay

Brackets

You'll find little use for brackets in general writing, but in academic writing you'll find four specific uses for them — usually when you are quoting someone else.

1. Use brackets with *sic*, a Latin term that means "thus it is," to indicate an error that you let stand in a quotation. Often the error will be a misspelling:

   Susanne Singer writes, "Muddled thinkers who confuse the slogans of ad writers with concrete comunication [*sic*] are doomed to live out their lives as puppets of well-paid hucksters."

2. Use brackets to correct a garbled quotation so that it reads clearly:

   In a tape-recorded interview, one coal miner reports, "I used [to] work twelve hours [daily] in the hole. Then [I'd] come home and cough till midnight."

3. Use brackets to clear up the relationship between antecedent and pronoun that may be clear in the complete text but unclear in the excerpt you're using:

   Top athletes understand the importance of slowly letting their bodies cool following a strenuous event. "After running a marathon, she [Helen Case] jogs another mile before doing thirty minutes of leg stretches."

4. Finally, use brackets to include important facts or to correct misinformation in a quotation:

Gadzbar claims, "In 1975 at the age of twenty-three [according to birth records, he was thirty-four in 1975] I encountered an Indian mystic who altered my world view."

Capitals

The guidelines for capitalization are constantly changing; however, there are certain ones that writers rigidly follow. We'll give you those along with the suggestion that you consult a dictionary to see if a particular word you wish to use needs to be capitalized.

1. Capitalize the first word of every sentence or word or phrase used as a sentence.

Carl sprinkles his papers with fragments.

Why?

Latent hostility.

Watch out!

2. Capitalize the first word in a full quotation.

The speaker states, "What we call a symbol may be an object, a name, a picture, or even a mental image that carries emotional significance for us."

Don't capitalize the first word in a quotation after an interruption.

"What we call a symbol," the speaker stated, "may be an object, a name, a picture, or even a mental image that carries emotional significance for us."

3. Capitalize the first word in every line of poetry.

To see a world in a grain of sand
And a heaven in a wild flower,
Hold infinity in the palm of your hand
And eternity in an hour.
— William Blake, "Auguries of Innocence"

However, if the poet does not follow this convention, follow the poet's style.

anyone lived in a pretty how town
(with up so floating many bells down)
spring summer autumn winter
he sang his didn't he danced his did.
— e. e. cummings,
"anyone lived in a pretty how town"

4. Capitalize the first word of a sentence that follows a colon if you want to stress the sentence.

> The future invites us like an unworked mine: The eighties will yield wealth.

5. Capitalize the first and last words and every important word in a title. Do not capitalize articles, conjunctions, and prepositions of fewer than five letters.

> *The Maltese Falcon*
>
> *All That Jazz*
>
> "The Love Song of J. Alfred Prufrock"
>
> *Atlantic*
>
> "How to Get Through the Day"

Don't capitalize *the* unless it is part of the title.

> I read the *Yale Review.*   *not*   I read *The Yale Review.*

Remember, too, that the convention holds for titles that include colons but with a slight twist: Also capitalize the word — even if it is a preposition, an article, or a conjunction — that follows the colon.

> *The Uses of Enchantment: The Meaning and Importance of Fairy Tales*

6. Capitalize the pronoun *I* and the interjection *O*.

> No matter how hard I study, I seldom do well in math.
>
> Thank you, O Lord, for this opportunity.

Don't capitalize *oh* unless it begins a sentence.

> Oh, I seldom do well in math.
>
> I studied math for two hours, but oh, how I failed the test.

7. Capitalize proper nouns, proper adjectives, and words used as essential parts of proper nouns. Don't capitalize common nouns. This convention may confuse you. To keep a clear head remember that proper nouns name specific persons, places, or things; that proper adjectives derive from proper nouns; and that common nouns name general categories of persons, places, and things.

Proper nouns	*Proper adjectives*	*Common nouns*
Freud	Freudian	psychologist
Shakespeare	Shakespearean	writer
Harvard	—	university
Nebraska	Nebraskan	state
Germany	German	country
Australia	Australian	continent

Specific persons, places, things

Norman Mailer	the Pacific Ocean
Judy Jernigan	Oak Creek Canyon
Tom Wert	the Washington Monument
the South	New York City
the West	Europe
the Northeast	Asia

Historic events, documents, periods, movements

the Civil War	the Middle Ages
the French Revolution	the Declaration of Independence
the Roaring Twenties	

Days of the week, months, holidays

Friday

May

Thanksgiving

Organizations, associations, government departments, political parties

Postal Service	Democrats
Department of the Interior	Republican party
Big Brothers of America	Peace and Freedom party
Young Men's Christian Association	20/30 Club
	League of Women Voters

Names of educational institutions, departments, courses, student classes, degrees

Huntington High School	the Social Science Department
Reed College	B.A. (Bachelor of Arts degree)
Math 54	Junior Class

Religious terms, religions, religious followers

God	Buddhism, Buddhists
Allah	Islam, Islamites
Holy Ghost	Hinduism, Hindus
the Virgin	Taoism, Taoists
the Christ Child	Christianity, Christians
Judgment Day	Judaism, Jews

Races, tribes, nationalities

Indian	French
Iroquois	Chinese
Negro	Mexican

Names of stars and planets

the Big Dipper	the Milky Way
the North Star	Mars

8. Capitalize common nouns when used as parts of proper nouns.

   Fairview Road

   Third Street

   Mayford Park

   Atlantic City

9. Capitalize titles when they come before proper names but generally not when they follow a name.

Professor Tamara Adams	*but*	Tamara Adams, professor of English
President Smith	*but*	William Smith, president of Edna College

10. Capitalize abbreviations that indicate time, divisions of government, national and international organizations and businesses, and call letters of radio and TV stations.

A.D.	FHA	NBC
B.C.	YMCA	IBM
A.M. (or a.m.)	NATO	
P.M. (or p.m.)	KTTV	

11. Capitalize the pronouns *he, his, him, thee, thou,* and *thine* but not *who, whom,* and *whose* when referring to God.

    God is a mystery; we cannot know who He is or what He is.

12. Don't capitalize geographical directions unless they refer to specific regions.

General directions	*Geographical regions*
west	the West
east	the East
south	the South
northeast	the Northeast

13. Don't capitalize seasons and academic years or terms.

spring	freshman year
summer	junior year
fall	fall quarter
winter	spring semester

14. Don't capitalize the names for relationships unless they are used instead of the proper name or with the proper name.

my father	My father lived until he was seventy-nine.
my uncle	I used to go swimming with Uncle Harry.
my mother	My mother played the flute, guitar, and piano.
my aunt	Give the book to my aunt.

Clutter

We subscribe to the notion put forth by Neil Postman and Charles Weingartner in *The Soft Revolution* that "if an idea cannot be expressed in language that a reasonably attentive seventh-grader can understand, someone is jiving someone else."

Plenty of jiving goes on. Advertisers, militarists, scientists, medical doctors, politicians, and even educators do it. For instance, what does it mean when an educator writes, "The ultimate goal is to motivate the client toward the successful completion of a quality educational experience"; or when a politician states, "Hope may be the one human factor absent from today's democratic landscape"; or when a physician announces, "The terminal infection began in the abdominal area then metastasized and permeated the entire system"?

No doubt these sentences hold some concrete information, but to get at it is something like eating through an eight-inch-thick ring of fat to reach the meat. Well, we'll start chewing.

Perhaps the educator means, "We want students to finish the course." The politician, "Things are dreary." And the M.D., "The cancer spread from the stomach through the rest of the body."

We're driving toward the idea that much of the writing we read is unnecessarily confusing. There's no need to use a difficult word where a simple one will do or three words where one accurate one will work better. It all adds up to cluttered writing, and cluttered writing leads to confusion.

Cut Intensifiers

You can cut out intensifiers, words such as *very, really, quite, totally, completely, definitely,* and *so.* In Getting Started we said these words carry over from speech habits. When speaking, people use them with vocal stress:

> The REALLY terrible storm ripped across the bay and TOTAL-LY destroyed business buildings and homes when it hit shore. The result was VERY disastrous: SO MUCH wreckage, SO MANY helpless people, SO MANY lost dreams. To see it was REALLY disturbing.

In writing, stress comes from using powerful words, not from using vacant intensifiers. In fact, intensifiers seem to "deintensify" by distracting from more muscular words. To see what we mean, reread the passage with the intensifiers cut out:

> The terrible storm ripped across the bay and destroyed business buildings and homes when it hit shore. The result was disastrous: wreckage, helpless people, lost dreams. To see it was disturbing.

Once you've cut out the intensifiers you can clearly see what you've said. Sometimes you'll want to revise by adding more detail because you'll sense some empty spaces, and sometimes you'll want to revise to create a better rhythm.

In the case of the example, the second sentence seems almost telegraphic, moving forward with quick bursts of information:

> The result was disastrous: wreckage, helpless people, lost dreams.

It could be revised by adding detail and by creating a more rhythmic movement:

> The result was disastrous: wreckage floating in the flooded streets, helpless people clinging to each other on high ground and rooftops, and lost dreams that seemed to have been carried away on the winds.

Maybe the phrase "lost dreams that seemed to be carried away on the winds" is too "poetic" for such a concrete passage. One more revision would take care of it.

You should cut statements that suggest modesty, phrases such as *I think, I feel, I believe, in my opinion,* and *it seems to me.* What do phrases like these tell readers that they don't already know? You wrote whatever they're reading; therefore, the piece must reflect your opinion, right? So cut modesty.

Also cut hedging. Sometimes you'll need to qualify your points; there's no doubt about that. But when it's overdone, you're hedging. You'll find yourself using words and phrases such as *for the most part, more or less, somewhat, rather, as it were,* and *virtually.* You may even write a passage like this:

> In my opinion the registration procedures at this college virtually require more discipline to complete than academic courses. For the most part, it seems to me, each of us is subjected to standing for hours in lines that twist from steamy registration

bungalows into the cement quad beneath the blazing sun. I feel the situation is not only unhealthy but also somewhat inhuman.

Do you feel the power in this passage? It's there, but hard to sense because of the excess language. After we cut the modesty and hedging, the energy comes through:

> The registration procedures at this college require more discipline to complete than academic courses. Each of us is subjected to standing for several hours in lines that twist from steamy registration bungalows into the cement quad beneath the blazing sun. The situation is not only unhealthy but also inhuman.

Now the passage has more impact and reads faster. Often speed and power result from cutting clutter from your prose.

Let's consider prepositions dangling from the ends of verbs that need no excess growth.

> Beth called and said she would be arriving down from San Francisco Friday.

> We need a strong leader to head up student government.

> Don't be nervous; face up to the danger.

> I'll be there if I can free up some time.

Why use *down* with *arriving?* Better to write

> Beth called and said she would be arriving from San Francisco Friday.

And why use *up* or *up to* with words such as *head, face,* and *free?* Better to write

> We need a strong leader to head student government.

> Don't be nervous; face the danger.

> I'll be there if I can free some time.

Are we nitpicking? Maybe, but remember a nit is a tiny parasitic insect that irritates its host. When readers go through a passage full of these verbal nits, they may not know what's irritating them, but they'll be scratching their scalps and complaining.

Roundabout phrases can also clutter your prose. Your goal is to write in a simple, clear style. Your words should be easily understood, and your sentences should move with some speed. But some writers, either out of ignorance or a sense of self-importance, impede clarity and speed by using several words when one or two will do. These circumlocutions muddy the verbal waters. Readers have to strain to see through the murk. As an example, read this handout distributed to members of a history class.

Prior to taking this course you should have completed History 100 in order to be prepared to meet the basic entrance requirements of History 110. It is often the case that after several weeks into the term students will come to the realization that they have not given proper consideration to the required prerequisite. If this is true in your case, make contact with me for the purpose of discussing the problem.

We have one major fear in offering this as an example. You have probably read so much writing like it that you may think it's high-quality stuff. Well it isn't. It's prefabricated junk — chunks of stock phrases strung together by a thin thread of thought. For instance, what does "prior to taking" mean in plain English? "Before," that's what it means. And what does "in order to be prepared to meet" mean? It means "to meet." And "to come to the realization that" means "to realize" or "to see." These phrases are roundabout ways of saying simple things. The writer needs to cut them out and cast them away. Once that's done, the writer will see other ways of making the passage even clearer. The first step, as you know by now, is to cross out the offending phrases and write in other words to keep the continuity.

Before ~~Prior to~~ taking this course you should ~~have completed~~ *take*

History 100 ~~in order to be prepared~~ to meet the ~~basic~~

entrance requirements ~~of History 110. It is often the~~ *Often*;

~~case that~~ after several weeks ~~into the term~~ students will

~~come to the realization~~ that they have not ~~given proper~~ *see/realize*

~~consideration to~~ the ~~required~~ prerequisite. If this is true *completed*

~~in your case, make contact with~~ me ~~for the purpose of~~ *for you;* *call* *to discuss*

~~discussing~~ the problem.

The editing done and the continuity established, all the writer has to do is revise the passage for simplicity and clarity.

Before taking this course you should take History 100 to meet the entrance requirements. Often, after several weeks, students will see that they have not completed the prerequisite. If this is true for you, call me to discuss the problem.

The passage is no longer murky. It's simple and to the point. But be on guard, because many of these wordy phrases have crept into our daily communication. You as a writer need to be aware of them or they may muddy what you try to say. To help you, here's a list of circumlocutions with shorter and clearer ways of saying the same things.

come to the realization	realize, see
of the opinion that	think
present with	give
for the purpose of	for
in the nature of	like
along the lines of	like, similar to
concerning the matter of	about
prior to	before
subsequent to	after
in connection with	by, in, for
during the course of	during
in the event that	if
for the period of a week	for a week
with respect to	about
with reference to	about
with regard to	about
in the amount of	for
regardless of the fact that	although
at this point in time	now
at that point in time	then
at any point in time	whenever
on the occasion of	when
in case of	if
in view of the fact that	as, since, because
for the reason that	as, since, because
with a view to	to
make contact with	call
it is often the case that	often
inasmuch as	since
the fact that	that

for the simple reason that	because
due to the fact that	because
despite the fact that	though, although
regardless of the fact that	though, although
on the occasion of	when, on
give consideration to	consider
have need for	need
make an adjustment in	adjust
is of the opinion	believes
give encouragement to	encourage
make inquiry regarding	ask
comes into conflict with	conflicts
give instruction to	instruct

And more, many, many more. These phrases hatch faster than anyone can crush them. They creep into the most diligent writer's prose. But don't be discouraged. We want to give you encouragement to ward them off regardless of the fact — which is often the case — that the language of public figures, college professors, and news reporters often comes into conflict with the value of clear, pointed writing. Don't be taken in. Fight clutter in your work.

The verb to be

One problem beginning writers share comes from using forms of the verb *to be*. Often they add clutter to your writing. Here are some examples of what we mean:

> Max Ernst was sixty-three and knew madness and death were before him.

> The sun was setting. The few clouds that were on the horizon were orange.

> Hemingway's "The Killers" is a story that is dominated by the feeling of impending violence.

When you reread a passage you have written, mark the various forms of *to be* and see if you can revise the sentences. Usually you'll be able to cut out some unnecessary words and use a stronger verb. Here are the sentences revised:

> At sixty-three Max Ernst saw only madness and death lying before him.

> The setting sun turned the few clouds hanging over the horizon orange.

> The feeling of impending violence dominates Hemingway's "The Killers."

Now these sentences are direct and clear; moreover, they read quickly.

For further illustration, study the following student example while watching for *was* and *were* structures.

> The motorcycles were sweeping into the park like 1000-pound bees. The lead rider was a huge man and was hunched over the handlebars. His face was behind a mirrored visor that was reflecting a miniature and distorted image of the road that was stretching before him.

A good piece of description, but it could be sharper. Concentrating on eliminating *was* and *were* structures, the writer revised it.

> The motorcycles swept into the park like 1000-pound bees. The lead rider, a huge man, hunched over the handlebars. His face was hidden behind a mirrored visor that reflected a miniature and distorted image of the road stretching before him.

The revision reads more quickly and carries more punch. The writer kept one *was* structure but added *hidden* to make the sentence stronger. That's fine; after all, we are not recommending that you restructure every sentence with a form of *to be* in it. We only suggest you restructure the ones that use it unnecessarily. Remember, we can't give you rules for editing and revising, but only suggestions. What to restructure is up to you.

There are/There is

Sometimes when you reread a passage you'll find sentences built on *there are* and *there is* patterns. We don't want to tell you not to use this pattern — it's an effective one — but we do want to tell you how to use it. *There are* and *there is* patterns simply assert the existence or presence of something; they do nothing more. The secret is not to abuse the pattern by asserting the obvious.

> There are differing opinions regarding women's liberation.

> There is a rift between America's Democrats and Republicans.

> There is conflict over who is responsible for the oil crisis.

To assert the existence of differing opinions, rifts, and conflicts regarding such controversial issues in this fashion is to waste a pattern that you can use more effectively to stress a fact that may be significant in your paper. In other words, save it to announce real news.

> There are more women than men enrolled in auto shop.

> There is only one answer to this problem.
>
> There are only two qualified candidates out of two hundred applicants.

More women than men enrolled in auto shop! One answer to a problem! Two qualified candidates out of two hundred applicants! This is news. News should be highlighted before the particulars are presented. *There are* and *there is* work this way.

But when something is beside the point, the pattern is useless:

> There is an old investment formula that says when the little man buys, sell.

If such a formula is commonly understood, why highlight it? Instead merely write

> An old investment formula says that when the little man buys, sell.

These are subtle differences compared to the way many beginning writers abuse this pattern. Often they unconsciously sprinkle their work with *there are* and *there is* sentences. Many times, while writing in this mental state, they'll also stir in some *it is* or *it was* patterns. To see what we mean, read the following passage:

> There are two types of characters in fiction: flat and round. It is the flat character who has only one outstanding trait, such as the drive of the relentless cop or the push of the power-hungry politician. It is the round character that is more complex, usually fleshed out with many traits and in a variety of detail. Often there is one trait that dominates the others, but the round character will be more fully drawn than the single-faceted flat character.

This is lazy writer's prose. The whole passage needs to be revised by reworking the sentences to eliminate *there are* and *it is*. Here's one way to do it:

> Flat and round characters dominate fiction. A flat character usually has one outstanding trait, such as the drive of the relentless cop or the push of the power-hungry politician. The round character is more complex, usually fleshed out with many more traits and in a variety of detail. Sometimes a dominant trait will stand out from the others, but even so the rounded character will be more complex than the single-faceted flat character.

If you find you write sentences using *there are* and *there is* ineffectively, rework them. Soon you'll find they will seldom appear in your rough drafts. Your first efforts will be sharper.

Coherence

One problem you need to avoid is the sense that your sentences seem disconnected — that they are running on watered fuel, spurting and coughing into action. When this happens coherence has broken down; your sentences aren't working together. Sometimes the flow is broken because you have tacked an irrelevant sentence onto your prose; this is a unity problem and can be corrected by simply cutting the offending statement. A coherence problem runs deeper; the parts belong but have not been properly joined.

As is usually the case in writing instruction, the problem is much easier to show than to explain. Take a look, therefore, at this example to see what we mean.

> Nowhere can I relax more than at my favorite lake. I like a lake with clear skies and fresh water. At the beach, salt water always makes me itch and the smog is often terrible. There's privacy at my lake with no more than a handful of campers scattered throughout the pines and meadows. The beach is usually packed, and I go away feeling more like an egg in a carton than a human being. I like fishing for trout, cooking the trout for breakfast, hiking the trails, cooking trout for lunch, napping in the shade, reading, cooking even more trout for dinner, and sleeping under the stars. Sometimes I go to Harry's, a beer bar that serves down-home meals and country sounds. After about ten days at my lake and Harry's, I'm ready for another semester.

Do you feel the disconnections, the spaces between the sentences? Reading it is almost like being led on a tour by a guide who has your nose between his fingers. Who yanks your head from side to side while rapidly declaring, "Look at this — Now this — And this!" Who makes no connections. Who doesn't show the relationships between sites. Who just yanks and announces. That's pretty much what this writer does to us. He hasn't smoothed our way. He hasn't connected his sentences. To write coherently a writer has to learn to blend sentences together. Often this means supplying more information for the reader so that the relationships are clear.

Now read the rewritten draft of the sample paragraph. The writer has supplied the connections and filled in the empty spaces.

> Nowhere can I relax more than at a lake I visit each August outside of Cedar City, Utah. I like the lake with its clear skies and fresh water more than the beach near my house with its smog and salty sea that leaves my skin itchy. My lake offers privacy with usually only a handful of campers scattered throughout the pines and meadows; the beach is usually packed,

and I go away feeling more like an egg in a carton than a human being. My days at the lake move in nice circles: fishing for trout at dawn, cooking trout for breakfast, hiking the trails, cooking trout for lunch, reading and napping in the shade, cooking trout for dinner, fishing for trout at dusk, and sleeping under the stars. Two or three evenings during my vacation I break the circle by going to Harry's, a beer bar that serves down-home meals and lots of country sounds. After about ten days of my lake and a few evenings at Harry's, I'm ready for home and another semester.

We can follow the writer's thought; the sentences connect. He has successfully rewritten the paragraph to make it coherent. One way he has achieved coherence is by filling in some empty spaces with more information. We as readers now know where the lake is located, why it's so important to him, and how he sees the time he spends there moving in circles. Since we haven't the power to mind-gaze, we need this kind of information to follow his point.

He has also achieved coherence by combining sentences, using subordinate clauses and phrases and punctuation techniques to tie them together. For instance, in the first draft he wrote

I like a lake with clear skies and fresh water. At the beach, salt water always makes me itch and the smog is often terrible.

After examining the ideas in these two sentences, he sees clearly that they relate through contrast. He decides to make them cohere by combining the ideas around "more than" to clearly show the contrasting relationship. He also uses a *that* clause to pack more information into the new sentence.

I like the lake with its clear skies and fresh water more than the beach near my house with its smog and salty sea that leaves my skin itchy.

Later he uses a semicolon to show another contrast. First he wrote

There's privacy at my lake with only a handful of campers scattered throughout the pines and meadows. The beach is usually packed, and I go away feeling more like an egg in a carton than a human being.

In the revision he ties these thoughts together:

My lake offers privacy with usually only a handful of campers scattered throughout the pines and meadows; the beach is usually packed, and I go away feeling more like an egg in a carton than a human being.

We've offered these opening examples and comments to awaken you to the importance of writing coherently. Guiding a reader through your writing is not a matter of catch-as-catch-can. It takes careful thought. You must anticipate the reader. But once you begin to think through what you're saying and develop a sense of a reader peering over your shoulder, you'll keep your writing coherent without too much effort.

Transitional Devices

Transitions are some mechanical tactics writers use to keep their work coherent. As we said in Getting Started, transitions serve as guideposts to direct the readers' attention. Let's study some of the standard transitional techniques. They will help you guide your readers.

Transitional words and phrases. When you give directions, develop illustrations, pack your writing with difficult information, or shift into a new pattern, you'll need to take some care in drawing your readers along. At these times we suggest you use obvious transitions. Plain ones. Ones that give a clear signal. You can select from a stock of standard ones. Here are a few, listed by how they function.

Similarity	likewise, similarly
Difference	but, however, still, yet, nevertheless, on the other hand, on the contrary, in contrast, at the same time
Addition	moreover, and, in addition, equally important, next, first, second, third, in the first place, in the second place, again, also, too, besides, furthermore
Illustration	for example, for instance, to illustrate
Time	soon, in the meantime, afterward, later, meanwhile, earlier, simultaneously, finally
Direction	here, there, over there, beyond, nearby, opposite, under, above, to the left, to the right, in the distance
End	in conclusion, to summarize, finally, on the whole
Restatement	in short, in other words, in brief, to put it differently
Result	therefore, then, as a result, consequently, accordingly, thus

Author, educator, and U.S. senator from California S. I. Hayakawa uses a few overt transitions to keep his reader awake while reading this paragraph.

> *To cite another example,* students trying to express themselves in writing may write poorly. In order to improve their writing, says the English teacher, I must teach them the fundamentals of grammar, spelling, and punctuation. *By thus* placing excessive

emphasis on grammar and mechanics while ignoring the students' ideas, the teacher quickly destroys student interest in writing. That interest destroyed, the students write even more poorly. *Thereupon* the teacher redoubles his dose of grammar and mechanics. The students become increasingly bored and rebellious. Such students fill the ranks of "remedial English" classes in high school and college.

Hayakawa is sparing in the use of overt transitions. But because they offer an easy way to link sentences, beginning writers tend to overuse them. We suggest you guard against this mistake. Too many *on the other hand*'s, *moreover*'s, *furthermore*'s, and *in contrast to*'s have about the same effect on a reader than a mistuned bass has on a music lover.

Also be sure you use the transition with a proper sense to connect your thoughts.

> We could go to the mountains; on the other hand, we could go to the desert.

Why "on the other hand"? The phrase announces a contrast — usually an extended one. Since no real contrast exists, the writer should have written

> We could go to the mountains or the desert.

Repetition of key words and phrases. Repeating key words and phrases — much more subtle than using mechanical transitions — will also help keep your writing coherent. One of the simplest tactics is to interweave pronouns along with the subject. This kind of repetition keeps the readers' attention focused. Conservationist Cleveland Amory uses this technique in discussing coyote survival behavior:

> In such situations, the *coyote's* only hope lies in *his* cleverness. And stories of *coyotes* outwitting hunters are legion. *Coyotes* will work in teams, alternately resting and running to escape dogs set upon them. *They* have even been known to jump on automobiles and flat cars to escape dogs. And *they* have also successfully resisted bombing. Lewis Nordyke reports that once when a favorite *coyote* haunt in Texas became a practice range for bombing, the *coyotes* left — temporarily. Soon *they* were back to investigate and found that the bombing kept people out. *They* decided to stay. Meanwhile, *they* learned the bombing schedule and avoided bombs.

In "The Death of Marilyn Monroe" Diana Trilling repeats personal pronouns to maintain coherence in a paragraph that compares Ernest Hemingway with the actress:

Of Ernest Hemingway, for example, I feel, much as I do of Marilyn Monroe, that *he* was unable to marshal any adequate defense against the painful events of *his* childhood, and this despite *his* famous toughness and the courage *he* could call upon in war, in hunting, in all the dangerous enterprises that seduced *him*. *He* was an innocent man, not a naive man, though not always intelligent. Marilyn Monroe offers us a similar paradox. Even while *she* symbolized an extreme of experience, of sexual knowingness, *she* took each new circumstance of life, as it came to *her* or as *she* sought it, like a newborn babe. And yet this was not what made *her* luminous — *her* innocence. The glow was not rubbed off *her* by *her* experience of the ugliness of life because finally, in some vital depth, *she* had been untouched by it.

Any repeated key word or phrase — not just pronouns — or any synonyms that carry the meaning of a key word or phrase can serve a transitional function. But remember, the word or phrase must be *key* — one that carries the meaning of the passage.

Poet Erica Jong uses this technique in a paragraph from "The Artist as Housewife." She says a major difficulty the female poet faces is "to raise a voice." She then links the idea to authenticity, a word she repeats throughout the passage.

The main problem of a poet is to *raise a voice.* We can suffer all kinds of kinks and flaws in a poet's work except lack of *authenticity. Authenticity* is a difficult thing to define, but roughly it has to do with our sense of the poet as a mensch, a human being, an author (with the accent on authority). Poets arrive at *authenticity* in very different ways. Each poet finds her own road to walking it — sometimes backward, sometimes at a trot. To achieve *authenticity* you have to know who you are and approximately why. You have to know yourself not only as defined by the roles you play but also as a creature with an inner life, a creature built around an inner darkness. Because women are always encouraged to see themselves as role players and helpers ("helpmate" as a synonym for "wife" is illuminating here), rather than as separate beings, they find it hard to grasp this *authentic sense of self.* They have too many easy cop-outs.

Transitional sentences. Besides obvious mechanical and repetitive transitional techniques, writers sometimes use transitional sentences to maintain coherence. Sometimes these sentences serve as resting points for readers by gathering up what has been said and pointing to what will be said. Jessica Mitford in a paragraph from *The American Way of Death* uses this technique.

The next step is to have at Mr. Jones with a thing called a trocar. This is a long, hollow needle attached to a tube. It is jabbed into the abdomen, poked around the entrails and chest cavity, the contents of which are pumped out and replaced with "cavity fluid." This done, and the hole in the abdomen sewed up, Mr. Jones's face is heavily creamed (to protect the skin from burns which may be caused by leakage of the chemicals), and he is covered with a sheet and left unmolested for a while. *But not for long — there is more, much more, in store for him.* He has been embalmed, but not yet restored, and the best time to start the restorative work is eight to ten hours after embalming, when the tissues have become firm and dry.

Parallel structure. Writers also use parallel structure — structures that repeat word patterns — to generate cohesiveness in their writing. The movement of parallel structures creates a rhythm that builds expectations in the reader. Lionel Casson in a passage from *Ancient Egypt* uses simple parallel structure to stress how far back Egyptian history goes. Casson opens with a brief topic sentence, then writes three sentences that repeat a pattern: *It was, It flourished,* and *It was viewed.*

Egypt was ancient even to the ancients. It was a great nation a thousand years before the Minoans of Crete built their palace at Knossos, about 900 years before the Israelites followed Moses out of bondage. It flourished when tribesmen still dwelt in huts above the Tiber. It was viewed by Greeks and Romans of 2,000 years ago in somewhat the same way the ruins of Greece and Rome are viewed by modern man.

In more sophisticated hands parallel structure can penetrate the psyche by going beyond a mere technique for organizing information and shaping an emotional cohesiveness for the reader. Joan Didion reaches for this impact in the opening paragraph of *The White Album.*

We tell ourselves stories in order to live. The princess is caged in the consulate. The man with the candy will lead the children into the sea. The naked woman on the ledge outside the window on the sixteenth floor is a victim of accidie, or the naked woman is an exhibitionist, and it would be "interesting" to know which. *We tell* ourselves that it makes some difference whether the naked woman is about to commit a mortal sin or is about to register a political protest or is about to be, the Aristophanic view, snatched back to the human condition by the fireman in priest's clothing just visible in the window behind her, the one smiling at the telephoto lens. *We look* for the sermon in the suicide, for the social or moral lesson in the murder of five. *We interpret* what we see, select the most workable of the multiple choices. *We live* entirely, especially if we are writers, by the imposition of a narrative line upon disparate images, by the "ideas" with which we have learned to freeze the shifting phantasmagoria which is our actual experience.

Transitions connecting paragraphs. So far we've illustrated transition as a way of maintaining coherence within paragraphs. But we want to point out the importance of connecting paragraphs. The standard tactic is to use a transitional word or phrase to make the connection. You've probably noticed that several paragraphs we've used as illustrations obviously connect with paragraphs that came before them. Hayakawa's begins "To cite another example"; Trilling's, "Of Ernest Hemingway, for example"; Amory's, "In such situations." All are using obvious transition as they glide from paragraph to paragraph. Sometimes writers will close one paragraph with a sentence or phrase that sets up the paragraph that follows. X. J. Kennedy uses this technique in an essay titled "Who Killed King Kong?"

> Why does the American public refuse to let King Kong rest in peace? It is true, I'll admit, that Kong outdid every monster movie before or since in sheer carnage. Producers Cooper and Schoedsack crammed into it dinosaurs, headhunters, riots, aerial battles, bullets, bombs, bloodletting. Heroine Fay Wray, whose function is mainly to scream, shuts her mouth for hardly one uninterrupted minute from first reel to last. It is also true that Kong is larded with good healthy sadism, for those whose joy it is to see the frantic girl dangled from cliffs and harried by pterodactyls. *But it seems to me that the abiding appeal of the giant ape rests on other foundations.*
>
> Kong has, *first of all*, the attraction of being manlike. His simian nature gives one huge advantage over giant ants and walking vegetables in that an audience may conceivably identify with him. Kong's appeal has the quality. . . .

Combining transitional devices. We don't want to leave you with the impression that writers select one method of transition and use it exclusively. If you glance back at Kennedy's piece, you'll see that he uses repetition and parallel structure as well as an overt transitional phrase. Most writing is webbed with transitional techniques. The following illustration is an excerpt from "Prediction as a Side Effect" by Isaac Asimov. Words and phrases that provide coherence have been underlined and keyed as follows:

P = pronoun
R = repetition
S = synonym
T = transition
* = pronouns not marked because there is no previous noun to which they refer

In the 1650s, the French duellist, poet, and science-fiction writer Cyrano de Bergerac (yes, <u>he</u> really lived, nose and all) wrote a tale of a
       P
trip to the Moon. In <u>it</u>, <u>his</u> hero thought of various ways of reaching the
         P   P
<u>Moon</u>, <u>each</u> logical after a fashion. One way, <u>for instance</u>, was to strap
   R   P   T
vials of dew about <u>his</u> waist. The <u>dew</u> rose, when the day grew warm and
               P   R
turned <u>it</u> to vapor. Might <u>it</u> not draw the <u>man</u> up as well, once <u>it</u> <u>rose?</u>
       P   P   S   P R
(The <u>idea</u> was wrong, but <u>it</u> had the germ of the balloon in <u>it</u>.)
     S   P   P
   Another of <u>Cyrano's</u> <u>notions</u> was that <u>his hero</u> might stand on an iron
   T   R   S   R
plate and throw a magnet up into the air. The <u>magnet</u> would draw the
                                              R
<u>iron plate</u> upward, together with the <u>man</u> upon <u>it</u>. When the <u>iron plate</u>
R   R   P   R
reached the <u>magnet</u>, <u>both</u> would tend to fall down again, but before <u>that</u>
            R   P   P
could happen, the <u>voyager</u> would quickly seize the <u>magnet</u> and <u>throw</u> <u>it</u>
                  S   R   R   P
up again, <u>drawing</u> the <u>plate</u> still higher and so on. (Quite impossible of
          R   R
course, but <u>it</u> sounds so plausible.)
            P
   And a third <u>idea</u> was to use rockets.
               R
   <u>It</u>* so happens that now, three centuries after the time of <u>Cyrano</u>, <u>we</u>*
                                                          R
do use rockets to reach the Moon. <u>It</u> is the only <u>method</u> by which <u>we</u> can
                                  P   S   R
<u>reach</u> the <u>Moon</u>, at least so far and for the foreseeable future.
R   R
   The first man to show that <u>this</u> was so in the scientific sense was Isaac
                              P

Newton, in the 1680s, and <u>we</u> still use <u>his</u> equations to guide <u>our</u> astro-
R   P   P

nauts in <u>their</u> flights. <u>However,</u> as it* turns out, the first to consider the
P   T

use of <u>rockets</u> was not <u>Newton,</u> but the <u>science-fiction writer</u> <u>Cyrano,</u>
R   R   R   R

thirty years before <u>Newton.</u>
R

Colon

The colon has several common uses, none of which will give you much trouble. The colon is used to separate subtitles from titles, for subdivisions of time, for parts of biblical citations, to separate a word or phrase from additional material, and to separate the salutation from the text in a formal business letter.

Title from subtitle

Origins of the English Language: A Social and Linguistic History

Time

    2:31 p.m.

    12:51 a.m.

Biblical citation

    Luke 3:4–13

Word or phrase from additional material

    For rent: three-bedroom house

Salutation from text in a formal business letter

    Dear Ms. Randolph:

    Dear Mr. Templeton:

These standard uses of the colon are not very troublesome. You probably already use the colon in several of these ways without much thought.

But the colon is also used after an introductory statement to signal that more will follow. Here are five ways you can use it.

1. Use a colon to introduce a series.

    She narrowed her vacation choices to three sites: the Greek islands, the Irish countryside, and the Swiss Alps.

    No matter how social historians of English look at their task, three dates stand out in the evolution of the language: 450, when the Germanic tribes invaded and occupied Britain; 1066, when the Norman French invaded and conquered England; and 1607, when English speakers colonized America.

2. Use a colon to introduce a statement or series preceded by *the following* or *as follows*.

Agreeing with Orwell, many linguists see the relation between language and thought as follows: a person's thought depends on the quality of a person's language, and, in turn, the quality of a person's language depends on a person's thought.

3. Use a colon to announce a long or formal quotation.

The author uses the weather to set the scene of his story: "I hear thunder roll through my neighborhood, and from where I sit before the front window, I see the wind lash leaves from the eucalyptus trees and swirl rain down through the branches and around the street lamps, the drops, like fragments of shattered mirror, splashing into pools of light reflected from the pavement."

4. Use a colon to announce a second main clause that explains the first.

His intention is clear: he is determined to become president no matter how far he must distort the truth.

Keep in mind that when the material that follows a colon is a complete sentence, you may begin it with a capital or a lowercase letter. The choice is yours. Remember, though, whichever you decide to use — capital or lowercase — use it consistently throughout a paper.

5. Finally, use a colon to introduce a final appositive.

Only one person is capable of handling the job: Elma Bowen.

A single trait gives man the power to dominate the kingdom of earth: speech.

In either of these examples, we could have used a comma or a dash instead of a colon. Keeping in mind that the comma is less formal than the colon and that the dash is more dramatic than either, select the one that best suits your tone.

Comma

By clearing up any errors you may be making in using commas, you will probably clear up a high percentage of your total mistakes in punctuation. Mastering commas isn't too difficult, for commas have nine main uses.

1. Use the comma to separate main clauses in compound sentences. The comma should be placed before any connector — *and, but, or, nor, for,* and sometimes *yet* or *so* — that links the clauses.

   > The man in the front of the boat gave hand signals, and the boy at the tiller steered by his directions.

   > Most of us who were raised in cities yearn for elbow room, but few of us ever venture farther than our city limits for quick glimpses of open space.

   When the compound sentence has brief main clauses, the comma is optional.

   > The dance lasted hours and we exhausted ourselves.

   or

   > The dance lasted hours, and we exhausted ourselves.

   > My feet hurt so I sat down.

   or

   > My feet hurt, so I sat down.

2. Use the comma to set off some introductory elements. When you begin a sentence with an adverb clause, a long prepositional or verbal phrase, a transitional word or phrase, or an interjection, use a comma to separate it from the main clause.

   Introductory adverb clauses begin with words such as *when, after, as, because, since, if, unless,* and *although.* The adverb clauses in the following sentences require commas:

   > After she returned from Paris, Barbara moved into a loft and began to paint.

   > If you hope to get a well-paying job, you had better develop some marketable skills.

   If an adverb clause comes at the end of a sentence, it does not need to be set off by a comma.

   > Barbara moved into a loft and began to paint after she returned from Paris.

   > You had better develop some marketable skills if you hope to get a well-paying job.

   If an adverb clause is short, there is no need for a comma:

   > When I dance she laughs and the cat hides.

   If you write a long prepositional or verbal phrase at the beginning of a sentence, separate it from the main clause with a comma:

   > In the early morning near the river, runners gather each Sunday for the Hash House Run.

Exhausted from hours of study, Joan closed her books and collapsed on the sofa.

To run successfully for a congressional seat, Hannah Becker expects to spend at least $100,000.

If you write a short prepositional or verbal phrase at the beginning of a sentence, omit the comma:

In scientific writing accuracy sometimes overwhelms style.

Facing east Ronald saw the sun rising above the hills.

When you begin a sentence with a transitional word or phrase, you will usually separate it from the main clause by using a comma:

Finally, I would like to point out the difficulty in funding a new student center.

On the other hand, the film treated a subject never before handled in cinema.

You should also set off interjections and direct addresses with a comma:

Great Scott, the world seems destined to self-destruct!

Sarah, why haven't you written?

3. Use commas to separate words, phrases, and clauses cast in series — three or more items of equal importance.

The colors of Old Glory are red, white, and blue.

William Faulkner, Flannery O'Connor, and Truman Capote are American writers with roots deep in the experience of the South.

In the trunk she found a faded dress, several dim photographs, two Easter bonnets, and a loaded pistol.

Sometimes he would become so emotional that he could relieve the tension only by running through the neighborhood, bursting spontaneously into song, or hammering relentlessly against the old workbench at the rear of the garage.

Some writers omit the comma before *and* and *or* when either is used in a series. We suggest you make a practice of including the comma so that you will not mistakenly lead readers to believe the last two items go together:

For the picnic he brought cake, apples, mustard, sourdough bread, ham, and eggs.

is clearer than

For the picnic he brought cake, apples, mustard, sourdough bread, ham and eggs.

Whenever you join each item in a series with *and* or *or*, don't use any commas:

The kitchen has no working oven or garbage disposal or dishwasher.

The wind swirled leaves from the ground and bent the treetops and swept the clouds east.

4. Use the comma to separate coordinate adjectives that modify a noun, a pronoun, or any word serving as a noun.

The tall, lanky, big-footed youth sauntered through the doorway.

You can spot coordinate adjectives easily. If you can rearrange the adjectives without changing the meaning or replace the comma separating them with *and,* then they are coordinate. If you can't make either of these alterations without changing the meaning, then the adjectives aren't coordinate and shouldn't be separated:

My uncle holds a Midwestern Populist view of economics.

She walked down the dimly lighted inner corridor.

5. Use commas to set off nonrestrictive clauses, phrases, and appositives. These nonrestrictive modifiers are used to give interesting information, additional details, or further description, but such additions are not essential to the meaning of the sentence.

Janice Smith, *who graduated from Johns Hopkins in 1978,* published an anthropological study this year. (Nonrestrictive clause)

He rubbed his eye, *circled by a bruise,* and moaned. (Nonrestrictive phrase)

The Cliff Palace, *a quaint but rickety hotel on the Maine coast,* provides vacationers monthly room and board for less than six hundred dollars. (Appositive)

Restrictive modifiers give information essential to the meaning of the sentence and should not be set off by commas.

I left the book *that has my notes written in the margin* at the library. (Restrictive clause)

The woman *teaching the only class in poetry writing* won the Most Outstanding Teacher award. (Restrictive phrase)

The novelist *Norman Mailer* has been more successful writing nonfiction than fiction. (Restrictive appositive)

How can you tell if a modifier is nonrestrictive or restrictive? One way, which works in most instances, is to read the sentence without the clause, phrase, or appositive. If the sentence still makes the same sense, the modifier is nonrestrictive and should be set off by commas.

Our earlier examples of sentences with nonrestrictive modifiers do make sense when the added clause, phrase, or appositive is left out:

Janice Smith published an anthropological study this year.

He rubbed his eyes and moaned.

The Cliff Palace provides vacationers monthly room and board for less than six hundred dollars.

If leaving out the modifying clause, phrase, or appositive leaves a sentence that does not make sense or is confusing, the modifier is restrictive and should not be set off by commas:

I left the book at the library. (Which book?)

The woman won the Most Outstanding Teacher award. (Which woman?)

The novelist has been more successful writing nonfiction than fiction. (Which novelist?)

Occasionally, a sentence will contain a modifier that can be either nonrestrictive or restrictive, depending on the intended meaning.

The students, in the back of the room, applauded wildly.

With commas setting off the modifier, this sentence means that all the students, who incidentally sat in the back of the room, applauded wildly.

The students in the back of the room applauded wildly.

Without commas, this sentence means that some students, those in the back of the room, applauded wildly.

If you write such a sentence, it's up to you to be aware of the possible confusion it might create for readers and to punctuate it appropriately. Remember not to set off restrictive appositives — appositives that give readers information they need.

The novelist Norman Mailer has been more successful writing nonfiction than fiction.

My brother Tom will be in Pittsburgh next week.

John the Baptist was an early Christian prophet.

6. Use commas to set off parenthetical expressions. Parenthetical expressions interrupt the flow of the sentence. Often they are transitional and guide readers' attention. Words and phrases such as *however, therefore, consequently, furthermore, accordingly, on the other hand, in the first place,* and *for example* serve this function.

Serious mystery writers, for example, try to reestablish sense in the senseless world of murder.

They are, consequently, destined for a life of struggle.

Gold, on the other hand, has a value that will not only endure but also increase over the years.

At other times parenthetical expressions will take the shape of afterthoughts or supply some additional information.

At eighteen, some fifty years ago, he struck out for Nevada in a broken-down Model T without a spare tire.

7. Use commas to avoid confusing readers. To maintain clarity, you will sometimes need to use a comma where one is not required.

When sixty-five, executives of many major American companies are forced to retire.

After eating, the cat curled up and began to purr.

8. Use commas to separate phrases that express contrast.

He is a confused man, not an immoral one.

The old man was thrifty, not stingy.

It was Jane, not Jan.

9. Use commas to separate absolute phrases. An absolute phrase is a parenthetical construction that modifies a whole sentence but is not attached to it by a connecting word. An absolute phrase usually begins with a noun or pronoun and is followed by a participle.

John ran through the rain, his feet pumping up and down in the puddles.

Their faces calm, the drivers sat behind the wheels and gunned the engines.

The film was dull, two hours stuffed with unremitting clichés.

10. Use commas according to established convention.

Salutations of informal letters

Dear Beth,

Dear Fred,

Dates

September 21, 1980 (*but not in* 21 September 1980)

Place names

New York, New York

Murphy's Bar and Grill, Chicago, Illinois

Addresses

2701 Fairview Drive, Costa Mesa, California 92626 (Don't use a comma to separate a state from a zip code.)

Numbers

345,678

78,632,112

Keep in mind that commas in numbers always set off groups of three digits and begin from the right. Also remember that in four-digit figures the comma is optional.

2,341 *or* 2341

Omission of understood words

This books belongs to Bob; this one, to Carol.

Burning Star does best at the start; High Prancer, in the stretch.

Comma Splice and Run-On

You probably already know that comma splices and run-ons are serious writing errors. But they are simple to correct. If you've joined two sentences with a comma, then you've written a comma splice:

Barbara French collects curios from around the world, William French collects maps of New England.

If you've joined two sentences without any punctuation mark, then you've written a run-on (sometimes called a "fused sentence"):

Barbara French collects curios from around the world William French collects maps of New England.

As you can see, there is very little difference between comma splices and run-ons. Both can be corrected in one of four ways.

1. Make two sentences.

   Barbara collects curios from around the world. William collects maps of New England.

2. Use a semicolon. You might write a comma splice or run-on because the thoughts you're trying to express are closely related. Writers use semicolons to show close relationships between the thoughts in two sentences.

   Barbara collects curios from around the world; William collects maps of New England.

   Primitive people have myths that reflect group consciousness, modern people have television. [Comma splice]

Primitive people have myths that reflect group consciousness; modern people have television.

American adolescence ended at the Pacific Ocean American maturity started with a turn toward the Atlantic. [Run-on sentence]

American adolescence ended at the Pacific Ocean; American maturity started with a turn toward the Atlantic.

3. Use a coordinating conjunction. The ideas in the sentences must be closely related, and the coordinating conjunction must be preceded by a comma.

Barbara collects curios from around the world, and William collects maps of New England.

When you use a coordinating conjunction to repair a comma splice or run-on, be sure to select the one that reflects the proper relationship between your ideas: *and* shows complementary relationships; *but* and *yet* show contradictory relationships; and *or* and *nor* show alternative relationships.

Note: Words such as *therefore, however, indeed, still,* and *nevertheless* are not coordinating conjunctions. If you use them to join main clauses, you must use a semicolon between the clauses.

Barbara collects curios from around the world; however, William collects maps of New England.

4. Use a subordinate structure. When one idea is more important than the other, you can subordinate the less important idea in a dependent clause by using a subordinating conjunction or relative pronoun.

Emphysema's ultimate effect on the body is deprivation of oxygen, it kills by suffocating. [Comma splice]

Since emphysema's ultimate effect on the body is deprivation of oxygen, it kills by suffocating.

Houston plays a gold-plated flute he got it as a gift. [Run-on sentence]

Houston plays a gold-plated flute, which he got as a gift.

Conclusions

Like introductions, conclusions come in variety; no single one serves all purposes. Your only obligation is to design one that naturally follows from the entire paper and clearly ends it. Avoid writing a conclusion that seems tacked on, and never — never, never, never — write one that raises a new question or apologizes for not covering the subject.

In college writing, the most common practice is to restate the central point and then summarize the subpoints to reinforce what has come before. Too often the summary method seems mechanical, but it can be effective if the writer handles it in an interesting way. A summary conclusion does have one strong advantage — it clearly links with the rest of the essay. The following paragraphs from a student paper that deals with investing in the stock market illustrate the summary method. Although we've left the discussion out, you can easily see what it covered.

The introduction:

> If you have any cash stuffed in jars or mattresses or just lying around in some passbook account, lazily accruing 5¼ percent interest, you would be wiser to fling it on a crap table. A crap game would give better odds at coming out ahead, for, as sure as a mouse with enough time will eat a pound of cheese, double-digit inflation will nibble your money away. At least on the crap table, although you would be bucking tremendous odds against winning, you would have a sporting chance. And there is always the payoff and the high you would get from watching the dice skip and jump over the green felt. But if you are too conservative for the Vegas thrill, then you might want to try the stock market. Even though the market is at an all-time low, it has some advantages for the cautious investor. First, you get paid for playing in the forms of dividends. Second, you get tax breaks. And third, there's better than fifty/fifty odds the market will rise.

Now the concluding summary:

> Is the market a good risk? It's clearly better than rat-holing your money or even stashing it in a savings account. Moreover, you get paid for playing, taxes work to your advantage, and the market, like an angry drunk pushed to the floor, will rise.

Besides the summary method there are several other standard ways writers use to write conclusions.

1. A writer may use the conclusion to deepen the dimension of an essay. One student ended a paper on being robbed and threatened at pistol point by shifting from the external details of the experience to an implicit psychological fact. Notice the following writer's use of questions to put the reader in a reflective mood.

> And what does it mean when somebody holds you up? Just the loss of a few dollars? Or just the loss of a wallet and some mementos — a few peeling photographs, worn identification cards, tattered ticket stubs? Yes, it means that. And it means more. It means you have become part of that chosen group that no longer feels safe after dark to walk the neighborhood streets.

Although the writer draws a fresh inference from the whole paper, she does not raise a new issue. She has, instead, highlighted an implicit aspect that ran beneath the surface of the entire essay.

2. A writer may also conclude an essay with an anecdote — a brief story — that puts the central idea in clear perspective. Nora Gallagher closes with this method in an article that deals with homosexual rights.

> A group of citizens tried to remove a gay group's name from a Bicentennial plaque. They met with resistance from City Councilman Leon Mezzetti, who said, "I wouldn't necessarily want the gays teaching my children, but the rules were that for 50 bucks you got your name on the plaque. And the gay people, God bless 'em, are following the rules. . . .
> "This is America. You can't change the rules after the fact, or you may as well tear the plaque down."

3. A writer may conclude by drawing a lesson that links the subject to the readers' condition. Tom Wicker in "Kennedy Without End, Amen" explores the significance of John Kennedy's brief term as president. Wicker adds a new dimension to his essay by linking the lessons Kennedy learned to the readers' learning process.

> In his life, I wrote those many years ago, "he had had his dreams and realized them," but he learned also the hard lessons of power and its limitations. After his death, the rest of us began to learn those lessons, too. The shots ringing out in Dealey Plaza marked the beginning of the end of innocence.

4. A writer may conclude with a quotation that deepens the meaning of an essay. One student who wrote a description of her creative process used a quotation from Joseph Campbell to knot the threads of her thought.

> At best my artistic process seems haphazard, a kind of inner blindman's bluff that finds its expression in chaotic collages. My groping and stumbling used to bother me until I came across a passage in Joseph Campbell's "The Inspiration of Oriental Art." He writes, "There is an important Chinese term, *wu wei, not doing,* the meaning of which is not *doing nothing,* but *not forcing.* Things will open up of themselves, according to their nature."

A writer may find that a quote is especially effective to end an interview or profile. Michelle Arnot concludes an article on the pleasures of massage that highlights the methods of New York masseuse Joan Witkowski.

> If you're not getting rubbed the wrong way, you may well become addicted. Joan finds that her vacations cause panic

among her clients. "I have to sneak away," she reports. "But it's always nice to come back. It's great to feel needed."

Or kneaded.

These samples are just a few of the many ways writers use to end essays. Notice, also, how methods tend to overlap. One has a quotation, but the quotation is a definition. Another holds an anecdote, but the anecdote includes a quotation. Several use questions. The label placed on a method isn't important. What is important is to write a conclusion that echoes the entire essay.

By the way — and we save this by the way for last to burn it into your mind — never, absolutely never, write "The End" after an essay's conclusion.

Dangling and Misplaced Modifiers

You run the risk of confusing your readers unless modifiers (words, phrases, or clauses used as adjectives or adverbs) clearly relate to the words they modify.

Sometimes the problem occurs because the modifier is misplaced — put in a position within the sentence that makes it appear to modify something it doesn't. Misplaced modifiers are sometimes confusing and sometimes nonsensical.

> Mr. Sheridan kept a record of all the money he made in his bureau drawer.

> She gave the candy to the neighborhood children that didn't turn out right.

The solution for this kind of misplacement is to reposition the modifier.

> In his bureau drawer Mr. Sheridan kept a record of all the money he had made.

> She gave the candy that didn't turn out right to the neighborhood children.

Other times the problem occurs because a modifier is left dangling with no word or phrase to modify.

> Walking along the country road, the sun rose gradually over the hilltops.

> While ordering hotdogs, "The Star-Spangled Banner" played over the loudspeaker.

These sentences seem to say that the sun was walking along the country road and that "The Star-Spangled Banner" ordered hotdogs. The writers have left something out — in these two examples, the pronoun *we*. Such sentences need to be revised to make the parts fit properly together.

As we were walking along the country road, the sun rose gradually over the hilltops.

or

Walking along the country road, we saw the sun rise gradually over the hilltops.

While we were ordering hotdogs, "The Star-Spangled Banner" played over the loudspeaker.

or

While ordering hotdogs, we heard "The Star-Spangled Banner" played over the loudspeaker.

Dash

Be cautious with dashes. When used properly they can be dramatic; when used improperly, tiresome and confusing. In a typed paper, you can make a dash by striking the hyphen key twice without spacing.

1. Use dashes to dramatize parenthetical elements.

   Harold ran — given the heat, slouched — six miles to come in last.

   Judge Sarah Riley sentenced Tom O'Keeffe — the treasurer of Local 1918 and once the friend of local politicians — to five years at Soledad prison.

2. Use dashes to dramatize appositives.

   Halfway through the party Phil Lambert — the man in the black cape and tuxedo who kept trying to bite Sam's neck — fell from the balcony into the tulip bed.

   He has only three vices — vice, vice, and vice.

   One love dominates my dreams — food.

3. Use a dash to separate a series that comes at the beginning of a sentence.

   Aching feet and ankles, throbbing shins, clicking knees, and crumbling hip joints — these are the physical joys that come with running on asphalt and cement.

4. Use a dash to show a break in thought.

   I don't know — it's just that — okay, I'll donate twenty dollars.

   He said, "You don't like it."
   "It's too — "
   "Too colorful?" he asked.
   "Too — well, too skimpy."

When using the dash in this way, be sure to omit the period or the question mark if the dash comes at the end of the thought.

5. Use a dash to precede an author's name after a direct quotation that has not been introduced or after one that stands separately from the text.

"If I had the use of my body I would throw it out the window."
— *Samuel Beckett*

Success is counted sweetest
By those who ne'er succeed.
To comprehend a nectar
Requires sorest need.
— *Emily Dickinson*

Editing and Revising

We've already talked a little about editing and revising in Part One, Getting Started, and we suggest you review that section if you feel the general concepts have slipped away. But now we want to illustrate the process in more detail and to give you more information about doing it.

If you're like most beginning writers, even some professional ones, you'll have a tough time accepting the idea that your prose isn't sacred. You've strained for ideas. You've found words to capture them. Nudged the words into sentences. Shaped the sentences into paragraphs. You've lavished time and energy on the whole creation. Why, you might ask, should you have to tinker with it any more?

Why indeed?

Because it's so easy to slip into the illusion that every word, every sentence, every paragraph has a clear meaning. You want to be clear. You wrack your brains to be clear. And somewhere deep in the imagination a seductive voice whispers. You become infatuated with the words and images it sets free. Ideas take off and soon you're floating in restless associations, the whole time writing under the illusion that your thought is clear. And it is — at least to you. But remember, except in your journal entries you're writing for a reader. You must keep a grip on the reality of what goes down on paper.

That's where editing and revising comes in. The act takes some courage. After all, to give up an illusion is hard, especially the illusion that you've been communicating clearly to another person — in this case, the reader.

To get started isn't too difficult, for it merely involves reading and rereading a rough draft as if you stood in someone else's shoes — the reader's. As you read, keep an eye out for words, phrases, and sentences that should be deleted, recast, combined with others, or replaced with more accurate ones (for example, a phrase such as *keep an eye out;* visualize the phrase — isn't it a horrible image?). With a pencil cross out the offending material. Rewrite between the lines or in the margins.

The problem in illustrating the editing and revising process is that it happens all at once, not in a nice orderly pattern. We wish we could demonstrate it by the numbers — you know what we mean: first, take up a pencil; second, sharpen the pencil to a fine point; third and fourth, return to the desk and with the rough draft before you begin to . . . but editing and revising doesn't work that way. The process is in part intuitive, a kind of faith healing. Before the intuition can come into play, you must see how the process is done and collect some information about how to improve what you've written in a rough draft.

By way of beginning, we want to offer a passage published a few years ago in *Playboy.* What! Edit and revise a piece of professional prose? Why not? If you can see flaws in publishing writing, you may begin to see them in your own work. The passage is a reminiscence, and the author captures some details from his early years.

> It begins very young up in the country whether you are raised on a big farm or in one of the small villages, which, though they often double as county seats, rarely number more than 1000 souls. There is a lumber mill down by the tiny river that manufactures crossties for the railroad systems, and the creosote the ties are treated with pervades the air. It is the smell of the town, depending on the wind: fresh-cut pine and creosote. In the center of the town there's a rather ugly yellow-brick courthouse, plain Depression architecture. The village is in northern Michigan and does not share the quaintness of villages in New England or the deep South, being essentially historyless. There are three baronial, rococo houses left over from the hasty passing of the lumber era, but most dwellings are characterized by their drabness, simply places for the shopkeepers to hide at night.

Confused? Absolutely! And your confusion doesn't come from our having lifted this single passage from a longer article. It comes from the author writing by midnight oil and failing to scrutinize the result in the sunlight. Truly, we don't know what this man is talking about. The intelligence behind the passage seems to be floating in a sea of personal associations. He seems to have no regard for a reader. For instance, what does "It" in the first line refer to? Moreover, what does "It begins very young up in the country" mean? Also notice how the writer begins by talking generally about villages and country but soon shifts to a particular village, one with a yellow-brick courthouse and three baronial, rococo houses. What are "baronial, rococo houses," anyway? What do they look like, really? Junk description like this often makes inexperienced readers feel stupid.

Since we wanted to find out what this passage was all about, we stripped it down, tore away the feathers to get to the meat. Where we could, we replaced difficult words with simple ones; we cut, rephrased, and combined. We worked with the intent of making the passage simple and plain. We weren't trying to clear up all the confusion; we only tried to edit away the decoration to see if anything could be saved and revised. Here is the result. We suggest you read it through, then reread it along with the marginal comments to get an idea of why we changed what we changed.

It begins ~~very~~ young ~~up~~ in the country whether you	*How young is "very" young? Why "up"? These two words say little. No need for them.*
are raised on a ~~big~~ farm or in ~~one of the small~~ village*s* (inserted: *a*)	*How big is a "big" farm? Ten acres? A thousand? Since no perspective for big is given, there's no need for it.*
~~which, though they often double as county seats, rarely~~	*The phrase "one of the small villages" is too many words to say "a village." Keep your prose concise. Village implies small. The information about the county seat doesn't seem to serve any purpose.*
~~number more than~~ 1000 ~~souls.~~ (inserted: *of*) There is a lumber mill	*"Souls" carries a connotation unnecessary to the passage.*
~~down~~ by the ~~tiny river~~ that ~~manufactures~~ crossties ~~for~~ (inserted: *stream* / *makes railroad*)	*Delete "lumber." Lumber mill is implied by other detail. No need for "down." A tiny river is a "stream." "Makes" is almost always better than the inflated "manufactures." Remember, simple is better.*
~~the railroad systems,~~ and the~~,~~ creosote ~~the ties are treated~~ (inserted: *smell of* / *and pine*) ~~with~~ ~~pervades~~ the air. ~~It is the smell of the town, depending~~ (inserted: *fills*) ~~on the wind: fresh-cut pine and creosote.~~ In	*The simple word "railroad" is more direct than "for the railroad systems."*
	This whole section is awkward; it needs reworking. All this stuff can be dropped or combined with other sentences. It's repetitive.
the center of the town there's a ~~rather ugly~~ yellow-brick	*Why "rather"? It doesn't do anything, really. "Ugly"? Readers should be able to see that for themselves.*
courthouse, ~~plain~~ Depression ~~architecture~~ The ~~village is~~ (inserted: *built during the*) (inserted: *village lacks history and*)	*"Plain Depression architecture" is awkward for "built during the Depression."*
~~in~~ northern Michigan ~~and does not share~~ the quaintness of	*This needs reworking. Awkward structure.*

feeling of *and Southern*

~~villages in~~ New England ~~or the deep South, being~~ *villages* ○ ~~essentially historyless~~. There are three ~~baronial, rococo~~ *mansions* ~~houses~~ left over from ~~the hasty passing of~~ the lumber

homes

era, but most ~~dwellings~~ are ~~characterized by their~~ ~~drabness, simply~~ places for ~~the~~ shopkeepers to hide at night.

What does "essentially" mean? Does this writer know? We don't think so. He's just mumbling to himself. "Historyless" is an awful misuse of language. The writer means without historical significance.

"Mansions" will serve for "baronial, rococo houses." No need for the "hasty passing."

"Homes" is simpler than "dwellings." In all your writing years you'll probably never need the phrase "characterized by." Always delete it. Always try to avoid sticking "ness" on the end of any word. Is there a need for "simply"? We don't see one.

Here's what the passage looks like with the changes incorporated:

> It begins young in the country whether you are raised on a farm or in a village of 1000. There is a mill by the stream that makes railroad crossties, and the smell of creosote and pine fills the air. In the center of the town there's a yellow-brick courthouse, built during the Depression. The northern Michigan village lacks history and the quaint feeling of New England and Southern villages. There are three mansions left over from the lumber era, but most homes are drab, places for shopkeepers to hide at night.

Now, what do we have left? Not much — a limp balloon that sputtered from our fingers, made two turns about the room, then fluttered to the floor. We hope that our letting out the wind from this inflated passage helped you see some of its problems. Can you see them?

Can you see that the piece lacks unity? The writer didn't set the focus. He allows us to stray.

Can you see that the point of view is fractured? The passage should have been written from the "I" perspective, not the "you."

And the coherence? Can you see how the thought seems to skip and flop? The writer has tried to move from a general comment on rural northern Michigan to a particular description of one village. He fails to do it coherently.

Finally, we hope you can see how the sentences seem crippled. The writer has built them on *there is* and *there are* patterns, the thoughtless writer's shortcut to description. These sentences need reworking.

With the editing done, we brazenly revised this writer's work; after all, under the writing teacher's blue pencil no one's prose is sacrosanct. We'll begin, as we suggest you begin when doing your own revisions, with the focus. This author's focus isn't clear. The focus must be made clear to achieve some kind of unity throughout the passage. Although the passage is confusing, we guessed from the first sentence that the writer was saying something about being young and becoming aware of the limited opportunities in his environment, which turns out to be Michigan:

> It begins young in the country whether you are raised on a farm or in a village of 1000.

He also wants to speak to the condition of all young people, not just himself — hence the use of the general "you." Keeping these thoughts in mind we rewrote the sentence this way:

> Like so many from rural northern Michigan, while still young I became aware of how little my village offered.

This revision solves another problem besides focus and point-of-view disruptions. The writer mentions growing up on a farm, then promptly drops any details of farm life. By using "rural" we suggest farm and country life but allow for a smooth movement to the particular village that dominates the rest of the passage.

Once the opening sentence was set, we went after the rest of the passage. We reordered the details with a concern for coherence, restructured the sentences, maintained the "I" point of view, and, since the passage echoes insignificance, waste, and a drab life, added a few words to capture that tone. Here's the result:

> Like so many from rural northern Michigan, while still young I became aware of how little my village offered. My village had fewer than one thousand people. It had neither significant history nor the quaint feeling of many New England and Southern villages. On its outskirts a stream flowed and carried away the waste from a mill that made railroad crossties and filled the town with smells of creosote and pine. In the town center stood a yellow-brick courthouse that was built during the Depression. Near it sat three decaying mansions left over from the booming lumber era, surrounded by drab homes, places for shopkeepers to hide at night.

This may not be the way the author would have rewritten this passage, but at least it is clear. Keep in mind, though, that editing and revising is not the reader's job; it's the writer's. In other words, it's yours.

You may be more concerned with writing information-centered pieces. No matter. The general approach to editing and revising holds up. Begin by rereading as if you stood in your readers' shoes. Ask yourself questions readers might ask you if they were present. "What does this sentence mean?" "Why have you repeated yourself?" "Why is this part muddled?" "Are you trying to confuse me with this word?" "What's your point, anyway?"

Exclamation Point

Be sparing in your use of the exclamation point. To overuse it is to create an immoderate, perhaps hysterical tone that exhausts most readers.

1. Use exclamation points after emphatic statements and commands.

Horses couldn't drag me to that reunion!

Be at my door at 7:08 p.m. exactly!

He roared, "Give me the change!"

"Off the roof!" Casey yelled.

Don't use exclamation points after mild commands.

When you finish the book, lend it to me.

Come over sometime.

2. Use exclamation points after interjections.

Wow! The party lasted ten hours.

Can they win the relay? No!

Fragments

Sentence fragments are groups of words that have been written as sentences: each begins with a capital and concludes with a period, question mark, or exclamation point but is not really a sentence. Sometimes writers consciously use fragments for dramatic effect. "Oh my god! I got an A on the final." More often they attach them to sentences. "Oh my god — I got an A on the final!" But when writers use fragments unconsciously, they mar their prose.

The *Grapes of Wrath* touched my life. Because Steinbeck vividly portrayed a struggle my grandparents went through.

Many fragments, like the one above, follow complete sentences. Often they are subordinate clauses introduced by words such as *although, because, if, since, until, while, that, which,* and *who.* Although a subordinate clause has a subject and predicate, it can't stand as a sentence. Fixing a fragment of this sort is fairly easy. Merely attach it to the preceding sentence or rewrite it so it can stand as a sentence.

The *Grapes of Wrath* touched my life because Steinbeck vividly portrayed a struggle my grandparents went through.

Faced with the prospect of not having enough money to buy food, the elderly poor must live each day in fear of slow starvation. Which some psychologists claim kills more of them than disease.

Faced with the prospect of not having enough money to buy food, the elderly poor must live each day in fear of slow starvation, which some psychologists claim kills more of them than disease.

Faced with the prospect of not having enough money to buy food, the elderly poor must live each day in fear of slow starvation. Some psychologists claim this fear kills more of them than disease.

Driving is still a cheap way to travel. Even though fuel prices have skyrocketed.

Driving is still a cheap way to travel even though fuel prices have skyrocketed.

Sometimes writers mistakenly treat verbal phrases as sentences. A verbal phrase begins with an infinitive (*to dance, to sleep*), a past participle (*danced, slept*), or a present participle (*dancing, sleeping*) and must always be part of a sentence. You can correct a fragment of this sort by combining it with a sentence or by rewriting it as a sentence.

We last saw Jane and Tom several hours after the game. Dancing in the street while the night poured rain.

We last saw Jane and Tom several hours after the game, dancing in the street while the night poured rain.

We last saw Jane and Tom several hours after the game. They were dancing in the street while the night poured rain.

Start your paper now. To have it ready by next Friday.

To have your paper ready by next Friday, start it now.

Start your paper now. Then you'll have it ready by next Friday.

Writers may also mistakenly treat prepositional phrases as sentences. Prepositional phrases beign with words like *toward, to, through, under, beneath, in, within, inside, over, above, outside, beside, behind, on,* and *about.* Generally, prepositional phrases can be attached to sentences but can never stand as sentences. Correct a fragment of this sort by combining it with the sentence that comes before or after it.

The newspapers carried the story. About the mayor hiring his son-in-law as a consultant for the city.

The newspapers carried the story about the mayor hiring his son-in-law as a consultant for the city.

It took three trips to Asia, two years of library research, and a mild heart attack. For Phillips to complete his study.

It took three trips to Asia, two years of library research, and a mild heart attack for Phillips to complete his study.

On days like today, when the sun is bright and the air is fresh and cool. I like to ice-skate on the pond at the edge of the woods.

On days like today, when the sun is bright and the air is fresh and cool, I like to ice-skate on the pond at the edge of the woods.

Sometimes writers treat appositive phrases — phrases that rename or describe nouns — as sentences. But, like subordinate clauses, verbal phrases, and prepositional phrases, appositives cannot stand as sentences. They must be combined with other sentences or rewritten.

The company is looking for a new sales representative. A person with a warm personality and an understanding of business.

The company is looking for a new sales representative, a person with a warm personality and an understanding of business.

Several popular weekend sports require exceptional hand-and-eye coordination. Handball, racketball, tennis, and squash.

Several popular weekend sports require exceptional hand-and-eye coordination — handball, racketball, tennis, and squash.

Hyphen

You can use the hyphen to divide words, form compounds, and attach prefixes and suffixes.

1. Use hyphens to indicate word breaks at the right-hand margin.

   Through storytelling the old communicate a family's history.

   Be sure to divide words only between syllables. Whenever you're unsure of the syllabication of a word, check a dictionary. The syllable break will usually be indicated by dots:

   com•mu•ni•cate

2. Use a hyphen to join two or more words that serve as a single adjective before a noun.

   That one-legged Easterner became a tobacco-chewing, rip-roaring broncobuster.

   Beth has finished some well-designed cabinets since taking a course in crafts.

   The twenty-year-old real estate tycoon will lecture tomorrow night.

When the compound adjective comes after the noun, don't use a hyphen.

Beth's cabinets are well designed because she took a course in crafts.

The real estate tycoon, who is only twenty years old, will lecture tomorrow night.

3. Use hyphens to form certain compound words:

mother-in-law	deep-freeze
cross-reference	good-bye
clear-cut	half-moon

Some compound words are hyphenated, and some are not, so check your dictionary for accuracy.

4. Use hyphens when spelling out numbers 21 through 99 and when writing fractions:

twenty-one	one-half
seventy-nine	three-fourths
two hundred ninety-nine	one three-thousandth

5. Use hyphens between prefixes and words beginning with capital letters.

un-American	post-Civil War
pre-Nixon	non-South American

6. Use hyphens between words and the prefixes *self-*, *all-*, and *ex-* (when it means "formerly"). Use a hyphen with the suffix *-elect*.

self-control	president-elect
ex-student	all-world

7. Use a hyphen between a capital letter and a word that serves as a suffix.

U-turn	T-shirt
X-ray	F-sharp

8. Use hyphens to avoid doubling vowels and tripling consonants.

anti-intellectual	co-owner
bell-like	wall-less

9. Use "suspended hyphens" for hyphenated words in series.

My mother-, father-, and brother-in-law all graduated from Locklin High School.

10. Use a hyphen to avoid ambiguity.

re-creation (something   *versus*   recreation   (a   diverting
created anew)   activity)

re-count (to count again) *versus*   recount (to narrate a past
                                      experience)

Introductions

When you write an introduction, you must clearly state or strongly imply the central point, and you must shape the beginning so that it leads naturally into the discussion. At the outset of a draft, you will be wise to write an introduction that flatly states, no matter how awkwardly, the central point. Later, once the entire draft is written, you can rework the beginning or throw it out and create a more vigorous one.

Also, since an introduction must lead readers into the discussion, don't back up too far to get a running start. For instance, if your subject is neighborhood vandalism, you would be unwise to start with a history of the Mafia.

Your introduction should also be appropriate and interesting. The kind you write will depend on the kind of essay and reader you envision. An essay written for an academic course would have a more formal introduction than one written for a student magazine. Here's a never rule: Never write an introduction that reports the rigors you underwent writing the essay.

To write an interesting introduction is almost always to write in concrete language and specific detail. If your prose limps along, the readers' interest will wane. Avoid general, imprecise language, like this:

> What do you buy when you buy an airline ticket? If you are going to fly in an airplane, it is important to know what you are guaranteed. If you read the fine print on the ticket, you will see you are not guaranteed much.

This introduction does little but present the subject and allow the writer to get twenty-eight extra words into the paper. He would show more consideration for the reader if he would merely start with the last sentence and toss out the first two. There are any number of effective ways to try to hook the readers' interest. All of them would use concrete language and specific detail.

> What do you buy when you buy an airline ticket? What does it entitle you to, and what are the airline's legal obligations to you? What's their responsibility if they cause you to miss a connection or blow a hotel reservation? Next time you're sitting in an airport, waiting for your delayed flight to get off the ground, you can pass the time and cool off your indignation by reading the

fine print on your ticket. A page headed "Conditions of Contract" could serve as a syllabus for a course in travel education.

Phrases such as "miss a connection," "blow a hotel reservation," "sitting in an airport," "waiting for your delayed flight," and so on add specifics most readers can relate to. This writer also uses a technique common to introductions: He begins by asking questions that the discussion will answer.

Since no set introduction is suitable for all purposes, a writer may begin an essay in any one of a wide variety of ways as long as it is appropriate, arouses some interest, and leads the reader into the discussion. Following are some examples of the most common introduction techniques.

1. Sometimes a writer will begin by cleverly using facts and statistics. Or, to put it another way, by dramatizing facts or statistics related to the central point. We want to stress the word *dramatize*. For most readers, wading through murky lists of facts and statistics is dull going. A good writer will dramatize the information so that readers will want to plunge into the rest of the essay.

Consider how Harry Stein dramatizes statistics in the opening paragraph of "How to Make It in the Water."

> First the bad part. It appears that swimming is here to stay. All signs point in that direction. Drop by a public pool on a ninety-five-degree afternoon and see for yourself; there they'll be, by the hundreds, churning through the water like a herd of water bugs. Then there are the statistics. A. C. Nielsen, the television ratings guy, reports that 103,000,000 Americans swim regularly. Which makes swimming by far the nation's most popular leisure activity, ahead of bicycling (with a mere 75,000,000), fishing (63,900,000), camping (58,100,000), bowling (44,400,000), and tennis (29,000,000).

In the following paragraph Eric Lax in "Quick, Make a Mussel!" dramatizes facts to hook the reader.

> This is about Mussels, not muscles. Consider: compared with an equal weight of T-bone steak, 3.5 ounces of mussels have the same amount of protein, one quarter the calories, one eighteenth the fat, eleven times the calcium and twice the phosphorus; mussels also pump fifty percent more iron into your body.

2. Often writers will begin by offering definitions. Good writers won't fall back on the dictionary to supply them with ready-made quotes and leave it at that. Instead they will generate some interest that goes beyond

the limits of a dictionary definition by casting descriptions in their own language and drawn from their own understanding.

In beginning a section on lions in *The Bestiary,* T. H. White opens by defining *beasts.*

> Leo the Lion, mightiest of beasts, will stand up to anybody. The word "beasts" should properly be used about lions, leopards, tigers, wolves, foxes, dogs, monkeys and others which range about with tooth and claw — with the exception of snakes. They are called beasts because of the violence with which they rage, and are known as "wild" because they are accustomed to freedom by nature and are governed by their own wishes. They wander hither and thither, fancy free, and they go wherever they want to go.

Leo Rosten in *The Joys of Yiddish* begins a description of a *shlimozl* with a definition.

> Pronounced shli-MOZ-zl, to rhyme with "thin nozzle." A chronically unlucky person; someone for whom nothing seems to go right or turn out well; a born "loser." Let me illustrate by combining four folk sayings: "When a shlimozl winds a clock, it stops; when he kills a chicken, it walks; when he sells umbrellas, the sun comes out; when he manufacture shrouds, people stop dying."

Often an introductory definition will be less formally structured than these just quoted and will seem to be closer to description (of course, definition is a form of description). For instance, in the opening paragraph of a short piece on packing in the Adirondacks, Anna La Bastille defines *lean-to,* a type of shelter available for public use on the trails.

> The lean-to is part of the history and tradition of the Adirondacks. A three-sided open shelter, it was originally designed as temporary quarters for hunters and fishermen in the 1800s but soon evolved into a more permanent structure, often used as a base camp by turn-of-the-century vacationers. There are some 200 lean-tos in the Adirondacks.

3. A writer may use a dramatic narrative to plunge the reader into the midst of an incident and then may follow with an exposition of the central point. Peter Eastman begins "Thermal Injury," an article on burns, with this technique.

> Robert, 27 years old, a graduate student; his wife, Anne; Frank, just graduated from Torrance High School; and Sue, Frank's best girl, are breaking an overnight camp on the west bank of Jenny Lake in the Sequoia National Forest.
>
> Morning mists move slowly off the little lake. Pine needles scent the air. Packs are ready to be hoisted.

> Robert pulls a cartridge from his tiny backpacker's stove. The shut-off valve sticks. Butane hisses for a moment, explodes loudly, and suddenly he is on fire. Knocked to the ground and shocked by the blasts, he sits numbly watching his blazing clothes.

George Orwell begins an essay on poverty in Marrakech with this narrative.

> As the corpse went past the flies left the restaurant table in a cloud and rushed after it, but they came back a few minutes later.
>
> The little crowd of mourners — all men and boys, no women — threaded their way across the marketplace between the piles of pomegranates and the taxis and the camels, wailing a short chant over and over again. What really appeals to the flies is that the corpses here are never put into coffins, they are merely wrapped in a piece of rag and carried on a rough wooden bier on the shoulders of four friends. When the friends get to the burying-ground they hack an oblong hole a foot or two deep, dump the body in it and fling over it a little of the dried-up, lumpy earth, which is like broken brick.

4. Straw man and reversal are two other effective techniques a writer can use for opening essays. Both should be used with caution because they reverse the train of thought that the opening sentences establish. Joseph Morgenstern in a review of the film *Easy Rider* uses the reversal. It comes in the last sentence.

> Time and again I wanted to reach out and shake Peter Fonda and Dennis Hopper, the two motorcyclist heroes of *Easy Rider,* until they stopped their damn-fool pompous poeticizing on the subject of doing your own thing and being your own man. I dislike Fonda as an actor; he lacks humor, affects insufferable sensitivity, and always seems to be fulfilling a solemn mission instead of playing a part. I didn't believe in these Honda hoboes as intuitive balladeers of the interstate highways, and I had no intention of accepting them as protagonists in a modern myth about the destruction of innocence. To my astonishment, then, the movie reached out and profoundly shook me.

The straw man device is similar to reversal: A writer sets up someone else's view in the introduction and knocks them down in the discussion. This technique usually begins with a direct quotation or summary that represents the position opposing the writer's. William Murray uses this method in the following quote.

> A recent issue of the "Calendar" section in the L.A. *Times* listed twelve theater openings, sixteen ongoing major pro-

ductions, 56 small-theater shows and 46 presentations in community playhouses. We would seem to be in the middle of a theatrical renaissance of unparalleled dimensions. Compared to what's available in L.A. and the immediate surrounding area, London is a backwater and New York a wasteland. Why isn't more being written about this phenomenon? Has L.A. bcome an Athens in a Periclean golden age of drama? Of course not.

5. A writer may begin by opposing a commonly held opinion about a subject. In the introduction to "The Joy of Maps," William Hjortsberg tries to shock the reader by challenging the general conception that maps are untrustworthy.

> "All maps are bad!" This draconian dictum survives from a math course I took as an undergraduate more years ago than I like to remember. The course, Math 1, known as Math for Idiots, covered such everyday matters as maps and calendars, seemingly simple items that grew increasingly complex as their mysteries were revealed.

Richard Reeves in "Equal Credit for Ghosts" attempts to hook the reader by shaking his belief that celebrities write their own books.

> In Jeb Magruder's Watergate book, one line of the acknowledgements reads: "I would also like to thank Patrick Anderson for his invaluable advice and assistance on this book." That was one of the three sentences in the book that Magruder wrote himself.
>
> John Dean, on the other hand, actually did write a manuscript. It wasn't, however, *Blind Ambition* — that was written by Taylor Branch. What Dean wrote was a pile of pages, unpublishable according to some sources, incoherent according to others. When last seen, Dean was on the book promotion trail, telling talk show hosts about the lonely agonies he endured as a writer.
>
> This is not about Watergate; it is about ghostwriting.

There are more, many more, kinds of introductions. We've offered a few of the most common to give you a sense of the possibilities. But no single method is suitable for all occasions, and none will work on any occasion if used awkwardly or mechanically.

Manuscript Form

Following standard manuscript form is a courtesy to the reader who expects things to be done properly. Manuscript form is merely a convention that defies logical explanation, but to ignore proper form is to risk annoying a reader — one who might be grading a college essay you have submitted.

Materials

For handwritten papers use 8½-by-11-inch lined white paper with neat edges, not paper torn from a spiral notebook. Use black or blue ink and write on one side only. Skip every other line to make reading and correcting your composition easier.

For typewritten papers use 8½-by-11-inch white typing paper but not flimsy onionskin. Double-space between lines and use one side only. Be sure that you have a good ribbon in the typewriter and that the keys are clean.

Unless otherwise directed, use a paper clip to hold pages together. Many instructors do not like pages stapled together, and no instructor likes the upper left-hand corner dogeared and torn to hold the pages in place.

Margins

Leave about an inch and a half margin at the left and top of the paper and an inch at the right and bottom to avoid a crowded appearance. On notebook paper the ruled vertical line indicates a proper left margin.

Indentations

Indent the first line of every paragraph uniformly — one inch in a handwritten manuscript, five spaces in a typewritten one.

Paging

Place the proper Arabic numeral (2, not II), without a period or parentheses, in the upper right-hand corner of each page. You may omit the number on the first page, but if you choose to include it, center it at the bottom.

Title

In handwritten papers place the title in the center of the first line of notebook paper and begin the first sentence three lines below it. In typed papers place the title about two inches below the top of the page and begin the first sentence three lines below it. Capitalize the first and last words of the title, any word that follows a colon, and all other words except articles, conjunctions, and prepositions of fewer than five letters. Do not underline your title or place quotation marks around it. If, however, the title of another work or a quotation is part of your title, then that part should be underlined or placed within quotation marks, whichever is appropriate. Underline titles of books, periodicals, newspapers, pamphlets, plays and films, long poems, and long musical compositions. Use quotation marks for titles of articles, short stories, short poems, songs, chapter titles and other subdivisions of books or periodicals, and episodes of radio and television programs.

Identification

Include your name, course title and number, the instructor's name, the date, and any other information your instructor requests. Write the information in separate lines, beginning in the upper right-hand corner of the first page.

Numbed Language

You're probably familiar with the feeling that comes from sitting for twenty minutes with one of your legs beneath your hips: The leg loses feeling because the flow of blood has been blocked; the leg goes to sleep; it becomes numb. Language, too, can become numb. Life is sucked from it so it no longer calls to mind an accurate vision of experience. To edit and revise successfully, you need to recognize any numbed language that's slipped into your prose. You need to cut it out and insert more accurate words.

Euphemism

One enemy of plain language is euphemism — pleasant words substituted for blunt ones or, in many cases, inaccurate words substituted for accurate ones. Although euphemism riddles every part of our culture, we can best illustrate it with some examples from the funeral industry. The *corpse* has become the *loved one*, the *deceased,* or the *dearly departed.* A *hearse* has become a *coach;* a *grave* has become a *final resting place.* A *coffin* was once a *casket* and is now a *vault* (no doubt for the loved one to be deposited in the ground like a contribution to a savings account). The person in charge of all this used to be called an *undertaker;* now that person is a *mortician,* and a *funeral* is commonly referred to as a *ceremony.*

Euphemism obliterates any imagery that blunt words carry. The word *corpse* may call up mental pictures, while *dearly beloved* creates a mental vacuum. Can you visualize what an undertaker might look like? You probably see a man in a black suit and string tie, maybe wearing a stovepipe hat and sitting on the seat of a buckboard with a pine box in the back — if you've been conditioned by Westerns. Now try to visualize a mortician. Not easy to do, is it? Can you visualize a grave? Probably. How about a final resting place? Probably not. Our point is that euphemism tends to fog the connection between language and experience. Euphemism numbs the mind.

Euphemism is sometimes acceptable, but more often it is harmful. In certain situations we feel more comfortable saying "men's room," "women's room," "bathroom," "rest room," even "powder room" for toilet. All well and good. These kinds of daily deceptions are no more harmful than a dangling modifier or a din of "you knows" scattered throughout someone's speech.

But euphemism can be dangerous to clear thought and plain writing. This danger is our main concern. Basically, euphemism is designed to deceive, and deception in language represents a danger to the way we see the world. If we fail to use words accurately, we will not have accurate pictures of experience; therefore, we will not transmit accurate information in our writing. We will be deceiving both ourselves and our readers.

Of course, you wouldn't set out to deceive a reader through the use of euphemism, would you? But merely having been born in contemporary America is to have been set adrift in a verbal sea of euphemism. A quick glance at advertising reveals that soap is called "body cleanser"; toilet paper, "facial quality tissue"; false teeth, "dentures"; used (or second-hand) cars, "preowned."

The government is probably the biggest euphemism offender. It has attempted to eliminate the word *poor* and replace it with *low income*. Slums and ghettoes are now called the *inner city*. Prisons are called *correctional facilities*. Employees are not fired but *selected out* or *terminated*. Old people are *senior citizens*. When officials claim one thing and something else turns out to be true, the first statement isn't a lie, it's *in-operative*.

Euphemism is designed to separate people from experience. If you've been raised in a society smothered in it, then you will be its victim and it will appear in your thought and writing. In fact, you might quite innocently write something like this passage taken from the opening of a student paper:

> Last summer I visited Mexico City's outskirts. The whole area was underdeveloped and swarming with the disadvantaged, who seemed to be living on a marginal diet. Several families often lived together in a small home, sometimes with no more than a single water source to serve them and several other homes together.

Too often beginning writers are trapped into believing that they should try to write like this. They think it sounds intelligent, perhaps official and authoritative. And why shouldn't they? After all, most beginning writers have had similar prose held up to them as representations of clear thought. Don't be deceived. This is the language of bureaucrats and sociologists unable to commit their emotion to what they see or to the language they use to describe what they see. They fluff their prose with euphemistic fuzz. Inhaling it numbs the reader's sensitivity. A revision of this passage with the euphemism cut out and plain language used to express what lurks behind the camouflage might read like this:

> Last summer I visited the outskirts of Mexico City. The whole area was a slum, a ghetto swarming with starving people who

seemed to have no more to eat than tortillas and water. Sometimes several families crammed themselves into two-room hovels made of cardboard and sticks. The only water they had came from a single tap shared by fifteen or twenty such dwellings.

Now the passage more closely represents what the writer saw. The numbed language has been replaced with vivid description that creates a picture of the experience. Readers don't have to guess what's behind the words. They can see. Whenever you revise a passage, replace any euphemisms you find with plain words. Your writing will become sharper, and you may even free yourself of some corrupt habits of thought.

Jargon and Pompous Language

Just as euphemism is a menace to good writing, so is jargon. It, too, is numbed language, words that have lost their teeth. Jargon comes from the specialized vocabularies of various professions and for one reason or another has slipped beyond its professional boundaries. There's nothing wrong with technical vocabularies. Technicians such as doctors, lawyers, educators, mechanics, and police need technical language to practice their trades. The problem comes about when the technical vocabulary crops up in places where it doesn't belong. Then the words become confusing, misleading, or downright deceptive. For instance, a student operating under the influence of a psychology course wrote this way about her fear of taking a test.

> I felt traumatically impacted when I read the first question on my history midterm. Normally I'm not one who suffers from paranoia, but I did feel my anxiety level elevate and I experienced a curious syndrome I often associate with a phobia toward standing on the top rung of a high ladder.

What does all this mean — "traumatically impacted," "normally," "paranoia," "anxiety," "syndrome," "phobia"? Is the writer afraid? Is the teacher out to get her? Is she headed for a fall? The sample may be exaggerated, but it makes a point. Language taken from a specialized field and applied to an everyday situation usually sounds like gibberish to a person trained to spot nonsense. To the untrained it often sounds impressive, perhaps even intelligent.

And that's the danger of jargon. We all want to sound intelligent. Consequently, in our beginning work we try to emulate the nonsense that we confuse with thoughtful discourse. We end up writing confused prose. In fact, jargon is so confusing that it has been suggested that the Food and Drug Administration compile a dictionary of current jargonese so that its employees can better cope with the babble.

What all this comes down to is that people use jargon to make ordinary comments sound important. Instead of saying, "I'm scared," writers schooled in jargonese might say "I feel anxiety." Instead of saying "I haven't learned to read well," they might say "I'm educationally handicapped." Instead of "you mke me angry," "I'm experiencing in-depth hostility toward you." Outside specialized fields, *anxiety, educationally handicapped,* and *in-depth hostility* are merely globs of jargon pasted to the page. Use of this kind of language says more about the writers than about the experiences they are trying to describe. It says their brains have been massaged by insensitive bureaucrats, manipulative politicians, misguided educators. We suggest you learn to nail down your thought with concrete words — in this case words such as *scared* or *fear, ignorant* or *failure,* and *angry* or *mad.*

Pomposity is related to jargon. People who write pompously use words and phrases that sound scientific, technical, or businesslike. Pomposity is nothing more than tortured detours writers send their readers on when they could have pointed out the direct routes. Here are some guidelines written by an air pollution agency for the staff and students of a college.

> Obligations of College Personnel and Students Regarding Air Quality Alerts in Area:
>
> ALERT ACTIONS
>
> STAGE I: REDUCE VEHICULAR USE BY A) UTILIZING BUS SERVICE, B) IMPLEMENTING CAR POOL PLANS, C) POSTPONING UNNECESSARY MEETINGS AND TRIPS.
>
> STAGE II: (IN ADDITION TO STAGE I). A) USE OF ALL CAMPUS MAINTENANCE VEHICLES WILL BE DISCONTINUED EXCEPT FOR EMERGENCIES, B) GREATER EMPHASIS UPON CAR POOLS, BUS SERVICE, BICYCLES, C) ALL ACTIVITIES THAT WOULD ADD POLLUTANTS TO THE AIR WILL BE DISCONTINUED.
>
> STAGE III: NO DRIVING AT ALL EXCEPT FOR EMERGENCIES. THE COLLEGE AND DISTRICT WILL BE CLOSED, BOTH FROM AN INSTRUCTIONAL AND ADMINISTRATIVE POINT OF VIEW.

The agency could have made a more accurate statement in plain English:

> Smog alerts come in three stages. Here are some directions for each one:
>
> Stage 1. Don't do any unnecessary driving. If you must travel, form car pools or use the bus.
>
> Stage 2. Continue with stage 1. No campus cars or trucks will be driven except for emergencies.
>
> Stage 3. Don't come to campus; it will be closed.

Writers flushed with pomposity might say

> The educational impact of our new media courses has surpassed our broadest expectations.

instead of

> Students are learning more than we expected from our TV courses.

or

> My paper will deal with the problematic area of the energy crisis.

instead of

> My paper deals with the energy crisis.

or

> When you think in terms of a major, you probably think in terms of future employment.

instead of

> When you think of a major, you probably think of finding a job.

or

> We don't perform at the same thinking level.

instead of

> We don't think alike.

or

> This college gives students more involvement type of experience in curriculum-making decisions.

instead of

> This college asks students what should be taught and how it should be taught.

or

> I had many meaningful relationships with various members of my psychology class.

instead of

> I like some people in my psychology class.

Words and phrases like *impact, broadest expectations, problematic, area of, in terms of, level, involvement, type,* and *meaningful* are often tipoffs that you're reading or writing pompous prose. Slow down. Ask yourself what the words really mean. Can the information be stated more directly? Don't be impressed with the person who writes pompously or with yourself if you are trying to do it.

Jargon and pomposity are wasteful. Although writers who use jargon and pomposity may sound intelligent, the chances are their material has no more substance than the eruptions from a bean-fed baby's rump. Do we exaggerate? Pause for a second and think of the frightening possibility that language of this sort actually does obscure an accurate vision of experience. Then listen to this kind of nonsense bursting from the lips of your elected officials. If you need a lesson in the use of jargon and pomposity, attend a school board or city council meeting. Listen carefully to hear if the language floating around the room connects to any kind of experience you recognize. But be on guard. Don't listen too carefully. Concentrating on official language for twenty to thirty minutes may affect the mind the way Novocain affects the gums.

How do you combat jargon and pomposity in your writing? Use common sense. Reread your work carefully to be sure you have written as plainly as possible. If you must use a technical term, be sure you know its precise meaning and use it precisely.

Paired Words

Paired words are another danger to thoughtful writing. After years of thoughtless use, words that got hitched now trip hand in hand through much of what we hear and read. Some people call them "married words" or "stock phrases," but the name doesn't matter. What matters is that they do little for concrete communication because a writer can quickly dip into the surface of his or her language pool and come up with a stock description to fill a blank space. Paired words may not be as deceptive as euphemism, jargon, or pomposity (we feel writers use them mainly out of laziness), but they can be just as numbing, often leading readers to believe they're getting solid information when they're really feeding on formula.

To see how available paired words are, read the following passage and mentally fill in the blanks with the first words that come to mind:

It was a grim-_____ group that gathered at the Huntsville

City Hall and contemplated the _____ future. _____ time

was slipping away. They had to _____ reality and make

_____ judgments about evacuating people who lived near the

town's nuclear power plant.

Although the responses may vary, yours probably aren't too different from ours.

It was a grim-FACED group that gathered at the Huntsville City Hall and contemplated the NEAR/DARK future. PRE-CIOUS time was slipping away. They had to FACE reality and make MATURE judgments about evacuating people who lived near the town's nuclear power plant.

These are just a few examples of the paired words floating around in our minds. There are more, perhaps thousands. For instance, whenever a man is accurate with a pistol, he's "deadly" accurate. And what kind of aim does he take? "Deadly" aim, of course.

When there's a need, what kind of need is it? A "dire" need — you're catching on. If a person is passionate, what kind of passion does the person exhibit? Easy, you say — a "firelike" passion. And when a person with a firelike passion has a purpose, what kind of purpose is it? A "compelling" purpose, naturally.

Finally, when a woman whose firelike passion drives her to fulfill a compelling purpose to become a brain surgeon, what kind of operation does she do, what kind of endurance does it take, where does the operation take place, and what do the people helping look like? (This is a tough one, but at this point in the brief lesson you should almost be a master of the formula.)

She performs *delicate procedures* that require *marathon endurance* in *operating theaters* while *grim-faced nurses* and *attending physicians* watch.

By the way, there was probably "precious little time" to save the patient's life since it was "hanging in the balance."

Clichés

Like paired words, clichés are also stock phrases that come easily to mind. We see them as being different from paired words because they often carry images. But the image is so blunted from overuse that it seldom pierces readers' imaginations. Once they were original expressions; now they're trite. You should avoid falling back on clichés when you're stuck for a more accurate description.

To give you an idea of what clichés are like, here are a few of the most exhausted ones:

flat as a pancake	quick as lightning
like a chicken with its head cut off	old as Methuselah

quick as a
flash

brown as a
berry

fog as thick as
pea soup

cool as a
cucumber

silent as the
grave

good as gold

happy as a
clam

rooted to the
spot

a barrel of
monkeys

as hard to
find as a
needle in a
haystack

hard as nails

like a child
with a new
toy

meek as a
lamb

smart as a
whip

claw to the
top

tumble to the
bottom

head over
heels

green as grass

Keep in mind that paired words and clichés are merely substitutes for fresh thinking. They spring to mind when you're in a rush, but they will always sound stale and will usually be confusing and inaccurate. It's easy to write something like

> We were so rushed we scurried about the house like a bunch of chickens with their heads cut off.

The image is a stock attempt to communicate rush and confusion, but it does that only for people who are numb to the visual power of language. Whenever you edit and revise your prose and come across clichés and paired words, strike them out and develop more accurate detail.

Numbers

Follow established conventions when handling numbers in general writing.

1. Spell out any number of one or two words.

       twenty-five   sixteen   one thousand

2. Use figures for any number that requires more than two words to spell out.

       102   345   4,679 *or* 4679

3. Use a combination of figures and words for numbers where such a combination will keep your meaning clear.

> six 90-year-olds

4. Use figures for the following:

Days and years

December 7, 1941   12 B.C.   A.D. 1066

Note: The forms *1st, 2nd,* and so on, as well as the *fourth, fifth,* and so on, are sometimes used in dates, but only when the year is omitted: June 6th or June sixth.

Time of day

8:00 a.m.   12:45 p.m.   1400 (military usage)

Note: When not using *a.m.* or *p.m.,* write the time in words.

> seven o'clock   half-past ten

Addresses

22 Meadow Sweet Way   Washington, D.C. 20036

Scores, statistics, and results of surveys

The Rams beat the Cowboys, 10 to 3.

The average class grade was 83.

The survey showed that of the group of forty, 36 supported the tax cut, 2 had no opinion, and 2 had never heard of the proposal.

Percentages, decimals, and fractions

52%   96.6   16½

Pages and divisions of written works

page 31   chapter 3   volume 11
act 2   scene 4   lines 10–18

Exact amounts of money

$12.91 $3,421.02   25 cents

5. Spell out any number that begins a sentence, or revise the sentence.

Incorrect	101 trumpeters blared the message — We won!
Corrected	One hundred and one trumpeters blared the message — We won!
Revised	The message — We won! — was blared by 101 trumpeters.

Parallelism

Parallelism exists when two or more ideas are expressed in the same grammatical form. In a pair or a series you must make the items parallel to avoid awkward shifts in construction.

> I enjoy going to concerts, hiking through the woods, and playing poker.

not

> I enjoy going to concerts, hiking through the woods, and poker.

> He learned to read rapidly, to speak fluently, and to translate easily in the new language.

not

> He learned to read rapidly, to speak fluently, and translating easily in the new language.

You can express a series of words, phrases, clauses, and even whole sentences in parallel form for both clarity and impact.

Words:	I plan to read, fish, and loaf.
Phrases:	Climbing the hills, dashing down the slopes, and racing through the valley became a daily routine.
Clauses:	The light dimmed, the curtains opened, and the play began.
Sentences:	We hope for the best. We fear the worst. We get what we deserve.

Some of our most memorable quotations achieve their impact through parallel structure.

> I came. I saw. I conquered.

> Give me liberty or give me death!

> Ask not what your country can do for you — ask what you can do for your country.

We shall fight on the beaches, we shall fight on the landing grounds, we shall fight in the fields and in the streets, we shall fight in the hills; we shall never surrender.

Parentheses

Keep in mind that of the three marks used to enclose nonessential elements (commas, dashes, and parentheses), parentheses indicate the greatest degree of digression.

1. Use parentheses to enclose numbers and letters marking items in a series within a sentence.

    To begin playing tennis well, you must remember three fundamental points: (1) tennis is a sideways game, (2) the backstroke makes a loop, (3) the follow-through should end high.

    Remember not to use periods with letters or numbers enclosed within parentheses.

2. Use parentheses to enclose nonessential information.

    One year after the war (his family didn't recognize him at first), he brought out the town's buried anger at draft resisters.

    There is nothing to seek and nothing to acquire (according to ancient Zen masters) because within every mind burns the flame of enlightenment.

Nonessential elements enclosed by parentheses take no special punctuation besides the parentheses themselves. At times you may have a punctuation mark following parentheses, but any such mark would be in the sentence even if the parentheses were not.

At times when I feel my stomach churning from fear (usually the morning of a midterm or final), I do deep-breathing exercises.

The dedicated detective buff spends hours each week prowling through used-book stores for first editions of the masters (Poe, Chesterton, Hammett, Chandler, and MacDonald).

Remember also to properly punctuate material you enclose in parentheses.

Arab students (Egyptians, Iraquis, Lebanese, Syrians) make up the majority of the foreign student population on campus.

Period

You probably have few if any problems using periods.

1. Use periods at the ends of sentences that are declarative, that make mild commands, and that ask indirect questions.

   The class starts Wednesday at noon.

   Come to class Wednesday at noon.

   He asked if class began on Wednesday at noon.

2. Use periods with most abbreviations.

P. K. Smith	Mr.	Mrs.	Engl.
Ms.	Ph.D.	M.B.A.	Hist.
U.S.	Mass.	B.A.	Soc. Sci.

   Don't use periods in abbreviations of the names of organizations and national and international agencies when more than two words are being abbreviated.

   IBM   (International Business Machines)

   NBA   (National Basketball Association)

   NCTE   (National Council of Teachers of English)

   Don't use periods with some abbreviations that are commonly used as words.

TV	VW	OK
5th	exam	lab
gym	memo	math

   When in doubt about whether to use a period in an abbreviation, check a dictionary for the acceptable form.

3. Use periods after numbers and letters in an outline.

   I. Subjects taught in the English Department
      A. Writing
         1. Communicative
         2. Expressive
      B. Reading
         1. Remedial
         2. Developmental

   Don't use a period if a digit or letter is enclosed by parentheses.

   (a)

   (1)

Point of View

By point of view we mean the way you present your material. In the broadest sense you can do it from either a personal or an impersonal stance. A personal point of view places you in the experience and leads you to use first-person pronouns (*I, me, my, we, us, our*). Or it may lead you to address your readers directly by using second-person pronouns (*you, your*). An impersonal point of view positions you out of the experience. It places you in an objective stance. When writing impersonally you'll seldom directly address the reader or use personal pronouns. One is the point of view of personal experience and observation; the other, of reports and research.

The material will usually dictate which stance to assume. You wouldn't take a journal entry that deals with childhood experience and rework it in an impersonal way; nor would you write historical, social, or scientific research in a personal way. So when selecting a point of view ask yourself where your material came from. From research? From reports of others? From personal experience? The point of view will follow naturally from the answer to the question.

To get a better feel for point of view, take a look at several examples. Jan Harold Brunvan uses an impersonal point of view in presenting information on folk riddles in *The Study of American Folklore*.

> Folk riddles are traditional questions with unexpected answers — verbal puzzles that circulate, mostly by word of mouth, to demonstrate the cleverness of the questioner and challenge the wit of his audience. The practice of riddling can be traced to the dawn of literary expression; it is referred to in the most ancient Oriental and Sanskrit writings, in the Bible, in classical legends and myths, in European folktales and ballads, and in some of the earliest manuscripts of Medieval literature. Compilations of riddles were among the first printed books in the Middle Ages, and books of literary riddles remained a popular diversion well into the Renaissance. Since the beginning of professional interest in folklore in the nineteenth century, massive collections of folk riddles have been published in most European countries and in many countries outside Europe. Riddles have been found in the native cultures of all peoples, even the American Indians, who until recently were thought to possess only a few that had been borrowed from Europeans.

Dry, isn't it? The passage is cleansed of personal pronouns; it doesn't address the reader. Brunvand is giving us the results of research. He's not giving life experiences.

The impersonal point of view is not always so dry. Many secondhand reports are written from the impersonal stance — by writers presenting the experience of others. Since they weren't part of it, they report as outsiders. Here's an example from *Alive* by Piers Paul Read. He reports the experiences of people who survived an air crash in the Andes. This paragraph captures the moment the plane crashes.

> Several passengers started to pray. Others braced themselves against the seats in front of them, waiting for the impact of the crash. There was a roar of engines and the plane vibrated as the Fairchild tried to climb again; it rose a little but then there came a deafening crash as the right wing hit the side of the mountain. Immediately it broke off, somersaulted over the fuselage, and cut off the tail. Out into the icy air fell the steward, the navigator, and their pack of cards, followed by three of the boys still strapped to their seats. A moment later the left wing broke away and a blade of the propeller ripped into the fuselage before falling to the ground.

Certainly not dry, but not overdramatized, either. Read keeps his distance: He reports the facts objectively and lets them carry the impact.

Sometimes when deciding which stance to take — personal or impersonal — you'll reach a crossroads. Your material hasn't come from research or from other people's reports. It may fall more into the area of personal experience, yet not be exclusively your experience; others may have had it as well. Let's call it common experience — experience that comes from your general background and knowledge.

Common experience goes beyond our individual lives. It tilts toward the communal. It comes from our participation in society. At this moment you probably have sufficient background to write intelligently about limited aspects of TV, politics, education, racism, sexism, parenting, sports, music, books, films, art, advertising, death, and catastrophes. You could write about them by generalizing from the information you've collected over the years. Your readers could follow what you're saying because they have shared these experiences. You may not be an expert in any of these areas, but to write about them is not to pretend to be an expert. You do have opinions along with enough information to develop them.

So what point of view do you use when writing from common experience? You can use either impersonal or personal. Either way, though, the writing will tend to sound more impersonal than personal — more authoritative.

Robert Paul Dye draws on common experience from radio to start "The Death of Silence." No doubt he's heard these programs and assumes his reader has also heard them or knows of them. His intent is to draw some general conclusions from them, not to reminisce about a mindless childhood spent sprawled in front of a Philco radio. He selects, therefore, an impersonal point of view.

Radio's funniest moment occurred on the "Jack Benny Program" when a thief demanded from the great tightwad, "Your money or your life." The long silence that followed was more violently hysterical than any of the quick retorts that are the stock in trade of most comedians. Benny's use of silence, his great sense of timing, made him one of the most popular comics of this century. Benny, of course, was not the only radio artist who recognized that silence could be more effective than sound: silence followed the crash of Fibber McGee's closet, preceded McCarthy's responses to Bergen. The chillers became more chilling when there were moments of silence. Silence was used to make the romances erotic and the quiz shows suspenseful.

Contemporary poet Adrienne Rich in "When the Dead Awaken: Writing as Re-Vision" also generalizes about common experience. She expresses the problems women writers face in confronting images of women developed throughout literary history. She writes with authority. The passage seems impersonal. However, Rich begins one sentence with *I think* to clearly indicate her perspective.

A lot is being said today about the influence that the myths and images of women have on all of us who are products of culture. I think it has been a peculiar confusion to the girl or woman who tries to write, because she is peculiarly susceptible to language. She goes to poetry or fiction looking for *her* way of being in the world, since she too has been putting words and images together; she is looking eagerly for guides, maps, possibilities; and over and over in the "words' masculine persuasive force" of literature she comes up against something that negates everything she is about: she meets the image of Woman in books written by men. She finds a terror and a dream, she finds a beautiful pale face, she finds La Belle Dame Sans Merci, she finds Juliet or Tess or Salome, but precisely what she does not find is that absorbed, drudging, puzzled, sometimes inspired creature, herself, who sits at a desk trying to put words together.

The following anecdote comes from the *Autobiography of Malcolm X*. Malcolm X talks about his childhood veneration of leading jazzmen during the 1940s. It's his private experience. No one else went through it. It calls for a first-person point of view.

Some of the bandsmen would come up to the men's room at about eight o'clock and get shoeshines before they went to work. Duke Ellington, Count Basie, Lionel Hampton, Coote Williams, Jimmie Lunceford were just a few of those who sat in my chair. I would really make my shine rag sound like someone had set off Chinese firecrackers. Duke's great alto saxman, Jonny

> Hodges — he was Shorty's idol — still owes me for a shoeshine I gave him. He was in the chair one night, having a friendly argument with the drummer, Sonny Greer, who was standing there, when I tapped the bottom of his shoes to signal that I was finished. Hodges stepped down, reaching his hand in his pocket to pay me, but then snatched his hand out to gesture, and just forgot me, and walked away. I wouldn't have dared to bother the man who could do what he did with "Daydream" by asking him for fifteen cents.

The first-person point of view is right. Notice how the writer avoids dropping the *I* on the reader's mind the way an ancient oriental jailer might drip water on a victim's head in unrelenting cadences. When you use the first-person singular, suppress the *I, my,* and *me* by putting them only where you need to. In this passage Malcolm X uses *I* five times, *my* once, and *me* twice. No drip, drip, drip of personal pronouns that might drive a reader daffy.

The first-person plural point of view involves the use of *we*. Never use the "royal *we*" or the "editorial *we*" — that is for one person trying to elevate personal experience to cosmic heights.

> Yesterday we went to class and found we had been given a C on our midterm.

Nor should you use *we* to avoid personal responsibility.

> We do not like the way this class is run. Our midterms, we find, were graded in too strict a manner.

This would be appropriate if the writer were speaking for the entire class, but the chances are that the writer is speaking from personal feeling and using the *we* point of view as a shield.

Do use *we* when you are talking for yourself and others, but try to make the general identity of the others clear.

> Six other class members and I got together and agreed that our midterms had been graded too strictly.

Now the *we (our)* fits.

The *we* point of view is often used to address a common group that includes the author. But the material sometimes has less to do with concrete personal experience and more to do with a general condition. Gerald Holton closes an essay titled "Constructing a Theory: Einstein's Model" with this point of view.

> As limited human beings confronting the seemingly endless parts and interlocking puzzles of the universe, we can nevertheless hope to play, as in Newton's metaphor, with pebbles at the shore of a vast ocean. If we do it well, that play can yield the most highly desirable kind of knowledge: a survey or overview of the

> world of nature that grants us the perception of an order guid-
> ing the phenomena in their infinite, individual variety and in
> their inexhaustible interactions with one another.

That's a mouthful, isn't it? But notice that Holton clearly establishes the members of the *we* group — all "limited human beings" who are "confronting the . . . puzzles of the universe." It's a glob of people, but a somewhat limited glob. When you confront the universe and have some others who are going to join you, talk to them from a *we* stance.

The use of *you* is right in any passage that directly addresses readers, particularly when it encourages or directs them to do something. If, for instance, you are sending readers on a journey or explaining a process, the use of *you* is natural.

Paul Roberts uses it in "How to Say Nothing in Five Hundred Words," an essay that explains how to go about writing college compositions.

> Say the assignment is college football. Say that you've decided
> to be against it. Begin by putting down the arguments that come
> to your mind: it is too commercial, it takes the students' minds
> off their studies, it is hard on the players, it makes the university
> a kind of circus instead of an intellectual center, for most schools
> it is financially ruinous. Can you think of any more arguments,
> just offhand? All right. Now when you write your paper, make
> sure that you don't use any of the material on this list. If these
> are the points that leap to your mind, they will leap to everyone
> else's too, and whether you get a "C" or a "D" may depend on
> whether the instructor reads your paper early when he is fresh
> and tolerant or late, when the sentence "In my opinion, college
> football has become too commercial," inexorably repeated, has
> brought him to the brink of lunacy.

Beginning writers seldom have problems addressing "you the reader" but sometimes stumble when using the indefinite *you,* which means "anyone."

> When you travel east along the southern route to Tucson, you'll
> enjoy stopping at Ajo Drug for a thick malt and hamburger.

The problem here is that the writer has failed to suggest that the reader has any intention of doing what the writer proposes. The writer is talking to an indefinite *you.* The sentence could have been written more effectively with *anyone.*

> Anyone who likes hamburgers and malts and is traveling east
> along the southern route to Tucson should stop at Ajo Drug for
> lunch or dinner.

But perhaps the writer wanted to use *you.* It does have a certain intimacy. The writer could have done it by using an *if* clause to identify the reader.

> If you're traveling to Tucson along the southern route and you like hamburgers and malts, then stop at Ajo Drug.

Although it works in a situation like this, we suggest you avoid using the indefinite *you*. It causes trouble.

Sometimes writers shift to the *you* once a passage is under way. The use of *you* draws readers in, makes them feel like participants. The shift takes some skill. It must come smoothly, and the experience must be one that readers can identify with:

> Last week I walked up to Kings Point and saw a spectacular sight. If you ever get up there at dusk, you'll see the desert stretching toward a deep blue sky mopped with red clouds. You'll see. . . .

When the shift is made awkwardly, it can be jarring.

> The physical threat to a quarterback passing from the "pocket" is intolerable. To stand there to the last millisecond, waiting for your receiver to reach the place the ball is supposed to go while you are being rushed by mammoth defensive linemen, takes sheer courage.

If directed toward potential quarterbacks, this passage would work. It wasn't, however. Writer Arnold J. Mandell directed it toward a general reader. Our guess is that not many general readers can identify with the experience. The shift is clumsy. Mandell would have written a more effective passage by avoiding the indefinite *you,* perhaps writing it like this:

> The physical threat to a quarterback passing from the "pocket" is intolerable. To stand there to the last millisecond, waiting for a receiver to reach the place the ball is supposed to go while he is being rushed by mammoth defensive linemen, takes sheer courage.

Now the point of view is impersonal. Don't you feel safer with a little more distance between you and the charging linemen?

Sometimes beginning writers really muddle a passage by shifting to *you*. Often the shift takes a form similar to this:

> At first, students may find enrolling in college confusing, but if they follow the orderly process established by Admissions, it will be easy. First, before your appointment, fill out and return the preregistration forms. Then you must be sure to keep your counseling. . . .

Did you catch the awkward shift from *students* to *you?* Don't make these kinds of shifts. If you know your audience, you probably won't. For instance, if this writer had intended his directions for students themselves, he might have written it like this:

> At first, you may find enrolling in college confusing, but if you follow the orderly process established by Admissions, it will be easy. First, before your. . . .

Or if the directions were for a more general audience — parents, teachers, clerks, and school administrators — he might have written it in this fashion:

> At first, students may find enrolling in college confusing, but if they follow the orderly process established by Admissions, it will be easy. First, before their appointments, they should fill out and return the preregistration forms. Then they must be sure to keep their counseling. . . .

There is a way this should not be written — with the deadly *one.*

> At first, one may find enrolling in college confusing, but if one follows the orderly process established by Admissions, it will be easy. First, before one's appointment, one should fill out and return the preregistration forms. Then one must be sure to keep one's counseling. . . .

Our recommendation is that one should avoid the use of *one* when one writes. Its use adds sand to a fluid process.

A last thought about point of view: Once you decide whether it will be personal or impersonal, stick to it. Stick to it through the entire essay. Keep in mind, though, that you can shift back and forth within a personal point of view. You may move from first-person singular to first-person plural and even to second person. But the shift should not come about out of mindlessness. It should be done skillfully. For example, examine the following passage from Jules Henry's *Culture Against Man.* Henry begins with *I,* swings to *we* ("our language," "urge us," "our culture," "we must search"), shifts to *you,* then returns to *we.* Notice that he uses the *you* to separate various members of his *we* group: "If you are propelled by drives," "if you are moved mostly by values." Henry has a strong grip on his point of view. It does not slip away.

> Fundamentally, values are different from what I call drives, and it is only a semantic characteristic of our language that keeps the two sets of feelings together. To call both competitiveness and gentleness "values" is as confusing as to call them both "drives." Drives are what urge us blindly into getting bigger, into going further into outer space and into destructive competition; values are the sentiments that work in the opposite direction.

Drives belong to the occupational world; values to the world of the family and friendly intimacy. Drives animate the hurly-burly of business, the armed forces, and all those parts of our culture where getting ahead, rising in the social scale, outstripping others, and merely surviving in the struggle are the absorbing functions of life. When values appear in those areas, they act largely as brakes on drivenness. Though the occupational world is, on the whole, antagonistic to values in this sense, it would nevertheless be unable to function without them, and it may use them as veils to conceal its underlying motivations.

In our own culture the outstanding characteristic of promotable executives is drive. It is no problem at all to locate jobs requiring an orientation toward achievement, competition, profit, and mobility, or even toward a higher standard of living. But it is difficult to find one requiring outstanding capacity for love, kindness, quietness, contentment, fun, frankness, and simplicity. If you are propelled by drives, the culture offers innumerable opportunities for you; but if you are moved mostly by values, you really have to search, and if you do find a job in which you can live by values, the pay and prestige are usually low. Thus, the institutional supports — the organizations that help the expression of drives — are everywhere around us, while we must search hard to find institutions other than the family which are dedicated to values.

Question Mark

The question mark has one principal use and three minor ones.

1. The principal use: Use a question mark at the end of a direct question.

   How will we solve this problem?

   Do you have the address?

   Why haven't the answers been distributed?

2. Use a question mark at the end of a question presented in a series even though it may not be a complete sentence.

   How many times have you missed? Six? Eleven? Fifteen times?

   Such a sentence might also look like this.

   How many times have you missed — six? eleven? fifteen times?

   Whether or not to capitalize *six, eleven,* and *fifteen* is the writer's option. We suggest that if you arrange questions in a series so that they stand alone, as in the first illustration, then you should capitalize them. But if you link them to the lead sentence, as in the second example, you shouldn't.

3. Use a question mark at the end of a question built into a sentence to make it more emphatic.

Will this situation ever end? I often wonder.

How many days will pass before the check comes? I keep hearing in my head.

Of course, if the question is a direct quotation, then the question mark is required.

"Will this situation ever end?" I heard John ask.

"How many days will pass before the check comes?" I asked Chuck.

Remember, use only a period after an indirect question.

Not

The police officer asked if there was anything he could do?

or

Taxpayers often wonder if they are getting their dollars' worth of government?

but

The police officer asked if there was anything he could do.

and

Taxpayers often wonder if they are getting their dollars' worth of government.

4. Use a question mark within parentheses to show doubt about the correctness of numbers and dates.

The *Times* said 22,231 (?) marched in the demonstration.

In 1945 (?) American English became the unannounced standard for the world's language.

Quotations

Whenever you use the exact words of a speaker or writer in your own writing, put quotation marks at the beginning and at the end of the quotation. This will show readers where the quotation begins and stops.

A cranky type, Turk would shout, "What of it" three times in rapid succession whenever anyone challenged his behavior.

A. R. Orage said, "There is one art — the greatest of all, the art of making a complete human being of oneself."

These are direct quotations — the exact words of the speaker and writer. They could be arranged differently, but the principle of clearly indicating a quotation by placing marks around it holds up.

> "What of it," Turk would shout three times in rapid succession whenever anyone challenged his cranky behavior.

> "There is one art — the greatest of all, the art of making a complete human being of oneself." A. R. Orage said.

Sometimes writers interrupt direct quotations. When they do, they are still responsible for separating their own words from those they quote.

> "There is one art — the greatest of all," A. R. Orage said, "the art of making a complete human being of oneself."

There will be times, however, when you'll want to give only a general idea of what someone has written or said. You would use an indirect quotation. Since an indirect quotation doesn't represent a person's exact words, you don't put it within quotation marks.

> A. R. Orage said that the greatest art of all is the art of becoming a complete person.

This indirect quotation more or less captures the gist of Orage's thought, but it needn't be set off by quotation marks.

Now that you have a general idea of how to indicate direct quotations, let's look at some particulars involved in punctuating, introducing, and editing quotations.

Punctuating and Capitalizing Quotations

Nothing makes writing easier than a hard-and-fast rule. We'll start with a couple. Periods and commas following quotations *always* go inside the quotation marks, just as they are placed in these examples. Study them.

> Bent over and patting the carpet, she said, "Finding a contact lens is like looking for a needle in a haystack."

> "A great writer always puts himself face to face with truth," Thomas Miller wrote.

This rule applies even when only one word is being quoted.

> My grandmother's favorite word was "Fiddlesticks."

When you use colons and semicolons with quotations, always put them outside the quotation marks.

> Some of my Aunt Maude's favorite expressions are "He runs around like a chicken without a head"; "Where there's smoke, there's fire"; and "Don't count your chickens until they've hatched": expressions from the common pot of American clichés.

Now the problem becomes more complex. Put question marks and exclamation points within the quotation marks when they apply to the quotations.

> The child asked, "When are we leaving?"

> The protestors shouted, "Hell no! We won't go!"

But put them outside the quotation marks when they apply to the whole sentence rather than just to the quotation itself.

> What's the meaning of the phrase "collective unconscious"?

> Did they shout, "Hell no! We won't go"?

> Stop demanding, "Let's leave"!

Also notice that you use only one kind of end punctuation. You would not write

> Did they shout, "Hell no! We won't go!"?

> Stop asking, "When are we going?"!

Very bad form. It looks silly.

If the quotation you are using comes after your sentence is under way, you must handle it in one of three ways. First, when leading into a quotation with any word such as *said, says, states, shouts, shouted, maintains, believes, writes,* and so on, you need to put a comma after the leading word but outside the quotation marks.

> Last week Dr. Peters said, "In ten years we won't see one whale off the southern California coastline."

Next, if the quotation is an integral part of your sentence and you do not lead into it with any word such as listed above, you don't need any punctuation before the quotation.

> Mr. Hallfield told us that he is "the world's greatest historian."

Finally, if your sentence is grammatically complete before the quotation comes, then use a colon to set it up.

> Conrad clearly states the theme of his story through Marlowe: "O Youth! The strength of it, the faith of it, the imagination of it!"

Beginning writers sometimes get tied up over capitalizing quotations properly. No need to. These simple guidelines should straighten the problem out. If the quotation is a complete sentence, capitalize the first word.

> Psychologist Jean Piaget writes, "In order to understand we have to invent, because we can't start from the beginning again."

If you identify the source in the middle instead of at the end or beginning of the quotation, it will look like this:

> "In order to understand," psychologist Jean Piaget writes, "we have to invent, because we can't start from the beginning again."

Notice that the interruption is set off by commas. The word *we* is not capitalized because it doesn't begin a sentence but continues it. If the second part of the quotation begins a new sentence, however, then you would capitalize the first word.

> "In the pursuit of learning, every day something is acquired," writes a Chinese sage. "In the pursuit of Tao, every day something is dropped."

Working Quotations into the Text

If you merely quote a complete sentence, you'll have no problem; just put quotation marks before and after it.

> "A writer is a person who writes."

But you'll seldom merely quote a complete sentence and leave it at that. More often you'll introduce a quotation by acknowledging its source. You already had a taste of the practice in the preceding examples. You can acknowledge the source of a quotation by giving just the person's name.

> Clint Linder has said, "A writer is a person who writes."

You may also work in some information about the person.

> Clint Linder, a leading novelist, has said, "A writer is a person who writes."

Or you may work in even more information.

> Leading novelist Clint Linder, best known for *Naked Jackal,* has said, "A writer is a person who writes."

For various reasons you might want to add a little color to the introduction. If you were on the spot when the comment was made and wish to give the reader a feel for the scene, you can add some detail.

> Standing before an audience of college students gathered in a local pub, leading novelist Clint Linder, after countless whiskeys, lifted a fist to pulp writer J. M. Finnegan's nose and screamed, "A writer is a person who writes."

Or your introduction can be muted yet still packed with detail. You can even let your readers know how you wish them to view the quotation.

> Erich Fromm, psychoanalyst and social philosopher, writes of the deeper lessons that come from studying the mind: "Psychoanalysis teaches one to be skeptical of what a man says, because his words usually reveal, at best, only his consciousness."

When a quotation runs beyond four lines, skip two lines before and after and single space and indent the quotation itself. If the quotation begins a paragraph, indent the first line. Also, since block form indicates you are quoting, there will be no need for quotation marks. Block form should look like this:

> In *The Bestiary* T. H. White describes the general eating patterns of lions:
>
> > Lions abstain from over-eating: in the first place, because they only take food and drink on alternate days — frequently, if digestion has not followed, they are even in the habit of putting off the day for dinner. In the second place, they pop their paws carefully into their mouths and pull out the meat of their own accord, when they have eaten too much. Indeed, when they have to run away from somebody, they perform the same action if they are full up.

Ellipses and Brackets in Quotations

Often to sharpen the focus and to speed the movement of your paper, you'll want to cut out the parts of a quotation useless to your point. This is done by an ellipsis — three dots indicating you have omitted something from the quotation. If the ellipsis comes at the end of a sentence, use four dots: one to indicate a period, followed by three to show omission.

You don't need ellipses to show all omissions. For instance, when you are excerpting single words or short phrases, the reader can see they've been taken from context, so you won't need ellipses. An operating guideline: avoid accumulating rows of dots; use them only when you sense that a reader needs to know of an omission.

For instance, the example from White's *The Bestiary* might be used more effectively if trimmed and integrated with the writer's text.

> Lions don't live up to all the myths we have created about them. For example, they are not the insatiable eaters that clichés such as "hungry as a lion" suggest. Instead, as T. H. White states in *The Bestiary*, "Lions abstain from over-eating . . . they only take food and drink on alternate days." Moreover, they may even put off "the day for dinner" if the previous meal has not been digested. They have even been known to "pop their paws carefully into their mouths and pull out the meat."

Brackets enclosing comments within a quotation indicate you are supplying the reader with information that for one reason or another is not within the quotation but is necessary for understanding.

> "Indeed, when they [lions] have to run away from somebody, they perform the same action [sticking a paw down the throat] if they are full up."

Semicolon

Some beginning writers see the semicolon as a mysterious squiggle designed by devious grammarians to addle the brain. Actually, the semicolon is easy to master.

1. Use a semicolon between main clauses not linked by a coordinate conjunction (*and, but, or, nor,* and sometimes *for, yet, so*).

   For some retired citizens Miami Beach is a glamorous lure; for others the city is a final dumping ground.

   The president delivered his speech; the protesters chanted and waved placards in the rear of the hall; the FBI took photographs.

   Remember that although the semicolon can take the place of a period between sentences, you should not substitute a semicolon for a period unless the sentences you join are closely related in meaning.

2. Use a semicolon between main clauses joined by a coordinate conjunction when there are several commas in the clauses.

   Today, families can eat at fast-food restaurants, such as Carl's, Kentucky Fried Chicken, Burger King, and McDonalds; but only a few generations ago, before people could hop in their cars and race to the nearest convenience center, families spent a greater part of their lives preparing food and eating it together.

   The semicolon before the coordinate conjunction *but* makes the break between clauses clearer than a comma would.

3. Use a semicolon between main clauses joined by a conjunctive adverb (*therefore, however, indeed, still, moreover, nevertheless, thus,* and *then*).

   Latin culture has its own sense of time; therefore, you should be prepared to wait as long as two hours for a scheduled appointment to start.

   People who want to know the look of the ocean need only walk straight ahead; moreover, by dipping their fingers into the sea they reach and licking off the drops, they will know the taste of the seven seas.

   After a night of worry, I saw the sun rise; still, I felt the darkness inside.

   Be sure to remember to put a comma after a conjunctive adverb.

4. Use a semicolon to separate items in a series if they are long and contain commas.

   The books that stand out in my memory are Jung's *Memories,*

Dreams, and Reflections, an autobiography that focuses on the psychologist's spiritual development; Fowles's *The Magus,* a mysterious novel that captures a character's personal growth and understanding of freedom; Lao-tzu's *Tao Te Ching,* a collection of reflections from an ancient Chinese philosopher.

Sexist Language

Changes are taking place in American English usage that reflect a growing awareness of sexism in American society. These changes affect what some social critics describe as a masculine bias embedded in our language. One striking illustration of this bias appears among masculine and feminine word pairs. Generally female forms are created from male forms:

actor	actress	host	hostess
heir	heiress	prince	princess
hero	heroine		

Although you may have a difficult time avoiding words such as these, you can avoid other words and usages that might be construed as carrying a masculine bias.

You may choose to avoid singular, masculine pronouns (*he, him, his*) to refer to both men and women when the sex of the antecedent is unknown or when the antecedent consists of both males and females.

Each manager must post his schedule.

Each manager must post *his* or *her* schedule.

All managers must post *their* schedules.

You can also avoid the generic use of *man* to refer to both men and women — "*Man* dominates the natural world" — by substituting *human* or *human beings,* terms that are generally considered inclusive and less offensive. Using recent coinages will also help you avoid sounding biased. For instance, you can replace *chairman,* which in the recent past was used to refer to both men and women, with *chairwoman* when a woman holds the position and *chairperson* when the person's sex is unknown.

At this time there is no comprehensive set of rules for avoiding the use of language that seems to carry a masculine bias. Writers, however, should become sensitive to the social issue and can choose whenever possible to avoid perpetuating masculine bias in their own work.

Subordination

Whenever you want to emphasize one idea over another, use subordination. To subordinate, present the less important information in a dependent clause or phrase and attach it to a sentence. Often, arranging your information in this way will eliminate a series of choppy sentences and make your prose read clearly and smoothly. Read the following examples to see how sentences that seem disconnected can be improved through subordination.

> We must budget carefully. I hope we can rent out the apartment above the garage. I want to buy a new car next year.

> If we budget carefully and if we can rent out the apartment above the garage, we can buy a new car next year.

> The storm damaged the crop. Strawberries are selling for a dollar a basket.

> Because the storm damaged the crop, strawberries are selling for a dollar a basket.

> The professor is an expert on weaponry used in the Civil War. He was raised in the South.

> The professor, who was raised in the South, is an expert on weaponry used in the Civil War.

When you subordinate information, be careful not to subordinate the main idea.

> Before becoming senator, he lived in the state for only one year.

> After living only one year in the state, he became a senator.

> Because good writers are writing them, mysteries, thrillers, romances, and works of science fiction earn huge sums of money.

> Because mysteries, thrillers, romances, and works of science fiction earn huge sums of money, good writers are writing them.

Titles

The title will be the first words your readers confront, so it deserves some attention. Often you'll write the exact title after the paper is polished because it will be only then that you will have a full view of the content of your paper. But we suggest you always begin with a working title, one that fences in the subject's range.

Whatever you do, don't write tricky titles designed to shock an audience into reading your essay; Gentlewomen Prefer Blondes, Plummeting Grades Suggest Brainrot, Thinking Can Land You in Jail, and such. In some eyes they may be cute, but to the steady gaze they are worthless. And never write empty titles: My Summer Vacation, Memories of Youth, A Work in Progress. Useless things seem to announce several paragraphs of boredom and tend to send readers into depression. The best policy is to use the title to let your readers know what's coming as accurately as you can.

When you write a title at the top of the first page, don't put it in quotation marks. It's your title; you're not quoting someone else's. If by chance your title happens to include a quotation, then put marks around that part. And never underline your own title. Words underlined in handwritten papers indicate that if they were printed, they would be put in italics.

Be sure to capitalize your titles properly. Always capitalize the first letter of the first word and the first letter of the last word. Also capitalize the first letter of all other words that are not articles, prepositions of fewer than five letters, or conjunctions.

High-Rise and Low Income

Tricks of the Ad Trade

Fairy Tales: Paths to a Child's Mind

Tone

> "I love your new coat," Bill said, touching the fabric. "It's soft. Where did you find it?"

Obviously, someone is paying someone else a compliment. The statements are straightforward, honest. But with some slight changes, we can get a new meaning from the dialogue.

> Raising his eyebrows, wrinkling his nose, and elevating his voice to a falsetto, Bill said, "I *love* your new coat. It's so . . . soft. Where did you *find* it?"

By making these changes in the descriptive detail, but without altering the dialogue, we've created a different tone. Do you hear the deception behind the words? For *soft,* interpret *floppy* or *shapeless.* And after the question "Where did you *find* it?" add the line "In a trash heap?" The speaker is no longer offering appreciation, but snide criticism.

If you overheard these comments the meaning would be carried in the tone the speaker used to say the words. You'd hear it. Most people convey tone in speech without much thought. If they feel pleasant, they sound pleasant. If they feel snotty, they sound snotty. But to achieve tone in writing you have to make more conscious choices.

To keep it simple we want to start off by talking about tone in general terms. First, tone has something to do with the kinds of English you use, and there are many kinds. Should you write in the kind of English a college president might use in reporting the state of the school? The kind a TV news reporter might use to write copy? The kind your favorite thriller or romance writers might use? Or maybe the kind you might use to write letters to friends?

There is no single kind of English to use for all circumstances. If you're writing a report for educators, then the circumstances might require that you write in the English of the college president. If you're writing for a universal audience, then the English the TV reporter uses might be appropriate. And, obviously, if you're writing to a friend, then you'd use the kind of English closest to the way you talk. What you always need to keep in mind are the situation and the audience.

Let's consider the way we speak to people. Although writing isn't recorded speech — far from it — it may help to understand how we use different kinds of English when speaking in different situations. Different situations force you to adjust your English and the way you use it.

For example, if you were talking to a toddler you might say something like "See the kitty. Pretty kitty. Fuzzy kitty. Touch kitty. Isn't it nice?" — and you'd be smiling a big I-love-you-baby smile. If, however, you were called on to respond spontaneously in psychology, you wouldn't talk as if speaking to a child: "Freud was a great man. He studied dreams. He also thought a lot." You'd address the group in more formal English: "Freud was the father of psychoanalysis, who thought through the concept of the unconscious."

After class with friends, your English would become more relaxed, full of slang, and more than likely stuffed with "ya knows" and "what'd you thinks." Talking with an employer or a professor or anyone who might have the power to evaluate your performance, you would probably avoid the casual street English you'd use with friends; your English, like a military recruit facing an officer, might come to attention. English, then, can be looked at as formal and informal. The informal kind is reflected in the everyday way we talk to family and friends; the formal kind in the way we talk to our loan officers, bankers, college deans, and so on. Of course, there are various levels of formal and informal English, but for your immediate uses, these two will serve as touchstones.

In a broad sense, written tone, like spoken tone, can be looked at as formal or informal. It just depends on what kind of English you're writing in at the moment. Now, since most of us have little trouble adjusting our speech to meet the circumstances of a face-to-face situation, we suggest that you consciously evaluate the writing situation as you automatically do the speaking one.

For instance, imagine you are going to write a report for a course in consumer economics. Your job is to write objectively — to present the information in an unbiased way by reporting facts, not your opinions. Your topic is truth in labeling. You decide to focus on the cosmetics industry and zero in on hair-dye manufacturers. Since you're limited to writing an objective report, you would write it in a formal tone, perhaps like this paragraph from *Consumer Reports:*

"Warning: Contains an ingredient that can penetrate your skin and has been determined to cause cancer in laboratory animals."

In January 1978, the U.S. Food and Drug Administration proposed a regulation that would require a warning label with those words to appear on all hair dyes containing a widely used chemical. But none of the estimated 33 million American women — and the unknown number of men — who dye their hair will ever see the warning. For obvious reasons hair-dye companies don't want it on their products. Some companies have therefore "reformulated" their hair dyes so that the cancer-causing chemical is no longer included.

This is no way to write home from summer camp. Much too formal. Much too objective. But this would serve for any unbiased report.

If, however, the situation changed, and you were to use the information to put forth your attitudes about the industry's attempts to avoid accurate labeling, the tone might shift from formal to informal. You might write a paragraph something like this one:

About two years ago, the Food and Drug people were on their toes. They forced hair-dye makers using a chemical called for short 4-MMPD to warn buyers that it might cause cancer. Cancer! The industry went into shock. Not because of the threat its product posed for 33 million women and an undetermined number of men who use the stuff. But because the hazardous labeling might cut into profits. Many companies, therefore, "reformulated" their dyes. They excluded 4-MMPD. Good, you might be thinking, a blow for truth and better health. Wrong! These companies haven't stopped using dangerous chemicals. They've merely switched to ones that have yet to be tested by the Feds.

In this example the sentences are simpler and shorter, the words are less complex, the details less ponderous, and the whole paragraph moves readers forward without giving them much time to stop and think. The tone, then, is more casual than the first example, less formal, a little more souped up. Word choice, sentence structure, the way details are used, even the imagery help create the tone.

From these last examples, you've probably come to suspect that there is more to tone than the use of formal and informal English. Besides formal or informal, readers often declare a writer's tone to be ironic, snide, wry, scholarly, pompous, dry, sardonic, witty, scathing, gentle, tongue-in-cheek — the labels are endless. Moreover, a writer's tone often implies, but never directly states, an attitude toward a subject.

For example, consider the tone of this opening paragraph from a piece titled "The Ultimate White Sale" published in *Mother Jones*. What do you think the writer's attitude is toward the Ku Klux Klan? How would you label the tone?

> The New Klan came riding in this decade right on the coat tails of the New South. Dry-look Grand Wizard David Duke has been making the talk-show rounds, promoting his Knights of the Ku Klux Klan. Its new face is cool, Madison Avenue, and cleaned up; it no longer claims to murder blacks — although Duke has been known to occasionally dust off his swastika.

The attitude? It would be safe to bet the writer doesn't like Duke's new Klan. And the tone? Well, naming a tone isn't as important as the impression it leaves with the reader. But clearly the tone suggests cynicism, a cynicism over the chances that the Klan would change its ways and perhaps even a wider cynicism over the way people and ideas are merchandised.

Notice, for instance, how the writer uses the title, "The Ultimate White Sale." Although we may not know it at first, by the end of the paragraph we can see that the title is used cuttingly. The idea of a department store's semiannual sheet and pillow case sale (keeping in mind that both pillow cases and sheets are part of the Klan's costume) links with Duke's attempts to sell white supremacy. The idea of cynical merchandising also connects with words and phrases such as *dry-look, promoting, Madison Avenue,* and *claims.* The writer wants us to see that his packaging offers nothing more than a new wrapper for the same old garbage — that the Klan's "new face" still fronts the old policies of terror and suppression: "Duke has been known to occasionally dust off his swastika." And Duke, like so many other hucksters, makes the "talk-show rounds."

A writer's tone isn't always as distinguishable as the tone in the above example. Sometimes a writer will deliberately write in a flat style while using humorous details and images. The result is deadpan humor — a kind of humor that results from a comedian delivering jokes while maintaining an absolutely expressionless face. Samuel L. Clemens, who wrote under the name Mark Twain, uses this technique in the following paragraph from *Mark Twain's Autobiography,* in which he describes the church in his birthplace, Florida, Missouri.

> Most of the houses were of logs — all of them, indeed, except three or four; these latter were frame ones. There were none of brick, and none of stone. There was a log church, with a puncheon floor and slab benches. A puncheon floor is made of logs whose upper surfaces have been chipped flat with the adz. The cracks between the logs were not filled; there was no carpet; consequently, if you dropped anything smaller than a peach, it

was likely to go through. The church was perched upon short sections of logs, which elevated it two or three feet from the ground. Hogs slept under there, and whenever the dogs got after them during services, the minister had to wait till the disturbance was over. In winter there was always a refreshing breeze up through the puncheon floor; in summer there were fleas enough for all.

The humor is here. Imagine a church floor with cracks so large a peach could almost drop through. Imagine a congregation sitting through Sunday service munching peaches, for that matter. But the incongruity of eating peaches in church with dogs and hogs battling below is humorous. Clemens tells it in a deadpan tone. The tone also reveals an unflappable attitude; Clemens doesn't judge the experience. Snorting hogs and barking dogs chewing on each other was merely a "disturbance." A winter breeze coming up through the floor was "refreshing." And the fleas? Well, at least everyone got a share.

In contrast to Clemens's understated tone, Richard Selzer, writer and M.D., launches this passage with an exaggerated praise: "I sing of skin, layered fine as baklava, whose colors shame the dawn. . . ." *Awe* seems to be the most accurate word to describe Selzer's attitude toward skin.

> I sing of skin, layered fine as baklava, whose colors shame the dawn, at once the scabbard upon which is writ our only signature, and the instrument by which we are thrilled, protected, and kept constant in our natural place. Here is each man bagged and trussed in perfect amiability. See how it upholsters the bone and muscle underneath, now accenting the point of an elbow, now rolling over the pectorals to hollow the grotto of an armpit. Nippled and umbilicated, and perforated by the most diverse and marvelous openings, each with its singular rim and curtain. Thus the carven helix of the ear, the rigid nostrils, the puckered continence of the anus, the moist and sensitive lips of mouth and vagina.
>
> What is it, then, this seamless body-stocking, some two yards square, this our casing, our facade, that flushes, pales, perspires, glistens, glows, furrows, tingles, crawls, itches, pleasures, and pains us all our days, at once keeper of the organs within, and sensitive probe, adventurer into the world outside?

Enough! We could spend a great deal of time giving you examples of various tones. But our mission is more practical. We want to make you aware of tone in your own work. Ask yourself, "What's the appropriate tone for my piece?" "Formal or informal?" "Should it express an attitude?" "What attitude?" And so on.

Let's face it. Tone conveys involvement. How can a writer express an attitude without feeling connected to the subject? Sure, there are scholarly pieces that at first glance seem toneless. But they're rare, and the chances are that a close look will reveal a tone, perhaps a reserved one, the voice of the meticulous explorer.

There are segments of the writing community, however, that attempt to scour away tone. Your college admissions office, for instance:

> We are pleased to inform you of your acceptance to Fairview College. In the upper right-hand corner of this page, you will find a number. This is your identification number. Please use it in any further communication you have with us in the future.
> Good luck in the pursuit of your education.

> *Office of Admissions*

And good luck to you, buddy!

This kind of tone is dangerous. When enough people who don't know any better read it throughout their lives, it becomes a standard in their minds for good writing. Don't make that mistake. Unless you are putting someone on — maybe an admissions officer — don't write in this official tone. It's deadly. In fact, it's so deadly we suggest that the admissions office would serve you better by writing something like this instead:

> You're in!
> Now, because we have so many people with the same last names and because we are swamped with letters, whenever you write to us use the number we've printed in the upper right-hand corner.
> Welcome to our campus, #92139.

At least it would be more honest.

One more thought on tone. In Getting Started we suggested you keep your tone consistent. Certainly writers shift their tone now and then, but as a practical practice, you should try to stay consistent. Whatever you do, avoid awkward shifts from an informal tone into a formal one — like this:

> My grandmother used to avoid black cats, ladders, and activity on Friday the thirteenth. Once I saw her stop in a crosswalk and hold up traffic while she bent over to pick up a penny with her arthritic fingers. What did she do with it? What else. She dropped it into her shoe for good luck. I guess she came from the old school of simple cause and effect, the school of superstition.
>
> Superstitions are often thought of as naive, popular beliefs that are logically or scientifically untenable. Hence, the alternative term *folk belief* is often employed, carrying with it the connotations of unsophistication and ignorance that the word *folk*

has in popular usage. Well, my grandmother may have been unscientific but she was not illogical. She operated with an iron-bound logic. . . .

This kind of fractured tone is unacceptable. It usually comes from confusion. In this case the writer has become confused in writing about personal experience while trying to sprinkle in bits and pieces of official information. This kind of effort needs to be rewritten. The writer needs to integrate the formally written information with an informal tone.

Word Choice

Accurate Verbs

Much of what we've suggested about sharpening your prose forces you to use active verbs. Verbs serve as the flywheels of your sentences. We suggest you strain very hard to find the most accurate one you can for each sentence. Consider the following example:

A man walked down the street.

If you wanted to tell how the man walked, you might write

The man walked quickly down the street.

Or you might say he walked rapidly. Okay, but a single verb could do it better:

A man scurried down the street.

A man strode down the street.

A man swaggered down the street.

Now the sentence is sharper; the verb is more accurate. If you stop to think for a moment, you'll realize how many words we have to describe the way a person might walk — *strut, stumble, promenade, saunter, stride, clump, tramp, tread, pace, step, ramble, march, toddle, waddle, file, glide, straggle, shuffle, scuff, meander, stroll, creep, stalk, wander, trudge, stamp, limp, stagger, ambulate,* and even *perambulate.*

So, whenever you reread a rough draft, check to see if you can sharpen your verbs. But remember to select verbs that fit what you're saying; don't pick them because they may sound fancy. For instance, you wouldn't be helping your prose much if you wrote, "A drunk perambulated down the street" — unless you wanted to get a laugh. Instead of *perambulate,* you would probably write *staggered.*

Sometimes selecting the right verb can change a fairly good passage into a stronger one. Here's a student's fanciful description of an experience in a bookstore:

The crowd wandered through the bookstore. Some couples talked softly with each other and others walked in silence, stopping at various stands to read a page or two. One woman looked up and called out, "OHMYGOD!" as a rider on a white stallion came through the door.

Now read the revised version to see how more active and accurate verbs create a better passage:

The crowd browsed through the bookstore. Some couples whispered to each other and some strolled in silence, pausing at various stands to read a page or two. One woman glanced up and blurted, "OHMYGOD!" as a rider on a white stallion clip-clopped through the door.

Browsed, whispered, strolled, and *pausing* help create a casual atmosphere one might find in a bookstore. Using *glanced* in place of *looked* is more effective because it seems more abrupt. *Blurted* works better than *called* because it conveys shock or surprise. *Clip-clopped* works better than *came* because it generates the sound of hooves and fractures the casual mood established in the opening sentences. By substituting active and accurate verbs the writer has sharpened the passage.

You might say that finding active verbs is easy to do for description, but what about using them in information-centered passages? Well, it can be done. Read the following passage from C. M. Bowra's *Classical Greece:*

The Greeks won their war with a famous ruse that military men and statesmen often try to repeat in other ways. They gave Troy a gift — a wooden horse with Greeks hidden inside. While the Trojans slept, the Greeks crept out and opened the city's gates to the rest of their army. Masters at last, the Greek soldiers saw Helen reunited with Menelaus, and everyone started for home. But one among them, the ingenious Odysseus who had devised the wooden horse trick, found the route 10 years long.

Verbs like *won, gave, crept, opened,* and *saw* make this passage active. Whenever you can, use active verbs to generate life in any writing you do.

A warning: We don't want to leave you with the impression that you should write hyperactive prose:

The Greeks annihilated the Trojans by using a famous ruse that military men and statesmen often try to repeat in other ways. They thrust a gift before Troy — a wooden horse with Greeks stuffed inside.

Hyperactive prose usually rings false and sounds silly. It's best left to cheap thriller and romance writers:

An ominous pall crushed the city as agent X slammed the turbo Mustang into second and jammed down the accelerator as he swept into the turn, fishtailed, and then skidded onto Broadway.

Laura, panting breathlessly, the freezing night air thrusting into her lungs like an ice pick, huddled against the castle wall where fear had paralyzed her.

Hmmmmm! Maybe there is money in it. Anyway, we suggest you sharpen your work by using accurate and active verbs. Whatever you do, don't stretch for the exotic when doing college assignments.

Hidden Verbs

Sometimes you may spend hours tinkering with verbs. You'll rummage through your vocabulary and browse through a thesaurus for the most active and accurate ones you can use. You'll end up with some finished sentences like these:

My research leads me to the solution of Travanian's identity.

Since John Simmons quit the committee, we must search for a replacement.

The P.E. Department encourages utilization of the pool during lunch hours.

To understand *The Deer Hunter* we must perform an analysis of its imagery.

Good verbs in these sentences, right?

Yes . . . but . . . And here the "but" is important. *Leads, search, encourages,* and *perform* are not the real verbs in these sentences. *Solve, replace, use,* and *analyze* are the real verbs, but they are hidden because they are disguised to look like nouns. These sentences would be more accurate if revised in this fashion:

My research solves the question of Travanian's identity.

Since John Simmons quit, we must replace him.

The P.E. Department encourages use of the pool during lunch hours.

To understand *The Deer Hunter,* we must analyze its imagery.

When you edit and revise a rough draft watch out for verbs that have been turned into nouns. Often they can be recast as verbs and used to make your writing more concise.

Concrete Language

Definite, specific, and concrete language pulls the reader to the page. General, vague, and abstract language pushes the reader from the page.

As an ad writer might phrase this thought: Vivid language gives an "up-close" feeling; obscure language gives a "far-back" feeling.

Far Back	*Up Close*
He was old when he gained success.	He had turned gray and seen his seventy-first birthday when he won the Nobel Prize.
The police arrested him in an alley.	Six police officers with drawn pistols captured him in an alley.
At Bernard's the sales staff greets customers courteously.	At Bernard's the sales staff greets customers with a smile.
Phil likes independence in his job.	Phil likes being his own boss.
For me to write an essay takes patience.	For me to write an essay takes hours of pacing and pencil chewing, at least a hundred pages covered with useless scribbling, and several pots of black coffee.

Although most writing assignments required in such courses as history, geology, sociology, and psychology will lead you into making general observations, you should never lose your grip on vivid language. Sometimes a line or two of vivid language mixed with the most general observations will bring the reader up close to the page.

Far Back

No student of human experience can deny one fact: once we were all children. We still carry that child inside. The childhood experience has shaped our world view. It has influenced the way we relate to others and created our approach to problem solving. When we find ourselves quarreling over petty issues instead of negotiating reasonable solutions, more than likely our inner child is behind the behavior.

Up Close

No student of human experience can deny one fact: once we were all children. We still carry that child inside. The childhood experience has shaped our world view. It has influenced the way we relate to others and created our approach to problem solving. When we find ourselves quarreling over petty issues instead of negotiating reasonable solutions, more than likely we have activated the tiny tyrant who used to toss himself to the floor, kick his feet, pound his fists, and scream and cry to get his wishes met.

The revised version ends with vivid language that brings readers closer to the experience. When you find yourself writing general observations, always work in a line or two of vivid language.

GLOSSARY OF USAGE

The advice and information we've included in this glossary — all gleaned from current dictionaries and usage guides — represents the practice of experienced writers. The entries themselves are composed of words and phrases that frequently cause problems for inexperienced writers. The glossary, of course, serves only as a supplement to a good dictionary, perhaps the most valuable resource you can use when writing.

a, an

Use *a* before a consonant sound, *an* before a vowel sound.

a university	a history	a one o'clock lunch	a C
an undertow	an hour	an orphan	an F

accept, except

Accept means "to receive." *Except* means "but for," "other than," or "to leave out." I can accept your argument except the last point. Do not except him from the guest list.

advice, advise

Advice is a noun that means "counsel." *Advise* is a verb that means "to give advice." I advise you to accept your attorney's advice.

affect, effect

Affect is a verb, meaning "to influence," and *effect* is a noun, meaning "result." The treatment did not affect her illness; in fact, it had several adverse effects. *Effect* can also be a verb meaning "to bring about." The senator effected significant changes in her district.

aggravate

Aggravate means "make worse." In writing you should not use it to mean "irritate" or "annoy."

ain't

Nonstandard English for *am not* or *aren't*.

all ready, already

All ready means "prepared." *Already* means "by now" or "previously." We were all ready to dance, but the band had already stopped playing.

all right

All right is always two words. *Alright* is a misspelling.

all together, altogether

All together means "in a group," "gathered in one place," or "in unison." *Altogether* means "completely" or "wholly." They went shopping all together rather than separately. They did not altogether believe his story.

allusion, illusion

An *allusion* is a reference to something. An *illusion* is a deceptive appearance. Dr. Catalano's lectures are filled with allusions from drama. After years of failure, he still believes the illusion that persistence is the secret of success.

a lot

A lot is always written as two words. *Alot* is a misspelling.

already

See *all ready.*

among, between

Among is used to refer to three or more people or things. *Between* is used with two people or things. Half the inheritance was divided between the two sisters, the other half among several charities. Sometimes *between* is used with more than two if the relationship concerns individual members of the group with each other. The nuclear treaty between the five superpowers was signed today.

amount, number

Amount refers to a quantity of something that cannot be counted. *Number* refers to things that can be counted. A large number of salt-water fish requires an aquarium that holds a tremendous amount of water.

an

See *a.*

and etc.

Et cetera (*etc.*) means "and so forth"; *and etc.*, therefore, is redundant.

and/or

A legalism that many people consider awkward in college writing.

anxious, eager

Anxious means "nervous" or "worried." *Eager* means "enthusiastically anticipating something." I am eager about my new job but anxious about the new responsibility.

anyone, any one

Anyone means "any person at all." *Any one* refers to a particular person or thing in a group. Similar definitions apply to *everyone, every one, someone, some one.* Anyone with the price of admission can come in. Any one of the membership might have started the rumor.

anyways, anywheres

Misused for *anyway* and *anywhere.*

as

Avoid using *as* for *because, since, while, whether,* and *who.* Because (not *as*) the train was late, the meeting was postponed.

as, like

See *like.*

awful

An overused word for *bad, shocking, ugly.* Also misused as a substitute for *very* or *extremely.*

bad, badly

Bad is an adjective and should be used in formal writing to modify nouns and as a predicate adjective after linking verbs. *Badly* should be used only as an adverb. John felt bad. The artist painted badly.

being as, being that

Do not misuse for *because*. Because (not *being as* or *being that*) life is short, grab all the gusto you can.

beside, besides

Beside means "next to." *Besides* means "except" and "in addition." The cowpuncher stood beside his horse. Besides one piano, the room was empty.

between

See *among*.

bring, take

Use *bring* to carry something from a farther place to a nearer one. Use *take* to carry something from a nearer place to a farther one. Take these pages to the printer and bring me yesterday's batch.

bunch

Bunch should not be used to refer to a crowd or group or people or things. Reserve it to refer to things that grow fastened together, such as grapes or bananas.

burst, bursted, bust, busted

The verb *burst* means "fly apart," and its principal parts are *burst, burst, burst*. The past tense *bursted* is unacceptable. *Bust* and *busted* are considered slang; therefore, they are inappropriate in college writing.

can, may

Can indicates ability, and *may* indicates permission. If I may use the car, I believe I can reach the store before it closes.

center around

Center on is more accurate than *center around*.

cite, sight, site

Cite means "to quote"; *sight* refers to the ability to see; and *site* refers to a place or location.

climactic, climatic

Climactic refers to a climax. *Climatic* refers to climate.

complement, compliment

Complement means "to add to something," "to complete something." *Compliment* means "to flatter" or "to praise." The roses complemented the table decoration. John complimented Sandra for her performance. *Complimentary* can also mean "free." The family received complimentary airline tickets.

conscience, conscious

Conscience refers to a moral sense. *Conscious* is an adjective meaning "aware." A country without a conscience is a country without a heart. He is unconscious of his behavior.

compare to, compare with

Compare to means "regard as similar." *Compare with* means "examine for similarities or differences." The boy compared his father's bald head to an egg. The investigator compared the facts of the Wellman case with the facts of the Billings incident.

continual, continuous

Continual means "often repeated." *Continuous* means "unceasing" or "without a break." My sleep is continually interrupted. The earth travels continuously around the sun.

convince, persuade

Careful writers use *convince* when someone changes his or her opinion. They use *persuade* when someone is moved to take action. The attorney convinced serveral students that capital punishment is immoral. The attorney persuaded several students to demonstrate against capital punishment.

could of

Often misused for *could have*.

couple of

Do not use *couple of* for *few* or *several*.

criteria, data, phenomena

Criteria is the plural form; the singular form *criterion* is seldom used. *Criteria* is often used as a singular noun, but careful writers use it only in the plural sense. The criteria were so ill phrased that they were hard to apply. Both *data* and *phenomena* are plurals of the same kind for the singular *datum* and *phenomenon*. They should be treated in the same fashion. New data suggest the drug is harmful. Today's unexplainable phenomena are tomorrow's scientific explanations.

data

See *criteria*.

deal

Misused for *bargain, transaction,* or *business transaction.*

differ from, differ with

Differ from means "be unlike." *Differ with* means "disagree."

different from, different than

Different from is widely accepted. *Different than* is acceptable when it precedes a clause. An elephant is different from a mastodon. Paris was different than I had expected.

disinterested, uninterested

Disinterested means "impartial." *Uninterested* means "bored" or "indifferent."

don't

Don't is a contraction of *do not* and should not be used for *does not,* whose contraction is *doesn't.*

due to

Do not use *due to* as a substitute for *because.* Jenkins became depressed because of (not *due to*) his heavy debts.

eager

See *anxious.*

effect

See *affect.*

enthused

The preferred adjective is *enthusiastic.*

especially, specially

Especially means "particularly" or "more than other things." *Specially* means "for a specific reason." The artist was especially pleased to receive the award. The design was specially created for her.

etc.

See *and etc.*

every which way

Do not use as a substitute for *in every direction* or *in disorder.*

everyone, every one

See *anyone*.

everywheres

Unacceptable English. Do not use for *everywhere*.

exam

In college writing use *examination*.

except

See *accept*.

expect

Do not use to mean "suppose" or "believe." I suppose (not *expect*) the beach will be crowded.

explicit, implicit

Explicit means "expressed directly or precisely." *Implicit* means "expressed indirectly or suggested." The threat was explicit — "I'll break your nose!" Although his voice was gentle, his body communicated an implicit threat.

farther, further

Farther refers to actual distance. *Further* refers to additional time, amount, or other abstract matters. I cannot run any farther. Further encouragement is useless.

fewer, less

Fewer refers to items that can be counted. *Less* refers to a collective quantity that cannot be counted. The marsh has fewer ducks living in it, but it also has less water to support them.

finalize

Avoid using *finalize* for *complete*.

flunk

Do not substitute for *fail*.

folks

Do not substitute for *parents, relatives,* or *people*.

former, latter, first, last

Former refers to the first named of two things or people. *Latter* refers to the second of two named. *First* and *last* are used to refer to items in a series of three or more. John and Bill are very successful; the former is a dentist, the latter a poet. Jogging, biking, and swimming require tremendous endurance; the last requires the most.

further

See *farther*.

get

A common verb used in a variety of common expressions: *get wise to yourself, her chatter gets me*, and the like. Using *get* in such ways is inappropriate in college writing.

goes

Inappropriate when used instead of *said* or *says* to introduce a quotation. It should not be used to indicate speech. He said (not *goes*), "Life is short."

good, well

Good is an adjective; *well* is an adverb. Burton is a good tennis player. He strokes the ball well. *Well* should be used to refer to health. You look well (not *good*).

had ought, hadn't ought

Often misused for *ought* and *ought not*.

herself, himself

See *myself*.

hisself

Incorrect for *himself*.

hopefully

Hopefully means "with hope." They prayed hopefully for the blizzard to stop. Often *hopefully* is used to mean "it is hoped" in place of *I hope;* however, *I hope* is preferred in college writing. I hope (rather than *hopefully*) the blizzard will stop.

illusion

See *allusion*.

implicit

See *explicit*.

imply, infer

Imply means "suggest." *Infer* means "conclude." Irving implied that he had studied for the quiz, but I inferred that he was unprepared.

in, into

In indicates a location or position. *Into* indicates movement or change. Barbara is in the study with a clairvoyant, who is in a trance. I must go into Murkwood, but I do not want to fall into danger. *Into* has also come to mean "interested in" or "involved in" something, which is an inappropriate use in college writing. My brother is interested in (not *into*) Dungeons and Dragons.

individual, party, person

Individual should be used to refer to a single human being when expressing that person's unique qualities. Each individual has a right to pursue his or her interests within the law. When not stressing unique qualities, use *person*. A romantic person will love the Austrian countryside. Except in legal documents, use *party* to refer to a group. Who is the missing person (not *party*)?

infer

See *imply*.

into

See *in*.

irregardless

Incorrect for *regardless*.

is because

See *reason is because*.

is when, is where

A common error in sentences that define. "Bandwagon" is (not *is where* or *is when*) a propaganda device by which advertisers urge consumers to become one of the millions buying their products.

kind, sort, type

These are singular words and take singular modifiers and verbs. This kind of butterfly is rare in North America. When referring to more than one thing, *kind, sort,* and *type* must be made plural and then take plural modifiers and verbs. These kinds of butterflies are rare in North America.

kind of, sort of

Do not use as a substitute for *somewhat* or *rather*. The course was somewhat (not *kind of* or *sort of*) dull.

lay

See *lie*.

less

See *fewer*.

liable

See *likely*.

lie, lay

These verbs are often confused. *Lie* means "to recline," and *lay* means "to place." In part, they seem to be confusing because the past tense of *lie* is the same as the present tense of *lay*.

lie ("to recline")	*lay* ("to place")
lie	lay
lay	laid
lain	laid
lying	laying

like, as, as if, as though

Like is a preposition and introduces a prepositional phrase. *As, as if,* and *as though* usually function as subordinating conjunctions and introduce dependent clauses. In college writing do not use *like* as a subordinating conjunction. The sky looks as if (not *like*) the end of the world is near.

like, such as

When introducing a representative series, use *such as*. To make a direct comparison with an example, use *like*. This decade has produced some playful novelists, such as Vonnegut, Coover, and Hawkes, but I still prefer to read classic writers like Hemingway.

likely, liable

Likely is used to express probability. *Liable* is used to express responsibility or obligation. She is likely to finish first. Dr. Crane is liable for his misdiagnosis.

lots, lots of
Do not substitute for *a great deal, much,* or *plenty.*

may
See *can.*

may of
Incorrect for *may have.*

media, medium
Media is the plural form of *medium.* Be sure to use plural modifiers and plural verbs with *media.* The mass media — television, radio, newspapers — influence our political attitudes.

might of
Incorrect for *might have.*

most
Do not use for *almost.*

must of
Incorrect for *must have.*

myself, herself, himself, itself, yourself
These and other *-self* pronouns are reflexive or intensive — that is, they refer to or intensify a noun or another pronoun in a sentence. The family members disagree among themselves, but I myself know how the inheritance should be divided. It is inappropriate in college writing to use these pronouns in place of personal pronouns. No one except me (not *myself*) will complete the job.

no way
Do not use for *no.*

nowhere near
Do not substitute for *nearly.* Walters is not nearly (not *nowhere near*) as intelligent as Smith.

nowheres
Do not use for *no where.*

number
See *amount.*

OK, O.K., okay

All are acceptable spellings.

party

See *individual*.

people, persons

People refers to a collective mass and emphasizes faceless anonymity. *Persons* refers to individuals who make up the group and emphasizes separate identity. People waited in lines for hours. Several persons fainted.

per

An English equivalent is usually preferable to the Latin *per*. The job pays $4.50 an (not *per*) hour. The raid was executed according to (not *per*) the captain's plans.

percent (per cent), percentage

Both *percent* (often spelled *per cent*) and *percentage* refer to numbers and should only be used in actual references to statistics. Avoid using them to replace the word *part*. The part (not *percent*) of the committee that causes trouble is small. *Percent* is always preceded by a number (twenty percent, 20 percent), and *percentage* follows an adjective (a small percentage). In college writing *percent* should always be written out (not %).

person

See *individual*.

persons

See *people*.

persuade

See *convince*.

phenomena, phenomenon

See *criteria*.

plus

Do not use as a substitute for *moreover*. Politics offers socially important work for young attorneys; moreover (not *plus*), it can help them get public attention.

quote, quotation

Quote is a verb. *Quotation* is a noun. Do not use *quote* when you mean *quotation.* The quotation (not *quote*) is from the Bible.

raise, rise

Two commonly confused verbs. *Raise* (*raising, raised, raised*) means "to force something to move upward." *Rise* (*rising, rose, risen*) means "to go up." Import quotas will raise the cost of American products. The mist rose from the swamp.

real, really

Real is an adjective; *really* is an adverb. The race was really (not *real*) tough.

reason is because

Use *that* instead of *because* in the phrase *reason is because,* or rewrite the sentence. The reason the business closed is that (not *because*) Carmen spent more money than she made.

respectfully, respectively

Respectfully means "with respect" or "showing respect." *Respectively* means "each in the order given." They respectfully expressed their doubts. ·*The Sun Also Rises, As I Lay Dying,* and *Day of the Locust* were written by Hemingway, Faulkner, and West, respectively.

rise

See *raise.*

said

See *goes.*

says

See *goes.*

sensual, sensuous

Sensual refers to pleasures of the body, especially sexual pleasures. *Sensuous* refers to pleasures perceived by the senses. The poet's sensual desires led him to create the sensuous images readers find in his work.

set, sit

Two commonly confused verbs. *Set* (*setting, set, set*) means "to place or to put." *Sit* (*sitting, sat, sat*) means "to be seated." When you mean "put something down," use a form of *set*. Beverly set her books on the table. When you refer to being seated, use a form of *sit*. Uncle Ralph would sit for hours without speaking.

should, would

Use *should* when expressing a condition or obligation. Use *would* when expressing a wish or customary action. We should attend the reception. He would always read for an hour before falling asleep.

should of

Incorrect for *should have*.

sight

See *cite*.

sit

See *set*.

site

See *cite*.

someone

See *anyone*.

such as

See *like, such as*.

sort

See *kind*.

sort of

See *kind of*.

specially

See *especially*.

sure

Do not misuse for *surely* or *certainly*. Richard was certainly (not *sure*) correct by refusing to support Kraft.

sure and, sure to, try and, try to

Sure to and *try to* are the preferred forms. Try to (not *try and*) attend.

than, then

Than functions as a conjunction used in comparisons. *Then* is an adverb indicating time. I would rather be dancing than (not *then*) studying.

theirselves

Incorrect for *themselves.*

then

See *than.*

try and, try to

See *sure and.*

uninterested

See *disinterested.*

use to, suppose to

Sometimes carelessly written for *used to* and *supposed to.*

wait for, wait on

Wait for means "await." *Wait on* means "to serve."

ways

Use *way* when referring to distance. The park is a mile a way (not *ways*).

well

See *good.*

which, who

Never use *which* to refer to people. Use *who* or *that* to refer to people and *which* or *that* to refer to things.

would

See *should.*

yourself

See *myself.*

INDEX

TO THE STUDENT

Please help us make *One to One* an even better book. To improve our textbooks, we revise them every few years, taking into account the experiences of both instructors and students with the previous edition. At some time, your instructor will most likely be asked to comment extensively on *One to One*. Now we would like to hear from you.

Complete this questionnaire and return it to:

>College English Developmental Group
>Little, Brown and Company
>34 Beacon Street
>Boston, MA 02106

School _____

City, State, Zip Code _____

Course title _____

Was this a conference-centered course? _____

Instructor's full name _____

Other books required _____

_____

1. Did you and your instructor regularly hold conferences to discuss your writing?

_____

2. Did you like *One to One*? _____

3. Was it easy to read? _____ Difficult to read? _____

4. In what ways did *One to One* improve or fail to improve your writing? _____

_____

_____

5. Which sections were the most useful to you? _____

_____

Why were they useful? _____

_____

6. Did you find the examples with parallel comments useful? _____

   How could they be improved? _____

   _____

7. Did you use the Index for Writers? _____ How was it helpful?

   _____

8. Did you find that the tasks in Part Three, Daily Writing, helped your writing

   skills? _____ In what ways? _____

   _____

   Did the tasks in Daily Writing help you in ways not related to writing? _____

   What ways? _____

   _____

9. Did you like the way *One to One* was organized? _____

10. Did you like the physical appearance of *One to One*? _____

11. Should the instructor continue to assign *One to One* next term? _____

    _____

12. Please add any comments or suggestions. _____

    _____

    _____

    _____

    _____

    _____

    Signature _____ Date _____

    Mailing address _____

    _____

    _____